Abraham has long been viewed as a source of common ground for monotheistic faith communities, yet the relationship between the various Abraham narratives is complex. In this book George Bristow rigorously analyzes biblical and qur'anic Abraham narratives and builds on the tight connection between narrative and worldview to lay the foundation for a careful and illuminating theological comparison between varying portraits of Abraham and the faith traditions in which they are embedded. In the course of building his argument, Bristow introduces an original model for analyzing the relationship of narrative to worldview and sheds important light on the function of Abraham for contemporary Turkish Muslims. Sharing Abraham is an essential resource for anyone interested in narrative and worldview studies, comparative theology, biblical and qur'anic hermeneutics, Abrahamic dialogue, or Islam in Turkey.

ISRME Studies in Religion and Theology

Sharing Abraham? Narrative Worldview, Biblical and Qur'anic Interpretation, & Comparative Theology in Turkey

ISRME Studies in Religion and Theology 1

ISRME Studies in Religion and Theology was established by the Institute for the Study of Religion in the Middle East to publish books about religious communities, religious texts, theologies and belief systems in the Middle East, North Africa, Turkey and Pakistan. The series solicits research studies from a range of disciplines and historical contexts, placing special emphasis on research about small, emergent or threatened religious communities and the interaction of these communities with majority traditions. The series will be of particular interest to students and scholars of religion, as well as to general readers concerned with the Middle East.

SHARING ABRAHAM?

Narrative Worldview,
Biblical and Qur'anic Interpretation,
& Comparative Theology

IN TURKEY

GEORGE BRISTOW

DOORLIGHT ACADEMIC
5 Newton Street, Cambridge, Massachusetts 02139 USA

Editorial offices
1164 Bradfield Road, Abington, Pennsylvania 19001 USA
www.doorlightpublications.com

Copyright ©2017 George Bristow

ISBN 0-9838653-3-7
ISBN13 978-0-9838653-3-9

Cover Design by Amy Schiltz
Interior Design by Ruth Anne Burke

Contents

LIST OF FIGURES

ACKNOWLEDGMENTS

As this book is largely based on my 2015 dissertation, it seems fitting to thank those whose support meant so much to me during that strenuous process. As in every area of our life and service together, I am deeply indebted to my wonderful wife, Donna, for her love, friendship and support. Not only did she encourage me throughout the writing of the dissertation on which this book is based and read substantial portions of it, but she has endeavored to keep me balanced and to lighten me up! My children and their spouses also cheered me on, especially my daughter-in-law Danielle, who tackled the difficult proofreading of some lengthy chapter drafts when they were still quite rough.

I am grateful to the faculty and staff of the International Baptist Theological Seminary in Prague, now the International Baptist Theological Study Center Amsterdam, for their determination to see us through the PhD process during some difficult years of institutional transition. I will not easily forget the wonderful, challenging weeks at the beautiful Prague campus during the annual Research Students and Faculty Colloquia and the stimulating conversations over meals and coffee. From the day I wrote to him, Parush Parushev was an unfailing encouragement and insightful guide on the research road, helping me to see the importance of narrative. My thanks also to Keith Jones and Norbert Csenyi for much administrative help and to librarian Zdenko Sirka, who consistently provided scanned material and guided me in finding online resources. Thanks to Peter and Katharina Penner and Rollin Grams for their encouragement to pursue this topic. Thanks to Jim Purves and Tim and Ivana Noble, who challenged me with tough questions during colloquia, to Hannes Wiher, who discussed missiological perspectives related to my work, and to Lydie Kucova and Marion Carson, who read and made very helpful comments on my chapters on the Genesis Abraham narrative and the New Testament use of Abraham respectively. Thanks to my friend and colleague in Istanbul, Daniel Brown, who read carefully through a lengthy chapter, raising significant issues for me to think about from his expertise in Islamic studies. I am now doubly indebted to Dan as he encouraged and guided me in turning the dissertation into a publishable book. His skillful editing of the whole manuscript has made it far more readable.

I am deeply grateful to my expert supervisors Andrew Kirk and Ida Glaser, not only for patiently helping me to shape my work through incisive comments and tough questions to strengthen my argument, but for extending warm fellowship and encouragement throughout. Many thanks also to my VU University supervisor Nelly van Doorn-Harder, who took on my nearly-finished research project during our transfer from the University of Wales and moved the work to completion.

I am grateful to Stewards Ministries and numerous friends and churches that provided financial support without which this dissertation would not have been possible. Likewise the warm fellowship and support of my beloved Turkish brothers and sisters in the Beşiktaş Protestant Church, where my family and I worship, has been a source of cheer and blessing for many years.

Thanks also to my Hasat colleagues in Istanbul, with whom I've had the privilege of serving Turkish churches for many years. What a great team! Thank you to Pieter, Tim, Elizabeth, Kayra, David, Joseph, Justin, Andrew, and Debbie who urged me on at various points and prayed for me. Thanks to Elizabeth for carefully proofreading this manuscript in its final stage. Special thanks to Yolanda, who uncomplainingly undertook the difficult task of transcribing my lengthy Turkish interviews along with all the other work she carries in helping make this team a family.

ABBREVIATIONS

AFStu	*Asian Folklore Studies*
AJISS	*American Journal of Islamic Social Sciences*
ANE	*Ancient Near East*
AÜİFD	*Atatürk Üniversitesi İlahiyat Fakültesi Dergisi (Ataturk U. Theology Faculty Journal)*
BBR	*Bulletin for Biblical Research*
BibInt	*Biblical Interpretation*
BJQH	*Al-Bayan Journal of Al-Quran and al-Hadith*
BSac	*Bibliotheca Sacra*
BYULR	*Brigham Young University Law Review*
CCO	*Collectanea Christiana Orientalia*
CE	*Comparative Education*
CSR	*Christian Scholar's Review*
CSSH	*Comparative Studies in Society and History*
CTJ	*Calvin Theological Journal*
CTM	*Concordia Theological Monthly*
CulPsy	*Culture & Psychology*
CurTM	*Currents in Theology and Mission*
DI	*Der Islam*
DTIB	*Dictionary of Theological Interpretation of the Bible*
EJTS	*European Journal of Turkish Studies*
ERS	*Ethnic and Racial Studies*
EvQ	*Evangelical Quarterly*
FPhil	*Faith and Philosophy*
FÜSBD	*Firat Üniversitesi Sosyal Bilimler Dergisi (Euphrates U. Journal of Social Science)*
HBT	*Horizons in Biblical Theology*
HTR	*Harvard Theological Review*
HUCA	*Hebrew Union College Annual*
HvTSt	*Hervormde teologiese studies*
ICMR	*Islam and Christian–Muslim Relations*
IDis	*Intellectual Discourse*
IJFM	*International Journal of Frontier Missions*
IJHSS	*International Journal of Humanities and Social Science*
IJPT	*International Journal of Public Theology*
ILS	*Islamic Law and Society*
Int	*Interpretation: A Journal of Bible and Theology*
IRM	*International Review of Mission*
İSAM	*İslam Araştırmaları Merkezi (Center for Islamic Studies)*
İÜİFD	*İstanbul Üniversitesi İlahiyat Fakültesi Dergisi (U. Istanbul Theology Faculty Journal)*
JAOS	*Journal of the American Oriental Society*

JArabLit	*Journal of Arabic Literature*
JBL	*Journal of Biblical Literature*
JBQ	*Jewish Bible Quarterly*
JBR	*Journal of Bible and Religion*
JEBS	*Journal of European Baptist Studies*
JEcStud	*Journal of Ecumenical Studies*
JETS	*Journal of the Evangelical Theological Society*
JGeog	*Journal of Geography*
JHumR	*Journal of Human Rights*
JIP	*Journal of Islamic Philosophy*
JMMA	*Journal of Muslim Minority Affairs*
JNES	*Journal of Near Eastern Studies*
JOTT	*Journal of Translation and Textlinguistics*
JQR	*Jewish Quarterly Review*
JQurS	*Journal of Qur'anic Studies*
JSNT	*Journal for the Study of the New Testament*
JSOT	*Journal for the Study of the Old Testament*
JSP	*Journal for the Study of the Pseudepigrapha*
JSR	*The Journal of Scriptural Reasoning*
JSS	*Journal of Semitic Studies*
KL	*(Amazon) Kindle Location*
LCWE	*Lausanne Committee for World Evangelization*
LJPS	*Lahore Journal of Policy Studies*
MAN	*MAN: The Journal of the Royal Anthropological Institute of Great Britain and Ireland*
MEQ	*Middle East Quarterly*
MERIA	*Middle East Review of International Affairs*
MissIR	*Missiology: An International Review*
Monograf	*Monograf*
MTheo	*Modern Theology*
Mus	*Le Muséon*
MusWor	*Muslim World*
OISO	*Oxford Islamic Studies Online*
PAAJR	*Proceedings of the American Academy for Jewish Research*
ParOr	*Parole de l'Orient*
PoeT	*Poetics Today*
ProEccl	*Pro Ecclesia*
RelC	*Religion Compass*
RPM	*Reformed Perspectives Magazine*
RQurR	*Review of Qur'anic Research*
RRelRes	*Review of Religious Research*
SBJT	*Southern Baptist Journal of Theology*
SCompR	*Studies in Comparative Religion*
ScotJT	*Scottish Journal of Theology*
SEÅ	*Svensk Exegetisk Årsbok*

SFM	*St. Francis Magazine*
SIntD	*Studies in Interreligious Dialogue*
ST	*Studia Theologica - Nordic Journal of Theology*
StudIsl	*Studia Islamica*
StutTT	*Stuttgarter Theologische Themen*
SweMT	*Swedish Missiological Themes*
TCulS	*Theory, Culture & Society*
TDOT	*Theological Dictionary of the Old Testament*
TDPSP	*Tradition & Discovery: The Polanyi Society Periodical*
Them	*Themelios*
ThNN	*Theology, News & Notes*
TJ	*Trinity Journal*
TJT	*Toronto Journal of Theology*
TS	*Theological Studies*
TurSt	*Turkish Studies*
TynBul	*Tyndale Bulletin*
UİBD	*Uluslararası İnsan Bilimleri Dergisi*
UÜİFD	*Uludağ Üniversitesi İlahiyat Fakültesi Dergisi (U. Uludağ Theology Faculty Journal)*
VT	*Vetus Testamentum*
WTJ	*Westminster Theological Journal*
ZAW	*Zeitschrift für die Alttestamentliche Wissenschaft*

And the LORD appeared to Abraham by the oaks of Mamre,

To Abraham Our messengers brought good news.

He lifted up his eyes and looked, and behold,

They said, "Peace." He answered, "Peace,"

three men were standing in front of him. . . .

and without delay he brought in a roasted calf.

Then he took curds and milk and the calf that he had prepared,

When he saw that their hands did not reach towards the meal,

and set it before them. And he stood by them under the tree while they ate. . . .

he found this strange and became afraid of them. . . .

The LORD said, "I will surely return to you about this time next year. . . .

Then, when the fear left Abraham and the good news came to him,

Then Abraham drew near and said,

he pleaded with Us for Lot's people, for Abraham was forbearing,

"Will you indeed sweep away the righteous with the wicked?

tender-hearted, and devout. "Abraham, cease your pleading:

He answered, 'For the sake of ten I will not destroy it.'"

what your Lord has ordained has come about."

And the LORD went his way, when he had finished speaking to Abraham.

(Qur'an Hud/11:69-76)

(Genesis 18:1-8, 33)

Joseph Anton Koch, detail of Landscape with Abraham and the Three Angels in the Valley of Mambre, 1797
Image courtesy of the Getty's Open Content Program.

INTRODUCTION

There is inherent logic to beginning with Abraham in Christian-Muslim encounter. Both Christians and Muslims trace their spiritual heritage to Abraham and tell many stories about him. Turkish Muslims emphasize Abraham's roots in the biblical city of Haran, whose ruins may be visited in Turkey today. According to well-known local tradition, a famous lake in today's Şanlıurfa (*Balıklıgöl: Fish Lake*) is the place where God intervened when the prophet Abraham was cast into the flames by the tyrant Nimrod, turning the fire into water and the wood into fish.[1] The city also boasts a cave reputed to be Abraham's birthplace. Turkey is an evocative location to discuss Abraham.

But to what extent do Christians and Muslims really share Abraham? The place of Abraham in the worldviews and sacred texts of Christians and Muslims diverges considerably. Christian Scriptures proclaim that Jesus Christ fulfills the Abrahamic promises and that Christ's followers are the true people of Abraham. On the other hand, the Qur'an proclaims that Islam is the religion or way of Abraham the prophet and that Muslims are the true people of Abraham. Differing narratives articulate different worldviews. Yet despite the dissonance, both apparent and actual common ground makes these stories a profitable place from which to begin or advance conversation with those who trace their roots to Abraham.

This study lays groundwork and explores the possibilities of employing the biblical and Islamic Abraham stories for interfaith encounter and Christian witness in Turkey. My understanding of Abraham in Muslim thinking grew from extended discussions with nine Turkish imams, who generously shared their beliefs about Abraham (Ibrahim) with me and allowed me to share my understanding of Abraham with them. Thus this study also considers "sharing" Abraham in the more colloquial sense used by some Christians who describe witness as "sharing one's faith."

I am a Christian minister, serving in theological education in the Muslim-majority country of Turkey, where I have lived since 1987. Most of those with whom I serve are followers of Jesus Christ in Turkish Protestant churches.[2] As a Bible teacher, personally involved in Christian mission, I am committed to the truth of the apostolic witness to Jesus Christ articulated in the New Testament (NT). As a researcher doing comparative theology, I am also committed to correctly understanding Muslim thinking and faith by learning from Muslims and from their interpretation of their primary sources. During this research my intent was to consider more deeply the qur'anic Abraham narratives and the Islamic worldview which these stories articulate, especially as they are retold in Turkey. I have also found my understanding of the Christian faith deepened in various ways. Studying the Genesis Abraham narrative and its NT use in this context has given me new insight into the gospel of Christ.

The Abraham stories promise to be a fruitful starting point for helping Christians and Muslims to understand each other's worldviews as well as to better understand their own. Attempting this in practice has significance for Abrahamic interfaith dialogue and comparative theology as well as for Christian missiology. As the initiators of several attempts to develop "Abrahamic dialogue" (which I consider in Chapter 1), Turkish Muslim scholars have a particular stake in Abrahamic studies. In the course of this study I have entered this Turkish dialogue and I hope to make a contribution to the growing body of biblical interpretation and comparative theology carried out by Christians in Islamic contexts. The study further aims to contribute to missiological best practice by encouraging more informed usage of narratives as part of Christian witness to Muslims. Finally, I hope my narrative approach to theological comparison will stimulate Christian-Muslim worldview studies and encourage a scriptural narrative focus in addition to the more common thematic approach to religious dialogue.

NARRATIVE AND WORLDVIEW

From the perspective of both Christians and Muslims, real events precede and give rise to both narrative and worldview. Christians, for example, believe that the death and resurrection of Jesus were real events, and Muslims believe that Muhammad's reception of the Qur'an happened in history. Narrative and worldview describe and interpret these events in different ways. While worldview is a useful way of abstracting and expressing the belief system arising from these events, narrative is primary or even indispensable for articulating the events themselves. In this study I develop a new model of the relationship of narrative to worldview that utilizes *polarities*—pairings that emphasize opposing attributes, tendencies, or principles—between Christian and Muslim worldviews to structure a comparison of the narratives. The African American poet Audre Lorde (1934–1992) noted the usefulness of polarities: "Difference must be not merely tolerated, but seen as a *fund of necessary polarities between which our creativity can spark like a dialectic.*"[3] It is my hope that the polarities identified here, while not obscuring commonality, will clarify differences and catalyze creative investigation.

Qualitative interviews with Turkish imams helped elucidate contemporary Muslim usage of qur'anic Abraham stories and test the usefulness of my model for engaging in Christian-Muslim interscriptural dialogue. I interviewed each of nine imams twice, firstly to learn about Abraham from their perspectives and secondly to confirm and calibrate my analysis of the Turkish Muslim perspective and to discuss some of my overall conclusions with them. As Moyaert correctly notes, "Interreligious dialogue is the place where we can listen to the stories of religious others and enter their world."[4]

CONTEXTUAL MISSIOLOGY, COMPARATIVE THEOLOGY, BIBLICAL AND QUR'ANIC INTERPRETATION

This research is located primarily within two related fields of study, which treat interfaith encounter from different perspectives and bear an uneasy relationship to one another: Contextual Missiology (CM) and Comparative Theology

(CT).[5] Missiology is a relative newcomer in the arena of traditional theological reflection, arising from the study of the practice of Christian foreign missions. Kim notes that historically "missiological reflection has emerged within a variety of disciplines including communications and evangelism, development and social studies, historical studies, religious studies, anthropology and cultural studies, ecumenics, biblical studies, and systematics."[6] My study involves several of these disciplines, particularly biblical and qur'anic studies for engaging the primary Abraham narratives. It makes some contribution to theological anthropology, defined as the "study of the human person in conversation with the doctrinal framework of particular religious traditions,"[7] by examining how Christians and Muslims appeal to Abraham in their self-identification. But this study's primary contribution to missiological reflection is to elucidate the relationship between biblical and qur'anic narratives and their related worldviews.

From a NT perspective, as I understand it, Christian mission refers first of all to the carrying out of the proclamation commissioned by the risen Jesus Christ, as recorded at the end of each of the four canonical gospels and at the beginning of the book of Acts.[8] The story of Jesus' life, teaching, work, death, and resurrection is to be told as a solemn testimony to all nations, who are to be called to obedient faith in him as Lord in their own context.[9] In this study I investigate the way in which Christians see this mission to all nations to be rooted in God's self-committing promise to Abraham: "I will bless you... in you all the families of the earth shall be blessed" (Gen 12:1-3; Gal 3:8).

I understand mission first of all as the activity of Christians living out their calling as followers of Jesus in every setting and part of the world. This calling includes the witness, community-building and teaching with which I have been personally involved in Turkey.[10] It also includes the church's calling to embody the presence of the kingdom of God in the world.[11] Wright expounds Christian mission in broad biblical terms: "Fundamentally, our mission . . . means our committed participation as God's people, at God's invitation and command, in God's own mission within the history of God's world for the redemption of God's creation."[12] Still we must evaluate the extent to which using Abrahamic promises for various missional purposes is justified by the biblical material.

The combining of *contextual* with *missiology* is somewhat redundant. Christian mission should be by definition contextual, entailing the purposeful bridging of various human and cultural divides to participate most effectively in what may be described as the mission of God.[13] The process of contextualization is likened by some to "incarnation"—taking on the form of those to whom one is sent for their good[14]—and by others to "translation"—changing the form of the message while maintaining the meaning.[15] One of missiology's contributions to other theological disciplines is the insight gained from Christian reflection in many different cultural contexts. An example of such reflection is found in the growing practice of reading sacred texts with those of other faiths, which has been described as "contextual reading."[16] Reading the Genesis Abraham narrative in comparison with the qur'anic Abraham narratives and in dialogue with Turkish Muslims constitutes an example of such contextual reading.

Reasons for giving missiological priority to Abraham emerge from three streams of contemporary Christian mission practice. Firstly, in *preparation and training* for Christian mission, the call of Abraham in Genesis 12 often serves as a source of missionary motivation rooted in the divine purpose to bring salvation to all nations. Beyond inspiring missionary candidates by appealing to Abraham's departure from homeland and family to follow the call of God, missiological writing underlines the centrality of this event from the standpoint of the "mission of God," the *Missio Dei*. For example, Showalter highlights the promise in Genesis 12:1-3:

> The missionary heart of God is nowhere more clearly revealed than in this great commission passage of the Old Testament and its essential reiteration in Matthew 28:19, 20. The two commissions are essentially one and the same. The promise (*epangelion*) to Abram is the gospel (*euangelion*) to the world.... Even the promise of his abiding presence is the same ... Gen. 28:14,15 with Matt 28:20.[17]

This priority is evident in mission curricula such as the widely used "Perspectives on the World Christian Movement," which begins with Abraham.[18] Biblical theological studies on mission draw attention to the sweeping missiological implications of this promise to Abraham, located at the critical juncture between the universal story of the nations and the first stage of Israel's story.[19]

Secondly, the Abraham narrative is important for mission *methodology*, as can be seen in approaches known as Chronological Bible Teaching (CBT) and biblical "storying." The CBT movement, developed toward the end of the 1970s, focuses on telling and retelling redemptive history and prophecy, "first communicating chronologically the great events and themes and then over time filling in the gaps."[20] If sequentially teaching the narrative of Scripture brings understanding of its message, a key part of the narrative for discussion with Muslims is the story of Abraham.

Storytelling, a communicative activity as old as humankind, is fundamental to the maintenance and transmission of traditions from generation to generation. It is also foundational to identity and worldview articulation. A special paper published by the Lausanne Committee for World Evangelization (LCWE), in conjunction with the International Orality Network (ION), contends that storytelling should be a significant tool in the process of "making disciples" of Jesus Christ: "Because stories possess the power to actually change how people think, feel, and behave, and to change the way they see the world, it is important to have a sequential, step-by-step process that leads them to a new, biblical worldview."[21] Steffen argues that the gospel needs to recover "its original character as a living storytelling tradition of messengers who told the good news of the victory of Jesus.[22] "Abrahamic" dialogue between Muslims and Christians might proceed better if these stories were first well told. Wise storytelling may soften the too-often confrontational nature of Christian-Muslim encounter.

In Turkish Ottoman life the public storyteller or "meddah" played an important role.[23] Recounting the lives of the prophets and, especially in Sufi circles, of the saints or "friends of God" has been central to Muslim formational practices.[24] Storytelling, especially the art of interpreting the Qur'an through the narration of hadith (reports concerning the words and deeds of Muhammad) as the stories behind the revelation of particular verses, is a significant aspect of Muslim life, with potential for dialogue with biblical storytellers.

Thirdly, the missiological importance of the Abraham narrative is seen in the concept of *transforming worldview*.[25] There is growing consensus in missiological circles that stories, particularly biblical stories presented more or less in their canonical order, are the most effective means of achieving this transformation at a deep, worldview level.[26] The Abraham narrative has potential to clarify the Christian worldview at one of the points where its metanarrative differs most from that of the Muslim worldview.[27] Muslims who encounter the biblical Abraham story may find their unexamined worldview challenged and disrupted, just as encountering the qur'anic Abraham stories may unsettle and challenge the unexamined worldviews of Christians.

COMPARATIVE THEOLOGY

This study also falls within the academic discipline known as Comparative Theology (CT), which Fredericks describes as "a way of dealing responsibly and creatively with the fact of the plurality of religions today."[28] The discipline is often identified with the work of Jesuit scholar Francis X. Clooney,[29] although it might be more correct to describe his approach as the New Comparative Theology, in contrast with the old comparative theology, which explicitly focused on missiology. Clooney describes CT as "the practice of rethinking aspects of one's own faith tradition through the study of aspects of another faith tradition."[30] According to Clooney:

> Comparative theology is particularly interested in highlighting the nature, dynamics, and use of doctrines and their referents within traditions but also across boundaries. Thus, for example, candidates for analysis will include: faith, truth, sin, grace, salvation, community, and worship, in general and in more specific doctrinal forms, plus an even wider range of vaguer but still fruitful terms such as union or communion, delusion, liberation, humility, devotion, spiritual knowledge, compassion, and healing.[31]

Many of these doctrines can be usefully compared with similar or related concepts in Islam. However, I am primarily interested in comparing the *scriptural narratives* and their *worldview implications* by detailed consideration of their respective Abraham narratives. I would therefore add narratives at the top of the list of Clooney's candidates for analysis.

Clooney says that the underlying motives of comparative theology are the pursuit of *mutual understanding* and peace, along with an *objective analysis* of religions. The first of these leads to "the determination to discern and stress what religious people have in common."[32] However while articulating areas of common ground is one goal of comparative theology, it is equally vital for mutual understanding to clarify points where faith systems diverge. The dissonance between biblical and qur'anic Abraham narratives uncovered in this study has potential both to reveal and to refine the worldviews of Christians and Muslims. In the end, my approach may have more in common with the analysis used by earlier practitioners of comparative theology described by Barnes: "They had no doubts about the object of their work—to make converts to Christianity. But, to do so successfully, they had to learn about and from the religious traditions they encountered; that learning profoundly changed the way they viewed their own tradition and the wider world."[33]

In the following chapter I will consider a related approach known as "Scriptural Reasoning" (SR) practiced by Jewish, Christian and Muslim scholars. Both SR and CT are related to interreligious dialogue, but CT is seen as more of a "private" scholarly enterprise involving less face-to-face encounter among representatives of religions and more prolonged study and self-conscious reflection on the sacred texts of "others," most frequently by Christian theologians.[34] Barnes puts it this way: "In CT . . . texts are read prayerfully and their ideas pondered interiorly; in SR the exercise is very much a group effort in which study builds up friendship and trust."[35]

To the extent that most of my time has been spent in private study and reflection on the biblical and qur'anic Abrahamic material, my research has been primarily an exercise in comparative theology. My dialogue with Turkish Muslims about Abraham and his stories has led to only a limited amount of reading of each other's texts together. Hence it does not fit as easily within the Scriptural Reasoning model.

BIBLICAL AND QUR'ANIC INTERPRETATION

My hermeneutical approach in examining the biblical text is commonly referred to as "theological interpretation of the Bible." Vanhoozer argues that because biblical texts are concerned ultimately with the reality of God, only a theological reading does justice to the subject and to the biblical writers' own understanding of what they were conveying:

> The principal thrust of theological interpretation is to direct the interpreter's attention to the subject matter of Scripture — God, the acts of God in history, the gospel — rather than to a particular theological tradition or, for that matter, to some other topic (e.g., the history of the text's composition, the secular history "behind" the text, the structure of the text, etc.).[36]

Although I also apply *narrative* criticism[37] (in chapter 3) and *canonical* criticism[38] (in chapter 4) I am primarily reading to know God's purposes as spoken in and through the biblical texts, applying a theological approach. This confessional approach highlights the biblical texts' testimony to the reality of God as the primary character in the narrative of Scripture. It is also a Christian approach to theological interpretation of the Bible, which regards the apostolic NT writings as continuing and complementing the Hebrew Scriptures, and thereby completing the body of authoritative divine writings read and studied as God's Word.

As a confessing Christian, interpreting the Qur'an is a somewhat different exercise for me from interpreting the Bible. Although I do seek to understand the Qur'an objectively on its own terms, I do not approach it as an insider. For this reason, in order to treat it fairly, I will accord priority to broadly received Muslim interpretation of the Qur'an, especially in terms of the development of an Islamic "worldview." While it is not common to speak of "theological interpretation of the Qur'an," the fact that the subject matter of both the Bible and the Qur'an revolves around various "theological" issues means that a comparative *theological* approach is appropriate for the purposes of this study.

My approach to interpreting qur'anic Abraham material may fit broadly within what Duderija describes as "progressive Muslims' methods of interpretation," to the extent that I employ a "thematic, corroborative-inductive (or systematic) approach to the Qur'an's interpretation" to understanding these texts.[39] Duderija divides contemporary Muslim approaches to qur'anic hermeneutics into two broad groupings—Neo-traditional Salafi Muslims and Progressive Muslims— and treats seven major areas where their interpretive approaches to the primary Islamic sources (Qur'an, Sunna, and Hadith) differ.[40] My approach aligns with the latter group in approaching the Qur'an with a presumption of some textual coherence at least at the sura level.[41] In both approaches, however, the "core principles" or "parameters of faith" are fixed and ultimately nonnegotiable.[42] It is these core, fixed elements of the Muslim worldview that I primarily engage while examining and interpreting qur'anic Abraham material for the purposes of comparative theology.

FIGURE 1.1 – MAP OF CHAPTERS

Chapters are mapped onto a broadly chronological overview of the ancient texts and areas of scholarly work to be engaged (shown in boxes) and onto the areas of "interscriptural dialogue" created by juxtaposition in the discussion:

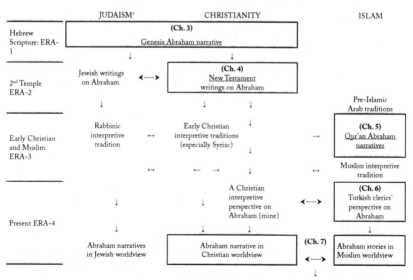

(Ch. 8) Implications for contextual missiology and comparative theology

CHAPTER 1 – ABRAHAMIC DIALOGUE

Burgeoning efforts in "Abrahamic dialogue" reflect increasing interest in investigating and utilizing the common appeal to Abraham by Jews, Christians and Muslims in today's pluralistic world.[1] Judaism, Christianity and Islam all trace their roots to Abraham.[2] Parks documents how Abraham has been seen as "the first Jew" by Jewish writers, as "the first Christian" by Christians, and as "the first Muslim" by Muslims.[3] Each tradition has at times claimed unique or even exclusive rights to the patriarch. The Qur'an takes note of these competing claims, addressing itself to Jews and Christians: "People of the Book, why do you argue about Abraham when the Torah and the Gospels were not revealed until after his time? Do you not understand? God knows and you do not. Abraham was neither a Jew nor a Christian" (Q3:65-67).

Ancient Abrahamic traditions have thus been utilized both to foster positive relationships and to instigate deep interfaith conflict. Kuschel describes this as a "family dispute" in which "each of the three faiths believes that it has preserved the paternal or maternal heritage in the purest form."[4] Yet in spite of this ongoing dispute, many today believe that Abrahamic identity opens up common ground that should be cultivated for the common good. For example, Moyaert holds that "Interreligious dialogue is the place where we can listen to the stories of religious others and enter their world."[5] Jewish writer Kogan draws attention to the way distinct identities have developed from the Genesis Abraham narrative: "That these [biblical] stories, *differently interpreted* (as they are in Christianity), or *differently told* (as they are in Islam), have become part of the core narrative of two related faiths attests to their profundity and their power."[6]

Abrahamic dialogue must be clearly distinguished from the larger field of which it is a subset. This distinction is not always adequately addressed in theologies of religion, which appeal to the natural revelation common to all peoples or common paternity as God's creatures.[7] The claim to possession of Abrahamic roots puts the issue on a different footing. Because of competing claims of special revelation, this dialogue is inextricably linked with what has been called *scriptures in dialogue* and the complex issues of *scriptural intertextuality*. Responsible study of our respective Scriptures is an imperative for this type of dialogue.

Abraham and Ecumenical Unity

Abraham is frequently recruited as a key ally in efforts to bring about peace and mutual understanding among conflicted groups and nations. Josua notes (though with evident concern) that many voices proclaim that "the three monotheistic religions should leave behind their competition up to now, reflect instead about their mutual father figure Abraham, and bear witness of intellectual and moral values to an increasingly areligious and unjust world."[8] Efforts of this sort are seen especially in places where pluralism and globalism have brought communities of different faith traditions into close contact. Catholic scholar Valkenberg recounts the benefits of his interfaith encounters with Turkish Muslims in the Netherlands:

> [This dialogue can] contribute to a form of God-talk in which Muslims and Christians may share their traditions as mutual incitements to a broader understanding of God. . . . European Christians have a lot to learn from the strangers who are our interlocutors in these dialogues.[9]

Valkenberg's significant dialogue partners from the influential Gülen movement[10] have sponsored a range of dialogue related programs centered around Abraham. For example, they organized "Abraham Meetings" in Şanlıurfa, Turkey, Abraham's ostensible place of birth, to build bridges between countries and religious communities.[11] These followed the first "Uluslararası Hz. İbrahim Sempozyumu" (International Abraham Symposium), a gathering of Muslim, Christian and Jewish clergy and scholars in the same city in April 2000. Yet the tensions inherent in Abrahamic dialogue were also evident in papers presented by Muslim contributors to the consultation, which emphasized the nonnegotiable nature of the Islamic understanding of Abraham.[12] For example, Moroccan professor Hassan Azzouzi made it clear that from a Muslim standpoint the only real Abrahamic unity is Islam: "It is the duty of those making an Abrahamic invitation to be clear that this concept carries only the meaning of Islam."[13] The "Abraham Meetings" in Şanlıurfa also provide the umbrella for annual gatherings of social aid organizations. The organizers of these events summarize their objectives:

> The International Project ABRAHAM MEETINGS has been launched as a humanitarian goodness movement which will bring the whole humanity together with [the] profundity [breadth] of Abraham's heart, his hospitality, abundance, benevolence, his understanding of sharing and his deep love of human beings.[14]

Another example of this Turkish Muslim appropriation of Abraham as a focus for dialogue was the "Abrahamic Traditions" dinner held on March 19, 2015, sponsored by the Niagara Foundation and the Turkish American Society of Wheaton, Illinois. Three speakers (Muslim, Jewish, and Christian) each examined the influences of Abraham on the world's major religions.[15] A small number of Turkish authors argue that the Abrahamic religions are essentially the same at their core. Ülkü, for example, whose works also include a study of Kabbalistic Jewish mysticism, asserts in his book, *Abraham Father of Nations (Ulusların Babası İbrahim)* that apart from differences in worship rituals, these religions are nearly one.[16]

In a Western academic context, the "Oxford Abrahamic Group" brings together Christian, Muslim and Jewish scholars with a goal of deepening mutual understanding of respective Abrahamic scriptures and traditions. Winter introduces a work by members of this group with optimism about the future of interfaith cordiality: "Today, despite the headlines, and the heated rhetoric of fundamentalist preachers on all sides, it is reasonable to claim that most Abrahamic believers find themselves on slowly convergent paths.[17] The scholars involved do acknowledge that there are no shortcuts in this process. Such initiatives are "most likely to succeed where the theology insists on the integrity of each religion, and refuses the logic of syncretism or relativism. Abraham's God, after all, is a God of truth, whose demands are absolute."[18] As I will argue, such integrity demands careful comparative theological reflection on the respective Abraham narratives.

Faith-based initiatives for peace are attractive because of what Breiner describes as the perceived "efficacy of religious faith to deal with contemporary problems."[19] Some initiatives show that Abrahamic commonality can be a basis for bringing people together on a local level. For example, one report examines texts in each tradition that seem to support violence, and then focuses on other perspectives within these traditions which can promote "Abrahamic alternatives to war" such as teachings and ethical imperatives within their sacred texts.[20]

Attempts to identify Abraham texts that might facilitate peacemaking will doubtless continue. For example, Sheridan finds such an opportunity in Genesis 25:9, where Isaac and Ishmael bury their father together. She argues that the text "may well found the basis for a new look at the role of Ishmael."[21] Pabst, writing from a feminist perspective, avers that Sarah and Hagar have been misused by the Christian tradition and suggests that if we "decide to see difference as enriching, and not as a threat to identity, Sarah and Hagar can become powerful figures within an interreligious dialogue today."[22]

Many of these efforts to ground peacemaking in the Abraham narrative are unconvincing. It is questionable, for example, whether the canonical narrative of Sarah and Hagar is as useful for this purpose as Pabst suggests, as I will argue in chapters 3 and 4. Similarly, Sensenig contrasts Abraham's "peace-making paradigm" with Israel's subsequent history: "The violent seeds of conquest sown by Joshua's 'scorched earth' crusade in this Promised Land ultimately bore the bitter fruit of a flawed and failed mini-empire, the Davidic monarchy."[23] Although it is true that Abraham's and Isaac's relationships with their neighbors were largely characterized by peaceful coexistence (e.g., the Philistine acknowledgement "We see plainly that the LORD has been with you. So we said, let there be a sworn pact between us" Gen 26:28; cf. 21:22-23),[24] nevertheless to contrast this neighborly interaction with the post-Exodus conquest of the land and destruction of its inhabitants by Israel's armies under Joshua's leadership is a questionable move, effectively ignoring the repeated promise of God to the patriarchs that he will give this land to their offspring (Gen 12:7; 13:15; 15:18-21; 17:3, 8, 26:3; 28:13). Such a move also ignores the specific notices made in the Genesis narrative of just such a future destruction of Abraham's present neighbors, who are presented as "wicked, great sinners against the LORD" (13:13).[25] While judgment will wait 400 years because "the iniquity of the Amorites is not yet complete" (Gen 15:13-16), this moral and religious corruption explains the drastic measures Joshua will take. Note also Joshua's warning to Israel that their end will be similar to the previous inhabitants of the land (Josh 24:19-20).

Using scriptural teaching on humanity's common identity as *created* by God may have far more potential for furthering peace and justice than using Abraham as a common source of faith. Goodwin points to successful efforts in which "religious leaders refer to the purposes of God for all humanity as set out in the creation narratives, and thereby expose exclusivist national ideologies as narrow and artificial constructions."[26] Common humanity is a less problematic bond than so-called Abrahamic faith, for reasons which will become increasingly apparent as we proceed.

CHALLENGES TO ABRAHAMIC ECUMENISM

Simplistic claims that all religions are essentially the same are neither sustainable nor helpful. While the claim that all religions are one may be well-intentioned, as Prothero insists, it is "neither accurate nor ethically responsible."[27] Similarly, Turkish theologian Ramazan Hurç argues that using Abraham as the basis for such dialogue is inadequate because the Qur'an clearly warns against it, citing the reminder in Q 3:65-67 that the scriptural books (Torah, Injil and Qur'an) were revealed after Abraham. He points out that Muslims cannot leave these books, especially the Qur'an, out of the discussion as if Abraham by himself were a basis for dialogue. His key example is Muhammad, who in his relations with Christians, continually called them to turn from their misguided Trinitarian faith to the pure Abrahamic monotheism of Islam.[28]

Islamic scholar Fazlur Rahman clarifies the qur'anic position, calling for some sort of coming together on a common platform:

> Religiously speaking, the high place that the Qur'an accords to the religious personalities of Abraham, Moses and others should provide an adequate basis for mutual understanding and cooperation, even though the Qur'an rejects Jewish particularism and has universalized monotheism and divine guidance, which every human being can share equally.[29]

But this is problematic. What Rahman calls "Jewish particularism" is one of the most sweeping aspects of the biblical worldview expressed not only in the Hebrew Bible but also in the NT. While Israel's God is the God of all humankind (e.g. Rom 3:29-30), the biblical story nevertheless traces a particular relationship with the Jewish nation as the channel of universal blessing. The NT makes it clear that as Jesus said, "salvation is from the Jews" (John 4:22; cf. Rom 9:3-5; 11:11-24; Eph 2:11-22). In a passing comment Paul sums up the relationship of Gentile believers to Jewish believers by saying "the Gentiles have come to share in their spiritual blessings" (Rom 15:27). So when the respective scriptures on Abraham are included in the discussion, we are faced with differences that make the common ground harder to find. From a Christian standpoint, the "high place that the Qur'an accords to the religious personalities of Abraham and others" is granted only at the high cost of denying the biblical particularism where Abraham's role is central.

From a Muslim perspective, scholars like Sachedina wrestle with the problem that the Qur'an seems to provide support both for religious pluralism and for exclusivism or absolutism toward other religions.[30] Pluralism can be argued based on a verse speaking of humanity as one community (Q 2:213). But the doctrine of the "supersession" of previous Abrahamic revelations, as a necessary result of the emergence of Muhammad, negates recognition of other religions' claims as legitimate ways of salvation. The primary way of resolving the apparent contradiction between qur'anic pluralism and exclusivism has been to argue that verses that may support toleration have been abrogated by verses that call for combating unbelief.[31] However, this concept of abrogation has been rejected by many modern scholars. Sachedina claims that "the principal problem that modern Muslim scholars face is deciding whether or not to accept the judgement of past scholars that qur'ānic verses which deal with interfaith relations have been abrogated."[32]

Hashmi firmly rejects "the notion of abrogation as an interpretive tool of the first resort."[33] He argues that when the Qur'an is read as an integrated whole, "the apparently belligerent verses emerge as limited in scope and application while an ethic of pluralism (best expressed in Q 5:48) is consistently upheld."[34] He interprets the qur'anic position as simultaneously calling various faith communities to Islam and assessing their distinctive paths as part of God's will: "All religion (*din*) is one, but the specific rules, norms, guidelines, laws (shari'a) for each community may vary."[35] However, I will argue that the distinction at issue is more than a question of rules and laws (paths within the one religion), but rather concerns deeper matters of worldview rooted in the main storylines of each faith.

Karl-Josef Kuschel builds a systematic argument for an Abrahamic *ecumene* in which, as he puts it, "Jews, Christians and Muslims are prepared to stop dismissing one another with polemic as 'unbelievers', 'apostates', or 'superseded'; in other words [treating one another] as brothers and sisters, in faith in the God of Abraham."[36] I question three areas of his argument. First, his explanation of Abraham and Christianity is particularly unconvincing, especially in explaining the beginning of Christianity after Israel's failure to "convert" under Jesus of Nazareth's teaching. He says, "Taking up a belief in the resurrection of the dead which had been widespread since the time of apocalyptic, Jesus' followers could not give up their conviction that the crucified Jesus was alive."[37] This is a seriously mistaken reading of the origins of the Christian belief in Jesus' resurrection as seen in the NT, which is inseparable from its understanding of Abraham (see chapter 4).[38]

Kuschel's second questionable assertion is that "in John we are confronted with the first exclusive Christianization of Abraham. . . . Johannine preexistence christology is the keystone in an argument about the exclusive truth needed for the Christian truth finally to be able to triumph over Jewish truth."[39] However, from the standpoint of the NT, the problem is not

Christian exclusion of Israel but Israel's rejection of the "son" of Israel's God. Jesus made this inescapable in the parable of the tenants (Matt 21:33-46). That Jesus was the Son of God is at the heart of the common NT kerygma (see chapter 5, preliminary comments).[40]

Thirdly, Kuschel too readily links *Ishmael* directly with the religion of *Islam* rather than with Ishmael's *Arab* descendants. By contrast, Arab Christian scholar Maalouf traces Ishmael through biblical history to argue that the oracle given to Hagar that Ishmael would dwell "in the proximity/presence" of his brethren (Gen 16:12) was a "word of integration rather than a word of alienation and hostility as is often believed."[41] He notes that Ishmael's descendants were an integral part of the restoration promises of OT prophecy (Isa 42:1-10; 60:1-7; etc.). In light of the biblical outworking of the Ishmael oracles, claims of fulfillment in Islam are weak at best.[42]

Muslim arguments for Abrahamic religious ecumenism based on common *ethical monotheism* are somewhat more plausible than efforts to make the biblical Abraham serve these interests. Nevertheless, as we will see, this is done at the expense of the overall biblical narrative which ties Abraham specifically to Israel and indeed to Jesus. An example of such a "generic Muslim" Abraham argument is expressed by Delorenzo:

> It is not a matter of favor won by an individual and passed on to others, so that a favored family develops and extends itself into a tribe, a community, a nation, a race. . . . From the very outset, beginning with Ibrahim . . . this notion was put to rest. . . . True guidance is God's guidance, and it is to be found in all the scriptures He revealed to humankind for their moral and spiritual edification. . . . Forget the labels! Forget the pedigrees![43]

Such an approach to common identity is problematic for Jews whose scriptures are unequivocal on Abraham's multiplication by God into the nation of Israel. It is just as problematic for Christians, whose founding documents not only affirm God's choice of Israel, but also redefine monotheism by including Jesus in the identity of Israel's God,[44] thus focusing the possibility of human beings' reconciliation with God on the singular divine intervention in Jesus' death and resurrection.[45]

Christian supporters of Abrahamic ecumenism are often critical of their own tradition's appropriation of Abraham. For example, Pulcini questions the validity of the interpretation of Abraham found in the NT: "Christianity reinterpreted the figure of Abraham to accommodate its needs. . . . Why was Christ the only descendent to whom the promises applied?"[46] He ignores the appropriation of the Abraham tradition by Jesus himself (see chapter 4) and apparently sees no importance in Jews receiving or rejecting Jesus as the Messiah. In Pulcini's view, Gentiles should be admitted into the Abrahamic line of blessing by faith in Christ while Jews should be seen as already there without Christ. This wholesale jettisoning of the uniqueness, universality and finality of Jesus as Lord and Messiah is found in many Christian efforts to widen the Abrahamic umbrella. Kuschel, for example, reduces Paul's Abraham theology to the following formula:

Gentiles who believe in Christ become children of Abraham in the spiritual sense. Children of Abraham after the flesh, the Jews, remain children of Abraham by following the faith of Abraham, which is not trust in the 'works of the law' but trust in a God who calls into being that which is not and thus breaks through and surpasses all earthly, human, criteria and expectations.[47]

Yet for Paul (consistent with the entire apostolic canon) there is no such difference: Jews, who have rejected Jesus as Messiah, are only "saved" and grafted back into the Abrahamic olive tree as they confess Jesus as risen Lord, just as Gentiles must (Rom 9:1; 10:1, 9-13; 11:23). Such suppression of biblical evidence is troubling. While the recruitment of Abraham as a neutral father figure in the effort to build and maintain peace arises from laudable intentions, much of what is written stumbles over the contradictory uses to which he is put. The approaches to Abraham in Judaism, Christianity and Islam are deeply different and at many points incompatible. Careful hermeneutics and comparative reading of texts confirm these differences. Josua examines this question in detail in his 2005 dissertation, concluding that there are very significant difficulties with Abrahamic ecumenism when the qur'anic texts regarding Abraham are examined with care: "Exegesis and reception of the qur'anic texts on Ibrahim not only show the different narrative perspectives, but, in particular, the different intentions of the same material, which only appear similar or even interchangeable when observed superficially."[48]

These challenges to Abrahamic dialogue make it clear that bringing the respective scriptures (the Tanakh, the Bible and the Qur'an) into careful comparative encounter is essential. Study of these scriptures yields resources for peaceful interchange and also clarifies areas of deeper difference that must be respected. Some models of dialogue intentionally focus on the mutual use of these Scriptures, specifically efforts to bring about encounter between Christians and Muslims through reading and discussion of their own and each other's scriptures.

Efforts in scriptural dialogue follow two different models: (1) those that seek a common scriptural basis for understanding differences and resolving conflicts; and (2) scriptural reasoning efforts that seek to enlighten and/or persuade those whose scriptures both overlap and differ from our own.

SCRIPTURAL DIALOGUE TO RESOLVE CONFLICT

Taking the first approach, we find an increasing amount of written work produced by scholars interacting with each other's texts, such as the "Essays in Scriptural Intertextuality" compiled by the Society of Biblical Literature.[49] We also find Christian and Muslim leaders/scholars in public forum dialogue, such as the Doha "building bridges" seminar in 2003 convened by Rowan Williams, Archbishop of Canterbury, which was an exercise in Christians and Muslims studying the Bible and the Qur'an together.[50]

Universities increasingly offer opportunities for such scriptural encounter. For example, the Trinity College Faculty of Divinity in the Toronto School of Theology offers a course entitled "Studies in Scriptural Reasoning: The

Abrahamic Traditions."[51] Similarly, the Center for Muslim-Christian Studies (CMCS), first in Edinburgh and more recently in Oxford, aims to facilitate student dialogue over scriptures.[52] This is not an easy process, as readers of texts bring their own presuppositions to their reading. Nevertheless, it is vital for Christians and Muslims to understand each other's scriptures and take their differences as well as similarities seriously.[53]

Some of the most significant reflection on this approach comes from "Scriptural Reasoning" movements, which pursue the practice of group reading and interacting with the scriptures of Judaism, Christianity, and Islam. Many practitioners of SR wrestle primarily with the encounter between "Islam" and the "West." A representative sample, or at least a formalized written dialogue between scholars, may be found in the volume edited by Koshul and Kepnes, which they introduce with the following purpose statement.

> The principal objective of this collection of chapters is to use the underlying allegiance to scripture in Islam, Judaism, and Christianity to underscore the deep affinities between the three monotheistic traditions and at the same time preserve the respect for differences between the traditions. . . . Beyond outlining the logic of scripture and interpretation, scholars in this book attempt to apply that logic in creative ways to develop responses to the contemporary Islam-West encounter . . . in a combined attempt to understand the contemporary conflicts between them and also in an enterprise to overcome these conflicts.[54]

The goal of this type of scriptural reasoning is primarily to utilize the resources of Abrahamic scriptures to *understand and resolve conflicts*, specifically "the present situation of conflict between Islam and the West." Despite some disclaimers,[55] much of the literature relates in one way or another to this state of affairs and to raising awareness of the importance of understanding one another's scriptures as part of the solution. While its description as a "wisdom-seeking engagement with Jewish, Christian and Muslim scriptures" points to a broader goal than conflict resolution narrowly defined,[56] this approach seems primarily addressed to the present Islam-West situation of "conflict" and the public square. Kepnes puts the goal of inter-religious conflict resolution this way:

> SR is a practice of group reading of the scriptures of Judaism, Christianity, and Islam that builds sociality among its practitioners and releases sources of reason, compassion, and divine spirit for healing our separate communities and for repair of the world.[57]

The methodology is designed to bring into existence long-lasting arrangements in which conversations are held jointly around these three scriptures and interpretive traditions. Through small groups gathering from time to time to read and interpret selected texts from the Tanakh, Old Testament/New Testament and Qur'an it is hoped that "an Abrahamic collegiality: not consensus but friendship" will be achievable. The groups operate with a "three-way mutual *hospitality*: each is host to the others and guest to the others as each welcomes the other two to their 'home' scripture and its traditions of interpretation."[58] In an interesting comment that sheds light on the model as it is being practiced,

Ford says that "the rabbinic debates around scripture in the Talmud . . . are probably the nearest traditional equivalent to scriptural reasoning."[59]

Ford gives eight suggested guidelines for scriptural reasoning, which outline both the process and the necessary attitudes of participants:[60]

> Acknowledge *the sacredness* of the others' scriptures to them (without having to acknowledge its authority for oneself).
>
> The 'native speakers' hosting a scripture and its tradition need to acknowledge that they do not exclusively own their scriptures—they are *not experts on its final meaning*.
>
> The aim is *not consensus*—that may happen, but it is more likely that the conclusion will be a recognition of deep differences.
>
> Do not be afraid of *argument*, as one intellectually honest way of responding to differences—part of mutual hospitality is learning to argue in courtesy and truth, and each tradition as well as each academic discipline embraces complex practices of discussion and dispute.
>
> Draw on *shared academic resources* to build understanding—members of different faith communities may be trained in the same field or share a philosophy.
>
> *Allow time* to read and re-read, to entertain many questions and possibilities, to let the texts unfold within their own traditions of interpretation and in (often unprecedented) engagement with each other, to stick with a text without premature resolution of its difficulties, and to sound the depths.
>
> Read and interpret with a view to the fulfillment of *God's purpose of peace* between all. . . .
>
> Be open to *mutual hospitality turning into friendship*—each tradition values friendship, and for it to happen now might be seen as the most tangible anticipation of future peace.

The final suggestion seems to me of particular value. Experience in Turkey has shown me that friendship is possible with Muslims who do not share my convictions even though they are aware of my work as a missionary-theologian (the Turkish term *misyoner* is historically and politically loaded and provokes strong reactions). Peaceful neighborly relations are possible among those of differing faith commitments, though usually the subject of religion and scriptures is avoided. Friendship works on a human level, especially when working together in job or community situations. Obviously the *institutional* setting opens possibilities for such structured, intentional scriptural dialogue in ways perhaps not so possible in day-to-day living or in familiar religious places of worship. In whatever setting, pursuing this intentionally requires a small group committed to reading together with some set of guidelines like the above. Ford uses the metaphors "house, campus and tent" to distinguish the locations where those involved in scriptural reasoning might be involved in different types of dialogue: "house" represents the common intra religious setting (synagogue, church, mosque communities and traditions); "campus" represents the university setting (where scholars belonging to different faith communities and disciplines might interact); and "tent" represents the small group setting where intentional scriptural reasoning actually takes place.[61]

An interesting challenge to this type of (largely) academic textual dialogue is raised by Melenie Prideaux, whose fieldwork in a mixed Muslim and Christian neighborhood highlights "the gap between theologians and communities." She claims that the study of Muslim-Christian dialogue is dominated by "the dialogue of the academic and theologian, the dialogue of texts," which in fact "does not necessarily seek to impact on or relate to religious communities, and in many senses becomes, as an academic exercise, an end in itself."[62] She contends that it is rather the practical and informal "living dialogue" which is the most significant kind of dialogue for most people. This highlights the importance of the friendship-building goal of this exercise.

The SR movement has numerous spokespersons in various locations. One is Peter Ochs (who reportedly coined the term "scriptural reasoning") and the Children of Abraham Institute (CHAI) at the University of Virginia, whose journal is the Journal of Scriptural Reasoning.[63] Another significant location is the Cambridge Inter-Faith Programme, where SR is an activity under the academic section of the programme.[64]

Ford comments that "scriptural reasoning does not encourage anyone to become an 'expert' in scriptural reasoning, as if it were possible to know all three scriptures and their traditions of interpretation in a specialist mode."[65] Adherents of each tradition have *their own* scriptures: Jews have the Tanakh, Christians have the NT and Muslims have the Qur'an. But this assumption of "ownership" becomes problematic, especially for Christian readers who receive the Tanakh in its present form as the Word of God and read it as *their own* scripture (not that of the 'other') along with the NT. The situation differs for the Jewish or Muslim reader. Judaism receives neither the NT nor the Qur'an as divine Scripture given by the one creator God of Israel; Islam affirms books given to Moses and Jesus but generally denies that the canonical scriptures (Tanakh and NT) are continuous with those original books in any meaningful way. But Christians, especially perhaps Jewish Christians, affirm the right to "host" the Tanakh/OT as equal heirs with Judaism, although this right is contested by many Jewish readers who consider the NT reading of the Tanakh to be a deviant interpretation.[66] Yet the Tanakh was the only scripture known and used by Jesus and his earliest followers. When the Jewish-Christian apostles speak of "the sacred writings" and "all scripture," they are referring to the Tanakh (2 Tim 3:15-16). As I show in the final section of chapter 5, Christians and Jews diverge from one another precisely along the lines of two readings of the same scriptures. This complicates the scriptural reasoning process. Who is the "host" of the Tanakh? Does SR require Christians to relinquish it to Jews?

Nevertheless, with the caveat that Christians claim the whole "Bible," it seems reasonable that the adherents of each tradition be recognized as the authoritative interpreters of their own scriptures. Thus Jews represent Judaism's positions, Christians represent Christianity's positions, and Muslims represent Islam's positions when explaining their relative readings of the scriptures in question.

But if adherents of each tradition "own" their scriptures, where is the common Abrahamic ground located? At the end of a special issue of Modern Theology devoted to SR, Daniel Hardy asks: "What are the most central seminal characteristics of the Abrahamic traditions, between them, and between them and the world?" and "How can we target the deepest suppositions of the Abrahamic traditions: the patterns of the activity of the Divine, the highest reaches of humanity (reason, passion, compassionate care, love, justice, social well-being, etc.) to which we are abductively attracted by the Divine?" [67] Hardy's questions show that the authors and practitioners of SR recognize a significant commonality between the so-called Abrahamic traditions. Yet what does "Abrahamic" mean here? What joins these three faiths in a common set and separates them from other world faiths? Presumably it is the doctrine of monotheistic creation (all that exists was created by one creator God), along with some notion of God's interaction with mankind through special figures like Abraham. Another common factor might be scriptures which overlap and have deep links, so that the NT, for example, affirms and continually quotes the Tanakh claiming that Jesus is the fulfillment of all that it points to, and the Qur'an claims to confirm the earlier scriptures of Moses and Jesus.

However, what Hardy calls the "deepest suppositions of the Abrahamic traditions" are mainly elements of uplifting and ennobling religious experience: "the highest reaches of humanity (reason, passion, compassionate care, love, justice, social well-being, etc.) to which we are abductively attracted by the Divine."[68] Are these not characteristics also claimed and aspired to by adherents of non-Abrahamic religions and humanists? Muslim background Turks, for example, disgruntled with religion or "religious" people, often declare that the important thing is to be human (*önemli olan insan olmaktır*). For the idea of something uniquely Abrahamic to be credible, defining both what is shared in common among these three traditions and also what distinguishes them from other worldviews must go beyond lofty aspirations for humanity.

Christian mission and Islamic Da'wa also raise important questions for this approach.[69] Would the structured, largely interfaith and institutional setting of SR be threatened by efforts to use scriptural dialogue to persuade those of other faiths to convert? Can "reasoning" in the SR sense include the "reasoning from the scriptures" approach used by Paul in the synagogues and multi-religious forums of his day (Acts 17:2, 17; 18:4, 19; 19:8, 9; 24:25), which aimed to persuade others and make disciples of Jesus Christ? Or can it include Muhammad's calling to debate with and warn unbelievers (e.g. Q 2:119), since, as Neuwirth remarks, "debate is one of the essential elements of the Qur'ān"?[70] If not, why not? One might reject efforts at persuasion from an understandable desire to avoid the divisions and even violence that could result from the rejection of such efforts to persuade others (sometimes against the messenger and sometimes against those who refuse to heed the warning). But if the very "DNA" of these faiths calls for mission or da'wa, how can deeper encounter avoid it?[71] Does not love of the God of truth require it? Yet SR does generally avoid it, and focuses rather on approaches that tend to maintain relationships, as Ford states:

A well-worn path into interfaith cul de sacs is to focus on "secure disagreements" which complacently reinforce the identity of each with minimal mutual exploration, learning or challenge. Rather, what has been found fruitful is continual engagement with the scriptures that have contributed both to such doctrines and to the shaping of a whole way of life (with worship, ethics, institutions and so on).[72]

Two "families" thus emerge from the mass of scriptural dialogue material and activity, distinguished by their objectives. The first pursues "scriptural reasoning" in order to create and deepen interfaith (especially Abrahamic) relationships which are often strained or nonexistent due to conflict (e.g. conflict between Islam and the West or the Israeli-Palestinian conflict). The second family of scriptural dialogue practitioners, while not rejecting these objectives, add the purpose of witness and persuasion.

SCRIPTURAL DIALOGUE TO PERSUADE

Honest involvement with our respective Abraham stories may lead to deeper communication and significant dialogue carried out for other purposes, among which is dialogue for the purpose of persuasive "witness" in mission. This purpose both includes and goes beyond the "dialogue as critical generosity" or the "dialogue of theological exchange" referred to in major Vatican statements on interfaith dialogue,[73] and goes further than that which the SR movement deems wise or fruitful. It moves to what may be described as challenging worldview by means of honest and respectful persuasion, based on the conviction that one's own faith is valuable and even necessary for the well-being of the dialogue partner. Many Christians, for example, are persuaded of "the inescapable particular, historical and exclusive dimension of the biblical revelation" and convinced of the importance of faithful witness to this revelation as part of genuine dialogue.[74]

Regrettably, much evangelical Christian response to Islam in recent years has been characterized by forms of discourse far removed from genuine dialogue. Cimino's analysis of American evangelical anti-Islamic discourse reveals that most of the post-9/11 literature draws sharper boundaries between Islam and Christianity than before 9/11 and asserts that Islam is an essentially violent religion. His survey reveals that "this polemic against Islam takes three forms: apologetics to prove the truth of Christianity against Islam; prophetic literature linking Islam as the main protagonist in end-times scenarios; and charismatic literature applying 'spiritual warfare' teachings to Islam."[75]

Christians involved in the forms of Abrahamic dialogue discussed in the previous section would disavow at least the confrontational tone found in this material, and most would reject all three of the polemical approaches. In addition to these approaches Cimino identifies a fourth evangelical position, *the contextualist approach*, which he finds as a missiological trend. "This approach teaches that the missionary must meet the Muslims on their own ground and that their culture and religious sensibility should be affirmed, even if ultimately 'fulfilled' through the Christian gospel."[76] I simply note that dialogue for the purpose of witness and apologetics does not necessarily share the defensive, aggressive tenor represented by the literature studied by Cimino.

While there is an allergy toward religious argument in many places today, particularly in North America and Europe, such disagreement can be the most meaningful and respectful of all. Valkenberg argues that genuine "dialogue is made possible by the fact that the partners differ, so that one should pay heed to the particularities of the traditions involved."[77] Rabbi Jonathan Sacks describes this as the "dignity of difference" and calls for the exorcising of "Plato's ghost," referring to the "false dream of unity based on universals, the idea that truth—reality, the essence of things—is universal."[78] Respecting and clarifying differences does not require adoption of pluralism as many advocates of interfaith dialogue seem to insist.

Among efforts to use scriptural texts in Christian-Muslim encounter, those in which Ida Glaser[79] is involved are particularly significant as models for my research because she works with the text of Gen 1–11, which the Abraham narrative continues; she exploits the narrative nature of that text; and her identified presuppositions and goals are not unlike my own. Glaser describes her 1994 dissertation as "an adventure in understanding a particular passage of the Bible in a particular inter-faith missionary context."[80] She describes "comparative theology," where she locates her work, as being "explicitly carried out from the point of view of believers in believing communities."[81]

As a Christian teacher I resonate both with the need for clearer understanding of other faiths' use of Abraham for more substantial dialogue and with the goal of peaceful interfaith encounter. I see no necessary conflict between these goals and those of witness and mission. It is possible, indeed essential, to combine sensitivity and awareness of different traditions not only with authentic Christian peacemaking, but also with witness and even apologetics. This conviction underlies many genuine efforts for deeper encounter. Christian-Muslim peace-making or conflict transformation efforts do not necessarily lead to giving up what Reisacher describes as "sharing God's love in Christ who died for our sins, rose again, and will return."[82] Perhaps some ground can be staked out through a theology of religions that emphasizes the *neighbor* and *hospitality*.[83] Muslim writer Al-Nowaihi voices similar desires:

> What is needed is for each party to force itself, at least temporarily, to see the other creed as its own believers see it. Only then can we arrive at a better understanding and a greater amount of mutual toleration. These goals cannot be reached by ignoring or minimizing the differences; rather should they be sought through a candid admission, coupled with an earnest attempt at a deeper sympathy and charity.[84]

My experience in Turkey shows that many Muslims respect openness about sincerely held faith commitments while strongly opposing efforts to hide mission behind a cloak of interfaith dialogue. Dialogue in mission should avoid reductionist or patronizing approaches to other faiths which give simplistic affirmation of their equal validity as ways to God and salvation, and the freedom of apologetics and witness must be part of healthy interfaith encounter. John Azumah defends the right to persuade in the context of dialogue: "My understanding of propagation and dialogue is that while the former is primarily concerned with a change in the belief of the other, the latter is primarily concerned with a change in perceptions of and attitude towards the other. The two cannot be mutually exclusive."[85]

Dialogue based on texts which interpret the significance of Abraham so differently may well include some form of *apologetics*. This is a more controversial purpose of dialogue, entailing both the articulate defense of a position and the related goal of proving the opposing position to be wrong. Yet interpreting the Bible honestly requires recognition of its polemical character in the face of the religions with which its human authors were in contact. As Wright states, "The Bible makes remarkably universal claims in the midst of this religious plurality in relation to the revealing and saving effect of particular events."[86] Certainly the NT enjoins witness and worldwide proclamation of the Gospel as an essential aspect of its message. Similarly, the Qur'an's polemical, debating approach is one of its best-known characteristics.[87] Citing Q 6:125, the London Central Mosque issued a fatwa encouraging Muslim participation in Abrahamic scriptural dialogue with this reminder: "According to the teaching of the Qur'an and the Sunnah of the Prophet Muhammad—Peace be upon him and all Prophets—Muslims are commanded to call to the way of Allah with wisdom and good admonition."[88]

There is a range of positions regarding the appropriateness of Christian apologetics. For instance, Karl Barth opposed apologetics, judging it a theologically mistaken enterprise to defend the faith on the basis of natural theology without the presupposition of faith in the Word of God.[89] There is, however, NT precedence for "reasoning with" (διαλέγομαι) people from different religious backgrounds in order to convince them of the truth concerning Christ (e.g. 17:2, 17; 18:4, 19; 19:8-9). Stackhouse spells out what this persuasive reasoning might look like under the title of *humble apologetics*, arguing that "the majority of Christians ever since have followed this pattern of constructive engagement with the ideas and minds of their day, in order that 'by all means I may save some' (1 Cor 9:22)."[90]

Three significant goals can be identified for sincere and open dialogue conducted for the purpose of mission and apologetics: (1) Substantial and respectful mutual understanding; (2) Mutual sharpening of understanding of each party's own texts and convictions; (3) Persuasion of dialogue partners to positions different from previously held, including conversion. The Abrahamic narrative is a good point for this process to begin, especially if the arena is credibly to be called Abrahamic Dialogue.

ABRAHAMIC DIALOGUE AND CONTEXTUAL MISSIOLOGY

Can Abrahamic interfaith dialogue serve contextual missiology? It is in fact at the heart of it. Taking people seriously as made in the image of God and engaging them humbly and honestly as our neighbors goes hand-in-hand with the learning process basic to interfaith witness. The further we advance into dialogue that is authentically "Abrahamic" in more than just name and common veneration, the more we will be forced to grapple with the Abrahamic texts of Genesis and the Qur'an.

Yet much interfaith dialogue is not particularly 'Abrahamic' except in name. My most profound discomfort has been with some Christian contributors, who seem so ready to abandon Jesus as the messianic son of Abraham in order to embrace an ethical monotheism in the interest of ecumenism. I also disagree with Rabbi Sacks' eloquently presented argument that the biblical narrative points us simply to acceptance of the different faiths as intended for different people.[91]

As a Christian I am persuaded that the sacred text points to one overarching narrative moving from the particularity of God's call of Abraham to his universal blessing of all peoples through the one particular man, Jesus, the true son of Abraham, ultimate heir and fulfiller of the patriarchal promise. Thus dialogue should not be limited to the pursuit of peace, justice and reciprocal enrichment, although these are valid goals for dialogue. But if the goals of Abrahamic dialogue are understood by both partners as mutual understanding, better communication and even effective persuasion, it is also essential to clearly articulate the Christian perspective.

CHAPTER 2 – NARRATIVE AND WORLDVIEW

How are biblical and qur'anic narratives to be studied and engaged with in such a way that fruitful comparison serves both deeper dialogue and more meaningful witness? We can begin with two provisional observations about narrative and worldview: (1) worldview is often articulated in narrative form, and (2) canonical master narratives undergird Christian and Muslim worldviews. Particular biblical and qur'anic stories are inseparable from larger narrative frameworks. While commonplace in Christian worldview studies, this connection between narrative and worldview appears to be infrequently acknowledged in Muslim approaches. Nevertheless, as Walsh and Middleton point out, narrative (history, stories, myths, folktales) is virtually "omnipresent" in faiths and philosophies worldwide, including Judaism and Islam, which both "articulate their worldview in narrative form."[1] Indeed, narrative has particular relevance and usefulness in Christian-Muslim engagement.

That the biblical narrative or "metanarrative"[2] and worldview are related is hardly a new notion in Christian thinking. The early church's "Rule of Faith" may best be understood as a summary of the biblical metanarrative, joining the confession of Jesus as Savior with the confession of God as Creator.[3] Early church father Tertullian described the rule with these words:

> That [rule] which prescribes the belief that there is one only God, and that He is none other than the Creator of the World, who produced all things out of nothing through His own Word, first of all sent forth; that this Word is called His Son, and under the name of God was seen in diverse manners by the patriarchs, heard at all times in the prophets, at last brought down by the Spirit and Power of the Father into the Virgin Mary, was made flesh in her womb, and being born of her; went forth as Jesus Christ.[4]

This narrative framework contains the essential elements of a Christian worldview. Blowers shows how early church fathers such as Irenaeus used the Rule of Faith, "articulating and authenticating a world-encompassing story or metanarrative of creation, incarnation, redemption, and consummation."[5] While I would adjust this list to highlight the "fall" and to begin the "redemption" phase with the Abraham–Israel narrative, the stages of the story represent the main elements of a representative Christian worldview.

Various definitions are given for the concept of *worldview*.[6] From a Reformed Christian perspective Wolters defines worldview as "the comprehensive framework of one's basic beliefs about things."[7] From a naturalist scientific perspective Vidal defines worldview as "a coherent collection of concepts allowing us to construct a global image of the world, and in this way to understand as many elements of our experience as possible."[8] The similarity of these definitions of worldview as a tool for comparing complex systems shows the usefulness of the concept of worldview for descriptive purposes. I will use the term to refer to the distinctive framework of core beliefs or concepts through which Christians and Muslims interpret God, the seen and unseen universe, human existence, history, and the future.

Wright lists four questions answered by all worldviews: "Who are we? Where are we? What's wrong? What's the solution?"[9] From these it can be seen that while worldview sometimes evokes a cerebral approach, it is in fact the stuff of ordinary living, mapping the well-worn paths of human behavior and culture. According to Meek, "worldview is about embodied humans who . . . feel their semiotics, hermeneutics and narrative as they do the fingers on their hands, and live their worldview as they would employ their digits to perform a sonata or prune a rosebush."[10]

As for *narrative*, Fee and Stuart's definition serves my purpose: "[Biblical] narratives are stories—purposeful stories retelling the *historical events* of the past that are intended to give meaning and direction for a given people *in the present*."[11] While we might also think of different *narrations* of one *story* (e.g. four gospel narratives of Jesus' life or four qur'anic narratives of Abraham's building the Kaaba), I will generally use the terms *narrative* and *story* interchangeably.

How do narrative and worldview relate? Which is formative of the other? When we say that *narrative shows worldview*, we imply that worldview is conceptually first, and that narrative is the way it is regularly expressed or articulated. Thus Wright argues that "narrative is the most characteristic expression of worldview."[12] However, when we say that *narrative shapes worldview*, we mean that at another level narrative is conceptually prior and that worldview arises from and is formed by narrative. This is the case especially for text-focused faith communities. Christians and Muslims ideally seek to have their worldviews shaped and corrected by reading and rereading their primary texts, which they traditionally understand to have authoritative priority as divine revelation. According to these communities, *real events* precede both narrative and worldview. Christians, for example, believe in the historical death and resurrection of Jesus, and Muslims believe in Muhammad's reception of the Qur'an. Narrative recounts these events in story form, while worldview abstracts concepts from the events and interprets them. Worldview is a useful way of articulating the belief system arising from these events, but narrative is indispensable for describing the events themselves. As Brockmeier says, there is an "inescapable historical aspect to human existence which narrative is uniquely capable of capturing."[13] Thus the biblical narrative, taken at face value, depicts or recalls the formative events which brought into existence and shaped the development of the people of Israel.[14] Similarly, while containing far less narrative material than the Bible, the Qur'an (together with the narrative of Islamic origins found in Muhammad's biography, known as the *Sīra*) is traditionally understood to reflect the formative events which gave rise to the Islamic Ummah.[15] These narratives may thus be construed as the collective memory of peoples who articulate their identity and worldview in these stories.

Christian worldview studies show how the overarching categories or lenses through which Christians understand and engage the world correspond to the broad framework of the biblical metanarrative. For example, N. T. Wright has written extensively on the relationship of narrative and worldview to argue that the Hebrew scriptural narrative focused upon Israel's place as the covenant people of the Creator placed in the midst of the world. He identifies "creation, fall, patriarchs, Israel, exile, expected restoration and vindication" as the main acts of the great story, which was therefore "inevitably read in the second-temple period as a story in search of a conclusion."[16] Divisions between factions in Judaism and between Judaism and Christianity are largely disagreements about the final act or acts of the play; the early acts are held in common.

The Qur'an, on the other hand, while claiming to confirm the previous books,[17] does not present a continuation, much less a concluding resolution, of this particular story. Rather it confirms and proclaims in its final form the message understood to have been proclaimed by the previous prophets and their books. Aslan argues that "as far as Muhammad understood, the Torah, the Gospels, and the Qur'an must be read as a single cohesive narrative about humanity's relationship to God, in which the prophetic consciousness of one prophet is passed spiritually to the next: from Adam to Muhammad."[18] As we will see, Islam indicates its narrative worldview in large part by prophet stories, including those regarding Abraham. While there is no chronologically articulated grand narrative, these repeated prophet stories, together with the truth of creation and the Last Day, reveal a framework for the sort of worldview categories mentioned above. Mining the qur'anic worldview from these prophet stories is thus a significant part of meaningful intertextual dialogue with the biblical narratives that articulate the Christian worldview.

LIMITATIONS OF A WORLDVIEW APPROACH

Despite its popularity in some Christian circles, the use of worldview as a category has a number of potential limitations. Firstly, using the concept of worldview to set out claims of universal validity may run counter to the perspectival understanding of reality which is inherent in the term worldview, meaning a particular "view" of the world. Wolters notes that a worldview "cannot transcend the experiences and perspectives of that particular nation, class or period. Thus 'worldview' forfeits all claim to universal validity, and becomes enmeshed in the problems of historical relativism."[19] Yet it is also possible to understand worldview in a less relativistic way, as in Vidal's *"philosophical worldviews* . . . aiming at a kind of universal validity . . . [providing answers] to worldview questions [which] correspond to the 'big,' 'eternal,' or 'age-old' philosophical questions."[20] In this study I use the concept primarily in this latter sense. Still the biblical worldview does not claim to be legitimated by an appeal to *universal reason*, as do the modern "metanarratives" toward which postmodernism (as defined by Lyotard) is "incredulous," but is rather received by a faith which in some ways precedes reason.[21] Studying biblical worldview is thus part of "faith seeking understanding."[22]

A second objection could be that a worldview approach entails reading the texts from a perspective created *a priori* out of dogmatic traditions.[23] A discussion of the relationship between dogmatic (systematic) theology and biblical theology helps to address this objection. Carson describes this relationship: "*Systematic theology*, precisely by its efforts at systemic wholeness and by its engagement with the culture, *openly attempts worldview formation*."[24] As systematic theology is refined by biblical theology's exegetical correctives, so a Christian worldview is shaped by the whole interpretive process starting from biblical narrative (and other genres). When a *scriptural narrative–exegesis–biblical theology–systematic theology–worldview* loop is functioning well, many of the weaknesses of an *a priori* worldview reading of texts are mitigated.

Thirdly, some Islamic writers see worldview as a Western construct which is inapplicable to the Qur'an, due to the cultural relativism inherent in a worldview approach and to the Qur'an's status as divine revelation. Yet others see it as a helpful approach when necessary qualifications are made. For example, Qutb confidently uses the term "worldview" after first distinguishing the Islamic worldview from "the philosophical concepts established by the human mind concerning the nature of God, the universe, and mankind, and the relations between them."[25] Sugimoto sees worldview as the "most relevant analytical framework to explain both conflictual and interactive relationships between and/ or within Islam and the West."[26] However, this is primarily Islam's response to modernism and the West, not its response to a Christian worldview. The comparison I pursue is between the qur'anic worldview and the Christian or biblical worldview, not with other worldviews currently dominant in the West.

The first three limitations show that not every approach to worldview will yield the comparison I am seeking. Bertrand outlines three approaches, of which "worldview as story" best clarifies points of convergence and divergence with Islam.[27] The narrative focus of this approach also makes deeper comparison of Christian and Muslim worldviews most accessible and meaningful in relation to Abraham, whose central role is story-based.

A fourth limitation is that it may be simplistic to speak of the "Muslim worldview" when my primary focus is on the qur'anic narratives and their use in Turkey. Daniel Brown points out that while the Qur'an does articulate a coherent worldview, this is not coextensive with an "Islamic" worldview. He writes, "What has passed for an Islamic worldview through most of history for most Muslims cannot be deduced in its entirety from the Qur'an. The idea of constructing a worldview from the Qur'an alone is an entirely modern idea, and is still marginal. It is better represented in Turkey than most other places."[28] My study does not, however, attempt to encompass everything that might be included in an "Islamic" worldview, but rather to outline the major, indispensable worldview elements that are evident in the Qur'an itself, as they are identified by many Muslims. Furthermore, in the Turkish context I have found extensive correspondence between the qur'anic worldview and that articulated by my

Turkish interlocutors. While the Muslim worldview incorporates more than what may be explicit in the Qur'an, it does not incorporate less. My biblical and my qur'anic worldviews rely on ways of thinking about the Bible and the Qur'an that have largely developed in recent times, but they are legitimate articulations of the core messages of these texts.

When these dangers and limitations are respected, using the concept of worldview for comparative theological engagement between Christianity and Islam is defensible. The interpretations of reality and views of life that arise from the Bible and the Qur'an may be addressed as coherent worldviews. Joining narrative and worldview concepts is especially important in comparisons of Christianity and Islam because of their appeal to stories of common figures.

A BIBLICAL-CHRISTIAN WORLDVIEW

Many studies present three primary elements of a Christian worldview in relation to the biblical narrative: *Creation, Fall,* and *Redemption*.[29] Others, including mine, add *Consummation*.[30] The first three elements are directly related to the Genesis narrative: creation (Gen 1–2), fall (Gen 3–11), redemption (Gen 12 and following). The Abraham narrative plays a pivotal role as the transition from the universal narrative of creation and fall of all humankind to the particular narrative of the call of the people through whom the Creator's blessing will be restored. The final element, *Consummation*, is the eschatological perspective of the biblical narrative and prophecy, which was inaugurated, according to NT proclamation, in the coming of Jesus Christ and will be consummated at his return in glory. I consciously follow a canonical reading of the Christian Bible, reading the OT and NT together.

The Bible begins with the all-encompassing fact of creation: "In the beginning God created the heavens and the earth" (Gen 1:1). Everything that exists, visible and invisible, belongs rightly to the Creator, who alone is to be worshiped (cf. Ps 24:1-2; Rev 4:11). Newbigin correctly describes the Bible as universal history, which "sets before us a vision of cosmic history from the creation of the world to its consummation."[31] In the biblical worldview,[32] God's creation was entirely "good," and was assessed as such by God in a refrain repeated throughout the creation narrative. God blessed his good creation and subjected it to mankind, who as male and female were created in the "image" (and likeness[33]) of the Creator, which indicates something comparable to the father-son relationship (cf. Gen 5:1-3).[34] This relationship entailed the mandate to "be fruitful and multiply and fill the earth and subdue it and have dominion" over all the creatures (Gen 1:28). The welfare of the created world was tied by divine design to humanity's special relationship with God; hence mankind's failure or success impacts the welfare of creation.

In the biblical narrative the appearance of strife, pain and death are the consequences of the disobedient act of the first human pair. Tempted by the serpent to distrust God, first Eve and then Adam break the creation covenant by eating the fruit of the tree of the knowledge of good and evil.[35] This scene is subsequent to and not part of the original creation, and the presence of the serpent in the garden is not explained.[36] Curses now intrude as "enemies" into God's good creation.[37] The Christian worldview sees the culpable rebellion of humankind against the Creator and their consequent subjection to evil inclinations and powers (the "fall") as the primary explanation for the complex realities of a good creation's often-tragic history. The way in which this event and its consequences are related to God's will is understood in a variety of ways by Christian theologians, but all recognize some universal effects of this "one trespass" (Rom 5:12-19).[38] Sin brings not only guilt, but also uncleanness, shame, bondage, fear and violence. As the narrative unfolds, the reality of sin and persistent, growing corruption is tragically evident.[39] Intimacy with God is lost, strife enters human relationships, enmity is placed between the seed of the woman and the seed of the serpent, humankind is exiled from the garden of God, the ground is cursed, etc. The narrative structure of the Pentateuch also shows the inadequacy of even divine law to resolve the problem. Comparison of the two desert journey accounts (Exod 16–17 and Num 11–17) shows that the giving of the Law at Sinai produces no improvement in Israel and leads only to punishment and death. While Christians differ on the extent of the fall's continuing effects on humankind, there is agreement that we are all alienated from God and that mankind is unable to bridge this gap, even with the aid of divine guidance (torah).[40]

God initiates the work of redemption (or restoration) with the election of Abraham and his offspring through Isaac and Jacob, followed by their deliverance from Egypt, the formation as a nation at Sinai, the settlement of the land, the establishment of the kingdom and temple under David and Solomon, and the return of a remnant from Babylonian exile. God performs these acts in the history of this one people, whom he has chosen and blessed (Deut 4:32-39; cf. Exod 19:4-6), so that all nations may know this God (Ps 67).[41] From within this long, mixed history emerges the promise of a royal "messianic" offspring and the return of God in a second "exodus" to secure the blessing of Israel's remnant and of all nations.[42] Within the Christian canonical framework, the coming of Jesus the Messiah is the next great act of God. [43] His birth comes through the line of Abraham and David (Matt 1), and his ministry is announced as the promised coming of the Lord himself to the land of Israel to inaugurate the kingdom of God (Mark 1:2-3; cf. Mal 3:1; Isa 40:3-5). The climactic act of God is the Passover death and resurrection of Jesus, understood as the divine (new Exodus) triumph over sin, Satan, and death, and the coming of God's Spirit to extend the blessings of Abraham to all nations (Matt 26-28).

Finally, the biblical perspective is thoroughly eschatological.[44] The narrative advances toward a long-awaited consummation, and the prophetic Scriptures unveil a grand future hope for the whole world. The creator God will come in the "last days" to restore all things after "the great and awesome Day of the Lord" (e.g. Joel 2:11, 31; Mal 4:5; 2 Pet 3). Jesus' return at the end of the age will bring final judgment and new creation, centered on a "new Jerusalem."[45] The story is full of hope and assurance for the future, as seen in these confident words of Paul, "He must reign until he has put all his enemies under his feet. The last enemy to be destroyed is death" (1 Cor 15:25).

FIGURE 2.1 – BIBLICAL-CHRISTIAN WORLDVIEW ELEMENTS

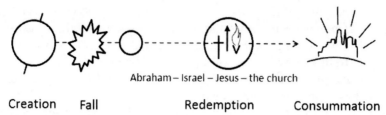

Abraham – Israel – Jesus – the church

Creation   Fall   Redemption   Consummation

Turkish pastor Turgay Üçal uses a favorite Turkish dish, *Şiş Kebab*, to illustrate that the key to the biblical perspective is the "shish" or skewer of God's unchanging purpose that keeps the disparate parts together in a linear view of history.[46] Yet it should be kept in mind that while the sequential order of the elements is essential to the biblical perspective, there is a sense in which they are ongoing, simultaneous realities. Creation is not only God's initial act of bringing into existence the cosmos but also his continuing creative act of sustaining and renewing all that exists. The "fall" is not simply an initial act of disobedience bringing condemnation on all Adam's descendants but indicates an ongoing "reign" of sin, death, evil powers, and futility (e.g. Eph 2:1-3; Rom 8:19-22). Redemption, though built on several great divine interventions, is God's ongoing work. All three elements continue until the consummation, when all things are made new.

A QUR'ANIC-MUSLIM WORLDVIEW

Based on my reading of the Qur'an and of relevant literature, and drawing on my interaction with Turkish imams, I identify the primary Qur'anic-Muslim worldview elements as *Tawhid*, *Prophethood*, and *Afterlife*. It might be argued that these are the elements of only the first of three realms or dimensions which are said to comprise the reality of Islamic worldview: *Iman* (faith or the objects of their faith), *Islam* (submission or the activities that a Muslim must perform), and *Ihsan* (defined as perfection or doing what is beautiful).[47] The "Hadith of Gabriel" is a classic summary of these dimensions: the angel Gabriel appears as an unknown stranger and asks Muhammad three questions, "What is faith (*Iman*)?" What is submission (*Islam*)?" and "What is perfection (*Ihsan*)?" To the first question the prophet answers, "Faith is to believe in God, the angels, the scriptures, the prophets, the Last Day, the measuring out [*Qadr:* fate or predestination]."[48] Murata and Chittick explain the relationship of these six articles of faith to the three principles that I identify as worldview elements:

> The truth that Muslims recognize and to which they commit themselves is expressed through the objects of faith mentioned in the hadith of Gabriel. . . . When theologians and philosophers undertook the classification and organization of religious knowledge, these six objects were divided up and placed in three broad categories known as *Tawhid*, prophecy (*nubuwwa*), and eschatology or the Return (*ma'ad*). These came to be known as the three principles or roots (*asl*) of the religion.[49]

I find these three principles or roots indispensable to the Qur'anic-Muslim worldview. If Muslims at times attend more closely to the other two dimensions of religion (Islamic worship duties and Muslim character or ethics/justice) than to theological scrutiny of the faith, these essential objects of faith are always presupposed. In this study I focus on the core worldview of the Qur'an expressed in its Abraham narratives, rather than the way in which Muslims seek to order their world based on these presuppositions.[50]

Berghout states that there is a "shortage of in-depth and objective research conducted by Muslims on worldview studies" and calls for more Islamic input.[51] Nevertheless, some significant work has been done. Navdi gives a basic definition: "Islamic worldview is considered and defined as general conception of the nature of the world in Islamic perspective. It contains a system of values principles [sic], which are based on the fundamentals of Islam."[52] Fazlur Rahman expounds themes such as God, man, society, revelation, and prophecy to demonstrate that the Qur'an possesses a "cohesive outlook on the universe and life."[53] Many Muslim studies of worldview (not unlike Christian studies) respond primarily to the challenge of modernity.[54] Revivalists like Turkey's Said Nursi and Egypt's Muhammad Abduh and Sayyid Qutb resisted "the relentless assault by 'the West' and its purported 'universal values' . . . in an attempt to articulate a worldview that is at once relevant to the modern world, yet adheres to the core of Islam as religion and civilization."[55] Scholars associated with "the Islamization of Knowledge" movement argue that the Islamic worldview presents an authentic and final view of reality, existence, and life, including the nature of God, Revelation (i.e., the Qur'an), creation, man and the psychology of the human soul, knowledge, religion, freedom, values, and virtues.[56]

While not all interpreters approach the relationships of verses to suras and suras to the Qur'an in the same way, most contemporary interpreters seek to bring the cohesive worldview of the Qur'an as a whole to bear upon the parts.[57] Ruthven asserts that "almost any one of the suras will contain, in a more or less condensed form, the message of the whole."[58] This relationship of the qur'anic parts to its whole, which is quite different from the biblical arrangement where the narrative framework is the organizing principle, complicates our comparative work. It is also important to recall that Islam does not address "theology" in the same way as Christian theology does.[59] However, by juxtaposing the major elements of the two worldviews in a broad narrative framework, it is nonetheless possible to make helpful theological comparisons.

As noted above, the central elements of a Qur'anic-Muslim worldview may be identified as *Tawhid, Prophethood,* and *Afterlife.* While terms vary, and while *Justice* is frequently identified as a fourth principle, this threefold analysis is found in both popular and academic descriptions.[60] Abdel Haleem enumerates "the basic beliefs in Islam [as] the unity of God as evidenced by His 'signs' (*ayah*), the prophethood of Muhammad, and the Resurrection and Final Judgment."[61] Chittick lists the same elements with different names: "All theological thinking in Islam is founded on the so-called three principles of faith: the unity of God, prophecy, and 'the return' to God."[62] The centrality of ethics and justice in the qur'anic worldview is linked with its *prophet-mediated* guidance for ethics and with the *afterlife*, when final justice will be done. Therefore, justice is subsumed under the categories of prophethood and afterlife in my model.[63]

The primary element of the Islamic worldview is unquestionably *Tawhid* (theism, divine unity), which is tied to God as the sole creator of all things. As Ramadan states, "[Tawhid] is the principle on which the whole of Islamic teaching rests."[64] Navdi clarifies this idea: "In the Islamic worldview, there is no bifurcation of the world . . . the nucleus of both [the Qur'an and the Sunnah] is the principle of Tawhid which provides all that there is in Islamic religious thought."[65] In the first half of the Islamic creed or *Shahada*, the essential declaration that "*there is no god but God*" includes within it an all-encompassing worldview. The words "*no god*" mean that all idolatry is utterly rejected, and the words "*but God*" affirm Allah to be the One, the absolute, transcendent Creator, the Lord and Master of all that is.[66] "God is one" in the sense that there is no likeness to him among things, and "God is one" in the sense that there is no multiplicity or division conceivable in Him.[67] Afzaal says that the principle of Tawhid is "the very life-force of Islam, for all aspects of Islamic belief, thought, and practice are rooted in its unifying and integrating vision."[68]

The qur'anic prophet narratives, which will be considered below, repeatedly affirm the basic message of Tawhid and its implications for the hearers. The truth that all things are contingent upon the one God calls for a response that integrates all of life in an ethical unity, as Smith summarizes:

> Tawhid is something that man does: It is the recognition of God's unity, at the lowest level, and in a series of ascending levels, it is the appropriation to one's self, also the proclamation, also the implementation of that unity: the living of a life that has integrity, because oneness is divine.[69]

Compared with the doctrine of creation in the Bible, which begins with the creation story, Tawhid is not so easily identified with narrative. Nevertheless the qur'anic message, that God has created all things and therefore all things are to be oriented to the creator, is strongly affirmed in the prophet stories.

According to Tawhid, all things and acts owe their existence and continuance to the ongoing creative work of God, and learning to see everything through this lens is a primary focus of an Islamic worldview. Any view that minimizes the role of God in actuating what exists runs the risk of *shirk*—associating partners with God.[70] This can mean that human actions and decisions are in fact the creation of God, in accord with an Islamic maxim, "the deeds and actions are created by Allah, and the efforts are from man."[71] Belief in divine unity works its way out in Sufi thought and practice in the pursuit of individual devotion and mystical union with God and in Sunni thought and practice primarily in the pursuit of communal practices of worship and development of a unified, just society.[72]

The Qur'an affirms God as the creator of both *the visible and the invisible* realms (39:46).[73] That the visible "signifies" the invisible is essential to its worldview. Mankind is responsible and presumed able to draw conclusions about the Creator from these "signs" in creation.[74] Noting that "the Qur'an employs the very same term *aya*, lit. 'signs,' to denote both the qur'anic text and cosmic phenomena," Turkish scholar Yamina Mermer explains the importance of this fact:

> The Qur'an complements the cosmos in that only through the Qur'an (and revealed scriptures), can one decipher what the cosmos is "saying." Furthermore, the cosmos complements the Qur'an, in that without the cosmos, the Qur'an would not make sense. . . . Listening to the Qur'an without observing the world would be like a blind person listening to a movie.[75]

The Qur'an asserts this repeatedly: "On earth there are signs for those with sure faith—and in yourselves too, *do you not see?*" (51:20-23; cf. 28:72).[76] The qur'anic worldview is above all else opposed to idolatry of any kind, and *shirk* is considered the one unforgivable sin: "God does not forgive the joining of partners with Him: anything less than that He forgives to whoever He will" (4:48, 116; cf. 39:65; 34:22; 31:13).

The second major element of the Islamic worldview is *Prophethood.* It is here that the qur'anic narrative material is most prominent. In qur'anic perspective prophets have been sent to every human community to provide divine guidance (16:36).[77] No community will be judged without first being warned by a prophet, who may also testify at their judgment (10:47). While these prophets are traditionally said to be many (124,000 according to some traditions), the Qur'an simply says that some were not made known to Muhammad (40:78). Twenty five are listed in the Qur'an; most are also biblical figures. In the Qur'an, Muhammad is the seal of the prophets (33:40), and as such his prophethood belongs to and exemplifies the general category of prophethood or prophecy.[78] But while previous prophets were sent to particular communities, Muhammad's prophethood is for all mankind (7:158; 22:107).[79] It is essential to the concept that each prophet brings the same basic message. Abu Zayd posits a mystical continuity among the prophets: "The Muhammadan Reality is the inward hidden reality which is manifested in all the prophets from Adam until its final and complete manifestation in the historical Muhammad."[80]

Most of the narrative portions of the Qur'an recount prophet stories, and Abraham's example is frequently cited in developing the concept of prophethood. Neuwirth describes these narratives as signs or lessons implied in history, because they generally follow a pattern in which the messenger is rejected by the people to whom he is sent but vindicated by God, who punishes the unbelieving community.[81] These typically fragmentary episodes provide moral examples, underscoring the danger of rejecting the messengers of God.

Qur'anic prophets bring their people *divine guidance,* which is understood to be mankind's fundamental need. God "saves" those rightly guided people who pursue moral excellence. Rahman says, "the whole fate of man, whether he will be 'successful' or 'shall perish,' depends on whether he can and does 'take the right path.'"[82] This guidance may be in written or oral form, which may be related to the overlapping two categories used to refer to these unique men, apostle/messenger (*rasul*) and prophet (*nabi*).[83] Prophets also function in the Qur'an as *ideal models* for believers. As the ultimate prophet, Muhammad is the pattern for every aspect of life, not only for individual believers who seek to emulate his ways, but also for spiritual, political, and military leaders.

The stark words of God in the Qur'an, "We have prepared an agonizing punishment for those who do not believe in the world to come" (17:10), capture the importance of the *afterlife* in the Muslim worldview. Life is understood as comprised of two aspects: life in this world (*al-dunyā*) and life in the hereafter (*al-*ākhirah). Al-Attas clarifies: "The worldview of Islam encompasses both *al-dunyā* and *al-*ākhirah, in which the *dunyā-*aspect must be related in a profound and inseparable way to the ākhirah-aspect, and in which the ākhirah-aspect has ultimate and final significance. The *dunyā-*aspect is seen as a preparation for the ākhirah-aspect."[84] *Afterlife, Resurrection, and the Day (of Judgment)* are dominating features of the Qur'an's landscape. The time will come when every person will come face-to-face with his or her deeds in life. Human deeds will be weighed and rewards and punishment meted out accordingly. This theme is related to that of prophethood as the prophetic message forms the basis of judgment. Citing Qur'an 4:41; 7:6-7; and 28:75 Rahman argues, "Every community shall be judged by the standards set for them by their prophet and in accordance with the teaching of their respective Revelations."[85] This aspect of the qur'anic worldview is distinctly related to the notion of all humans being directly accountable to God, and is linked to a primeval confession obtained by God from all of Adam's offspring that they know him as their Lord (7:172).

The three key principles—Tawhid, Prophethood, and Afterlife—are interdependent and relatively constant throughout Islamic thinking. In fact, they are as inseparably linked to one another in the qur'anic worldview as Creation, Fall, Redemption, and Consummation are in the biblical. This is evidenced in the often-repeated qur'anic phrases "God and his Messengers"[86] and "God and the last day."[87] The Qur'an summarizes these tightly linked elements, "Anyone who does not believe in God, His angels, His Scriptures, His messengers, and the Last Day has gone far, far astray" (4:136).

FIGURE 2.2 – QUR'ANIC-MUSLIM WORLDVIEW ELEMENTS

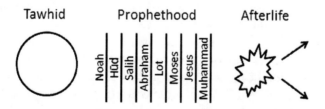

Figure 2.2 illustrates the similarity of the prophet stories by representing their stories as parallel segments, following a repeated pattern, and not consecutive in the same way as in the Bible. It would be wrong however to suppose that there is no linear or sequential logic within their scattered presentation. In fact, the very idea of juxtaposing the two worldviews in a narrative framework depends on some sort of overarching order. First of all, as McAuliffe notes, the qur'anic

worldview conceives of a series of prophetic interventions in human history. The Qur'an "clearly expresses an awareness of divine revelation as a chronological sequence, a series of time-specific disclosures intended for particular peoples. Q 2:136 marks the milestones in that chronology." [88]Secondly, analysis of the prophets named in the Qur'an shows that they are often recounted in an order more or less corresponding to the biblical chronology. Of course, no diagram can do justice to these worldview concepts, even if they are based on narratives. These can only be worked out in the detailed analysis of the narratives, with which the following chapters are occupied.

WORLDVIEW POLARITIES

Juxtaposing the main elements of the biblical and qur'anic worldviews in three pairings yields the following three polarities:

Creation-Fall	–	Tawhid
Redemption	–	Prophethood
Consummation	–	Afterlife

At first glance the motif of Creation seems similar in biblical and qur'anic perspective, with differences concentrated in the Redemption-Prophethood polarity. Both faiths give theistic accounts of reality, teaching that "God created the heavens and the earth" (Gen 1:1).[89] Humanity's dependence on the Creator for life and all things is bedrock in both faiths. However, Christians and Muslims highlight quite different aspects of this core. Muslims emphasize the Tawhid implications of creation, and Christians emphasize the narrative outcome proceeding from the creation's "beginning."

Studies of these distinct creation narratives highlight several differences: First, regarding the degree of autonomy which God grants to his creation, Lodahl argues that where the Qur'an emphasizes "the sheer and utter power of God's commanding speech in the act of creation," Genesis 1 portrays "a Maker who creates the world by inviting it to be, and by the power of this divine invitation empowering the world to be creative."[90]

Second, we see two areas of difference regarding the creation of man and woman and what it means to be human: First, while in the biblical narrative mankind is created in the "image" of God, the qur'anic narrative names man as God's "vice-regent" or "successor";[91] and, second, while in the biblical account God entrusts to Adam the job of naming the animals (Gen 2:19), in the Qur'an God "taught Adam all the names," elevating him above the angels who were not taught the names (2:31-33).[92] Adam's role was to remember and reproduce the names he was taught. Genesis seems to highlight the value of human autonomy and creativity, while the Qur'an underscores the value of humans remembering what God teaches.

Third, regarding the failure of Adam and Eve, three areas of contrast are highlighted by these writers: (a) In Genesis the tempter is a serpent, part of the animal creation (3:1), whereas in the Qur'an the culprit is of a different order— Satan, Iblis, who is a rebellious angel or jinn;[93] (b) In Genesis the man and woman make excuses and shift the blame with no clear repentance, whereas in the Qur'an the pair confess and repent; (c) The consequences of this event in the Bible are curses and permanent expulsion from God's presence,[94] whereas in the Qur'an Adam is sent down to earth from the "garden," furnished with guidance as the first prophet.

These areas of dissonance are further reflected in the polarities between the biblical creation-fall perspective and the qur'anic creation-Tawhid perspective. I consider this below under three headings: God in creation, humankind in creation, and evil (suffering) in creation.

God in Creation

The word "in" draws attention to the manner and extent to which God is understood to be "present" within the created order. Does God "come into" this created universe and "appear to" his creatures? If God is prior to and beyond the entire created order, does he enter into time and space? How does transcendence relate to immanence?

In the Christian worldview, God condescends to come among human beings, appearing visibly within his creation.[95] The transcendent God becomes immanent within creation not only in universal omnipresence, but also in concrete, localized reality. As the chief protagonist, God's "elusive presence" pervades the biblical narrative.[96] Adam and Eve hear the "sound" of God "walking in the garden" and hide from his "presence" (Gen 3:8). God personally interrogates and sentences the serpent, the woman, and the man. God warns Cain personally (not through an angel), questioning him and announcing his punishment. God tells Noah how to build the ark, and personally shuts Noah in (Gen 7:16). God's tangible presence continues as the narrative turns to Abraham and the other patriarchs. Exodus recounts visible appearances of God on Horeb/Sinai (3:1-7; 19:16-20; 20:21; 24:9-11) and narrates the preparation of a sacred tent where God will dwell in the midst of his people (Exod 25–31, 35–40). The NT narrates God's ultimate appearance, as the Word of God becomes flesh and dwells among his people (John 1:1-2, 14) as Emmanuel, "God with us" (Mat 1:23; cf. 28:20). In this intensification of divine immanence, the NT moves in the opposite direction from other Second Temple Jewish writings, which minimize theophany in their readings of the Hebrew Scriptures where divine appearances are depicted.[97]

For Muslims, such descriptions of tangible divine presence run contrary to the Tawhid principle. For example, Shah examines the depictions of God in the three Abrahamic traditions, concluding that only the Qur'an presents a deity free of such profane depictions, which have led to widespread rejection of God by rational modern people. The tension caused by the "amalgamation of anthropomorphic and transcendental tendencies" of the Hebrew Bible becomes unbearable for him in the NT: "Incarnational theology is not paradoxical. It is thoroughly and utterly contradictory."[98] He appeals to the Tawhid principle in the Qur'an as rectifying the biblical compromise of the divine transcendence by "identifying itself with the original pristine message sent by God to mankind."[99]

In considerations of the Creator-creation relationship in Islamic scholarship, creation is almost a corollary to Tawhid.[100] Diminishing the oneness and transcendence of God by wrongly expressing divine immanence within creation is inevitably viewed with suspicion. During a discussion with a group of Muslims in Istanbul, I used the word "condescend" to explain this narrative attribute of God as coming among humanity and was sternly told that God does not condescend! This issue raises sharp worldview dissonance, because such depictions of divine immanence balance divine transcendence throughout the biblical narrative and contribute significantly to the Christian worldview.[101]

A second issue regards the unity of God. Islamic theism's overwhelming emphasis on oneness and unity is not found in the same way in the biblical picture, especially in Genesis.[102] In the Genesis creation account the oneness of God has elements of complexity. In a Christian approach, references to God's spirit and word involved in creation (e.g. Gen 1:2-3; Ps 33:6) are generally informed by teaching about plurality within the one God, classically summarized in the NT understanding of God as Father, Word/Son and Spirit (John 1:1-5; Matt 28:19) and narrated in the birth and baptism narratives of Jesus (Luke 1:26-38; 3:21-22). The divine plurals, "*Let us* make . . . in *our* image, according to *our* likeness . . . God created man in his own image" (Gen 1:26-27; cf. 3:22; 11:7) have sometimes been taken by Christians to suggest complexity.[103] The NT clearly affirms plurality within unity, at times using plural terms (John 14:23; 1 Cor 8:6; 2 Cor 13:14).[104] However, any suggestion of plurality within unity conflicts with the Tawhid understanding of the absolute unitary oneness of the Creator. The Qur'an condemns nothing more harshly than the sin of *shirk* or attributing "partners to God" (e.g. 4:48; 6:22-23), and it charges Christians with error in this area (5:116).

Humankind in Creation

In Genesis, the story of humanity opens with the words "in the beginning," marking the beginning both of the created cosmos and of the human story. The opening account (1:1–2:3) is the story's prologue.[105] The words that follow —"These are the generations of the heavens and the earth" (2:4)—head an extended storyline concerning what became of this good creation entrusted to mankind.[106] It links this story of human failure directly to the subsequent stories through the repetition of similar tôlēdôt headings ("these are the generations of . . ."). Humanity's story follows a special genealogy, traced carefully from Adam to Shem to Terah (5:1-32 with 11:10-26); even while outlining the general development of human culture and the nations (4:17-24; 10:1–11:9). As Kaminski shows, "the blessing given to humankind in Gen. 1.28 and 9.1 advances in one family in particular . . . who have become bearers of the creation theme."[107] This line is traced through the patriarchal period, through Israel's history and beyond (e.g. 1 Chr 1–9, from Adam to post-exilic times), and brought to completion by the genealogies of Jesus (Matt 1 and Luke 3), who is seen as the "last Adam / second man" who ultimately restores all that was lost by Adam.[108]

In the Qur'an, the human story "begins" with a pre-creation covenant made with mankind such that every person will be held accountable for the knowledge of God (7:172). The creation of Adam and his wife is recounted several times, with a particular emphasis on the refusal of Satan to worship mankind (2:30-39; 7:10-27; 17:61-65; 20:115-124). Human beings are addressed in several places as the "Children of Adam" (7:35). The period between creation and Judgment Day is world history, with a loose metanarrative formed by the prophets (see below). But the main narrative focus is on the stories of individuals and especially peoples who are confronted in one way or another with the message of the Creator. It is arguable that the qur'anic story of God's creation of a single pair, from whom he "spread countless men and women far and wide" (4:1), is primarily tied to the Islamic metanarrative of Muhammad and his people which is evident behind much of the qur'anic text. Hence this sura (An-Nisa') moves directly from the creation of the first pair to instructions for Medina regarding inheritance, marriage, and the treatment of women, children, and orphans. Much of the narrative material in the Qur'an functions in this way, to illustrate the message addressed to Muhammad and his audience.

The Qur'an does not emphasize linear history in the way the Bible does, though the prophet stories in series do convey the sense of humankind's history. Hermansen argues that the qur'anic concept of history is conveyed with a "concept of time that is frequently less linear than that of the Christian and Jewish traditions."[109]

Another area of divergence regarding humanity arises from Islamic rejection of the possibility of any representation of God.[110] This diverges from the biblical account of mankind being created in "the image and likeness of God" (Gen 1:26-27), since "image" can imply the unfitting idea of representation. Thus Kaltner says, "the notion of humanity being created in the divine *image* is completely absent from the Qur'an and the reason for this is that the idea violates one of the central beliefs of Islam."[111] Roth adds that even if image might be acceptable in some way, "likeness" is unacceptable to Muslim thinking.[112] Still we may ask how different the biblical *image* is from the qur'anic *khalifah* (viceregent) concept taught in Muslim worldview studies.[113] Glaser argues that while *khalifah* indicates status and function assigned by God, *image* emphasizes nature and relationship to God. Thus the biblical Adam and Eve "are like God," being in a particular *relationship* with him by nature, whereas "the qur'anic *khalifah* is not like God, having authority only as delegated by his Creator."[114] The Bible intimates that the image of God has been marred by the sin of mankind, not erased (e.g. Gen 9:6), and that there is a long-term purpose of God to restore this intimate likeness and relationship which seems to be related to the idea of the father-son likeness.[115] This dissonance is sharpest when Jesus, as the unique image and Son of God, enters the biblical story.

Evil in Creation

The existence of evil in God's creation is acknowledged by both the Qur'an and the Bible, but their approaches are different. The biblical creation narrative is inseparable from the story of the "fall" in Genesis 3. Kempf shows how the effects of the judgments of Gen 3:14-19 are worked out in the chapters which follow.[116] Sin is an enemy "crouching at the door," which Adam's son Cain must overcome (Gen 4:7). Rampant wickedness, corruption, violence, and continual evil intentions bring "all flesh" (not just Noah's people) to the point of divine judgment (Gen 6:5-13). But the Bible insists that God is good and that he created all things good at the beginning, including mankind in his own upright image (Eccl 7:29). Several carefully narrated incidents in Genesis allude to fall-like events in the lives of Noah, Abraham, Jacob, and Joseph.[117] A number of major biblical narratives also raise the problem of the suffering of righteous people.[118] Together creation and fall provide part of the basis for a Christian argument, namely that, as Stump argues, "there are morally sufficient reasons for the omniscient, omnipotent, perfectly good God to allow suffering in the world."[119]

Islam rejects the Christian understanding of the effects of Adam's disobedience, limiting it rather to a brief interlude which had no effects on future humanity. Miller argues that "the fundamental difference between Islam and Christianity is . . . hamartiological. Adam did sin, he was indeed punished, but in no way did his guilt develop into what Christians have variously called original sin or original stain."[120] According to the Qur'an, "Adam disobeyed his Lord and was led astray—later his Lord brought him close, accepted his repentance, and guided him" (20:121-124). God took the initiative in restoring Adam, granting him the words he should use in repentance (2:37-39). Ruthven sums it up this way:

> In the Quran . . . Adam is forgiven immediately (20:122). Adam becomes the first of the prophets, God's vice-regent (*khalifa*) upon earth. His place of exile, far from being accursed as in the Old Testament, is to become man's "dwelling place" and a "source of profit" to him (7:10).[121]

In the qur'anic narrative, Satan is implicated and the human couple is exiled from the heavenly garden, but the results of Adam's sin are not an ongoing narrative reality. Rather this original scene is replayed as other peoples are deceived and disobey their Lord. The Qur'an repeatedly warns of the punishment for sin and promises forgiveness to those "who avoid grave sins and foul acts" (53:32). The primary need of humankind, like Adam in 2:39, is "guidance." The qur'anic narrative repeatedly recounts ignorant people's willful rejection of this guidance brought to them by prophets.

Muslims reject the Christian reading which separates creation from fall,[122] and view the reality of evil and suffering through the wide-angle lens of Tawhid, which necessarily includes both the doctrine of creation and (at least the appearance of) evil in the world. The oneness and sovereignty of God whose will is absolute must be the explanation of evil in the world. As one of my interlocutors made clear to me as we discussed this polarity, good and evil both come from God (*Hayır ve şer Allah'tandır*).[123] The Qur'an indicates God's awareness that his creature man would cause much evil, which caused the angels to challenge his intent. But God answers, "I know things you do not" (2:30). It affirms that all that exists is within God's ongoing creative sovereignty. Some say Islam has little place for theodicy as such; God's words are answer enough.[124]

Others like Turkish theologian Akbaş engage the question: "Firstly, suffering is a punishment for sin. Secondly, suffering is an outcome of the failure of human free-will. Thirdly, suffering in the Qur'an is described as a test and a discipline. [Fourthly,] iniquities and sufferings of this world will be recompensed in life after death."[125] Much of this relates to guidance for facing life's difficulties with submission, rather than to the issues of the existence of natural and moral evil. Regarding the broader issue, he concludes that "God as a powerful deity must be the creator of evil."[126]

Osman Demir argues that "good and evil are both necessary realities in the cosmos in order that humankind is put on trial during her/his life on the earth."[127] I have frequently encountered this concept in discussions of suffering in Turkey. Ease is only understood by contrast with difficulty, and so on, and these apparent evils serve God's good purpose for human beings.[128] The argument appears to be twofold: 1) Things that appear evil may actually on a deeper level not be evil at all; and 2) The presence of some evil enables us to understand the good. While there is commonality here with biblical studies on the mysteries of suffering and divine providence,[129] a fundamental disagreement is still evident with the biblical worldview which distinguishes carefully between the essential goodness of creation and the evil introduced by the fall.

When we allow the biblical narratives to speak for themselves regarding who God is and what he does, dissonance with the qur'anic picture soon surfaces. I have devoted significant space to this issue, because in my view the discord here is often underestimated in comparative theological approaches.

Redemption–Prophethood Polarity

The second major pairing of biblical-Christian and Qur'anic-Islamic worldview elements, the Redemption – Prophethood polarity, raises the questions "What is the solution?" and "What is the meaning of human history?"[130]

Redemption and prophethood might be seen as an asymmetrical pair, in that redemption is *what is being* accomplished and prophethood is *the means* of accomplishing it. But here these words function as shorthand for the biblical narrative of redemption and the qur'anic narrative of prophethood, which are amenable to comparison. The Qur'an envisions the sending of prophets as the means by which people are "saved" through the guidance brought to them.[131] In the biblical worldview God provides redemption, whereas in the qur'anic worldview he provides guidance (through prophets), reflecting differences in Christian and Muslim understanding of the fundamental need of humankind in the world. The Bible also gives great significance to prophets of God, as those who explain the significance of the saving acts of God and the concomitant obligations on the beneficiaries. Much biblical material narrates the acts and messages of the prophets. Nevertheless, as I show below, as primary worldview and narrative framework categories, *redemption* and *prophethood* present contrasting tendencies.

In both cases the focus is on the meaning of human history, but while the Bible underscores *God's coming* into and acting within history, the qur'anic version of human history highlights *God's sending* of prophets. The Bible primarily narrates the story of *one people* chosen to be the means of blessing for all peoples, and the Qur'an relates stories of the *various peoples* of humankind to whom these prophets have been sent. The Bible expounds *one developing story* of God's deliverance of mankind from bondage to Satan and evil, and the Qur'an elaborates on *one repeated message* to provide the guidance needed by mankind to resist satanic inducement to evil and idolatry.

The Bible narrates an overarching history in which God the Savior initiates and provides salvation for all nations, ultimately through the Jewish Messiah. This is distinctly different from the qur'anic narrative of God sending many prophets with one message of guidance and warning to many different peoples. In this regard, it is revealing to compare qur'anic summaries or lists of prophets with biblical summary passages.[132] Generally speaking, where the Qur'an lists prophets of God and the fates of the peoples to whom they were sent, the biblical passages rehearse key acts of God in one ongoing story (see Appendix 1).[133]

The prophets mentioned by name in the Qur'an (excluding Muhammad) are generally recounted in an order corresponding to the biblical chronology, though sometimes the order varies significantly (see Appendix 2). The names found most frequently in suras recounting prophet stories are *Noah* (in all but five), *Moses* (in all but seven) and *Abraham* (in all but eight). With the exception of Jesus, prophets after Moses tend to be found in suras mentioning at least four prophets. Suras 6, 21 and 38 are the richest in prophet stories, followed by suras 3, 4, and 19. Two types of accounts may be identified: First, several compact lists of prophets are given in certain verses or groups of two or three verses.[134] The longest list of this type is in sura 6, Al-An'am:

> Such was the argument We gave to *Abraham* against his people—We raise in rank whoever We will—your Lord is all wise, all knowing. We gave him *Isaac* and *Jacob*, each of whom We guided, as We had guided *Noah* before, and among his descendants were *David, Solomon, Job, Joseph, Moses,* and *Aaron*—in this way We reward those who do good— *Zachariah, John, Jesus,* and *Elijah*—every one of them was righteous— *Ishmael, Elisha, Jonah,* and *Lot.* We favored each one of them over other people. (6:83-86)

Second, a number of other suras recite a series of short, largely parallel prophet stories.[135] These have come to be known as "punishment stories," because most of them refer to God's destruction of stubborn people-groups to whom the prophets were sent. The longest of these series is found in sura 21, where the stories of seventeen different prophets are briefly recounted: *Moses and Aaron* (21:48), then separately *Abraham, Isaac, Jacob,* and *Lot* (21:72-75), *Noah* (21:76-77), *David and Solomon* (21:78-82), *Job* (21:83-84), *Ishmael, Idris, and Dhu'l-Kifl* (21:85-86), *Jonah* (21:87-88), *Zachariah, John ,and Jesus* (21:89-91). It can be seen from these two examples and the details in the appendix that while there are a number of suras in which the prophets are mentioned in precise biblical order (7, 10, 11, 22, 42, 54), and while there is clear evidence of familiarity with the basic biblical outline of history (Adam through Jesus), the order of the prophet narratives or their mention in lists is rarely important to the purpose for which they are narrated.[136]

When these prophet stories are considered together, an overall metanarrative underlying the qur'anic worldview takes shape.[137] From Adam to Muhammad, qur'anic world history consists in a long series of prophets sent by God, including nonbiblical prophets Idris, Hūd, Salih, Shu'ayb, and Dhu'l-Kifl.[138] The order of the named prophets frequently consists of little more than a list of names without a sequential storyline. Frequently the emphasis is on the resistant people to whom the prophets were sent rather than on the prophets themselves.

The biblical story of God's covenant relationship with Israel is mentioned in the Qur'an but shaped differently. The Jews are criticized for repeatedly ignoring the message sent to them and for departing from the original faith of Abraham, which is now to be centered on Mecca rather than Jerusalem (Q2:140-41).[139] The Qur'an tells of Abraham, Isaac, Jacob, Moses and Aaron, David, Solomon, John and Jesus, but the progressive biblical story in which they play distinct roles is barely distinguishable. Allusions to the exodus are limited mainly to God's confrontation with Pharaoh and Israel's apostasy with the calf. While there is reference to a covenant with the Children of Israel (Q2:40), nothing is told of this covenant's renewal (2 Sam 7; 1 Chr 17; Jer 30-33). The Qur'an presents these figures as prophets of Islam and retells their stories as prototypes of Muhammad's.

Hence a polarity can be identified relating to God's intervention in human history, with a biblical emphasis on God's acts and a qur'anic emphasis on his prophets. This should not be taken to mean that the Bible does not emphasize the prophets of God or that the Qur'an is not interested in the acts of God in history. But insofar as *the narrative of human history* is concerned, the biblical-Christian worldview is built upon and expounds God's coming in redemptive intervention and the Qur'anic-Muslim worldview is built upon and expounds God's will disclosed in prophetic intervention. In terms of God's provision for mankind's deepest need within this world, the Bible points to divine saving acts and the Qur'an to divine saving guidance.

One people or many peoples?

Where the Bible tells the human story particularly in terms of the history of one people, Israel, the Qur'an sees the human story as the repeated history of many peoples. The biblical view sees the descendants of Abraham chosen and redeemed to be God's special nation, and called into a unique covenant relationship with Him for the sake of all nations (Exod 19:1-6).

> Israel's election was . . . explicitly for the sake of all nations. This universality of God's purpose, that nevertheless embraces the particularity of God's chosen means, is a recurrent and a constant theological challenge (to Israel as much as to contemporary theologians).[140]

God dwells among the people of Israel, and entrusts them with his oracles. God repeatedly disciplines them, even with exile, for their sins and utter unfaithfulness to their calling (Amos 3:2). Yet because of God's faithfulness, through them comes the Messiah for the nations, as promised by the prophets. The biblical worldview is built on a narrative in which a special dynamic is created by the relationship of Israel with the other nations. Following the primeval narratives, the story narrows as Israel's OT history is told and explained by the prophets. Then the story widens to embrace all nations after Christ's death and resurrection as the NT narrates and interprets the final act of God in Christ by which redemption is provided for the nations and God's final word is spoken to mankind (Heb 1:1-4).

The Qur'an presents its view of history primarily through the stories of prophets being sent to different peoples of the world with similar results. Akhtar sums up the Quran's constantly reiterated philosophy of history:

> God sends messengers along with adversity so that the nations may suffer and thus repent in humility. Instead, perversely their hearts harden and they reject the divine message and the messenger.... Strategically, God then increases the amount of luxury in the lives of sinners, dramatically increasing the good things of this life. Then, suddenly, divine punishment seizes the rejecters in the midst of their new enjoyments; and the community is eradicated (Q 6:42-5; 7:94-5; 17:16; 25:18; 34:34-5).[141]

Consistent with this repeated pattern of punishment stories and their application, the genre of the Qur'an may be described as primarily homiletical discourse. As Abu-Hamdiyyah expresses it, "The Qur'an is mainly a preaching discourse occupied to [sic] making the human being conscious of God."[142] As such, its stories (of prophets and their reception by various peoples) are told with a hortative purpose. The Qur'an uses familiar monotheistic tradition to support its homiletical argument, making use of the stories of prophets and their peoples for new messages.[143] Whatever compositional history may lie behind their place in the qur'anic text, these recurring stories serve what Kaltner calls the Qur'an's "primary interest in the message or meaning of a text, its preference for purpose over plot."[144] God himself narrates the incidents and draws the lessons from them for the prophet and his listeners. In this "typological" relationship, the difficulty of the ancient messengers is shared by the Prophet himself, and the fate of those people is potentially to be shared by the community to whom Muhammad is sent.[145] Waldman notes how the qur'anic narration of the Joseph story in Sura 12 ends with a lengthy homily: "The Qur'an is interested mainly in Joseph's role as exemplary God-fearing man and Messenger."[146] This assessment is applicable to other prophet stories as well. It is notable that qur'anic prophets are models of virtue and faith, exhibiting none of the foibles so typical of even major characters in the biblical narrative.[147]

Yet while the qur'anic narratives are stories of the prophets, they are equally the stories of the peoples to whom they were sent. They are "punishment stories" as well as prophet stories.[148] The message is clear: Take care how you receive the Prophet (Muhammad) and his message; remember what happened to the peoples who refused their prophets in the past! The qur'anic versions of these stories repeat different parts of them for different contexts and purposes as a preacher might use parts of Bible stories in sermons to illustrate different points.[149] Reynolds and El-Badawi show that the Qur'an's use of these stories resembles some Syriac Christian homilies of the same era, which used related biblical traditions to persuade their listeners.[150]

That this forms a contrast with the biblical narrative of God redeeming a particular people has not gone unnoticed by Muslim scholars. Al-Faruqi, in his discussion of Islamic and Christian approaches to the Tanakh, rejects the concept of salvation history.

> The so-called 'saving acts of God' in Hebrew Scripture, Islam regards as the natural consequences of virtue and good deeds. . . . The 'Promise' of Hebrew Scripture, or the unearned blessing of any man or people, the Qur'an utterly rejects as inconsonant with God's nature and His justice; the Muslims being no more unfit for such favoritism than any other people."[151]

If al-Faruqi correctly represents the Islamic worldview, serious dissonance is inevitable, for nothing is more central to the biblical worldview than God's saving acts within history.[152]

Human fallenness or human forgetfulness?

The biblical redemption narrative corresponds to a worldview that sees all humanity as fallen, expressed with terms such as "dead in trespasses and sins" and "by nature children of wrath" (Eph 2:1-3). Jesus taught that the source of defilement was internal: "from within, out of the heart of man" (Mark 7:20-23). The Qur'an, on the other hand, views human beings as inherently God-oriented by nature, but tending to ignore their creator because of forgetfulness, societal influence and satanic deception. So where the biblical narrative as read by Christians recounts a long story of God redeeming "fallen" humanity, the qur'anic narrative as read by Muslims articulates a repeated message through which God is reminding "forgetful" humanity of God and the day of reckoning. As with Adam (Q 20:115), humanity's problem is "forgetfulness," hence the need for divine "reminders" which are communicated by prophets. As Abu Zayd puts it, God "helps man to remember that eternal pact by sending prophets with messages. . . . All prophets, including Prophet Muhammad himself, are, accordingly, representatives of 'reminders.'"[153]

The Christian diagnosis of the human condition is more radical than the qur'anic analysis, as seen above. In the Bible more than guidance is necessary for everlasting happiness, because more is wrong than forgetfulness. In Genesis, God assesses post-flood mankind gloomily: "the intention of man's heart is evil from his youth" (Gen 8:21).[154] Related to the narrative's emphasis on the fallout from Adam and Eve's disobedience is the less-than-exemplary behavior of key biblical characters such as Noah, Abraham, Lot, Jacob, and David. These narratives are often rejected by Muslims as slander against the prophets of God and as falsification of the earlier Scriptures. Yet this picture is found throughout the canonical Scriptures; mankind is not only forgetful but sinful. The open record of the sins of the best-known figures is accompanied by the open history of Israel's recurrent failure and tendency toward idolatry. The same transparency is found in the narratives of chief apostles Peter and Paul. In fact, confession of personal sin is a central virtue of biblical prophets and apostles.

On the other hand, the Islamic understanding of "*fitrat/fitrah*" (human nature) is that all are born with an innate God-centeredness: "Stand firm and true in your devotion to the religion. This is the natural disposition God instilled in mankind—there is no altering God's creation" (Q30:30).[155] Rahman summarizes the consistent qur'anic perspective:

> Man has not yet developed a fully adequate sense of responsibility. His cognitive faculties are great, but his faculty of the moral sense of responsibility fails most of the time . . . (33:72) . . . We see then, that while '*ilm* is there, the sense of responsibility fails, most of the time when a crucial test comes, man is unable to discharge this trust.[156]

According to the Qur'an, Satan caused Adam and his wife to "slip and removed them from the state they were in," and in consequence God sent them to live on earth (2:36). Islam recognizes no need for deliverance from the penalty or power of sin. The guidance brought by the prophets, and religious practices that bring to mind the ultimate realities (God and the afterlife), are the sufficient means for human beings to "remember" their calling and reach their divinely intended purpose in creation.[157]

If from the qur'anic perspective the key to the human plight is guidance from God, from the biblical perspective the key is the Creator God becoming the Savior God, and the role of biblical prophets is to announce and explain God's works of salvation. This process involves the divine *election* of a particular human line through which the redeeming purposes of God would ultimately reach all nations and indeed all creation.

One aspect of the biblical redemption narrative is deliverance by means of a sacrifice, suggested in the Passover lamb's blood shielding from death, and in the blood shed at the altar of the tabernacle/temple as atonement for sins (Lev 1–7). Jerusalem becomes the locus of atonement in the temple sacrifices, and the story culminates in Jesus as the Lamb of God who takes away the sin of the world by his sacrificial death. In the NT his death is interpreted as completing this OT redemption motif once and for all.[158]

This biblical theme is rejected by the Islamic worldview. Hermansen says, "Muslim rejections of the crucifixion arise both from the fact that since there is no original sin, redemption is neither necessary nor possible, and the fact that as the 'Messiah' Jesus would not be killed by his opponents (Qur'an 4:157)."[159] The Qur'an explicitly rejects both "intercession" and "ransom" in the "Day when no soul will stand in place of another" (2:48; cf. 6:164; 17:15).[160]

Other significant aspects of the biblical narrative-worldview element of redemption could be developed, yet here it is important to underscore the point that from the beginning of the biblical narrative the ultimate answer to the human situation depends on aspects of God's redeeming work, not primarily on his guidance as in the qur'anic narratives.

Thus the dissonance between biblical and qur'anic narrative becomes pronounced when we juxtapose the narrative of redemption with the narratives of prophethood: The acts of God in the biblical narrative do not resonate well with the stories of the prophets of God in the Qur'an; the narrative of human history focused on the story of one people within cosmic history does not harmonize with the qur'anic prophet stories concerning many different peoples to whom prophets came; and the biblical answer to the condition of sinful humanity does not blend well with the qur'anic position that the need of a forgetful but basically God-oriented people is not salvation but prophetic guidance.

Consummation—Afterlife polarity

Some find a substantial polarity between *history* and *eschatology* as the respective foci of biblical and qur'anic perspectives. Neuwirth, for example, compares Psalm 136 and Sura 55, concluding that where the Psalm celebrates *God's faithfulness in history*, the qur'anic sura exalts *God's power in resurrection and the afterlife*: "The position that history occupies in the psalm is occupied in the Qur'an by the idea of God's power to resurrect the dead and to complete His creation in Paradise."[161] Yet I will argue below that just as the qur'anic view of history is an extension of its overwhelming prophetic focus on the day of judgment (relating instances of divine judgment in the punishment narratives), so also the biblical view of the consummation is an extension of its major focus on redemptive history. Therefore, juxtaposing biblical and qur'anic eschatology also reveals significant worldview dissonance. Hermansen gives a helpful summary of some of the concepts to be compared:

> Eschatology embraces not only teachings about death, resurrection, immortality and judgement, but also the tradition's understanding of *beginnings, the meaning of history and the direction and purpose towards which everything in creation tends.* Theologically it orients our ultimate purpose, and this should be central in its interpretation.[162]

This is an important clarification, for in many ways the Bible and the Qur'an teach similar things about death (death of physical body not the end of human existence), resurrection (bodily, at the end of the age, to eternal bliss or eternal shame), immortality (no end to resurrection life), and judgment (a great day of judgment based on deeds in this life). Yet their understandings of *beginnings* (creation and fall versus Tawhid) and the *meaning of history* (redemption history versus prophet history) are significantly different, as we have seen. Significant dissonance may also be heard in the two competing versions of the "direction and purpose towards which everything in creation tends," as I will show after a few comments about common ground.

We see significant areas of similarity between the two worldviews when we consider eschatology as primarily the future life of the individual. Both anticipate the day of resurrection of the just and the unjust, when each individual will be judged according to their deeds. Both foresee a blissful paradise for the righteous and an awful fire for the unrighteous. Both present a hope of the faithful being in the presence of God (e.g. Rev 22:4; Q9:72). But if we consider eschatology as the consummation of the whole biblical narrative rather than individual destiny in the afterlife, the similarity diminishes.

Both the Qur'an and the Bible use eschatology as a medium of exhortation. Warnings and exhortations about the Day of Judgment are scattered extensively throughout the Qur'an:

> [Prophet], your Lord's punishment is coming—it cannot be put off—on the Day when the sky sways back and forth and the mountains float away. Woe on that Day to those who deny the Truth, who amuse themselves with idle chatter: on that Day they will be thrust into the Fire of Hell. (52:7-14; cf. 41:19-24; 44:10-16; 46:33-35; 50:20-30).

Such warnings are also part of the biblical appeal to "the day." Israel's prophets repeatedly warn the people to repent and turn to the Lord in view of the coming day, a day of "destruction from the Almighty," when God will openly intervene to settle the score for the wickedness of the nations (Joel 1:15-16; 2:2, 11-17; 3:1-21; Amos 5:18-27; Obad 15). The NT also depicts the return of the Lord and the final day of judgment when the divine King will settle accounts with his servants and judge the nations (Matt 24-25; 2 Thess 2:1-10). These sections are all accompanied by warnings to be prepared with true righteousness, not religious activities.

But despite this common appeal to eschatology in both biblical and qur'anic exhortation, we also see significant differences arising from the connections between the eschatological perspectives (consummation and afterlife) and their respective primary narratives of human history (redemption and prophethood).

Return of God or Return to God?

Islamic teaching on eschatology often highlights the concept of a "return" to God—both personal and collective. While this is not absent in biblical eschatology, the biblical narrative as a whole moves toward what may be described as the climactic "return of God"—the great day when in the prophet's words, "the Lord my God will come, and all the holy ones with him" (Zech 14:5). "Then shall all the trees of the forest sing for joy before the LORD, for he comes, for he comes to judge the earth" (Ps 96:11-13). In OT prophecy this "coming" was the time when Israel's God would appear at the end of this age to bring judgment on the nations (including Israel) and deliver his remnant, ushering in the "age to come." In the NT, this coming "Lord" is identified with the risen Lord Jesus and the "coming of the Lord" with his return.[163] His coming will bring the resurrection of the dead (e.g. 1 Cor 15:22-26, 51-57; 1 Thess 4:13-17; 2 Tim 4:1; Titus 2:13).

The qur'anic perspective conceives of "the Day" largely in terms of man's return to God: "They will come out [from their graves] on that Day, the Day when they hear the mighty blast in reality. It is We who give life and death; *the final return will be to Us*" (50:42-43). It is central to Islamic eschatology that the soul of man must "return" to its Creator at the Day of Judgment (7:29; 32:11).

Among Sufi Muslims there is a related emphasis on a "return" or journey to God during life which is accomplished by Muslim praxis, especially the daily prayer, which according to Muhammad after his ascent to heaven, is the "ladder of the believer."[164] Muslims even now may experience intimacy with God in this way, through mystical personal "entrance" into the contemplation of God. But in the qur'anic perspective, the final return dominates. This undergirds much of its warning of those who do not believe in the Day (17:10), including tyrants like Pharaoh (40:27). On the other side are those "who believe in the Day of Judgement and fear the punishment of their Lord–none may feel wholly secure from it" (70:26-27).

While belief in resurrection and final judgment is common to Christians and Muslims, they ground their belief differently. For Christians, it rests on Jesus' resurrection from the dead (John 11:24-25; 2 Tim 1:10). Jesus is the "firstfruits" of the future resurrection of all believers from the dead (1 Cor 15:23).[165] Muslims hold this belief in general resurrection while rejecting the crucifixion-resurrection narrative from which its Christian form arose.[166] Qur'anic discourse calls for belief in the resurrection, afterlife, and judgment as a logical necessity, arguing from God's creative and life-giving power, especially as seen in human birth (e.g. Q 22:5-6; 36:77-81; 56:57-74). Where the Bible shows Jesus' resurrection as assurance of future resurrection, the Qur'an presents "logical proofs for the resurrection of the body, including the description of the resurrection as a second creation (Q 32.9–10; 53.45–7)."[167] This is the Qur'an's overall approach, basing arguments on evidence that is equally available to all human beings.[168]

Consummation of history or final judgment?

In the biblical view of the consummation an innumerable multitude of redeemed people from every nation will gather before the throne of God (Rev 7:9-17; cf. 5:9-10; 14:4).[169] Thus the biblical eschatology is the fulfillment and consummation of the long story of redemption. Dumbrell finds five biblical theological themes that reach their consummation in the final vision of biblical canon in Revelation 21–22.[170] The new Jerusalem, the new temple, the new covenant, the new Israel, and the new creation each bring to completion themes which run through the biblical narrative and coalesce at the end of the age. Each can be developed in detail as integral to the biblical narrative and as the fulfillment of the biblical promises.

The Islamic narrative, however, supersedes these themes with its own. Jerusalem is replaced by Mecca, the temple by the Kaaba, the selective biblical covenants by the universal primordial covenant of all souls, the church made up of believers from all nations by the Islamic Ummah, and the new creation where God dwells among men by the Garden where the faithful dwell in bliss. Thus the biblical eschatology, which consummates the creation-fall-redemption narrative, is countered by a qur'anic eschatology which correlates with both Tawhid (creation) and prophethood.[171] We see a similar relationship between prophethood and eschatology whereby qur'anic punishment stories regularly recount stories of judgment on unbelieving peoples who reject their prophet's messages, thus functioning as signs pointing towards the ultimate day of judgment.

The Christian worldview looks at the future day as "our blessed hope, the appearing of the glory of our great God and Savior Jesus Christ" (Titus 2:13). At the center of this joyful hope is the promise of God to dwell among mankind.

> Sing and rejoice, O daughter of Zion, for behold, I come and I will dwell in your midst, declares the LORD. And many nations shall join themselves to the LORD in that day, and shall be my people. And I will dwell in your midst, and you shall know that the LORD of hosts has sent me to you. (Zech 2:10-11)

This theme has its concrete beginning in the tabernacle narrative where God commands Moses to speak to the people of Israel, newly delivered from Egyptian bondage: "Let them make me a sanctuary, that I may dwell in their midst" (Exod 25:8). In spite of the golden calf episode, which threatens the whole arrangement, the narrative ends with God's arrival to dwell among them (40:34). From this time until the exile God dwells among them in a unique way, distinct from universal omnipresence. The NT presents the birth of Jesus as God's glory coming to "tabernacle" among his people: "the Word became flesh and dwelt among us, and we have seen his glory" (John 1:14).[172] The biblical narrative moves toward the finale where God dwells among his people:

> Behold, the dwelling place of God is with man. He will dwell with them, and they will be his people, and God himself will be with them as their God. . . . the throne of God and of the Lamb will be in it, and his servants will worship him. They will see his face." (Rev 21:3; 22:3-4)

In its extensive literature regarding Paradise, the Islamic tradition tells of a vast reception God throws for the blessed upon their arrival in Paradise, which climaxes with the removing of the veil between God and his worshippers so they may look on him.[173] A hadith report promises faithful Muslims a vision of God at the summit of Paradise: "A veil shall be lifted, and the believers shall gaze upon the face of God." [174] But despite these common themes, the concept of God dwelling in the midst of his people seems to run counter to the qur'anic sense of God's transcendence.

New Jerusalem or Paradise?

In the book of Revelation, "new Jerusalem" represents a people and a creation wholly delivered from sin, the curse, Satan, and death itself. The idolatrous world system known as 'Babylon' is judged and destroyed (Rev 17–18). Organized opposition to God is put down by the returning "Lord of lords" (Rev 19). The devil is bound and cast into the lake of fire, and finally so also are death and hades and all whose names are not written in the Lamb's "Book of Life" (Rev 20).[175] The old cursed creation is done away with altogether and is replaced with a new creation (Rev 21). Only then, after the final removal of evil, is the new Jerusalem—the corporate "Bride of the Lamb"—revealed, coming down out of heaven with the glory of God.

In the qur'anic picture there seems to be no concept of the end signifying the removing of sin and evil except in the sense of justice being done at last. Unbelievers receive their just deserts in the Fire and the believers also receive their reward for faithfulness, the Garden of Paradise. Whether this is to be understood as a strict *quid pro quo* or as tempered by the limitless mercy of God, the Qur'an places a huge emphasis on the weighing of each person's deeds on that day.[176] For example, "On a Day when people will be like scattered moths and the mountains like tufts of wool, the one whose *good deeds are heavy on the scales* will have a pleasant life, but the one whose *good deeds are light* will have the Bottomless Pit for his home" (Q 101:6-9; cf. 81:14). Yet while everything in the Muslim worldview is in the shadow of the Day, the narrative does not move toward a final removing of evil by God as the biblical narrative does.

To summarize, while the consummation-afterlife polarity does not exhibit as many dissonant notes as the redemption-prophethood polarity, we nevertheless see significant areas of divergence. In the Christian worldview the end is the consummation of a narrative of God *redeeming* a people from the world and bringing an end to the evils that have corrupted mankind. In the Muslim worldview the end is the outcome of a narrative of God *sending prophets* with guidance to communities so that people may be "mindful of their Lord" and not be among those who disbelieve on that Day (Q 39:71-74).

Because the Abraham stories are part of a larger set of biblical and qur'anic narratives, and since narrative both shapes and shows worldview, this material needs to be juxtaposed carefully to achieve balanced and meaningful comparison. The model I have introduced here for Christian-Muslim narrative and worldview comparison delivers useful results. Despite some potential limitations, the concept of worldview elements corresponding to the respective metanarratives provides a valid and valuable framework as we begin our detailed comparison of Abraham as understood by Christians and Muslims.

CHAPTER 3 – ABRAHAM IN GENESIS

Biblical material relating to Abraham begins with the primary narrative of Genesis 11:27–25:11, a discrete section or cycle marked out by the headings "these are the generations of Terah" (Gen 11:27) and "these are the generations of Ishmael, Abraham's son" (Gen 25:12).[1] Most of the biblical references to Abraham are found in this single fifteen-chapter narrative.[2] We begin however, with a survey of the Abraham material in the Hebrew Bible outside of this main narrative.[3]

The narratives of Abraham's sons and grandsons, which focus on Isaac, Jacob, and Joseph (Gen 26–50), contain 27 references to Abraham. Some of these are simply historical notes, genealogical or otherwise, referring to Abraham's era. Others begin to identify God as "the God of Abraham" (or similar words) and to refer back to his promises to Abraham. This era was so determinative that afterward God is identified as "the God of Abraham, the God of Isaac and the God of Jacob" (Exod 3:6, 15–16).[4] This divine identification communicates a unique relationship between the "God of Abraham" and the people of Israel:

1) The God of Abraham is the God of specific, purposeful election who has *"called"* (Isa 51:2) and *"redeemed"* Abraham (Isa 29:22). This election is referred to by future generations as the root of their relationship to God (Neh 9:7; Ps 105:6; Isa 41:8).

2) He is the living God who *reveals himself personally*. In addition to the times when he "spoke" to Abraham, God also "appeared" to him (Exod 6:3), as well as to Isaac and Jacob. Abraham is seen as a "prophet" to whom the word of the Lord has come (1 Chr 16:22; Ps 105:15).

3) Abraham's God is the *maker of solemn and binding promises*. He has promised or "sworn an oath" to bless Abraham and give him numberless descendants and an eternal inheritance (Gen 26:3; 50:24; Exod 6:8; 32:13; 33:1; Num 32:11; Deut 1:8; 6:10; 9:5; 29:13; 30:20; 34:4; 1 Chr 16:16; Ps 105:9; Mic 7:20). Abraham receives a "covenant" (Exod 2:24; Lev 26:42; 2 Kgs 13:23; 1 Chr 16:16; Ps 105:9). For future generations issues relating to the "land" are linked with God's promise (Gen 26:3; 28:4, 13; 35:12; 50:24; Exod 6:8; 32:13; 33:1; Lev 26:42; Num 32:11; Deut 1:8; 6:10; 9:5; 30:20; 34:4; 2 Chr 20:7). Nevertheless, they should not be presumptuous about their possession of the land simply because it was given to Abraham (Ezek 33:24).[5] Abraham's burial site is a down payment on the future possession of the whole land (Gen 49:29-32; 50:13).

4) He is a *God of restoration*, whose covenant with Abraham (and to some degree with Isaac and Jacob) becomes the basis on which his rebellious descendants are forgiven and restored to God's favor. This is especially seen when this Abrahamic covenant is pleaded by an intercessor (Exod 32:13; Lev 26:40-42; Deut 9:27; 2 Kgs 13:23; Neh 9:7; Jer 33:26). Help in situations of national crisis is asked for and granted on this basis (2 Chr 20:7; 30:6). The latter prophets' message of hope after God's judgment is also established on this foundation (Mic 7:20). In fact, in "the most remarkable echo of Genesis 12:3 outside Genesis," Isaiah prophesies that "on that day" even Israel's great enemies Assyria and Egypt will be "blessed" along with Israel (Isa 19:24-25).[6]

5) He is the *God of a particular people*. God's promise to Abraham is the ground of Israel's status as God's particular "people" and his identity as their God (Deut 29:13). They are prayed for on this basis to remain faithful to God (1 Chr 29:18). Israel is addressed as the "seed" or "descendants" of Abraham (Ps 105:6; Isa 41:8; Jer 33:26) and Abraham is described as Israel's "father" (Josh 24:3; Isa 51:2). Yet, a day will come when people from the Gentile nations "are afforded the same status *'as the people of the God of Abraham'*" (Ps 47:9).[7]

Thus the Abraham narrative is inseparable from both the primeval narrative of Gen 1-11 and the ongoing narrative of Israel's development as a special nation. Nevertheless, it must also be considered as a cohesive narrative in its own right.

THE CANONICAL ABRAHAM NARRATIVE: PRESUPPOSITIONS

For the purposes of this study I take the canonical Abraham story at face value as a single historical narrative. I do not engage historical-critical questions arising from apparent difficulties in the text, such as motif repetition, doublets, uses of the divine name and numerous apparent inconsistencies of which ancient interpreters were also aware.[8] The hermeneutical importance of treating the biblical stories as a literary unity is now widely recognized, and I proceed on the basis that there is purpose in these seeming anomalies.[9] I seek to understand the intent or meaning of the Abraham story as it is, particularly its theological interpretation: what does it tell us about God, his purposes, and his acts in history?[10] Leaving aside questions of compositional history and the date and setting of final redaction, I also presume the essential historicity of the narrated events while remembering they are more like a painting of an ancient event than a modern photograph. I take the events portrayed by adroit storytelling to have a historical reference, based on reliable oral and/or written testimony, even if their final narrative composition is done centuries later.[11]

Christians and Muslims have traditionally presumed that the events recorded in their sacred scriptures *have happened*. At the same time, using the conclusions of biblical scholars whose theories regarding sources and redaction seem to support their claim, Muslim writers often argue that the Torah and Gospel have been corrupted. I wish to distance myself from these theories for the purposes of theological comparison with qur'anic Abraham narratives.

Second, it seems evident that ahistorical presupposition is not an intrinsic element of narrative theology. Gooding contends that the history produced by biblical narrators using the "dramatic" method is none the worse for that: "The use of symmetrical structure by an ancient historian or biographer is simply his way of achieving interpretation which a modern historian would achieve by different methods."[12]

The *meaning* or *theology* of the text is best sought through examination of the text as we have it. The story is constitutive of the theology. As Janzen puts it, "The theological meaning of the text cannot be neatly detached from its literary form, any more than a person's spirit can be neatly detached from one's body."[13] While I seek to approach this text judiciously, my presuppositions are those of Christian theism and my acceptance of the Christian canon inevitably shape my insights into its Hebrew Scripture portion in many ways.[14]

GENESIS 11:27–25:11

The overall structure of Genesis is marked by the tenfold use of the heading formula *'ēlleh tôlēdôt* – "these are the generations of X" or "this is the account of the line of X," (2:4; 5:1; 6:9; 10:1; 11:10; 11:27; 25:12; 25:19; 36:1, 9; 37:2).[15] As Janzen notes, the repeated word *tôlēdôt* captures the themes of blessing and generation, which tie together the creation narratives and the patriarchal birth narratives.[16] Within this framework Abraham's life forms the vast bulk of the account of his father Terah's line (11:27–25:11), which comprises one unit within the larger story, presented in twenty "clearly defined episodes" as a continuous narrative.[17] These episodes fall into two major parts, separated by a genealogical section in 22:20-24, comprised of (1) the main narrative, beginning with Abram's call and concluding with his testing (12:1–22:19), and (2) an epilogue, wrapping up Abraham's life and looking to the next generation (23:1–25:11).[18]

The first and main section is a carefully crafted chiastic ring, framed by genealogical material relating to Terah's descendants in Haran, especially Abram and Nahor. In this structure the Lord's initial call of Abram (12:1-9) corresponds to his testing of the patriarch (22:1-19);[19] Sarai and Abram's encounter with Pharaoh in Egypt (12:10-20) is balanced by her endangerment in Gerar and Abraham's encounters with Abimelech (20–21); Abram's initial separation from Lot and rescue of him in connection with Sodom (13–14) corresponds to Abraham's intercession for Sodom and Lot's rescue (18–19); the Lord's promise and confirmatory covenant with Abram (15) is balanced by his renewed promise and covenant of circumcision (17). The birth of Ishmael to Hagar is thus in the middle (16),[20] in what Douglas describes as the "pivotal central point" in this ring composition.[21] As Klinghoffer says, "That chapter—Hagar's pregnancies [*sic*], the birth of Ishmael—is the pivot on which Abram's life turns."[22] The narrative advances as a single story in which the primary characters are God, Abraham, Lot, Sarah, Hagar, and their sons. The major sections may be shown in somewhat more detail in the following table.

FIGURE 3.1 – GENESIS ABRAHAM NARRATIVE STRUCTURE

GENEALOGY OF ABRAM'S CLAN WHO MOVE TO HARAN	11:27-32	Terah's descendants Abram, Nahor, and Haran
A. THE CALL AND OBEDIENCE OF ABRAM	12:1-3	The Lord calls Abram, promises to bless all nations through him.
	12:4-9	Abram obeys the Lord's call, goes as called. At Shechem the Lord promises land; builds altars at Shechem and east of Bethel
B. ABRAM, SARAI, AND THE KING	12:10-20	Abram in Egypt, "Sarai is my sister" deception, Pharaoh frees Sarai (Heir-line is preserved)
C. ABRAM, LOT AND SODOM	13:1-13	Abram and Lot separate as Lot chooses the lush valley near Sodom.
	13:14-18	Abram promised the land, builds altar at Hebron
	14:1-16	Abram rescues Lot from the Shinar alliance
	14:17-24	Abram blessed by Melchizedek., rejects Sodom's king
D. COVENANT	15:1-21	The Lord promises offspring, Abram believes the Lord, the Lord makes covenant with Abram, promises numberless seed and a land
E. THE "FALL" SARAI OUT, HAGAR IN	16:1-16	Sarai proposes that Abram take Hagar, Hagar driven out, the Angel of the Lord sends Hagar back to Sarai now, Ishmael born
D'. COVENANT SARAH PROMISE	17:1-22	The Lord appears to Abram, makes covenant of circumcision, changes names; excludes Ishmael, promises Isaac
	17:23-27	Abraham circumcises Ishmael and household and is circumcised himself
C'. ABRAHAM, LOT AND SODOM. SARAH PROMISE	18:1-15	The Lord appears to Abraham with two angels, announces son
	18:16-33	Abraham intercedes for Sodom
	19:1-29	Angels rescue Lot and daughters, destroy Sodom.
	19:30-38	Lot's daughters have children by incest: Moab and Ammon
B'. ABRAHAM, SARAH, AND THE KING, SARAH & ISAAC IN, HAGAR & ISHMAEL OUT	20:1-18	Abraham in Gerar, "Sarah my sister" deception, God visits Abimelech, who frees Sarah, Abraham prays for him. (Heir-line is preserved.)
	21:1-21	The Lord visits Sarah; Isaac born, circumcised, weaned; Hagar and son cast out. God promises Hagar to make Ishmael a great nation.
	21:22-34	Abimelech seeks treaty with Abraham, covenant at Beersheba, Abraham calls on the Lord's name
A'. THE TEST AND OBEDIENCE OF ABRAHAM	22:1-14	God tests Abraham, sends to Moriah. Abraham obeys, goes, builds altar, offers Isaac; the Lord's Angel intervenes, ram provided
	22:15-19	The Lord's Angel calls second time repeating promises of offspring, blessing of all nations, adding victory over enemies
GENEALOGY OF ABRAHAM'S CLAN WHO LIVE IN HARAN	22:20-24	Nahor's descendants in Haran

This chiastic structure suggests that the fulcrum of the narrative is barren Sarai's proposal to her husband so that she can have what she wants: "Go in to my servant, it may be that I shall obtain children by her" (16:2).[23] A serious complication is thus introduced into the central plot of God fulfilling his promises through Abraham's barren wife. From this point forward Abraham's affections and household are divided. This complication occupies a major place in several narrative sections as firstborn Ishmael is explicitly demoted by the promise and birth of Sarah's son Isaac (17:18-21; 21:1-21).

This focus on Ishmael's birth adds confirmation that the primary theme of the overall narrative is the difficult and complicated fulfillment of God's promise of offspring (seed) to Abraham. Grüneberg argues that "the Abraham cycle focuses primarily on the question of whether and how Abraham will have descendants."[24] The question of who will be Abraham's *heir* is central to the entire narrative and crucial to God's promise of a *heritage* (blessing, ultimately for all nations) and an *inheritance* (land, ultimately the world).[25] In the following, I consider the Abraham narrative episode by episode, looking for pointers to its overall purpose and indicators of the worldview that it embodies.

11:27-32 Genealogical background of Abram's family.

The Abraham narrative is linked to the primeval narrative (Gen 1:1–11:9) through two sections of genealogical material. First is the ten-generation linear genealogy from Shem to Terah's three sons Abram, Nahor, and Haran (11:10-26), entitled "the generations of Shem." This genealogy serves, along with the similar ten-generation genealogy from Adam to Noah (5:1-32), to link God's new beginning with Abraham both to the original creation and to the fresh beginning after the flood.[26] In this selective approach to history other lines are quickly set aside as they constitute little more than the backdrop to the main drama. Hendel's comment is insightful: "An important implication of the past organized as a genealogy is that it is clearly goal oriented, pointed toward a particular future."[27] Thus the section beginning in 11:27, entitled "the generations of Terah," dispenses with Terah and Abram's two brothers with a minimum of information, moving quickly on to Abram's story, which is the main narrative focus. We are only told that Terah took Abram, Lot, and Sarai and left Ur "to go into the land of Canaan, but when they came to Haran, they settled there" (11:31).[28]

Thematically a key phrase for the overall narrative is evident in the simple notice at the structural center of the short section,[29] that "Sarai was barren; she had no child" (11:30). Much of the story's drama builds on this issue. As Stump says, the Abraham narrative as "bounded by and focused on a concern with children. Among the first things we learn about Abraham is that he is married to a woman who cannot bear him children."[30] As Sarai is barren, so also are Rebekah and Rachel, the wives of her son Isaac and her grandson Jacob (25:21; 29:31). God's blessing includes his special intervention to overturn this particular curse (Exod 23:26; Deut 7:14).[31]

The location of Abram's homeland has been the subject of much research.[32] The Sumerian site of Ur in southern Mesopotamia has been the majority position since its discovery in 1922. However, the biblical text seems to identify the land to which Abraham sends his servant to get a wife for Isaac—"go to my country and to my kindred"—with the place from which God called him initially when he left Ur—"from the land of my kindred" (Gen 24:4, 7; cf. 11:31; 12:1; 15:7). This land where Isaac and Jacob found wives among Abraham's kindred was near Haran in northern Mesopotamia, the region called Paddan Aram or Aram Naharaim (25:20; 28:5). If this identification is correct, Abram's homeland may have been Edessa, now known as Şanlıurfa, located some 44km northwest of Haran.[33] On the other hand, accounting for the "Chaldean" label in the phrase "Ur of the Chaldeans" (Gen 11:28, 31; 15:7; Neh 9:7) is more problematic in the northern identification.[34]

Wherever it occurred, the early life of Abram before his migration to Haran is significant for this comparative theological study. Where the Genesis narrative says almost nothing about this period of his life, the Qur'an and Islamic sources relate many stories about his conversion to faith in one creator God, his conflicts with idolaters and the persecution he endured as a prophet of monotheism.[35]

12:1-9 The Lord calls Abram and Abram obeys

Whether understood as the initial word spoken to Abram while still in Ur ("the Lord had spoken") or the word calling him to complete the journey to Canaan begun with his father and delayed in Haran for years ("the Lord spoke"), this call and its accompanying promises (12:1-3) are constitutive of the story that follows.[36] With no indication of any prerequisite action leading to divine choice, God summons Abram to "go . . . to the land that I will show you," with a threefold call to leave: "your country and your kindred and your father's house."

The summons is accompanied by a threefold promise: "And I will make of you a great nation, and I will bless you and make your name great." In the narrative and genealogies that follow, this "great nation" is clearly identified with the twelve tribes of Israel. The summons and promise are in turn followed by another imperative (or result) leading to the threefold result that will flow from Abraham's obedience and God's fulfilling his promise to him: "Be a blessing. I will bless those who bless you, and him who dishonors you I will curse, and in you all the families of the earth shall be blessed."[37] God's purpose in calling Abram is ultimately to bless all nations.[38] Repetition of the terms "clans/families" and "nations" makes clear verbal links with the preceding narratives, which recount their origin in the Table of Nations (Gen 10) and their dispersing from Babel (Gen 11:1-9). All these families of the earth are in view as the Lord calls Abram (see 10:5, 20, 31-32; 11:9).[39] Noort rightly identifies this promise as "the hermeneutical key to the whole narrative."[40]

These promises of blessing stand in tension with Sarai's barrenness, setting up the need for God's special intervention. It may also allude to the divine work of making the world "fruitful" in Genesis 1, as "seed" is an important result of divine action in both sections (Gen 1:11-12; 12:7; 13:15-16). Divine blessing is also significant in both,[41] so when the narrative of redemption begins in 12:1-3, its agenda is announced with the fivefold repetition of the word "bless/blessing," perhaps intimating the divine purpose to overturn the earlier divine curses.[42] Janzen rightly notes that chapters 1–11 "are not the preface to the main story called salvation history; rather, the salvation history is a remedial process within the larger story of God's creation."[43] God's promise to make Abram's name great answers the ill-advised purpose of the tower-builders in Shinar, "let us make a name for ourselves" (11:4). Such details reinforce the organic bond of the Abraham narrative with the preceding chapters.

Taking Lot and Sarai with him (as Terah had done, 11:31), along with livestock and servants acquired in Haran, Abram obediently journeys to "the land of Canaan."[44] Stump suggests that taking Lot indicates "a certain double-mindedness in Abraham's attitude toward God," as Lot should have been among those Abram left behind.[45] While the narrative does not directly indicate this, the repeated difficulties Abram experiences because of Lot may support her reading.

In Canaan, the Lord "appears" to Abraham in the first of a number of such appearances and promises him an inheritance: "To your offspring I will give this land" (12:7). This foundational passage says little about how or in what form God appeared, but it is later emphasized that the Lord "appeared" and did not simply send his word to the patriarchs (Exod 6:3).[46] The God of Abram is characterized throughout the patriarchal narratives as a God who comes near, "appearing" in quite tangible ways (15:1-21; 17:1-22; 18:1-33; 26:2-5, 23-25; 28:11-17; 35:1-15).[47] To these appearances of God/the Lord may be added the appearances of the Angel of God/the Lord in Gen 16:7-14; 32:24-32.[48] Abram's response is worship, building an altar to the Lord, "who had appeared to him" (12:8). As Dempster says, "this resumption of true 'worship' places Abram squarely in the lineage of Seth (Gen 4:26), whose descendants were marked by such activity."[49] Abram's sojourning is emphasized throughout the section as he moves on from Shechem to near Bethel, where he builds another altar and calls on the name of the Lord, before moving again toward the Negev. Beale argues that building altars and calling on the name of the Lord indicates both a claim on this particular land for the Lord and (in the larger canonical context) even a connection with the temple that would eventually be built in this land.[50] There is no record of any of the patriarchs building altars in any other lands during their journeys. The climax of the narrative finds Abraham building a final altar on which to offer the ultimate sacrifice, his beloved son (22:9).

The narrative emphasizes God's summons and the compound promise that enables or stirs Abram to act. This pattern of God's command-promise followed by Abraham's faith-act is found a number of times in the Abraham cycle. Additional revelation frequently follows acts of sacrificial obedience.[51]

12:10-20 Abram endangers Sarai in Egypt

The blessing promised to Abraham in the land is threatened in this section both by famine[52] and by Abram's fearfulness in Egypt. The central issue of the section is Sarai's endangerment in the royal harem due to Abram's insistence that she identify him as her brother. While the narrator does not condemn Abram's self-protective subterfuge, Pharaoh's three questions make it inescapable that it was deceitful and wrong: "What is this you have done to me? Why did you not tell me that she was your wife? Why did you say, 'She is my sister,' so that I took her for my wife?" (12:18–19).[53] The overall result of this short account is that Sarai is protected as God sends plagues on Pharaoh's household and the first threat to the promise is averted.

The story presents Abram (and his family) as altogether human and susceptible to human frailty. "This family is in no way superior to the rest of the human race. The ancient stories repeatedly emphasize that the conduct of the 'pagan' is more noble and righteous than that of the elect."[54] In fact it is characteristic of the biblical narratives to display the foibles of the patriarchs, even as the later narratives hide nothing of the failures of the Israelites. It is noticeable however that later Jewish exegesis of this story tends to emphasize more the wickedness of Egypt and the exemplary righteousness of Abraham.[55]

13:1–14:24 Abram, Lot and Sodom—Part One.

Following the return from Egypt, emphasis falls on issues relating primarily to use and control of the land. Abram returns specifically "to the place where he had made an altar at the first. And there Abram called upon the name of the Lord" (13:4). Two stories concerning Abram and Lot are narrated, each with a closing section in which blessing is announced for Abram. In the first, Abram and Lot separate as Lot chooses the lush valley near Sodom (13:2-13), and as soon as Lot leaves, God promises to give Abram and his offspring the whole land in perpetuity—"forever" (13:14-18). God gives the first of two pictures that illustrate how innumerable his offspring will be: "If anyone can number *the dust of the earth*, then your descendants can also be numbered" (cf. "stars" in 15:5; 22:17). The announcement also confirms, and adds specificity to, the first brief land promise (12:7), which preceded the trip to Egypt. It thus emphasizes the importance of this particular land for God's purposes for Abraham.

In the second story, Abram rescues Lot from the Shinar (Babylonian) alliance in what constitutes the only military activity recounted about him (14:1-16). Lowin points out that Abram's sole campaign differs significantly from those of Moses and Joshua (as well as from those of Muhammad).[56] Upon returning in victory with the spoil Abram is blessed by Melchizedek, "priest of God Most High" and sovereign of Salem, the city better known as Jerusalem (14:17-24; cf. Ps 76:2).[57] The enigmatic king-priest Melchizedek has been the object of much speculation, including ancient traditions identifying him with Abraham's ancestor Shem.[58] More important is his invocation of God's blessing on Abram (cf. 12:2-3), perhaps as part of a covenant-making ceremony in which he personally brings out "bread and wine" (14:18).[59] In Psalm 110 God addresses the exalted messianic warrior as a Mechizedekian priest, appointed by divine oath: "The LORD has sworn and will not change his mind, 'You are a priest forever after the order of Melchizedek'" (Ps 110:4). Taken together these passages may suggest the mediation of God's blessings to Abraham's offspring through a future messianic figure, particularly the blessing of *victory over enemies* (cf. Gen 22:17).

In both of these stories Sodom plays an important part, as Lot is taken captive with the Sodomites, while Abram refuses to take any reward or spoil from Sodom's king. This brief tale of two cities thus identifies the Abrahamic promise with Salem and places it in a certain opposition to other kingdoms, particularly Sodom and its infamous opposition to the Lord (13:13).

In relation to the main storyline of the Abraham cycle, that of who will be Abraham's heir, this section serves to show how and perhaps why Lot is excluded. Helyer says, "The crisis here is that Abram's heir-apparent virtually eliminates himself from the promise by leaving the land of promise. Now Abram is without any heir."[60] Lot's choice leaves him with no share in either Abram's promised inheritance or relationship with Abram's offspring (Lot's descendants Moab and Ammon become enemies of Israel). It is clear that the promises of blessing will have nothing to do with Lot's line, though for the patriarch's sake Lot is rescued from Sodom. In a similar way, Abraham's other sons and his grandson Esau receive subsidiary blessings as they are left out of the line of promise. It becomes clear that God's promised blessing is linked with the promised land.

15:1-21 The Lord confirms his promises with a covenant

Two dialogues between the Lord and Abram (15:1-6, 7-21) comprise this section in which the Lord makes a covenant with Abram. Each segment begins with God's promise, followed by the patriarch's questions and God's answer with a symbolic action to confirm his promise. For the first time we encounter the phrase commonly introducing records of revelation given to Hebrew prophets; "*the word of the LORD came* to Abram" (15:1; also in 15:4). The first such prophetic "word of the Lord" is a promise, not a warning or a command.[61] Urging Abram not to fear because God himself is his "shield," God promises that his "reward shall be very great." In the Genesis narrative Abraham is not a prophet proclaiming a message from God, but a believing recipient of God's call and promise.[62]

Abram's response shows that his primary interest is not the reward, but his heir. The only remaining candidate is his servant Eliezer, whom he could theoretically adopt.[63] He reminds the Lord twice of this central concern: "I continue childless. . . . Behold, you have given me no offspring." In direct answer to this concern, "the word of the Lord" comes again: "This man will not be your heir; but one who will come forth from your own body, he shall be your heir." The Lord (or the word of the Lord[64]) takes Abram outside and shows him the innumerable stars, reaffirming his promise of a vast number of offspring: "So shall your descendants (seed) be" (cf. 13:16). The narrator recounts that Abram, perhaps enabled by this visual sign, "believed the Lord" in spite of the long delay and that the Lord "accounted as righteousness" Abram's faith in God's promise and ability to do this humanly impossible thing.[65] In an alternative reading

Abram both believes and reckons righteousness or justice to God, since who is reckoning righteousness to whom is unspecified in the text.[66] Grammatical arguments that seem to militate against this reading are considered in detail by Johnson.[67] Nevertheless, the primary concern here is not forgiveness or acceptance by God but covenantal commitment to Abram, as emphasized by the formal covenant ceremony that follows. Holland says this ceremony signifies "God's commitment to Abraham in covenant to make him the father of a great nation that, in turn, would bless other nations (Gen 18:18). It was about how God acted righteously toward him, keeping faith with his promise, and the faith Abraham expressed was in response to the promise the Lord had given him."[68]

The second dialogue follows immediately, beginning with the Lord's word of self-revelation and purpose: "I am the LORD who brought you out from Ur of the Chaldeans to give you this land to possess." Similar words often introduce the Lord's commandments, particularly the Decalogue (Exod 20:2; cf. Lev 19:36; 22:33; 25:38; 26:13; Num 15:41; Deut 5:6; 6:12; 8:14; 13:5, 10), showing that God's identity is linked with his particular interventions in human affairs. This word to Abram, with its parallel in Exodus 20:2—"I am the LORD your God, who brought you out of the land of Egypt, out of the house of slavery"—suggests that Abraham's is a story of redemption by God, not unlike Israel's miraculous deliverance from Egypt. Isaiah's mention of Abraham's call confirms this impression: "Thus says the LORD, *who redeemed Abraham.* . . ." (Isa 29:22)[69] The Isaiah passage, like the Genesis patriarchal narrative, links God's redeeming Abraham with the future of Jacob's descendants in one continuous story.

This phrase also serves as the historical introduction to what seems to be a covenant convention in the ANE, used here to confirm the immutable nature of God's purpose.[70] Abram's question, "How am I to know that I shall possess it?" is answered by a solemn ritual act. The Lord first reveals the future of Abram's descendants, including 400 years in Egypt and their eventual return to possess the land, and then, in the form of a "smoking fire pot and flaming torch," passes between the divided pieces of sacrificial animals laid on the ground. Divine initiative is in the forefront of the narrative, as only God's presence moves between the pieces; Abram is passive.[71] The actions are summed up in the words, "The LORD made a covenant with Abram, saying, 'To your offspring I give this land, from the river of Egypt to the great river. . . .'" (15:18) For the first time, the word "covenant" is used of God's commitment to carry out his promises to Abram, combining two key elements: "offspring/seed" and "land." The God of Abraham is the covenant-making God.[72]

The personal interaction between God and Abram is notable here, as is the sometimes-visible immanence of God mentioned in passing by the narrator. God's theophanic presence often attends covenant-making contexts in biblical narrative (e.g. Exod 3–4; 19–20; 23:20-33; 34; Judg 2:1-5; Mal 3:1).[73] As Kaiser and Silva note, "One of the most notable features about biblical narrative is the pervasive presence of God. Often, God is one of the two characters in these scenes."[74]

16:1–16 Barren Sarai gives Hagar to Abram, Ishmael is born

This two-part scene, situated between the two covenant-making scenes of chapters 15 and 17, forms the pivot point of the main section of the Abraham cycle.[75] It begins with a notice that Sarai is still barren after ten years in Canaan, with no sign of the promised offspring from Abram's body. Sarai's proposal that Abram "go in to" her servant Hagar, while having both biblical (Gen 30:1-13) and ANE[76] parallels, seems to stem from an attempt to circumvent the will of God: "the LORD *has prevented me* from bearing children."[77] Contrary to Culver's assertion that "the Genesis text does not cast any moral stigma on Sarah's plan as such,"[78] the scene clearly alludes to the famous scene known as the "fall" with the words "Abram listened to the voice of Sarai . . . [she] took . . . and gave . . . to Abram her husband" (16:2-3), which closely parallel those of Genesis 3:6 and 17. Wenham concludes, "The narrator suggests we are witnessing a rerun of the fall."[79] This will lead to a series of complications and a reaffirmation or clarification of God's purpose, which will require particular divine intervention.[80] But the repeated intervention of God to fulfill his purposes in spite of this disruption indicates that, like the earlier fall, this is part of the larger story of human failure and faithlessness into which God comes as deliverer. The Abraham narrative continues the story of fallen humanity even as it records the beginning of the divine initiative of redemption.[81] Joseph's words at the end of the book reflect this theme: "As for you, you meant evil against me, but God meant it for good, to bring it about that many people should be kept alive" (Gen 50:20).

The outcome of this affair evidences discord rather than blessing. Hagar "despises her mistress"; Sarai blames Abram and deals so harshly with Hagar that she flees from her. "The first scene ends in total disaster for all concerned. Hagar has lost her home, Sarai her maid, and Abram his second wife and new-born child."[82] It is only divine intervention by the Lord that brings some restoration of order and hope in place of affliction and separation until the time when the promise will be fulfilled as planned by God. In view of its importance for the biblical worldview, this human failure may be seen as part of an emerging picture in which even "prophets" are all too human. Scenes of drunkenness and unseemly events in Noah's and Lot's life, or of David's adultery and killing of Bathsheba's honorable husband to cover her pregnancy are not altogether surprising, but are rather symptoms of universal human sinfulness.

The first appearance of the special "Angel" or "messenger" of the Lord/God in the Bible is to the outcast Hagar. He promises to personally ("I will . . .") multiply Hagar's descendants so that they cannot be numbered for multitude. The text seems to indicate that the one who talked to Hagar was the Lord, and that she had understood this in some sense: "she called the name of the Lord, who spoke to her, 'You are a God of seeing,' for she said, 'Truly here I have seen him who looks after me'" (16:13).[83] Hannah comments that in nearly every case when the angel of the Lord/God appears in a patriarchal narrative "there is a curious oscillation between the angel and the Lord; at times the [angel of the Lord] speaks not as a messenger, but as if he is to be identified with the Lord."[84]

The angel speaks to Hagar four times, beginning by addressing her by name and questioning her about her journey. Then in response to her explanation that she is fleeing from her mistress the angel speaks to her three times regarding three matters: 1) a humbling command to return and submit to Sarai, whom she had despised; 2) a promise that he (the Lord) will greatly multiply her offspring (cf. 13:16; 15:5); and 3) an announcement that she is pregnant (as she already knows) and will bear a son whom she will call Ishmael, whose future will be marked by both freedom and feuding.[85] Whether interpreted as a positive oracle of "free-roaming, bedouinlike existence,"[86] or a negative one of conflict,[87] it is clear that Ishmael is not the one through whose offspring the nations will be blessed. Hagar returns home and bears Abram (not Sarai) a son, whom Abram names Ishmael, as she is directed.[88] Kepnes argues that Hagar foreshadows Israel: "Since Hagar flees Sarah's home in Canaan, heads for Egypt and then returns to Canaan, her wanderings remind us of Abraham's journeys. Like Abraham, Hagar is a wanderer who comes to hear the word of call and fulfill a divine mission."[89] He cites feminist Bible scholar Tikvah Frymer-Kensky, who shows another startling connection based on the name Hagar (*Ha-Ger: the stranger*) and the prophecy to Abraham in the previous chapter about his descendants being "strangers" (*Ger*) in Egypt (15:13):

> Hagar the stranger, Hagar the servant, Hagar, the wife of Abraham and mother of Ishmael *is* Israel! She presages, she prefigures, Israel's suffering in Egypt. And in her deep connection to God, and in the fact that God sees and listens to her suffering and rewards her with a multitude of offspring, Hagar also prefigures Israel's ultimate redemption![90]

The divinely given name "Ishmael" means "God (El) has heard," and gives expression to the immanence and interest of God in the afflictions of needy people. God's "hearing" is brought out three times in relation to Ishmael (16:11; 17:20; 21:17). He is to be blessed, multiplied, and made into a nation through God's gracious intervention in this scene, both because of Abraham's request and as his seed (17:20; 21:13). Yet as will become evident in the following scene, in the overall Abraham narrative the misguided conception of Ishmael must be seen as a serious complication or diversion from the fulfillment of God's covenant with Abram.

While the Abraham narrative gives little basis for "demonizing" Hagar, Ishmael, or their descendants, it does develop a clear trajectory for a unique role for Abraham's descendants through Isaac, not Ishmael (Gen 26:4), and through Jacob, not Esau (28:14). That mission is on behalf of the *nations*, among whom Ishmael's and Esau's descendants will be numbered (25:12-18; 36:1-43).[91] Regarding this passage Kepnes says, "because of the fundamental vagueness of scripture, the reader is called upon, indeed required to interpret the text . . . [Scripture] is an opaque semiotic system whose meaning is fulfilled in its interpretation by us."[92] I would argue that as part of an overarching narrative, scripture is not as malleable as Kepnes implies.

This theologically rich passage is significant for at least two major themes of the book of Genesis: the introduction of difficulty through human failure/sin, and the Lord's ultimate victory in spite of the resulting enmity, bringing good out of evil, particularly through the seed of promise. The complications arising here are finally resolved in chapters 21-22, where God clarifies the relative roles of Ishmael and Isaac in his purposes. The Lord is revealed as the present God who both hears (16:12) and sees (16:13) the afflicted one, even when afflicted by the chosen people.[93]

17:1-27 The Lord reaffirms and deepens his covenant with Abram and Sarai

Thirteen years pass as Ishmael grows up with Abram, Hagar, and Sarai. Nothing has happened to explicitly indicate that Ishmael is not the heir-apparent.[94] Now the Lord appears to Abram to re-affirm and clarify his intention to fulfill his promise of offspring through barren Sarah. The narrative, beginning with a theophany, is comprised of a five-part divine discourse (17:1-2, 3-8, 9-14, 15-16, 19-21), followed by a notice that "when he had finished talking with him, God went up from Abraham" (17:22). Characteristic of the Abraham cycle, obedience follows immediately: Abraham, his son Ishmael and the males of his household are circumcised "that very day" (17:23-27).

The Lord introduces himself for the first time as "El Shaddai," a name with royal associations and connected in Genesis with the promise of multiplied offspring (17:1; 28:3; 35:11; 48:3; 49:25). Abram is first commanded to walk before him and be blameless, and then to be circumcised as the sign of the covenant God has made with him. While some new elements are added, such as abundant use of the word "covenant" (13 times), the "everlasting" quality of the covenant (17:7, 13, 19), the promise of "kings" (17:6, 16), and the promise to "be God" to him and his offspring, it is clear that God is expanding and focusing the previous promises of offspring and land.[95] The announcing of names is prominent throughout: God's name is given as *El Shaddai*, Abram is renamed *Abraham*, Sarai is renamed *Sarah*, the promised son is to be named *Isaac*. The names Abraham and Sarah are particularly linked with God's plan that a "multitude of nations" will come from them (17:5-6, 15-16).[96] The change of both names highlights the intensified divine focus on this couple as the joint heads of the line through which God's blessing will be brought to the nations through their "royal" offspring.[97] The promise of the land, now "for an eternal possession," is tied to the intention of the Lord to "be their God," a pair of concepts also related to God "dwelling among" his people.[98]

In a variety of ways, the Lord ratchets up the intensity of his commitment and makes it clear once and for all that his covenant purposes for Abraham will be fulfilled only through offspring born from Sarah's womb. God's purposes will depend entirely on his special act in overriding human barrenness and old age. Significantly the sign of the covenant is given only now, a sign placed in the flesh of the male reproductive organ. Abraham's incredulous laughter and his prayer for Ishmael are decisively overruled: "No, but Sarah your wife shall bear you a son, and you shall call his name Isaac. I will establish my covenant with him as an everlasting covenant for his offspring after him" (17:19). Though Ishmael will be blessed abundantly and become a great nation (17:20), God insists one final time, "I will establish my covenant with Isaac, whom Sarah shall bear to you at this time next year" (17:21). Ishmael receives circumcision as the sign of the covenant along with all the men in the household; nevertheless it seems that he, his offspring, and all others will be outsiders to the covenant itself, which is focused on one royal lineage.[99] Williamson assesses this evidence somewhat differently, arguing that Ishmael himself is as much included in the covenant as any other person in Abraham's household, and that the feature that is applied exclusively to Isaac is the "perpetuity of the covenant" to his offspring. Because of the importance of Ishmael for discussion with Muslims, I quote Williamson's nuanced conclusion at length.

> Whereas Ishmael, as part of Abraham's family, was himself included within the covenant community, this covenantal status was not explicitly extended to his progeny, as is clearly so in the case of Isaac (Gen. 17:19). Thus this eternal covenant was to be perpetuated exclusively through Isaac's seed. It was in and through them (i.e. the special Abrahamic line of descent, beginning with Isaac) that the promissory aspects of this covenant would be fulfilled.[100]

This dramatic scene contributes significantly to the main theme of the Abraham narrative, which is the complicated issue of who will be Abraham's heir. The universal covenantal blessings intended for the "nations" will be mediated through a particular seed in a particular land. Once again barren Sarah is brought onto center stage in spite of all the human impossibilities this entails.

18:1–19:38 Abraham, Lot and Sodom—Part Two.

These two chapters comprise a complete unit in four main sections, united by the presence of the Lord, angels, Abraham, Lot and Sodom. Both chapters begin with acts of generous hospitality shown by Abraham and Lot to their special visitors. The connection between 13–14 and 18–19 is strengthened by the special dining scenes in both. Melchizedek brings out bread and wine for Abraham in chapter 14, and Abraham sets his table for the Lord and two angels in chapter 18.

The Lord appears again to Abraham, shortly after his previous appearance.[101] Though Abraham sees "three men standing in front of him,"[102] it gradually becomes clearer to him and the reader as the scene unfolds that one of these "men" is the Lord himself, and the other two are angels (see 19:1).[103] This apparently unmediated presence of God is a frequent feature of the Abraham narrative. Following the lavish meal, the Lord focuses attention on Sarah, though speaking to her husband, and promises again that she will have a son (18:10). The narrator reminds us of the physical impossibility of Sarah bearing a child, and Sarah laughs at the idea, as Abraham had done (17:17). But the Lord's challenge rivets attention to the central issue of the narrative: "Is anything too hard for the Lord?" He repeats: "Sarah shall have a son."[104]

Two related scenes follow as the two "men" turn their attention toward Sodom,[105] where their wicked reception by the inhabitants of the city is contrasted both with Abraham's hospitality and Lot's.[106] First the Lord reveals what he is about to do in judging the evil cities[107] to his "friend" or confidant Abraham in light of his calling to be the channel of blessing to the nations of the earth and to instruct his household in righteous living (18:17-21). Abraham's intercession for the city of Sodom seems to be a sample of this calling to mediate blessing for the nations. Based on his conviction that, as "the Judge of all the earth," the Lord will be just, Abraham secures the assurance that the city will be spared if even ten righteous inhabitants are found there. Yet only Lot and his daughters are ultimately rescued, with much difficulty, and the unrighteous city is obliterated in a divinely directed "ecological disaster." The summary states the basis of Lot's deliverance: "God remembered Abraham and sent Lot out of the midst of the overthrow when he overthrew the cities in which Lot had lived" (18:29).[108] The contrasting land theme begun in chapter 13 is concluded as Abraham "looks down," from "the place where he had stood before the LORD," toward the once fertile "land of the valley" which is now a smoking devastation (19:27-28). God's purposes are with the land of Abraham's possession.

The final scene, in which Lot's daughters sleep in turn with their drunken father, concludes Lot's largely unattractive portrait in the biblical narrative. Despite his promising beginning, accompanying Abraham and enjoying abundance, Lot leaves Abraham for the verdant valley near Sodom. In the end he has to be pulled reluctantly out of the wicked city and loses his home, his wife, and any honor he had left.

20:1–21:34 Abraham, Sarah and Abimelech; Sarah & Isaac in, Hagar & Ishmael out

In the overall Abraham cycle, these two chapters correlate at least in part with 12:10-13:1, where Abram and Sarai are in Egypt. Here again much of the focus is on Sarah, as for a second time Abraham deceives a ruler by calling her his sister.[109] Both of these narratives, along with Isaac's similar action (26:6-11), show impediments to the fulfillment of God's promise of posterity, which are caused by the patriarchs' own timidity and dishonesty.[110] Nevertheless God's dialogue with Abimelech does underscore Abraham's role as a "prophet" and an intercessor (20:7). Abraham is called a "prophet" (nabi) only here in Genesis. It is significant that this passage gives no support to the later Jewish and Islamic concepts of Abraham as the father or prophet of monotheism. It is God who intervenes to keep Abimelech from the sin for which Abraham's lie has opened the way and it is Abimelech who rebukes the patriarch (20:6-9). Yet, despite Abimelech's "integrity" and "innocence" in the matter, only Abraham's prayer will bring healing to the women's closed wombs.

Following the divine deliverance of Sarah, the Lord at last opens her womb, and the long-awaited son of promise is born at last. Every phrase emphasizes the Lord's keeping his word, "as he had said . . . as he had promised . . . at the time of which God had spoken to him . . . as God had commanded him" (21:1-4). Here is the fulfillment; this son is the seed through whom God will establish his everlasting covenant (17:19, 21).

Yet the complication introduced by Sarah's proposal in chapter 16 continues to create difficulty, as Hagar's son Ishmael is seen "laughing" during the celebration of Isaac's weaning (21:9).[111] The situation is only resolved when she and her son are sent away. Abram's failure in Genesis 12 may have contributed to his failure in Genesis 16—he may have acquired Hagar during his stay to Egypt (12:16).[112] God clearly confirms Sarah's seemingly harsh judgment: "Whatever Sarah says to you, do as she tells you, for through Isaac shall your offspring be named" (21:10-13). Ishmael is blessed as Abraham's seed, but the line of God's purpose is through Isaac, so Ishmael must leave.

Nevertheless, as in chapter 16, Hagar is not abandoned by God, who hears the voice of the dying boy, and the angel of God speaks from heaven words of comfort and promise: "Up! Lift up the boy, and hold him fast with your hand, for I will make him into a great nation." We are specifically told that "God was with the boy" as he grew up, and Hagar takes a wife from Egypt for him (21:21).[113] Throughout the narrative there is a careful balance between God's care for Ishmael on the one hand and his fulfillment of the promises through Isaac on the other.

Nikaido draws attention to various similarities and links between Gen 21:1-21 and 22:1-19. Both sons are sent off with meagre provisions with no return expected. Both Hagar and Abraham are addressed by the angel of God calling out of heaven. "In both cases, the voice from heaven reaches the characters at a critical moment, in a remote place, as they are preparing for their child's imminent death."[114] Both Hagar and Abraham "lift up their eyes and see" the deliverance (a well and a ram respectively) provided by God (21:19; 22:13). Nikaido sees Hagar and Ishmael as positive figures: "In contrast to her negative role as Sarah's antagonist, Hagar is portrayed in a manner that compels us to see her as a matriarchal figure on a par with such figures as Abraham and Hannah."[115] He argues that seeing their story as merely background for the main story of Isaac does not do justice to the literary detail devoted to the characters of Hagar and Ishmael. However, this seems to neglect the way in which details are given of other figures that, while protected by God, are soon set aside from the ongoing plot (e.g. Cain). It also minimizes the shape of the overall narrative and the weight given in the narrative to the lineage of the covenant from which Ishmael is explicitly excluded. Lastly, it neglects the ongoing theme of enmity between brothers which seems to be the part of the outworking of the curse on the serpent in Gen 3:15.

Finally, Abraham is seen in relation to Abimelech again. Perhaps word of the miraculous birth of Abraham's son has reached him. For whatever reason, God's hand on Abraham is evident to him: "God is with you in all that you do" (21:22). Abraham agrees to a covenant between the two men and their posterity for honest and kind dealings, confirmed by the exchange of mutual oaths. For the final time we hear of Abraham "calling on the name of the Lord," this time identified as the "everlasting God."

22:1–19 The Lord tests Abraham and Abraham obeys

Time passes as Isaac grows up with Abraham, apparently near Beersheba in the land of the Philistines, where Abraham had planted a tamarisk tree.[116] Then in the climactic scene of the main narrative, God tests Abraham with a command echoing his initial word to "go . . . to the land that I will show you" (12:1), saying, "Take . . . and go . . . and offer him there as a burnt offering on one of the mountains of which I shall tell you" (22:1). As Abram had once parted from country, kindred, and father's house, now he is to part with his offspring, "your son, your only son Isaac, whom who love." Abraham surely grieved in parting with Ishmael, but that farewell was understandable in light of the conflict between Sarah and Hagar and God's insistence on Isaac. But now, he is to sacrifice Isaac, the son of promise in whom all his hopes are centered. I accept the text naming Isaac as Abraham's "only son" as it stands, which fits with other motifs of the narrative as a whole, despite the fact that Isaac was not literally the only son.[117] Repeatedly in Genesis the firstborn is displaced by a later son who is the focus of the divine initiative (Cain in replaced by Seth, Ishmael by Isaac, Esau by Jacob, Reuben by Judah and Joseph). Abela notes, "This is the episode that delves deepest within the son theme. . . . For the first time in the Abraham narrative the protagonist is addressed as 'father' by his own son."[118] In fact, the whole narrative has developed around the theme of Abraham's longed-for heir. I suggest that this sonship theme is in fact related to the image-of-God theme in the creation narrative, which suggests the son's likeness to the father.[119] The father-son relationship, which is so central to the Aqedah narrative, is also part of the renewing of this "image" which was damaged by the first sin.[120]

Despite the difficulty of the test, Abraham's obedience is proven complete, and his trust in God is expressed clearly and movingly: "God will provide for himself the lamb for the burnt offering, my son" (22:8). After the step-by-step preparation of the altar and the binding of Isaac, the unforgettable moment arrives; the father's hand is raised with the knife to slaughter his son; for the second time his name is called "Abraham, Abraham. . . ." The ram is found and Isaac is delivered. The narrative underscores Abraham's awareness that the Lord had indeed "provided," just as he had assured Isaac, and he names the mountain place, "the Lord will provide/see."[121] The purposes for which the land has been given to Abraham's offspring now seem to be focused in a particular way on this site: "On the mount of the Lord it shall be provided" (22:14).[122]

The angel of the Lord then calls the second time, and for the final time expands and confirms, with an *oath*, his commitment to bless Abraham and his offspring:

> I will surely bless you, and I will surely multiply *your offspring* as the stars of heaven and as the sand that is on the seashore. And *your offspring* shall possess the gate of his enemies, and in *your offspring* shall all the nations of the earth be blessed. (Gen 22:17-18)

The repeated focus of blessing is on Abraham's *offspring* (see italics), but to the now-familiar promises of great multiplication and blessing for all *the nations* is added triumph over enemies.[123] Enmity to this singular/plural seed is part of the picture along with promised blessing.[124] A strong link is established between this verse, the announcement regarding the seed of the woman in 3:15, and the prediction regarding Judah's line in 49:8-10. These three passages contain the only references to "enmity" in Genesis, and in each case the enmity is to be overcome by the promised offspring.

This culmination highlights again the central issue of the Abraham narrative, which is the problem of the heir in the fulfillment of God's promise of offspring (seed) to Abraham. Scene after difficult scene, with complication after complication, all lead to the apparent conclusion that the heir question is settled through Isaac's birth to Sarah, followed by Hagar and Ishmael's expulsion. But now God commands that Isaac be sacrificed! The test of faith in the realization of the promise is now identified solely with this son. Abraham's faith is expressed in obedience, and seems to rest on the confidence that his God who has done the impossible will "provide" a solution. God's provision turns out to be a substitute, a ram providentially caught in a thicket: "Abraham took the ram and offered it up as a burnt offering instead of his son" (22:13), naming the place as the mount of God's provision (seeing). The canonical identification of this location with Temple Mount (2 Chr 3:1) and with the place of Jesus' crucifixion in the NT coincide with both Jewish and Christian typological understanding of the near sacrifice of Isaac as foreshadowing divinely provided atonement.[125] Notably "the Hebrew words for 'burnt offering', 'appear', and 'ram' are found together only in Lev. 8-9, 16 and Gen. 22."[126]

In Gen 12:2-3 and 18:18 God promises Abraham both that he is to become "a great and mighty nation" and that "all nations" are to be blessed in him. As Frishman notes, it is telling that in later times Jewish and Christian readings emphasized one or the other and not both of these:

> It will come as no surprise that the rabbis offer no commentary on these verses [promising blessing to 'all nations' Gen 12:3/22:18; 17:4]. Whereas Ephrem ignored the verses concerning the blessing of *the people* while commenting precisely on Gen 22:18, the rabbis chose to ignore the repercussions of Abraham's blessings for *the peoples*.[127]

Yet rather than this either-or dichotomy, the biblical picture keeps together as complementary the particular line (both the nation Israel and the royal offspring) through which the blessing will come and the worldwide beneficiaries (both Israel and the nations) of the blessing.

Abraham's obedience is now taken up into the covenant as part of the basis on which God reaffirms his purpose to bless all nations: "*because you have done this* and have not withheld your son, your only son, I will surely bless you . . . and in your offspring shall all the nations of the earth be blessed, *because you have obeyed my voice*" (Gen 22:16-18, italics added; cf. 26:5). As Moberly says, "It is not that the divine promise has become contingent on Abraham's obedience, but that Abraham's obedience has been incorporated into the divine promise."[128]

While God's promise remains at the center of the outworking of his purposes, Abraham's obedience is nevertheless cited by God as the reason for God's blessing of his son Isaac (26:5).[129] God's intends that Abraham will teach his commands and ways to his descendants and even says that this is the purpose for which he has chosen him (18:19).

One final feature of the narrative that should not be missed is the Lord's intensely personal involvement (22:1–3, 10–12, 15–18). Such immanence is evident throughout the entire Abraham cycle, but particularly in dialogue concerning the future of the promised offspring (12:7; 13:14-17; 15:1-21; 17:1-22; 18:1-19; 20:3-7; 21:1, 11-13). God has a stake in Abraham and his offspring; Abraham's response is of great significance to him.

22:20-24 Genealogy of Abraham's clan, Nahor's descendants in Mesopotamia

This brief genealogy, placed in the narrative as news reaches Abraham from his homeland, together with 11:27-32 brackets the main narrative section of Abraham's life (12:1–22:19). It highlights the relative slowness of the multiplication of Abraham's promised offspring in comparison with that of his brother Nahor. Elements unifying the smaller second section are renewed contact with the clan in Haran (22:20-24; 24:4, 10-61), the death of Sarah, who is both Abraham's wife and Isaac's mother (23:1-2; 24:67), Sarah and Abraham's burial in the field purchased from the Hittites (23:3-20; 25:9-10), and the transition to Isaac as the next recipient of the divine blessing (24:1; 25:11).

23:1-20 Sarah's death and burial in the land

The narrative of Sarah's death and burial focuses on Abraham's careful purchase of a field and cave in the land of Canaan, and thus underscores his certainty that this land would belong to his offspring. God had told Abraham that significant time would pass before the ownership of land was transferred to his descendants (15:13-21). Yet there is no thought of returning to his family in Mesopotamia, because God has called Abraham here (cf. 24:6-8). The story highlights Abraham's faith in God's promise, and the field is an installment of his descendants' inheritance.[130] Each of the patriarchs will be buried in this location (Gen 25:9; 49:29-30; 50:13).

This episode emphasizes once again the unmistakable narrative trajectory of the land promise: though for now only a field is possessed, this is to be the place for the fulfillment of God's promises to Abraham. This purchase narrative is most closely paralleled in the Hebrew Bible by the narrative of David's purchase of the Jerusalem threshing floor which became the site of the temple (2 Sam 24:18-25; cf. 1 Chr 21:18-22:2 with 2 Chr 3:1). The verse following this Abraham story begins with the same words as the verse following the David story: "Abraham/David was old and advanced in years" (Gen 24:1; 1 Kgs 1:1). McDonough suggests that "David's action in purchasing the temple site thus serves as a fulfillment of the promise made to Abraham, a fulfillment that had been anticipated in the purchase of the cave and field at Machpelah."[131]

24:1-67 A bride for Isaac

Although chapter 22 is the dramatic climax of the Abraham narrative, the lengthy story of finding a bride for Isaac contains many themes from the whole narrative. The Lord's leading of Abraham's praying servant reveals his "steadfast love and his faithfulness" (24:27; cf. 24:4). God's direction of events is evident to all: "the thing has come from the Lord . . . as the Lord has spoken" (24:50-51). The narrative also emphasizes that God has "blessed" Abraham abundantly, as promised (24:1, 31, 35, 36, 60).

A mother is needed for Isaac's future offspring, to whom the promises will be transferred. But the situation is again seen to be humanly difficult: Isaac must not return to his father's homeland and the bride must not come among from his present neighbors. God must provide. Walton says, "The narrator goes to such great length to demonstrate the role that God played in bringing the marriage to fruition. . . . Survival of the line still hangs by a thread."[132]

The elaborate story of divine leading stands in contrast to the simple statement regarding Ishmael's wife: "his mother took a wife for him from the land of Egypt" (21:21). Isaac's importance as the son of promise is shown by the detailed divine provision of his wife. Fuchs points out that the fourfold repetition of Rebekah's act of providing water (24:14, 18-20, 43-44, 45-56) emphasizes "that the encounter with Rebekah and the consequent betrothal are divinely sanctioned."[133] Rebekah's show of hospitality and her willingness to leave her father's household and "go" in accord with the evident call of the Lord is also significant: "Rebekah shows herself to be cut from the same cloth as Abraham. The call of Abraham may thus be said to be repeated in the second generation—not in Isaac, but in Rebekah!"[134] The stage is set for the mission of God to advance with Isaac, who is now "the blessed of the Lord" (26:29) and to whom God will renew his promises (26:2-6).

25:1-11 Abraham's latter years and death

The final episode of the Abraham narrative summarizes the 38 years of his life after Sarah's death with a bare minimum of information. Abraham takes another wife, Keturah, who bears him six sons. Among these only the offspring of Jokshan and Midian are named. The point of the section is that these other sons are sent away from Isaac, just as Ishmael had been, so that Isaac's position as the sole heir is protected. Abraham died when he reached 175, "in a good old age, an old man and full of years," and was buried alongside his first wife, Sarah.

GENESIS AFTER ABRAHAM

The Abraham narrative continues into the Isaac narrative after a brief review of the generations of Ishmael, who in fulfillment of the announcement to Hagar, "settled over against all his kinsmen" (16:12; 25:18).[135] The Lord repeats his promise to Isaac for the sake of Abraham (26:2-5, 24) and Isaac is recognized as the "blessed of the Lord" (26:28-29). Genesis 26:5 indicates that the basis of God's blessing of Isaac is Abraham's obedience: "because Abraham obeyed my voice and kept my charge, my commandments, my statutes, and my laws." This verse is sometimes taken as showing Abraham as a righteous keeper of *torah*, and it provides a basis for later Jewish embellishments of the story portraying Abraham with Levitical terminology. For example, Levenson argues from the four technical terms used—"my charge, my commandments, my statutes, and my laws"—that he kept God's commandments even before they were given to Moses.[136] Against this reading, Childs argues on grammatical grounds that Abraham's obedience was to Noachian prohibitions, circumcision and the general laws of humanity rather than the Mosaic Code.[137] It may also be argued that aspects of Abraham's behavior in Genesis violate the Levitical code. For example, Abraham describes his wife Sarah as "the daughter of my father" (21:12) a marriage forbidden in Lev 18:9. Similarly Jacob marries two sisters while both are living (Gen 29:30), which is clearly forbidden in the Law: "You shall not take a woman as a rival wife to her sister ... while her sister is still alive" (Lev 18:18). Embellishment is needed to see Abraham as an ideal observer of Torah.

Genealogical records at the beginning signal the transition between generations. As noted above, in the ongoing narrative the Lord begins to be identified as "the God of Abraham," particularly with reference to his promises to Abraham which are repeated to Isaac (26:24) and to Jacob (28:13; 31:42, 53; 32:9). In the formulas introducing the generations of Abraham's first two sons, a subtle language distinction emphasizes the key link of Isaac with Abraham. Ishmael is identified as "Abraham's son, whom Hagar the Egyptian, Sarah's servant, bore to Abraham" (25:12) and Isaac as "Abraham's son: Abraham fathered Isaac" (25:19). The narratives are clearly structured by means of differing lengths, with twists of plot and with specific appearances and words of God, all showing divine selection. First Isaac rather than Ishmael, then Jacob rather than Esau are identified with the purpose of God to bless all nations through Abraham's offspring (26:3-4; 28:13-15; 35:1-12). The narrative of Jacob's descendants gradually draws attention to the two key lines of Joseph and Judah (see Gen 37–38 and 49:8-12 and 22-26). This process of selection is not based only on the relative merits of the different offspring—one could make a case for the merits of Joseph, but Judah is hardly exemplary.[138] Alexander argues that from Genesis 3:15 through 49:10, a specific line of offspring is identified, through which the divine purpose to restore creation and bring blessing to all nations will be accomplished.[139]

The links between the Lord's promises to Abraham and His ongoing commitment to Abraham's descendants are made explicit at various points in this narrative. Thus Isaac is told that he will be blessed because of his oath to Abraham (26:3), Joseph gives directions concerning his bones based on this promise (50:24), and Moses is assured that the there is no doubt about the future: "I will bring you to the land which I swore to give to Abraham, Isaac, and Jacob, and I will give it to you for a possession" (Exod 6:8; 33:1). Sonnet notes that the name "Yahweh" is linked with these promises: "God's promise to Moses in Exodus 3:12, 'I will be (εηψεη) with you,' for instance, gains a powerful rationale when related to God's foundational commitments to Isaac and Jacob, 'And I will be (εηψεη) with you' (Gen. 26:3 and 31:3), in relation to the oath sworn to Abraham."[140]

SEVEN PRIMARY MOTIFS IN THE ABRAHAM NARRATIVE

(1) The hinge of history. In Genesis, the Abraham narrative serves as a hinge in the history of God's dealings with humankind, turning from universal history to the particular history of the lineage chosen to mediate the restoration of blessing for all nations. Because the narrative is situated in the larger narrative of cosmic history, which begins with the creation of the heavens and the earth by God, the sole creator and sovereign, it can only rightly be understood in light of this broader context and these multilevel connections. The narrative is linked by genealogical headers and by many story details to both the primeval history, which it continues, and the patriarchal narratives (Isaac and Jacob), which it begins. In relation to the former, the Abraham narrative is the first act of God in response to the corruption and dispersion of the nations of mankind, inaugurating what I described in the previous chapter as the narrative of redemption. As to the latter it is clearly intended to form the first stage of the history of the people of Israel who are the descendants of these patriarchs.

(2) God as protagonist. God, the creator and sovereign of all things, is the active protagonist throughout most of the episodes of the Abraham story. We encounter him speaking, promising, and appearing to Abraham, afflicting Pharaoh and his household, making and confirming covenants, closing, healing and opening wombs, listening to and finding Hagar and Ishmael, visiting and eating at Abraham's table, descending to investigate reports, ascending after discussion, destroying cities, doing the "impossible," testing Abraham and providing a ram as a substitute sacrifice. God is often visibly present within the story, in both the appearances of the Lord and the appearances of the unique "Angel of the Lord." God "comes" into his creation in particular places and tangible ways which are distinct from his omnipresence or immanence in every place. These appearances are specifically connected with God's making and confirming covenants with Abraham. The Abraham narrative then is a significant segment of the advancing story of God's condescension, entering into covenant relationship with particular human beings.

(3) The acts of God. God's revelation of his own identity is linked with particular acts that he has done and intends to do: "I am the LORD *who brought you out* of Ur of the Chaldeans" (15:7). God identifies himself to Abraham as "God Almighty" as he makes a series of promises to perform a series of actions (17:1-8). This "narrative identity" developed in the Abraham story gives substance to his consequent title as "the God of Abraham." By the term "narrative identity," I refer to the idea that *who God is* may often be understood through the narratives of *what God does.* The identity of the God of Abraham is thus ultimately inseparable from the long series of divine interventions and acts which form the high points of the biblical narrative.[141] Among these self-revealing divine acts is giving of life to the nearly "dead" bodies of Abraham and Sarah, doing the humanly impossible: "Is anything too hard for the LORD?" (18:14).

(4) Abraham's faith and failure. The birth of Ishmael to Hagar comes at the suggestion of Abram's wife Sarai, and stands at the center of the narrative as a sort of "fall" event, following which God intervenes repeatedly to reaffirm his commitment to fulfill his purposes through Sarah's son. This event highlights the biblical emphasis on the lasting consequences of sin, often in family conflict that affects future generations. Other examples of such failures may be found in Abraham's lying about his wife's identity to protect himself from pagan kings and in Lot's committing incest with his daughters at the end of his story. Abraham stands not so much as an exemplar of unblemished faithfulness to divine law, but as a failing human being who believes God's promise and acts in obedience to his call. Abraham believes and moves out to Canaan, leaving his roots and family behind. He believes God's promise of offspring, and God accounts this to him as righteousness. He obeys God's covenant of circumcision, his command to send Ishmael and Hagar away, and finally his command to sacrifice Isaac, trusting that God will keep his promise. Despite failures he is ultimately characterized by obedience to God's commands, based on his faith in God's promises.

(5) Offspring. God promises Abraham three primary things: innumerable offspring, a specific land, and universal blessing for all nations. All are important, but the dominant theme is the difficult and complicated fulfillment of the promise of offspring (seed). Time after time the hope of offspring and an heir is threatened: by Sarah's barrenness, by Lot's departure to Sodom, by Sarah's endangerment in Pharaoh's palace, by the passage of time which renders procreation less and less likely for Abraham and Sarah, by the birth of Ishmael and Abraham's attachment to him, and ultimately by God's command that Abraham sacrifice Isaac. The emphasis is on God's faithfulness to his own promises and his mysterious ways in fulfilling them. This theme also draws attention to the crucial matter of who will be Abraham's heir, through whose line the purposes of God are to be realized. Genesis takes pains to narrate God's exclusion of Ishmael (as well as other sons of Abraham) from this covenant purpose. The motif of one brother selected in place of another runs throughout the book of Genesis.[142] Ishmael fits this pattern, as he is set aside in favor of Abraham's second son Isaac.

(6) The Land. The issue of the land promised to Abraham and his descendants in perpetuity runs throughout the narrative. The Lord leads Abram to a specific land and promises to give this land to his descendants, whereupon Abram begins to build altars to the Lord who appeared to him (12:1-8). When Lot selects the rich land near Sodom and Abram remains in the highland of Canaan, the Lord repeats the promise and Abram builds another altar (13:14-18). Abram receives the blessing of Melchizedek, king of Salem (14:17-24), perhaps pointing to the future importance of that city. God says, "I am the LORD who brought you out from Ur of the Chaldeans to give you this land to possess" and formalizes a covenant to this end (15:7-21). After the false start with Hagar and Ishmael, the Lord reaffirms that he will give this land to Abraham and Sarah's offspring "for an everlasting possession" (17:8). Abraham is sent to a particular site to offer his beloved son, a place that will become the site of the temple and the center of future divine activity (22:2, 14, 18). Sarah is buried in the land which Isaac's

descendants will inherit, and Abraham sends away Keturah's sons, as he had previously sent away Ishmael. A faithful appropriation of the Abraham narrative will have to take seriously the "territorial particularity" of God's promise of the land.[143]

(7) Blessing for all nations. God's promise that through Abraham and his offspring "all the families of the earth will be blessed" is repeated at key moments, most notably at the opening and closing "bookends" of the narrative (12:3 and 22:18; also at 18:18; 26:4-5; 28:14). The Abraham narrative is intended as the groundbreaking stage in the Creator's enterprise to bring blessing to all nations. The story shows little about the reintroduction of monotheism to the world, a theme only introduced by extrabiblical exegetical traditions regarding Abraham. Rather it seems to focus on a "messianic" promise of universal blessing mediated through a particular dynasty, which is progressively unfolded and repeatedly alluded to throughout the biblical canon (note Gen 49:10).[144]

Each of these themes is a crucial thread running throughout the narrative. Other themes include altar-building, strife among brothers, and endangerment, but the overall Abraham story has a discernible shape which focuses attention on Abraham's call at the beginning and his testing at the end of the main narrative, and on the problematic birth of Ishmael at the central pivot point. These crucial episodes underscore God's primary promise to bless all nations through Abraham's offspring, and its difficult first step toward fulfillment through the birth and preservation of Isaac. Within the context of the Hebrew Scriptures this persistent purpose of the God of Abraham relates not only to the issues of creation and fall in the first chapters of Genesis but also to the ongoing story of Israel and the nations.

CHAPTER 4 – ABRAHAM IN THE NEW TESTAMENT

While Christian reflection on Abraham extends beyond the NT, I will treat the NT usage of Abraham as representing the core Christian reading. Patristic writers frequently refer to Abraham[1] and often draw on a wider selection of Jewish sources than the NT does, specifically on Jewish "embellished narratives." But the interpretive approach used by the earliest Jewish Christians, perhaps learned from Jesus himself, appealed almost exclusively to the Hebrew Scriptures, rather than to Second Temple Jewish exegetical narratives. Moreover, while the NT prioritizes the order of OT Abraham narrative, with its movement from promise to fulfillment, from the end of the first century onward there was a discernible shift away from emphasis on the historical sequence of OT narrative in Christian writers' use of the OT.[2] This gradual de-emphasizing of the narrative framework and the trajectory that it entails diverges from the NT approach to Abraham.

While the so-called "Great Tradition" is of immense value, it is my conviction that the normative source for assessing orthodoxy in Christian approaches is the canonical Bible.[3] New Testament references to Abraham form an integral part of a *unified set of convictions* about what Israel's God had newly done through Jesus Christ.[4] This common core of NT convictions corresponds with its appeal to Abraham. The intertextual appeal to Abraham is thus a significant but small subset of the use of the OT in the NT, for which there is voluminous scholarly literature.[5]

A Canonical Approach

I approach the NT from a Christian canonical perspective, taking these twenty-seven apostolic texts as together forming the second (and final) section of Holy Scripture, of which the canonical Hebrew Scriptures form the first section.[6] It is the Christian position that these two "testaments" together form one canonical "Bible," which is the written Word of God.[7] Jews who do not recognize Jesus as the Messiah dispute this, of course.[8]

The question of canon is an area of significant dispute, beyond the scope of this study, but a few comments are necessary because of the canonical framework I presuppose here.[9] The approach known as "canonical biblical interpretation" is identified particularly with the work of Brevard Childs.[10] For my purposes the most important emphases of the canonical approach are its insistence on focusing on the final form of the text as a whole and its efforts to give what Seitz describes as a "sensitive account of how the Old Testament actually does Christian theology from its own plain sense."[11]

Often the term "canonical" is used to refer only to the process through which apostolic writings were recognized as authoritative by the early church, emphasizing a late date for "canon."[12] Kruger argues that a fuller definition includes looking at canon "from the divine perspective, rather than from only an ecclesiological perspective."[13] This is closer to the way most Muslims and evangelical Christians understand their Scriptures, and such an approach respects the NT writings' own emphasis on the Spirit-inspired eyewitness testimony uniting these works as apostolic "Scripture," building on and complementing the revelation of the OT prophets (1 Pet 1:10-12; 2 Pet 1:16-21; 3:1-2, 16-17).[14] The canonical approach, which focuses on the text as we have it and seeks to treat individual books as part of an ordered whole, is the most appropriate approach for my study.

Three discernible points of canonical unity of the New Testament undergird my presuppositions in this area. Firstly, there is a *theological* aspect. Eugene Lemcio traces the presence of a specific *"kerygmatic core"* throughout the pluralism of the NT writings, and argues the essential unity of the canonical writings:

> At the heart of this stabilizing core beats theology *per se.* God is the initiator of the redemptive act in Christ.… Finally, it is the doctrine of God, in both his person and activity, that binds the Testaments together. The existence of this unifying kerygma legitimates the task of further defining the nature of biblical *theo*logy.[15]

The second unifying factor is *christological.* The God of Israel is now acting and revealing himself once and for all in and through Christ. In Paul's words, "God was in Christ reconciling the world to Himself" (2 Cor 5:19; cf. Heb 1:1-2; John 1:18). As Bird has argued, the common conviction found throughout the NT documents is that Jesus of Nazareth is the *Christ* or Messiah of Israel, the Son of the living God.[16] The risen Jesus is worshipped and served as both "Christ" and "Lord," a messianic and divine identity encapsulated in the title "the Lord Jesus Christ."[17]

Thirdly, this canonical unity is based on the *metanarrative* within which the books are situated. The overall canonical narrative (OT with NT) engenders a Christian worldview lens through which individual stories may be seen. The NT writings testify to and interpret the conclusion of the narrative as one in which the Creator-Savior God is the chief protagonist. As Vanhoozer says, "The Old Testament testifies to the same drama of redemption as the New, hence the church rightly reads both Testaments together, two parts of a single authoritative script."[18] From this perspective, then, the canonical NT writings bring to consummation the story of God, creation, and humankind, with an essentially common voice.[19] These texts reveal a common if multifaceted reading of Abraham in light of God's work in Christ.

According to the Gospels, Jesus claimed to be the authoritative interpreter and teacher of the Hebrew Scriptures (Matt 5:17-48; 7:24-29; 23:10; 28:20), and said he had more to teach which would only be understood after he rose from the dead (John 2:22; 12:16; 16:12). After his resurrection he taught his followers to read the Scriptures in light of his suffering and subsequent glory (Luke 24:25-27, 32-34, 44-49; Acts 1:3). It is therefore no surprise to find the apostolic writers expounding Jesus' work by repeatedly and extensively citing the ancient texts. As Farkasfalvy summarizes,

> From its very beginning, Christianity had an exegetical agenda which belonged to the core of its program. . . . The Jewish scriptural texts quoted by the Christian kerygma are involved in a twofold dynamic. On the one hand, the first Christian preaching sought to obtain an understanding of Christ from the Scriptures and, on the other, it sought to understand the Scriptures from words and deeds of Christ.[20]

The NT explicitly claims that the new things accomplished by God though Christ are "according to the Scriptures," not only by fulfilling specific predictions and promises, but as the goal and trajectory of the "Law and the prophets" as a whole (Matt 5:17; 11:13).[21] It cites and alludes to hundreds of OT passages to support and illustrate its arguments.[22] There is a range of scholarly opinions concerning the degree to which the NT authors respected the original context of the passages they cite to support their arguments. Some like Enns see NT appropriation of the Hebrew Scriptures as largely divorced from concern about the original context, articulating instead a free Christological reinterpretation.[23] I see evidence, however, that Jesus and the apostles used the Scriptures not only creatively, but also carefully and with respect for the context.[24] While clearly bringing a Christocentric perspective to the Hebrew Scriptures, the NT writers draw on the Scriptures in ways that respect the context within the eschatological trajectory of the OT.[25]

NEW TESTAMENT USE OF ABRAHAM

The name Αβρααμ (Abraham) is found seventy-three times in eleven books of the NT.[26] Of these references, twenty-three are in the Synoptic Gospels (fifteen in Luke, seven in Matthew, one in Mark). Luke refers to Abraham more than any other NT author with twenty-two references in Luke–Acts. This is followed by nineteen Pauline references in Romans, Galatians, and 2 Corinthians, eleven references in John's Gospel (all in chapter 8), ten references in Hebrews, two in James, and one in 1 Peter. Discussion of Abraham in Acts is found only in sermons: Peter in the temple (3:13, 25), Stephen before the Sanhedrin (7:2, 8, 16, 17, and 32), and Paul in the Antioch synagogue (13:26).[27] My analysis considers all of these references on a genre basis, asking how and for what purpose the texts in question are appealing to Abraham and the Abraham narrative.

The Synoptic Gospels and Acts

The Gospels do not appeal to Abraham in a uniform way, although the Synoptic Gospels do show significant commonality in their usage. Matthew's seven references and Mark's single reference to Abraham (Mark 12:26) are paralleled in

Luke with the exception of Matthew's two summary statements at the beginning and end of his genealogy (Matt 1:1, 17).[28] The uniquely Lukan Abraham passages are the prophetic celebratory words of Mary and Zechariah (Luke 1:55, 73), the story of Lazarus and the rich man (16:19-31), and the accounts of two people identified by Jesus as "daughter/son of Abraham" (13:16; 19:9).

Matthew. Abraham has a significant place in the origin narratives of Matthew and Luke (Matt 1:1-17; Luke 1:54-55, 69-75; 3:23-38). Matthew begins his gospel with Abraham, through an "annotated genealogy" evoking those in Genesis.[29] The opening formula, "the book of the generations" (βίβλος γενέσεως), recalls the Septuagint translation of the *tôledôt* headers beginning in Gen 2:4. He frames the linear genealogy (1:2-16) with a twin reference to Jesus' descent from Abraham and David (1:1, 17). Matthew's special emphasis on *fulfillment* thus begins by showing that the whole Abraham lineage is fulfilled in Jesus the Messiah,[30] who is the "son of David, the son of Abraham." By beginning with Abraham and ending with Jesus' commission to "make disciples of all nations" (28:18-20), Matthew highlights God's "all nations" promise to Abraham (Gen 12:3; 18:18; 22:18). As the promised "offspring," Christ "fulfills" both the all-nations promise to Abraham and the kingdom promise to David.[31]

Matthew's narration of Jesus' birth and early childhood, following the genealogy, shows him recapitulating in his person and ministry all that Israel should be, fulfilling the whole story from its Abrahamic beginnings, through the Exile and beyond.[32] The narratives are punctuated with citations from the prophets, whose promises of Israel's restoration are being fulfilled in Jesus' coming.

John the Baptist challenges Jewish expectations regarding who will inherit the blessings of the promised restoration, treating them as spiritual Gentiles who could join the family of Abraham only through "proselyte baptism."[33] With the "kingdom of heaven" impending, he warns, "do not presume to say to yourselves, 'We have Abraham as our father,' for I tell you, God is able from these stones to raise up children for Abraham" (Matt 3:9). This saying challenges the "merits of Abraham" concept, widely held in rabbinic writings, according to which God remains faithful to Israel because of the righteousness of their ancestors, the greatest of whom was Abraham.[34] But the baptizer disallows this confidence, calling Israel to repentance for forgiveness of sins and pointing to the coming One.

Jesus advances John's challenge to Jewish trust in Abrahamic kinship for eschatological salvation, declaring that "many will come from east and west and recline at table with Abraham, Isaac, and Jacob in the kingdom of heaven, while the sons of the kingdom will be thrown into the outer darkness" (Matt 8:10-12). Wright points out several implications from this scene: (1) Faith in Jesus rather than ethnic descent from Abraham defines membership in the eschatological kingdom of God; (2) Jesus "restores the messianic banquet to its properly universal extent," whereas Jewish apocalyptic tradition had narrowed it to include only Israelites; (3) Texts originally speaking of God "gathering" Israel from exile now include Gentiles in the great restoration; (4) the all-nations blessing thrust of the Abrahamic promise (Gen 12:1-3), which will be connected with the Great Commission at the end of the Gospel, is pictured in this eschatological banquet scene.[35]

Luke–Acts. Luke and Acts may be treated together, for the reasons summarized by Tannehill: "This unity is the result of a single author working within a persistent theological perspective, but it is something more. It is a narrative unity, the unity appropriate to a well-formed narrative. . . . Luke–Acts has a unified plot because there is a unifying purpose of God behind the events which are narrated."[36] Where Matthew emphasizes fulfillment of the OT through the *genealogical* trajectory from Abraham to Jesus, Luke underlines Jesus' birth-events as fulfilling God's oath-sworn *promise* to Abraham (Luke 1:54-55, 69-75).[37] Under the Spirit's influence Jesus' mother and John the Baptist's father rejoice over the birth of their respective sons. God is "visiting" and "redeeming" his people, as Mary says, "in remembrance of his mercy, as he spoke to our fathers, to Abraham and to his offspring forever" (1:54-55), and, in Zechariah's words, "to show the mercy promised to our fathers and to remember his holy covenant, the oath that he swore to our father Abraham" (1:72-73).

Citing Isaiah 40:3-5, Luke emphasizes that the messenger voice crying in the wilderness presaged the promised coming of God, the time when "all flesh shall see the salvation of God" (Luke 3:6). He ties John the Baptist's argument that physical birth is not enough to make one a child/heir of Abraham (3:7-8) to Isaiah's prophecies of the "last days." Isaianic references to Abraham declare that a "remnant" of Abraham's estranged offspring will be comforted and saved (Isa 29:22; 41:8; 51:2; 63:16). The faithful in Luke 1–2 (Zechariah, Elizabeth, Mary, Simeon, Anna) are part of the righteous remnant "waiting for the consolation of Israel" (Luke 2:38; cf. 2:25; 23:51; 24:21).[38] This aspect of Luke's reading of Abraham is deeply eschatological; by calling Israel to repent and receive the coming Lord, John is announcing that the time of fulfillment has arrived.

During one of many table scenes in Luke's so-called "travel narrative" (9:51–19:27), Jesus warns the guests that not all who show up at the door will be able to enter: "there will be weeping and gnashing of teeth, when you see Abraham and Isaac and Jacob and all the prophets in the kingdom of God but you yourselves cast out" (13:28-29; cf. Matt 8:9).[39] In another challenge to expected outcomes, he tells them of a rich Jew, poor on compassion, who is excluded from Abraham's table while the poor beggar he neglected ends up in "Abraham's bosom" (Luke 16:19-31). This phrase may refer to being seated with the patriarch at the messianic banquet.[40] Two other Abraham-related examples add detail to the Lukan picture of those who will possess the "salvation" Jesus is bringing: A crippled "daughter of Abraham" is freed from Satan's bondage (13:10-17), and a once greedy, now repentant "son of Abraham" is visited with salvation (19:1-10). Salvation is the rightful inheritance of the true daughters and sons of Abraham, who humble themselves as "sinners" (e.g. 5:8; 7:37-50), coming to the "friend of sinners" (7:34; 15:1-2). Four times helpless people confess their need to Jesus, his saving power is extended to them, and they are affirmed with the words, "your faith has saved/healed you" (Luke 7:50; 8:48; 17:19; 18:42).[41] True children of Abraham are those saved by faith in Jesus, who call on the Lord for mercy, like the persistent widow, the tax collector in the temple, the blind man on the road, etc. They are those who, like Abraham (Gen 12:1-5), are willing to leave all to follow his call (Luke 9:57-62).

The final direct reference to Abraham in the Synoptic Gospels comes in the final week of Jesus' ministry, as he is challenged in the temple courts on the question of resurrection (Matt 22:23-33; Mark 12:18-27; Luke 20:27-39). After correcting the Sadducees' misconceptions about resurrection life in relation to marriage, he challenges them to think more deeply about resurrection by considering God's words to Moses from the bush (Exod 3:1-6): "Have you not read what was said to you by God: 'I am the God of Abraham, and the God of Isaac, and the God of Jacob'? He is not God of the dead, but of the living" (Matt 22:31-33). Scholars differ as to whether or not Jesus' reasoning here is an example of "rabbinic" argumentation.[42] Jesus' argument may turn on the present tense, "I *am* the God of Abraham," implying that for this to be true, Abraham must have been alive in Moses' day.[43] It presumes the eternal nature of God's promises, so that the patriarchs must be raised to receive the fulfillment.[44] Another intriguing aspect of the argument is developed by Janzen, who points out the relationship between Abraham's plight (biological sterility) and that of Moses' people in Egypt (political oppression and murder): both of these predicaments are forms of the threat of "death." He shows the link between Abraham's story and the situation dreamed up by Jesus' opponents:

> The Sadducees have told Jesus a story of sterility persisting through much conjugal effort and futile hope, ending in death. By using the formulaic sentence from the burning bush, Jesus responds to . . . their story with a reminder of the ancestors' story. That story too is one of sterility . . . [which] persists in the face of divine promise and repeated promise.[45]

The God who gives life to the dead did the impossible for Abraham, even though he was as good as dead, and he was about to do so for Israel as he called Moses. A deep relationship between resurrection and the Abraham narrative is entailed by Jesus' creative answer.

Abraham is referred to several times in Acts in ways related to those found in Luke. The prophetic announcement first heard in Luke 1–2 that the Abrahamic promises are now being fulfilled, becomes even stronger after the resurrection of Jesus from the dead. Peter explains an astonishing healing with the words, "The God of Abraham [has] glorified his servant Jesus." (Acts 3:13-16). He calls on Israel to repent and turn to the risen Messiah, telling them that "these days" are those announced by Israel's prophets. He then quotes God's promise of universal blessing: "You are the sons of the prophets and of the covenant that God made with your fathers, saying to Abraham, 'And in your offspring shall all the families of the earth be blessed.' God, having raised up his servant, sent him to you first, to bless you" (Acts 3:25-26; cf. Gen 22:18).[46] Scott notes the relationship between the nations represented at Pentecost in Acts 2:9-11 and the table of nations in Gen 10, showing that the Abrahamic promise of blessing to those nations is being fulfilled in a reversal of Babel (Gen 11). He adds, "As Acts brings out in a subsequent chapter, Peter had reported the reversal of Babel in yet another respect: God himself has intervened in order to take from the nations (ἐξ ἐθνῶν) a people (λαὸν) for his name [15:14]."[47]

In his fiery last words to the Sanhedrin, Stephen narrates Israel's story, beginning with a rehearsal of Abraham's call in Mesopotamia, his subsequent two-stage journey (first to Haran until his father died, then to "this land in which you are now living"), and his life in the land until the birth of Isaac (Acts 7:1-8). In this compressed retelling of Abraham's story Stephen conflates Gen 11:31–12:5, specifically quoting 12:1.[48] In recounting God's promising the land to Abraham and to his offspring (7:5), he conflates Gen 12:7; 13:15; and 15:18. He focuses on God's prediction to Abraham of his descendants' future bondage and subsequent deliverance from Egypt (7:6-7), specifically quoting Gen 15:14 but replacing the last phrase ("with great possessions") with words borrowed from Exod 3:12, "you shall serve God on this mountain." Finally, he links the covenant of circumcision when Abraham and Ishmael were circumcised (Gen 17) with Isaac's birth and circumcision on the eighth day (Gen 21). He draws particular attention to the Exodus as fulfilling the promise to Abraham (7:17), and recounts how God identifies himself to Moses as "the God of Abraham, and of Isaac, and of Jacob" (7:32). Stephen's selective retelling of Israel's history highlights the Abraham narrative as the beginning of a divinely initiated sequence of events leading ultimately to the "the coming of the Righteous One" (7:52).[49] The story runs from Abraham to Jesus.

Paul addresses the Jews in the synagogue in Antioch as two groups: "men of Israel/sons of Abraham's family" and those who "fear God" (Acts 13:16, 26), showing that for him ethnic Israel as Abraham's physical descendants is an on-going category. Nevertheless, only a remnant within Israel believes this word. The message of salvation was "spoken first" to the Jews and proselytes, but as the subsequent events make clear, it was ultimately intended for all nations (13:44-48). Paul explicitly equates this saving message of Jesus' resurrection with the fulfillment of the Abrahamic promise: "we bring you the good news that what God promised to the fathers, this he has fulfilled to us their children by raising Jesus" (13:32-33). By linking the promise to *"the fathers"* with Davidic citations (Pss 2 and 16; Isa 55:3), Paul joins the Abrahamic and Davidic covenants as fulfilled in Christ.

So Acts reveals an early Christian appeal to Abraham which includes addressing ethnic Jews as Abraham's family, recounting key points of the Abraham narrative as the launching pad of Israel's story, and proclaiming God's new act of salvation in Jesus, particularly raising him from the dead, as the fulfillment of the promise to Abraham.

This survey of Abraham references in the Synoptic Gospels and Acts reveals several distinct strands of usage: 1) A genealogical appropriation of Abraham links Jesus with the messianic line through Abraham and David, identifying the birth of Jesus as the beginning of the final movement of God's royal program for world history; 2) God's promises to Abraham and to the remnant of Abraham's offspring are being fulfilled in the coming of Jesus as the Messiah. In fact, the good news or "gospel" is that God has begun to fulfill these promises; 3) The hope of resurrection from the dead is identified both with God's unbreakable covenant to Abraham (and David) and with Jesus' resurrection as the fulfillment of these Abrahamic promises; 4) The true "sons" and "daughters" of Abraham are Jesus' followers. The guest list for the Abrahamic/messianic banquet has on the one hand been narrowed to those repentant Jews within Israel who trust in Jesus as the Messiah and on the other hand expanded to embrace people from all nations who believe in him. The beginning of this ingathering is seen in Acts as the gospel spreads from Jerusalem to the nations.

John's Gospel. The Gospel of John explicitly refers to Abraham only in one extended dialogue (8:31-58), though it contains numerous allusions to the Genesis narrative (see below). In Jerusalem Jesus argues with "the Jews" who were challenging his messianic claims, telling them that if they were truly Abraham's offspring, they would believe his life-giving words rather than seek to kill him (John 8:31-41). As the argument proceeds they grasp more clearly what he is claiming: "Are you greater than our father Abraham, who died?" (8:53). In John 8, Jesus is presented as greater than "our father Abraham" by his promise that whoever kept his words would never see death, and in chapter 4 as greater than "our father Jacob" by his offer of spiritual water welling up to eternal life, in contrast to the normal water from Jacob's well. Jesus' comparison of himself with Jacob ends with an "I am" claim in 4:26, as does his comparison with Abraham (8:58).[50]

Jesus extends his charge that the Jews were not doing "the works of Abraham" by claiming that Abraham actually did believe in him: "Abraham rejoiced that he would see my day. He saw it and was glad" (John 8:56). If they had understood and believed their Scriptures, they would believe in him and rejoice in his presence as Abraham did. Levenson misses the point: "What precisely is meant by . . . 'the works of Abraham,' (v. 39) is unclear, but the message is patent: 'the Jews' ought to be doing the same thing. . . . John's term 'the works of Abraham' could not be further from the characteristic use made of Abraham by the apostle Paul."[51] On the contrary, when the Jews ask Jesus "What must we do, to be doing the works of God?" Jesus answered them, "This is the work of God, that you believe in him whom he has sent" (6:28-29). According to John, Jesus asserts that this is precisely what Abraham did: he saw and rejoiced in Jesus' day—he believed. The question of which event Jesus refers to with the words "he saw [my day]" has been much discussed.[52] Brunson argues that Jesus' words "was glad" point to the joy of Isaac's birth and may be alluding to the celebration account in *Jubilees* 16:20-31.[53] Ronning notes a possibility suggested by the Targum of Isa 43:12, where the Lord's passing between the pieces in Gen 15 foreshadows the Red Sea deliverance through the divided waters. This OT "day of the Lord" would then be the "day" that Abraham "saw," as Jesus' death and resurrection answers to the Exodus deliverance.[54] Keener suggests the words may imply that "Abraham foresaw Christ's glory just as did Isaiah (John 12:41).[55] Boyarin suggests that in light of John's thoroughly Jewish, pre-incarnate Logos theology (1:1-14) it refers to the "word of LORD" coming to Abram (Gen 15:1).[56] Most likely Jesus alludes to the Aqedah, where Abraham was commanded to offer up his beloved son. Jesus' statement that Abraham "saw" his day may point to the Hebrew word "see" (provide), which is repeated several times in relation to God's "providing" the lamb: "On the mount of the LORD it shall be provided/seen" (Gen 22:8, 13, 14). Understood this way, Abraham caught a believing glimpse of the day when the true Lamb of God (John 1:29) would be offered as the ultimate sacrifice.[57]

Jesus then goes further and declares, "before Abraham was, I am" (John 8:58), thus radically subordinating Abraham to himself and stirring even greater antagonism to his claims to be greater than and prior to the patriarchs (cf. 1:15; 4:12). With this allusion to the Lord's self-identifying words, "I am the God of Abraham" in Exodus 3:14, Jesus presents himself as Abraham's pre-existent Lord.[58] Bruner sums up the implications of these words:

> This may be Jesus' supreme self-reference in the Gospel of John, for it makes more temporally clear than almost any other claim the difference between Jesus and all other human beings, even all other exalted Old Testament human beings.... Can Jesus express his Deity more profoundly or succinctly?[59]

In summary, John's uses of Abraham, though confined to one chapter, undergird three themes in relation to Jesus in the Gospel of John. 1) If the Jews wish to be true children of Abraham, they need to listen to and abide in Jesus' words, becoming truly his disciples. 2) Abraham looked forward to Jesus' "day," most likely in connection with the Aqedah and the death and resurrection of Jesus. 3) With the bold words, "before Abraham was, I am," Jesus claimed to stand in relation to Abraham as God stood in relation to Moses at the burning bush when he pronounced his name as "I am."

The Epistles

Authors of the NT Epistles most commonly employ the Abraham narrative as part of a theological argument concerning how people are justified before God and how such people of faith are to live their new lives. We see this focus not only in Paul's Roman and Galatian epistles, but also in Hebrews, where Noah "became an heir of the righteousness that comes by faith" just before the discussion of Abraham begins (11:7), and in James' appeal to Abraham (2:21-23), apparently engaging with the Pauline argument. Two notable exceptions to this thematic focus on faith and justification are, first, Peter's appeal to the example of Sarah, who calls Abraham "lord," to urge wives ("you her children") to pursue inner beauty and submission (1 Pet 3:6); and, second, the use by the author of Hebrews of the Melchizedek episode in conjunction with Ps 110:4 to demonstrate the superiority of Jesus and his priesthood.[60]

Romans. Paul appeals to Abraham in Romans 4 to substantiate his two-fold claim that "the righteousness of God has been manifested apart from the law" and that "the Law and the Prophets bear witness to it" (3:21).[61] God "justifies"[62] both Jew and Gentile without reference to their keeping the Mosaic Law, through their faith[63] in the crucified, risen Jesus, provided as a once-for-all redemptive sacrifice. At the same time the Law (here meaning the Pentateuch, not the Mosaic commandments) testifies to this reality when it declares that Abraham was counted righteous on the basis of his *faith alone*, apart from any works which could warrant "boasting" (3:27; 4:1-8, citing Gen 15:6).[64] The Abraham narrative first bears witness that even the "ungodly" who believe in Jesus are justified by this grace, apart from law-works.[65] Secondly, the narrative testifies that *circumcision* (representing the covenant status of Jews here) is not necessary for justification; after all, Abraham was justified before he was circumcised (4:9-12, citing the historical order of events in Gen 15 and 17 as proof). Thus uncircumcised Gentiles may be declared righteous before God and included in the people of God.

Thirdly, the Abraham story is used to show that the *promise* must be inherited by faith rather than by adherence to the law. The "promise" is mentioned for the first time here, in sweeping terms: "that he would be heir of the world."[66] "Heir of the world" may represent a universalizing of the land promise as found in the prophets (e.g. Isa 55:3-5).[67] But the focus of the section is on offspring from many nations, and so the phrase may refer to the promise that Abraham's offspring would "possess the gates of his enemies" (Gen 22:17b), a royal heir ("his") ruling the nations in blessing (Gen 49:10; Pss 2:7-12; 72:8-9). The law cannot be the means of fulfilling the promise for two reasons. First, scriptural testimony[68] shows that the "law works wrath" (4:15; cf. 3:9-20) by turning sin into trespasses (5:13) and ministering condemnation and death (7:9-11; cf. 2 Cor 3:6-7).[69] Second, this promise that Abraham would be the "father of many nations" was given to one whose "body was as good as dead."[70] Yet since it is evident that the law cannot "give life" (cf. Gal 3:21), this promise of multiplying life could only be fulfilled through grace. Paul's appeal to Abraham in 4:13-25 shows that the only way God's grace can be operative is through faith in God's life-giving power. Abraham's confident faith that "God was able to do what he had promised" (4:21) is associated with faith in God "who raised from the dead Jesus our Lord" (4:24).

In Romans 9–11, the apostle again calls Genesis to testify as he grapples with the persistent unbelief of the majority of his fellow Israelites and the inclusion of the growing number of Gentiles along with the remnant of Israelites as true "sons of Abraham" who confess Jesus Christ as Lord and believe God has raised him from the dead (9:30–10:12). He demonstrates that "they are not all Israel who are descended from Israel" (NASB) by showing that not all of Abraham's or Isaac's physical descendants are truly their offspring (9:6-13; citing Gen 21:12; 18:10, 14; and 25:22-23).[71] Only a remnant of ethnic Israel obtains "the righteousness that is by faith" along with many Gentiles. Paul, himself a "descendant of Abraham" (cf. 2 Cor 11:22), is evidence of this present-day "remnant, chosen by grace," the beginning of the restoration of "all Israel" (11:1-5, 26). The patriarchs, beginning with Abraham, are blessed by God as "the nourishing root of the olive tree" from which many natural Israelite branches have been cut off and into which Gentiles have been grafted alongside the remnant (11:16-25).[72] This is God's mysterious way of bringing the promised blessing to the nations and of provoking to jealousy the majority of Israel, who are still beloved for the sake of the irrevocable call of God on their "forefathers" (11:28-29). The existence of the remnant shows that God has not forsaken them. The "forefathers" refers to Abraham, Isaac, and Jacob. Yet this relationship is limited by the key concepts of sonship and election, which for Paul are inseparably tied to Jesus Christ, the Son of God and firstborn.[73]

Galatians. Paul musters several Abrahamic arguments in his impassioned response to the "Judaizers," who were insisting that Gentile believers in Jesus must be circumcised to be true "sons of Abraham."[74] He appeals to the Abraham narrative in chapter 3 to show that physical kinship and Law are not essential to such "sonship"blessing, but that in Christ the blessing of Abraham has come to the (Gentile) "nations"just as foreseen by the Scriptures (3:5-14, citing Gen 12:3). As Silva argues, "the apostle's point is not simply that we should believe as Abraham believed (though that is true enough and critically important), but that those who believe become the recipients of the redemptive blessings associated with the patriarch."[75] This comprehensive "blessing" is identified by Paul both with the "righteousness" accounted to Abraham when he believed God's promise (citing Gen 15:6), and with the promised Spirit whose power the Galatians have already tasted. Christ's curse-bearing, redeeming death has made this possible: "that in Christ Jesus the blessing of Abraham might come to the Gentiles, so that we might receive the promised Spirit through faith" (3:14). Lee shows that Scriptures such as Isa 44:3 and Ezek 36:26–27 with 37:14, which refer to the future outpouring of God's Spirit, are in Paul's mind as he points to the presence and power of the Spirit as evidence that the Abrahamic blessings have come through Christ. "Not only are the Sinai-covenantal blessings fully restored at the eschatological restoration of Israel, but also all the elements of the Abrahamic promise are fully realized"by the revivification and empowerment of the Spirit.[76]

Paul also argues from the chronology of promise and law (3:15-18). The "promise"to Abraham and to his offspring was an unmediated "covenant,"which was "ratified by God"centuries before Sinai; it follows that the inheritance cannot come by the law. The fact that the "offspring"to whom the promises were made is singular, not plural, supports his contention that this "seed" is Christ (3:16; citing most likely Gen 12:7, but also pointing to Gen 22:17-18).[77] Thus the Abrahamic promises are ultimately fulfilled in Christ, the royal descendant to whom the nations are given.[78] The law was given to clarify transgression, holding Jews under its guardianship "until the coming faith [in Christ Jesus] would be revealed" (3:23). Now that Christ has come, all who believe in him are "sons of God . . . Abraham's offspring, heirs according to promise" (3:29).

Finally, in his famous allegorical use of Sarah-Isaac and Hagar-Ishmael, Paul illustrates/argues that not all physical children of Abraham were heirs of the promise in Christ. In his reading of the Genesis narrative (Genesis 16, 17 and 21), Isaac was the "son of promise" (Gal 4:22; cf. Rom 9:7), while Ishmael was disallowed as Abraham's covenant "heir." Isaac represents those who belong to Christ (the promised "seed"), as opposed to those who are in still in bondage under the Law, whom he links with Ishmael (circumcised, but not the promise-son).

As the prophetic promise of the Spirit is related to the Abrahamic blessing in chapter 3, here also the prophetic call to Zion to rejoice over her many sons is employed to demonstrate the fulfillment of the Abrahamic promise (3:27; citing Isa 54:1).[79] According to Jobes, "The overarching hermeneutical issue in this passage is how Paul can use the story of Hagar and Sarah from Genesis 21 to effect an exegetical reversal that ends up identifying Jews as the children of Hagar and Christians as the children of Sarah."[80] She argues that Paul's quotation of Isa 54:1 builds on an earlier reinterpretation of Sarah as the "mother" of those in future restored Israel who "pursue righteousness" (Isa 51:1-2). Isaiah's picture of two "mother Jerusalems," one cursed with exile (earthly Jerusalem), and one blessed through the outpoured Spirit (Jerusalem above), provide Paul with the basis for his characterization: present Jerusalem (barren, still seeking righteousness through the law) and present heavenly Jerusalem (fruitful, through the resurrection "birth" of Christ the son of promise).[81] Thus Paul's use of Abraham here serves his overall reading of the Abraham narrative in Galatians. The blessing promised to all nations through Abraham (3:8; Gen 12:3) and through his offspring (3:16; Gen 22:18) is explicitly focused on Isaac's line (4:22-23; Genesis 21) and from thence to Jesus, whose death, resurrection, and outpoured Spirit bless all who "have believed in Christ Jesus," Jew and Gentile alike (2:16).

Taken together, Romans and Galatians use Abraham in arguments which show that God justifies sinners apart from the law through faith in the crucified and risen Jesus, that God's promise precedes and takes priority over God's law, that in the gospel of Christ God has faithfully fulfilled all the promises made to Abraham, and that all those who believe God's promise irrespective of ethnic identity are true sons of Abraham through Christ.

Hebrews. The epistle to the Hebrews makes use of the Abraham narrative in ways that are not unrelated to Paul's usage. The priority of the promise to Abraham, now being fulfilled in Jesus, over the Mosaic covenant, is repeatedly and variously argued. Believers in Jesus as Son of God are the true "offspring of Abraham" who are "helped" by his priestly ministry (2:16). In nearly Pauline fashion, historical order is emphasized from the first verses onward, identifying the author's era as "these last days."[82] Chapter 11 traces the story of OT exemplars of faith from creation to the heavenly city, with the greatest detail given to Abraham's obedient faith in God's promise, consummated by his offering up Isaac. His faithful life as a landless "stranger and exile" is emphasized (11:9, 13; cf. Gen 23:4). Nevertheless, in Hebrews 11, "faith" (πιστις), which is so closely identified with Abraham, is not simply "faithfulness." For example, the assertion that "by faith we understand that the universe was created by the word of God" (11:1-3), means believing God's word regarding this unseen act of creation. This "faith," by which "righteousness comes" (11:7), indicates trustful reliance on God's word regarding things as yet future or invisible, rather than the unswerving, torah-keeping "faithfulness" attributed to Abraham in contemporary Jewish writings.[83]

God's "unchangeable purpose" of preparing "many sons" for an eternal inheritance, which he has guaranteed with two oaths (to Abraham in Gen 22:16-18 and to the Messiah in Ps 110:4), is specifically identified as the outworking of his promise to Abraham and his offspring (6:12-20), through the mediation of the Son/Priest. Hebrews is an example of early Christian exegesis of the canonical Abraham narrative read in the light of Jesus as the Davidic Messiah of Psalm 110. Abraham here, as in other books, is both the primary *recipient* of God's promise (6:13; 11:17) and a principal *paradigm* of obedient faith (11:8-10, 13-16). Like Paul in Rom 4:18-22, the author shows that Abraham grew strong in faith in spite of his age, and fathered Isaac through Sarah (11:11-12).

Hebrews' most distinctive contribution to exegesis of the Abraham narrative is a detailed reading of Genesis 14:16-24 with Psalm 110:4, in which Abraham is shown to be subordinate to the king-priest Melchizedek, after whose priestly order the eternal priesthood of Messiah is patterned (Heb 7:1-10).[84] Jesus, as the eternal priest in Melchizedek's order is the guarantor, mediator, and source of all that is promised. The author attends to three points regarding Abraham: (1) Abraham's position as head or representative of all his offspring, including Levi, from whom come priests under the Law; (2) Abraham's subordination to the priest-king Melchizedek, who mediates God's blessing to him; and (3) Abraham's place as the primary possessor of God's promises: "him who had the promises" (7:6). Jesus Christ is the eternal, "Melchizedekian" mediator of all that is granted to the "heirs of the promise" (6:17).[85]

Abraham's near offering of Isaac, trusting God to raise him, is correlated with resurrection faith in Heb 11:17-19. Cockerill argues that these verses form the heart of this section. "While the hypothetical raising of Isaac may have been only a temporal resurrection (like v. 35a), Abraham's faith was in a God who 'could raise the dead' (ἐκ νεκρῶν ἐγείρειν δυνατὸς ὁ θεός, v. 19) in a general resurrection, a 'better resurrection' to eternal life (v. 35b)."[86]

To sum up, several usages of Abraham are evident in Hebrews which we have already noted in the Gospels, Acts, and Pauline epistles: The fulfillment through Jesus of the oath-guaranteed promise to Abraham is the heart of "this great salvation," the true "offspring of Abraham" are Jesus' persevering followers, Abraham's exemplary faith is equated with faith in the resurrection, and Abraham's story is primary in the narrated history of God's people. In the one usage unique to Hebrews, Abraham's encounter with Melchizedek is expounded in light of Ps 110:4 and Jesus' acts as mediator of the new covenant in order to show Jesus' supremacy as the eternal King-Priest, who is "able to save to the uttermost those who draw near to God through him" (7:25).

The Epistle of James. James brings together two passages from the Abraham narrative–Genesis 15:6, where Abraham is "counted righteous" and the offering of Isaac in Genesis 22–which recount events separated by many years. He does not emphasize the historical time frame as Paul does. Neither, however, does he conflate these events completely as some Jewish writings do; instead James makes a distinct connection between the two events which he describes as fulfillment: "the Scripture was *fulfilled* that says, 'Abraham believed God, and it was counted to him as righteousness'" (2:20-24). That is, the earlier faith was worked out in obedience, "filling out" the faith. Fulfillment here has the sense "bring to ultimate significance."[87]

James uses Abraham and Rahab as examples of being "justified by works and not by faith alone" (2:24-25). While arguing different points, it is notable that both Paul and James conflate the situation of the patriarch with two characters notorious for sexual actions that according to the law were punishable by death (adulterous David and prostitute Rahab).[88] Thus whatever difference in emphasis may be seen in their treatment of justification, clearly being blameless before the law was not central to either one's definition. Both Rahab's action and Abraham's were extraordinary acts of obedient faith, but were not acts of keeping the law.[89] James is dealing with the nature of genuine faith: "Can that faith save him?" (2:14). Faith which is "alone" is not the genuine faith which always results in "works" as its fruit in Paul's letters as well (e.g. 1 Thess 1:3; 2 Thess 1:3, 11). In his appeal to Abraham, then, James' teaching is not in conflict with Paul's emphasis on "the obedience of faith" or "faith working through love" (Rom 1:5; 15:18; 16:26; Gal 5:6; Eph 2:8-10).[90]

New Testament Allusions to Abraham

In addition to the explicit references considered above, several indirect references or allusions support the overall NT appeal to Abraham.[91]

The "fathers." During his defense speeches recorded in Acts, Paul gives the patriarchal promise as the reason he is on trial for preaching Jesus' resurrection and the resurrection of the dead: "I stand here on trial because of my hope in the promise made by God to *our fathers*. . . . Why is it thought incredible by any of you that God raises the dead?" (Acts 26:6-8; cf. 13:32-33; 23:6; 24:15, 21; 28:20). The resurrection of Jesus is seen as inseparable from the Abrahamic promise and as its fulfillment.

Paul affirms the key link between Abraham and Messiah in listing Israel's privileges: "To them belong *the patriarchs*, and from their race, according to the flesh, is the Christ" (Rom 9:5). In an extraordinary statement of hope for Israel's "hardened" majority, Paul asserts that they are beloved for the sake of their "*forefathers*," meaning the patriarchs (Rom 11:28-29). Paul alludes to the Abraham narrative once more in chapter 15, asserting that Christ's mission as Israel's "servant" was to demonstrate God's integrity, by fulfilling his promises to the patriarchs. Christ's service to "the circumcised" also serves the universal goal: "that the Gentiles might glorify God for his mercy" (15:8-9). A series of quotations regarding the Gentiles (15:10-12) concludes with the LXX of Isa 11:1, emphasizing that the call of Abraham becomes the means of God's blessing coming to "all nations" through Jesus' ministry as the messianic king.[92]

Various other passages allude to the patriarchs. For example, in John's Gospel, Jesus claimed to be the link between earth and heaven, the antitype of the one which Jacob had seen in his dream (John 1:47-51; cf. Gen 28:11-15). As Köstenberger says, "Jesus is the 'new Bethel,' the place where God is revealed, where heaven and earth, God and humanity, meet."[93] In another example, Jesus' words reveal an awareness of the historical order of events, noting that circumcision preceded the Law: "Moses gave you circumcision; not that it is from Moses, but from *the fathers*" (John 7:22).

Birth narratives. The phrase "they had no child, because Elizabeth was barren, and both were advanced in years" (Luke 1:7, 18) unmistakably echoes Abraham and Sarah's condition (Gen 11:30; 16:1; 18:11). Zachariah is rebuked for not believing (as his ancestor had done?). Likewise, the human impossibility of the angel's words to Mary being fulfilled (Luke 1:33-37) echoes Sarah's condition, but the divine response to their confusion or questioning is the same in both situations: nothing is "impossible with/too hard for God" (cf. Gen 18:14). These allusions emphasize the continuity between God's promises to Abraham and the miraculous births that begin the era of their fulfillment through Jesus.

Offering of the beloved son. Paul echoes Gen 22:12, "you have not withheld your son [οὐκ ἐφείσω τοῦ υἱοῦ σου LXX], your only son, from me," to elucidate the death of Jesus Christ: "He . . . did not spare his own Son [του ιδιου υιου ουκ εφεισατο] but gave him up for us all" (Rom 8:32). In this understanding, as Seifrid says, "God takes Abraham's place. The roles of the Aqedah have been reversed: God did not 'spare,' but 'delivered up' his own Son."[94] The well-known phrase in John 3:16, "God so loved the world, that he gave his only Son," may allude to this event as well: "his own son" echoes "your beloved son" (Gen 22:1, 12, 16).[95] Jesus is called God's "beloved son" at his baptism (Matt 3:17; Mark 1:11; Luke 3:22) and during the transfiguration (Matt 17:5; Mark 9:7). Like Abraham, God did not withhold but gave his beloved son. The Baptist's identification of Jesus as "the lamb of God" in John 1:29 may also refer to this event, especially in light of Abraham's confidence that God would provide for himself the lamb for the burnt offering (Gen 22:8).[96] In John's Gospel Jesus is presented both as the sacrificial Lamb and as the beloved Son, given by God to take away the sin of the world, with a basis in both Isa 53 and Gen 22.[97] These allusions highlight the typological relationship between the near-offering of Isaac the son of Abraham in the Aqedah and the completed offering of Jesus the Son of God.[98]

Inheriting the earth. In Jesus' famous words, "Blessed are the meek, for they shall inherit the earth" (Matt 5:5), Abrahamic themes of blessing and inheritance are invoked, as mediated through Psalm 37. "The meek" are thus declared to be the true children of Abraham under the reign of God.[99] Similarly in Hebrews those who are "called" under the new covenant are "heirs" of the "world to come" which is the promised "eternal inheritance" (Heb 2:5; 6:17; 9:15). To a significant extent the NT identity of believers as "heirs of God" is in continuity with the Abrahamic promise of which Jesus Christ is the primary heir (e.g. Rom 8:17; Eph 3:6; Rev 21:7; cf. Gal 3:18, 29).[100]

Blessing for "all nations." Jesus' command in Matthew 28 to made disciples of "all nations" is plausibly linked to the Abrahamic promise of blessing for "all nations" and to the prophetic expectation of a harvest of Gentiles.[101] Wright notes, "Matthew begins his gospel affirming Jesus the Messiah as the son of Abraham and ends it with the mission mandate that would encompass all nations. He thus sets the church also under the authority of the Abrahamic mission."[102] The visions of the throne of God and of the Lamb, around which is gathered an innumerable crowd of the blessed from "every tribe and language and people and nation" (Rev 5:9), strongly evoke the promise to Abraham of innumerable offspring: "a great multitude that no one could number, from every nation" (7:9).[103]

These Abrahamic allusions could be multiplied further, but those I have mentioned are consistent with the use of Abraham in the explicit references surveyed above. Because the promises of God to Abraham are understood in the NT as being fulfilled in Jesus Christ, the Abrahamic allusions are in continuity with them even when he is not explicitly referenced.

Summary of New Testament themes

The various usages of Abraham identified in the survey above may be gathered under seven themes: lineage, Christology, resurrection, soteriology, ecclesiology, geography, and eschatology. These themes are integral to the theology of the NT and constitute the worldview lenses through which Christians understand the Abraham narrative. Below I correlate these NT Abraham themes with the seven motifs from Genesis identified in the preceding chapter.

(1) Jesus is Messiah, son of Abraham. Nothing is more central to the NT perspective than that Jesus is the Messiah. The NT establishes this messianic identity by tracing Jesus' royal *lineage* through genealogical tables (Matt 1:1-17; Luke 3:34). These genealogies tie the Jesus narrative(s) into the story beginning in Genesis, and unite Jesus' Davidic or messianic lineage with his Abrahamic lineage. We saw that Gen 11:27–25:8 is linked by genealogies and narrative elements to the primeval narrative which it continues and to the ensuing patriarchal narratives which it initiates. The birth of Jesus culminates a biblical storyline carried in part by genealogies, thus uniting the two testaments into one long story of one royal (messianic) line. A final aspect of this messianic identity is underscored by Paul, who finds in the singular "seed" or unique "offspring" promised to Abraham a reference pointing to the Christ rather than simply to the patriarch's numerous offspring (Gal 3:16).

(2) Jesus is identified with the God of Abraham. NT Christology classically attends to both the humanity and the divinity/deity of Jesus Christ. The NT use of Abraham supports both aspects. On the one hand, Jesus' Abrahamic lineage is part of his identity "according to the flesh" (Rom 1:3). On the other hand, his divine identity and his preexistence are claimed in explicit relationship to Abraham in John 8:52-58, where Jesus declares, "before Abraham was, I am." Thus Jesus is both the son of Abraham and the God of Abraham. This affirmation is consistent with the broader picture of New Testament writers applying to Jesus Hebrew Scripture texts referring to the Lord.[104] His preexistence is also established through a Christian reading of Genesis 14 together with Psalm 110 in Heb 7:1-28. In Genesis the Creator God is the protagonist of the Abraham story, entering actively into his creation to carry out his purposes. The NT in various ways identifies the coming of Jesus, who is the main character in this new stage of the narrative, as the climactic coming of the God of Abraham.

(3) Abraham's God of resurrection has raised Jesus. In the NT God is identified in relation to Abraham preeminently as him "who raised Jesus from the dead" (Rom 4:16-24). Abraham's God is the life-giving "God of the living," who raises the dead, fulfilling his eternal commitments to his promises. The divine power that gave miraculous conception to barren Sarah is the same power that raised Jesus from the dead.[105] Salvation blessings are granted to all who trust in the God who raised Jesus, just as Abraham believed God's promise in the face of bodily deadness. Abraham receiving Isaac back from expected death exemplifies trust in this resurrecting power of God (Heb 11:17-19). The gospel promises the blessings of salvation to all who believe in the God who raised Jesus from the dead, just as Abraham believed God's promise of offspring in the face of impossibility (Rom 4:24; 10:9). Paul equates his ministry of proclaiming the resurrection with his hope in the promise made by God to Abraham (Acts 26:6-8).[106] The fact that many NT appeals to Abraham are tied in some way to the resurrection correlates with the hermeneutic of resurrection by which the Hebrew Scriptures are interpreted in the NT.[107] The apostolic announcement that God has raised Jesus from the dead is inseparable from the apostolic reading of Genesis where God's "narrative identity" is linked with his past and promised acts.[108]

(4) Abraham's "saving" faith. In the NT's soteriological appropriation, God's accounting of Abraham's faith to him as righteousness (Gen 15:6) is read as the definitive prototype of God's ways in saving sinful people through faith in his promises. Abraham is as much in need of salvation as any other human being. Paul's argument in Romans begins with an extended demonstration that Jews and Gentiles alike are all "under sin," because of the "fall" (Rom 1:18–3:20; 5:12ff), and are equally in need of a gift of righteousness from God, including Abraham and David, who are presented as Scriptural examples. The argument that justification comes by faith in Jesus is demonstrated from the Abraham narrative (Rom 4:12-16; Gal 3:6-14). At the same time Abraham's "saving" faith is understood in the NT as obedience to God's commands based on trust in his promises (Heb 11:8, 17; Jas 2:21-23). Numerous scenes in Luke and Acts continue this salvation-by-faith-in-Jesus motif.[109] In this usage Abraham is the paradigm of all who believe and are made partakers of the salvation of the messianic age to come. This correlates with the complicated and frequently threatened fulfillment of God's promise of offspring in the Genesis narrative. Abraham's "saving" faith is understood in the NT as obedience to God based on trust in his promises.

(5) Abraham's true offspring. Numerous passages in the NT use the Abraham narrative to demonstrate the identity of the people of God, the true "children of Abraham." Natural Jewish identity is expressed in the NT with the phrases such as "your fathers" (including Abraham), "our father Abraham," and "descendant of Abraham." Nevertheless, the physical kinship claim is strongly rejected as insufficient basis for true relationship with God and inclusion as "children of Abraham." Authentic heirs of Abraham are identified as those (from Israel and from all nations) who receive salvation from Jesus the Messiah and are identified

with Abraham by virtue of being "in Christ." Paul wades into the difficult debates over how Gentiles may participate along with Jews in the blessings to be inherited by "Abraham's offspring," appealing to the Genesis narrative to establish a precedent for all who will receive such covenantal "righteousness" apart from the law (Gal 3:7-29). Abraham is both the primary recipient of the promise of God's redemption, fulfilled in Jesus Christ, and the principal paradigm of faith for all nations who are called to believe in God, who has raised Jesus from the dead. This correlates with the thorny issue arising in Genesis with the birth of Ishmael at the pivot point of the narrative and the series of events underscoring the identity of the legitimate heir of Abraham, through whom the purposes of God are to be realized. The Hebrew prophets show that not all Jews are God's people,[110] and the concept of a righteous *remnant* becomes the primary focus this true Abrahamic identity. In the NT this remnant is identified as the people of Jesus: "If you are Christ's, then you are Abraham's offspring, heirs according to promise" (Gal 3:29).

(6) Abraham's inheritance. The NT appeals to God's *promise of a homeland* to Abraham in several distinct ways. First, while not exhausting the promise, Israel's historical conquest of Canaan is understood as a fulfillment of the Abrahamic land-promise (Acts 7:16-17, 45; Heb 4). Second, the land promised to Abraham is the geographical setting for the fulfillment of many land-specific prophetic words that are organically related to the Abrahamic promises. God's saving act in Jesus Christ thus takes place in Jerusalem, to which the gospel narratives move, and from whence the good news goes out to the nations. Third, the full Abrahamic inheritance is developed as a universalized land-promise and the expectation of the new creation (Rom 4:13; Heb 11:8-10). Strom describes this as "the transposition of land to cosmos."[111] Abraham's longed-for heavenly country, the coming messianic banquet with Abraham, Isaac, and Jacob, and multitudes from "all nations" gathered before the throne, are all pictures of the consummation which are expressed in Abrahamic language and are inseparable from the NT resurrection hope of a re-created cosmos resulting from Jesus' resurrection. Fourth, related to this transposition, is the NT insistence that there is no longer a central place of worship and pilgrimage on earth (John 4:21). The holy place of Abrahamic pilgrimage is now the heavenly city (Heb 9:11; 11:14-16). This of course correlates with the promise of land to Abraham and his descendants that runs throughout the Genesis narrative. Abram begins to build altars in this land to the Lord who appeared to him. The region where Abraham nearly offers Isaac is named and identified with Jerusalem as the scene of God's future provision, presumably of an ultimate sacrifice. Even after the exile Israel's prophets foretell a return to the land in the coming days, when God will make a "new covenant."

(7) Blessing of the nations. The most sweeping category of the NT use of Abraham is the eschatological appropriation of Abraham. From the NT perspective the coming of Jesus is the culmination of the divine enterprise to bless all the nations of the world, of which Abraham's story was the groundbreaking stage. The impending births of John and Jesus are celebrated with prophetic announcements that the messianic "day" anticipated by Abraham has dawned at last. The God of

Abraham has "raised up" Jesus his servant precisely in fulfillment of his promise that through Abraham's offspring all nations will be blessed (Acts 3:13-26; cf. 13:32-34). That the "blessing of Abraham" has now come through the work of Jesus and the giving of the Spirit is the "gospel of God." God's giving of his Son, foreshadowed in the Aqedah, the resurrection of the dead, and the promised Spirit being poured out on the nations are all Abrahamic "gospel" themes. All of this was included within the promises Abraham believed (Rom 4:13-16; Heb 6:13; 7:6). This correlates with God's promise that through Abraham and his offspring "all the families of the earth will be blessed," which is repeated most notably at the opening and closing "bookends" of the main Abraham narrative (12:3 and 22:18). In the NT perspective, the promised age arrives with the coming of Jesus.

Each of these areas of NT appropriation of Abraham contributes to the Christian worldview introduced in chapter 2. The significance of these Abrahamic worldview elements for comparison with the Islamic worldview will be clear when we consider the qur'anic Abraham material in chapters 5 and 6.

Second Temple Jewish Use of Abraham

Noting some contemporaneous Jewish uses of Abraham that the NT ignores, rejects, or warns against may further refine our understanding of the NT use of Abraham. The movements that became known as Rabbinic Judaism and Christianity emerged from the same Second Temple Jewish milieu, and the earliest form of the Christian movement has been referred to as "Nazarene Jewish Christianity"[112] or even "Nazarene Judaism."[113] Understanding how the NT reading of Abraham diverges from other Jewish readings of that period will help us understand the significance of Abraham for Christians. As Carson says, "it is correct to say that the Christian Paul read these Scriptures through the lens of the resurrected Christ—but that tells what triggers the hermeneutical shift, not what the shift itself is."[114] Clarifying this "shift" will also help us understand Islam's reading of Abraham, which is substantially closer to most of these Jewish readings than the NT reading outlined above.

Second Temple Jewish interpretive approaches to the Pentateuch are available to us in extant texts of that period, specifically the writings of the Apocrypha, Pseudepigrapha, Qumran, Josephus, and Philo.[115] These post-canonical writings from the era relevant for the NT make many references to Abraham which reveal his great significance for Jewish identity and history. The general picture that emerges from this literature shows Abraham as the prototype of faithful obedience to the Torah. Hansen summarizes the findings of his survey of Abraham in the literature of the Apocrypha and Pseudepigrapha as follows:

> In most of these texts Abraham is exalted as the perfect model of Torah observance (Sir. 44; Jub. 15.1, 2; 16.20, 26; 17.17-18; 23.10; 1 Macc. 2.50; T. Levi 9.1-14; T. Benj. 10.4; T. Abr. 17.2; 2 Baruch 57.1-3). His faithfulness at times of testing (Sir. 44.19; Jub. 17.17-18; 19.6; 1 Macc. 2.52; Jdt. 8.25), his circumcision (Sir. 44.20; 1. Macc. 2.52), his rejection of idolatry (Jub. 12.1-14; Apoc. Abr. 1-8), and his hospitality (T. Abr. 17) all receive special attention and elaboration as marks of his perfect righteousness.[116]

It is evident that the canonical portrait has been substantially enhanced in this literature.[117] Three areas in particular stand out. First, whereas the Abraham of Genesis shows no direct rejection of idolatry, in these writings he is essentially the founder of monotheism and a zealous opponent of idolatrous practices. Second, whereas in Genesis Abraham evidences no awareness of explicit Torah practices,[118] here Abraham is "the perfect model of Torah observance." Third, whereas in Genesis Abraham is specifically "tested" by God only in the Aqedah incident, here Abraham is tested throughout his life and found faithful at every point.

The book of *Jubilees*, sometimes referred to as the "Little Genesis," is an important example of the so-called "rewritten Bible" of Second Temple literature.[119] VanderKam describes it as "an older, authoritative work inherited and cherished by the Qumran community associated with the Dead Sea Scrolls," which predates these sectarian divisions (Jubilees is commonly dated to 160–150 BCE).[120] Its importance for this chapter is that it represents very early Jewish exegetical work on the book of Genesis. The retelling of Abraham's story found there is a significant strand of the interpretive trajectory that led to the early rabbinic approach. In VanderKam's words, Jubilees "allows us to see that exegetical motifs expressed in later literature (e.g. the midrashim) existed already in the second century BCE."[121] It was also highly esteemed by Byzantine and Syriac Christian chronographers working on Genesis. Adler notes, "In spite of occasional warnings and prohibitions against it, these chronographers quote more extensively from Jubilees than from any of the other Jewish pseudepigrapha of the Second Temple period."[122]

The book is introduced as an overview of world history based on a Jubilee-based solar calendar (1.1). God calls Moses to the top of Mount Sinai and commands "the angel of the presence" to write for him a narrative covering the period "from the beginning of creation till My sanctuary has been built among them for all eternity" (1.27-28). The remainder of the book records the angel's retelling of Genesis and the first half of Exodus, with omissions, alterations, and particularly additions, which carry the polemical freight of the book. According to Hayward, the focus of the book of Jubilees is the people of Israel: "This already constituted nation stands at the head of the anonymous narrator's introduction, just as she stands at the head of the creative process: the gradual process whereby Israel becomes constituted on earth then becomes the major theme of the angelic narrator's discourse."[123]

Abraham's story is narrated from his birth (Jub 11.14) to his death (23.1-9; see my summary of events according to *Jubilees* in Appendix 4). The angel recaps the patriarch's life with these words: "Abraham was perfect in all his deeds with the Lord, and well-pleasing in righteousness all the days of his life" (23.10). His life is interpreted as a series of events in which the Lord *tried him* in many ways and found him completely faithful (17.17-18).[124] Great emphasis is given to Abraham's careful keeping of the law, particularly in relation to the feasts of Tabernacles and Passover. Following the announcement of Isaac's birth Abraham is the first person to celebrate this seven-day festival (16.15-31). Huizenga shows that the Aqedah functions here as a "patriarchal etiology of the Passover festival."[125]

Several aspects of *Jubilees'* reading and interpretive rewriting of the Abraham narrative differ from the NT reading:

(1) A lengthy addition to the Genesis account narrates Abraham's first 60 years in Ur of the Chaldees, where God first "tried him through his country" (17.17). At age 14 (2 "weeks" of years) he separates himself from his father, "that he might not worship idols with him" and "began to pray to the Creator of all things" (11.16-17). At age 28 (2 more "weeks") he challenges his father Terah about the worship of man-made, dumb idols which are "misleading of the heart to those who worship them" (12.1-5). After staying with his resistant family another 21 years (making a jubilee 7 weeks of years), Abram marries Sarai. Some 11 years later he burns down the idol house and Terah takes his clan to Haran, where Abram lives for another 14 years. *Jubilees* reconstructs the background for the famous call of Genesis 12:1-3: Abram stays up all night (on the new moon of the seventh month) to seek a sign in the stars regarding the rain. But "a word came into his heart," and he realized that the heavenly bodies are in the hand of the Lord, and prayed to the Creator God to deliver him from evil spirits, guide him, and establish him and his seed forever, "that we go not astray from henceforth" (12.16-20).[126] This narrative explains why God would call Abraham: His idol-rejecting righteousness and God-seeking heart made him deserving of it. As Levenson rightly notes, this is absent from the Genesis narrative: "Unlike later rabbinic exegesis, the Torah itself offers no grounds for the selection of Abram for this awesome assignment. It makes no claim that he had earned it or that he was endowed with some innate predisposition that made his selection rational."[127]

The NT knows nothing of this added episode, but finds the basis for Abraham's call in nothing other than God's unwarranted election (Rom 9:11; 11:28-29). In the two passages mentioning his migration nothing is said of any prehistory (Acts 7:2-6; Heb 11:8). This omission is striking when we consider that these heroic stories were prevalent in Jewish literature. There is rather a restriction of focus to the canonical narrative, highlighting Gen 12:1-3 as the inaugural promise of God (Acts 3:25; Rom 4:13; Gal 3:8).

(2) Jubilees' interpretive moves are communicated by means of embellishment of the Genesis story. This is typical of the "exegetical narratives" on the forefathers (known as *midrash aggadah*), of which Jubilees is one of the earliest examples. Lowin describes the origin of these stories: "The narratives frequently began life as Jewish exegesis of a biblical issue intended to explain a textual difficulty or elucidate a homiletically problematic matter."[128] Careful reading of Jubilees shows which parts closely follow Genesis and which were rewritten for exegetical purposes. For example, where God's testing of Abraham to offer his son is apparently uncaused in Genesis 22, here the evil spirit "prince Mastema" incites God, as Satan incites him against Job (cf. Job 1:6-12): "Bid him offer [Isaac] as a burnt-offering on the altar, and Thou wilt see if he will do this command, and Thou wilt know if he is faithful in everything wherein Thou dost try him" (17.16). This leads to the Aqedah account in 18.1-19. The narrative expansion provides a solution to the difficulty of God's commanding the patriarch to do

something forbidden by the Law, an answer inspired by Job's story.[129] In time these additions take on a status nearly equal to the original narrative, as Lowin notes: "In explaining these 'problems', the rabbis drew from all over the Bible, seeing all of its parts as interconnected. Importantly, since the explanation of a particular pericope thus derived from materials drawn from the Bible itself, the rabbis understood the exegesis to have been part of the biblical text itself, part of the divine plan in its composition."[130]

By contrast, the NT does not achieve its reading by such textual embellishments of the OT narrative. Rather it references the canonical narrative in support of its reading. In this example the absence of incitement only adds to the mysterious command for Abraham to sacrifice his only son, which finds its deepest meaning as a prophetic picture of God's sacrifice of his Son.

(3) Jubilees develops a particular liturgical chronology as it expands the canonical narrative. In the worldview of Jubilees, God's law-based covenant relationship with Israel began with creation, and therefore Abraham is presented as a shining model of a law-keeping Jew despite the fact that he lived centuries before the Law was given to Moses. Segal argues that "Jubilees brought the election of Israel backward to the week of creation, and therefore the stipulations of the covenant . . . were also brought backward to the pre-Sinaitic period. . . . [Hence we find] the juxtaposition of legal passages to the rewritten stories of Genesis."[131] The NT, on the other hand, focuses on distinct, progressive periods of God's rule in the biblical narrative. Paul treats various relationships to the law within a chronological framework, so Abraham, who lived in the period before the Law was given to Moses, was not "under the Law." From the NT perspective the importance of the narrative flow is lost in Jubilees' reading and replaced with law-centered stories embodying its distinct worldview.

(4) Jubilees' retelling of Abraham's story has what Huizenga calls a "paranetic [sic] function—the author wishes to make clear that only strict obedience to covenant stipulations secures deliverance from earthly and heavenly threats against the covenant people."[132] While the NT does use Abraham with a hortatory function, it does not appeal to his example to compel obedience to "covenant stipulations." Rather the emphasis is on Abraham's relationship to God while still uncircumcised, living centuries before the Law was given (Rom 4; Gal 3) and as an example of obedient faith in response to God's promises and startling one-off commands: leave your homeland (Heb 11:8-10), listen to Sarah about Ishmael (Gal 4:30), offer your son (Heb 11:17-19).

(5) God's palpable presence is omitted from some theologically difficult places in the narrative, though some theophanies are retained. So where Gen 18 has the Lord himself appearing to Abraham and announcing that Sarah will have a son, *Jubilees* has only angels: "we [the angel of the presence and two other angels] appeared unto Abraham, at the oak of Mamre, and we talked with him, and we announced to him that a son would be given to him by Sarah his wife" (16.1). Where Genesis mentions no angelic mediator at Abram's first call, Jubilees has the word of the Lord coming to Abram through the angel of the presence (12.22). On the other hand, the NT affirms the appearance of the

Lord himself to Abraham to call him (Acts 7:2-3). *Jubilees* exhibits the Second Temple tendency to emphasize the transcendence of God and delete seemingly problematic (anthropomorphic) appearances of God, especially where the Angel of God is identified with God himself.[133]

In light of God's OT appearing to Abraham and others at major revelatory moments, it is striking that the NT records no such appearances of God or his unique angel to Jesus.[134] Rather Jesus' coming is the coming of the Lord. He is the Lord, appearing in human flesh (1 Tim 3:16). Isaiah's and Malachi's prophecies of the Lord's coming are being fulfilled in the coming of *Jesus* (Mark 1:1-4, 14-15). Jesus is the Lord whose glory Isaiah saw in the temple (John 12:40-41 with Isa 6:1-10). One who sees him sees God (John 14:9).

It is evident from this brief analysis that the picture of Abraham in the worldview of *Jubilees* has evolved from its depiction in canonical Genesis. Abraham is now the discoverer and defender of monotheism and the model Torah-keeper. This Torah-centered reading of Abraham was likely engendered by Judaism's struggle to maintain monotheism and ritual purity in the face of the sophisticated pressure of Hellenistic idolatry.[135] But whatever its formation, *Jubilees* represents an emerging Jewish reading of Abraham from which the NT diverges significantly.

Areas of divergence between NT and Jewish readings of Abraham

Differences in Jewish and Christian approaches to the Hebrew Scriptures are evident in competing readings of Abraham.[136] I see three major points of divergence:

(1) The NT and non-Christian Jewish readings represent *different endings to the same story.* As Wright shows, Josephus's sequel had Israel's God going over to the Romans, Sirach has the conclusion in the glorious worship in the rebuilt temple before Antiochus Epiphanes arose, and the Maccabees find the conclusion to Israel's story in their own stunning victory over the Greeks.[137] Moralistic writings such as *Jubilees, Pseudo-Philo,* and the *Wisdom of Solomon* foresaw an appropriate sequel to come if only Israel would pursue faithfulness to all the requirements of the covenant.[138] These writings hold forth hope that Israel's restored commitment to Torah will lead to a finale centered on Israel, or at least on a purified remnant of Israel.[139] The NT presents a radically different sequel to this story, centered on the coming of Jesus the Messiah.

(2) NT writers *privilege biblical narrative over law* and Abraham over Moses. Davies contends that from a Jewish perspective, Christian interpretive focus on a "linear structure that moves from figure to fulfillment gives to biblical narrative a dangerous precedent over biblical law."[140] However, the NT sees biblical law pointing beyond itself to the last days and even confirming its own temporal status. Where NT retelling emphasizes aspects of the narrative which stress the acts of God and a forward trajectory toward the gospel, much Jewish retelling of the story of Israel emphasizes the legal portions by reading aspects of it back into the patriarchal narratives, as

seen above in *Jubilees*. Van der Lans cites Jewish writings (e.g. Josephus, *4 Maccabees, Jubilees*) that make obedience to the Law a primary condition for being counted as the seed of Abraham, and portray Abraham as a Torah-observant.[141] The NT resists this effort to make the law primary or to make it normative for the era from Adam to Moses.[142] Carson argues that when first-century Palestinian Jews were asked the question, "How does a person please God?" they were likely to answer, "By obeying the law," and that this answer reveals the dominant hermeneutical lens through which the OT was read. Paul, on the other hand, places the weight on the narrative sequence as a crucial interpretive key: "Abraham was justified by faith *before* the giving of the law, and the promise to him and to his seed similarly came before the giving of the law . . . this is one of the hermeneutical differences between the apostolic interpreters of Scripture and their unconverted Jewish counterparts."[143]

(3) In these Jewish readings, Abraham is a model of holy zeal, opposing idolatry and Gentile dominance. He is the perfect model of Torah observance and a hero of monotheism, of which he is in fact the founder. Klinghoffer describes this tradition:

> There is another Abraham [from the one portrayed in the book of Genesis]: the patriarch as portrayed in ancient oral tradition, Oral Torah. . . . By tradition's account, remarkably vivid where Scripture's is modest and circumscribed, Abraham was a missionary who converted tens of thousands to monotheism. He was also an occultist, astrologer, healer, and writer of esoteric texts whose home was a regular gathering place for angels.[144]

The NT ignores such heroic depictions of Abraham and other OT figures which are found in these Jewish exegetical narratives (though not in the Hebrew Scriptures). In the Gospels Jesus draws attention to Israel's history as a narrative of failure rather than of glory, in which the story of sin and rejection of the prophets is now culminating in the rejection of the Messiah (e.g. Matt 21:33-46). While Abraham is a man of faith, it is not his faithfulness but God's that is defining. Paul conflates Abraham with guilty but forgiven David, "against whom the LORD [did] not count his sin" of adultery and manslaughter (Rom 4:2-8). In the NT reading these people are not inherently righteous, but are like all other sinners for whom God's grace in Christ provides cleansing and righteousness.[145]

Explicit NT disavowal of Jewish "tradition"

The NT writings appeal directly and widely to the Tanakh while directly appealing only minimally to the body of Jewish exegetical materials, whether written or oral, available at the time. Nevertheless, many scholars see deep indebtedness to the noncanonical Jewish writings in the NT documents, and some even see similar approaches.[146] Yet the exclusion of extant Jewish writings from citation is surely significant.[147] This reflects a conviction, probably based on Jesus' own appeal to the Scriptures over against the "traditions of the fathers," that the traditional Jewish interpretive approaches of the Second Temple period were misguided at best. Certainly it is clear that within decades of Jesus' death two separate communities were appealing to the Hebrew Scriptures in very different ways.[148] The Gospels, Pauline literature, and Hebrews allude to or directly address Second Temple Jewish readings of Abraham in a variety of ways.

The Gospels. The relationship of Jesus, as represented in the Gospels, to the Jewish interpretive traditions of his time is a vast field of study.[149] The Gospels portray Jesus as inaugurating a massive reassessment of Jewish tradition-guided reading of Torah. According to Matthew, Jesus asserts that he and his teaching *fulfill* the Law and the prophets as a whole (Matt 5:17-20).[150] He sets his *authority above* that of the traditional reading: "you have heard that it was said . . . but I say to you" (Matt 5:21-48). In this sermon Jesus engages traditional or common readings and effectively supersedes them with his own commands, which "fulfill" them. Jesus' teaching, as found in the Gospels, essentially ignores Jewish oral law and interpretive traditions, interpreting the Tanakh afresh through the lens of his arrival and kingdom. He effectively substitutes himself for the temple and the whole Levitical system in a comprehensive challenge to Judaism's Torah-centered reading.[151]

Another aspect of this reading is seen in Jesus' use of the Scriptures to explicitly *overturn positions* held by his contemporaries who interpreted these Scriptures through the lens of oral tradition—"the traditions of the elders" (Mark 7:1-15; Matt 15:1-20). According to the NT accounts, so distorted was this lens in Jesus' judgment that its authoritative users had become "blind guides of the blind" (Matt 15:14; cf. 23:1-36; Luke 11:37-52), unable to see what God was accomplishing in front of their eyes. Through symbolic actions and direct teaching, Jesus charged the traditionalists with obscuring the original purpose of God, of which his ministry was the climactic phase—the "day" that Abraham "saw" (John 8:56). He told his opponents that if they were really Abraham's children as they claimed to be, they would believe the truth as Abraham did (John 8:39-43), and that if they believed Moses, they would believe him because Moses wrote of him (John 5:46). Jesus was what R.S. Good calls the "protagonist of the old,"[152] denouncing their dependence on the oral tradition: "Why do you break the commandment of God for the sake of your tradition? . . . For the sake of your tradition you have made void the word of God" (Matt 15:6). He makes here a fundamental distinction between the "the commandment of God" (as found in Scripture) and the Jewish tradition. Edwards concludes, "the oral tradition, which was the defining element of Pharisaic and rabbinic Judaism, is in the present pericope [Mark 7:1-13] categorically nullified."[153]

There are indications that Jesus, while not citing Abraham in this regard, emphasized the *narrative shape* of the Torah in ways similar to that noticed above regarding Paul's argument in Galatians 3 and Romans 4. For example, Jesus told the doubtful crowds "all the Prophets and the Law prophesied *until* John, and if you are willing to accept it, he is Elijah who is to come" (Matt 11:13-14). The new moment was upon them in the arrival of John and Jesus. In another incident, Jesus argued priority from the narrative order of the Pentateuch: "Moses allowed you to divorce your wives, but *from the beginning* it was not so" (Matt 19:8; cf.

Mark 10:5-6). He reads Deut 24:1-4 as a temporary concession in light of the narrative order.

Jesus' repeated challenge "have you not/never read?" (Matt 12:3, 5; 19:4; 21:16; 22:31), does not question their acquaintance with the Scriptures but their interpretive approach, which obscured the primary meaning of the text in light of the larger plan of God. On this basis he challenges the Sadducees' mistaken reading of Exod 3 about the "God of Abraham." Perhaps the clearest example of Jesus challenging his contemporaries to recognize the climax reached in Israel's narrative is the parable of the vineyard tenants who ultimately reject the owner's son (Matt 21:33-46).

Pauline writings. In the book of Acts Paul is represented as arguing with fellow Jews in synagogues from the Hebrew Scriptures, with mixed results (e.g. Acts 13:14-52; 17:1-4; 28:23-24). That Paul's letters controvert major aspects of Judaism's reading of the OT is not in dispute; the live question is whether he is a good reader of the texts.[154] Some argue that Paul's "hermeneutic of faith" is in fact a careful reading of the texts, which may be compared with (other) Jewish readings of *the same texts.*[155] Sprinkle's compares the soteriological structures of Paul with Qumran (and with *Jubilees, Sirach, Psalms of Solomon, Wisdom of Solomon, 4 Ezra, Pseudo-Philo's Biblical Antiquities,* and *the Testament of Moses*), noting points of continuity and discontinuity. He argues that Paul's theology, while remaining within the Jewish spectrum of beliefs, "still seems to push the envelope of God's role in salvation with a complexity and precision that is unparalleled in the literature of early Judaism."[156] He finds more discontinuity than continuity between Paul and early Jewish writings.

Francis Watson sees Paul, in purposeful "conversation" with Jewish readings of Abraham, exploiting two related sets of tensions in order to subvert the non-Christian readings: (1) between the "unconditional Genesis promises and the conditional offer of 'life' that derives from the law given at Mount Sinai," and (2) between this offer and the situation resulting when it is "overtaken by the realities of sin and death, so that those who are under the law are under its curse"[157] The other Second Temple readings mitigate these tensions in various ways by recasting Abraham as a heroic model of every religious virtue.[158] We saw this "hero" reading above in Jubilees. It is also seen in 1 Maccabees 2:50-54, where Abraham is linked with zealous Phinehas, to whom God also "reckons righteousness" (Num 25:10-13; Ps 106:28-31).[159] By conflating Gen 15:6 with 22:1, Abraham is rendered a hero and justified for his great obedience "*when he was tested,*" rather than when he believed God's promise. Paul opposes this reading, linking Abraham instead with sinning, forgiven David (Rom 4:2-8). Philo reads Genesis as embodying unwritten laws, already "incarnated" in Abraham. But in the very texts where Philo and Jubilees discover harmony between Abraham and Sinai, Paul finds antithesis and sees promise preceding command. In Josephus Abraham leaves Chaldea because of his rational deduction of the Creator from the creation and to escape the persecution arising from his proclamation of monotheism. The contrasts identified by Watson are summarized in Figure 4.1.

FIGURE 4.1 – PAULINE AND OTHER JEWISH READINGS OF ABRAHAM

	According to other Jewish interpretations:	According to Paul:
A)	Abraham is an exemplary role model (virtuous, zealous, perfect), duly honored by God for his faithfulness.	Abraham is primarily the recipient of God's sovereign promise to act on his behalf, whose righteousness is constituted merely by his faith.
B)	God's promises are primarily occasioned by Abraham's acts of piety (e.g. renunciation of idolatry).	God's promises of future, world-wide saving action originate in the unmotivated divine election.
C)	Abraham holds the central position in the story.	God holds the central position in the story.

On this understanding, the view Paul rejects in his hermeneutical approach is not his own anti-Jewish construct, but an existing Jewish exegetical reading of a larger-than-life Abraham who "*has something to boast about*" (Rom 4:2). If Sprinkle and Watson are correct, Paul's letters are best understood as rejecting significant aspects of the dominant Jewish interpretive traditions of the period, including not least their reading of Abraham.

The Pastoral Epistles explicitly warn against "Jewish myths" and "endless genealogies, which promote speculations" (1 Tim 1:4; 4:7; Titus 1:14). These phrases most likely refer to haggadic stories of creation and genealogies of the patriarchs found in the exegetical narratives mentioned above. According to Hirshman, "It would seem that the author is warning the audience against the Jewish misunderstanding of Scripture on two fronts, aggadah and halakhah, interpretation and observance."[160] Jewish exegetical traditions were seen as obscuring the inspired, useful canonical Scriptures (2 Tim 3:15-17), especially insofar as they major on the law rather than the promise of God fulfilled in Jesus Christ. Yet, "the law is good, if one uses it lawfully," as that which reveals sin and testifies to the gospel of God's salvation for "sinners," such as the people of Israel (and the patriarchs) have been shown to be by the law itself (1 Tim 1:8-11; cf. Rom 3:19-24).[161]

Hebrews. In Hebrews' extensive appeal to the Scriptures, all other readings, especially those that are Torah-centered, are implicitly ignored and set aside. Recent scholars argue that Hebrews is not supersessionist, replacing Judaism with Christianity, but rather addresses "new covenantal" Jewish believers as possessing in Christ the fulfillment or fullness of their ancestral faith.[162] The letter's conclusion explicitly warns against competing Jewish teachings: "Do not be led away by diverse and strange teachings, for it is good for the heart to be strengthened by grace, not by foods, which have not benefited those devoted to them" (Heb 13:9).[163] This rejects, as strange and unnourishing, all readings (including those of mainstream Jewish and sectarian groups, or even Jewish Christians) that do not consistently recognize the Law as an anticipatory word leading to Christ.[164] One additional emphasis is that the goal of pilgrimage, particularly Abraham's sojourn, is now directed to the heavenly Jerusalem.[165] This sidelines the earthly temple site by showing how the earthly cult in Jerusalem foreshadowed the eternal holy place.

This survey of Jewish Second Temple writings yields a depiction of Abraham quite different from that in Genesis. He has evolved into the discoverer and defender of monotheism, a diligent Torah-keeper and a model of success in every test. The NT disavows Jewish interpretive tradition and even warns against it. This comparison helps to clarify our understanding of the NT appropriation of Abraham that reads the canonical Abraham narrative in the light of Jesus as the Messiah.

We noted in passing that the Jewish portrayals of Abraham and others as exemplars of great virtue resemble Islam's portrayal of the sinless prophets. This is particularly true of Abraham, as will be seen in the next two chapters. Comparing the NT reading of Abraham with Judaism's reading not only helps clarify the Christian appropriation, but also sheds light on Muslim's usage. The NT emphasis on using the canonical narrative to the exclusion of later traditions has significance for contextualized Christian witness to Muslims. As we will see in chapter 6, Turkish Muslims regularly recount para-qur'anic Abraham stories to supplement the qur'anic ones. Discussing Jesus' approach to the traditions of Judaism in the NT may be useful for clarifying areas of difference.

The NT uses the Genesis Abraham narrative as an integral part of a set of convictions about what God had newly done through Jesus Christ. This NT use of Abraham, seen in light of the coming of Jesus, diverges widely from the use of Abraham in other Jewish writings of the Second Temple period. These *torah-centered* readings of Abraham rise out of its postexilic conflict with pagan idolatry, and have little common ground with the NT appropriation. Sandmel argues that "To see what the writer makes of Abraham is often to see most clearly what the writer is trying to say,"[166] and "Abraham is to the rabbis and to Philo (as well as to Paul) the foremost example of the man who did what each is urging; but each is urging a different thing."[167] I agree with Sandmel's first statement, but I disagree in part with the second. Yes, the use of Abraham in the NT and in Judaism does help us see what the writers are trying to say. But while, to Paul and the NT writers, Abraham does exemplify the obedience of faith, he is first and foremost the recipient of divine promises that are now being fulfilled in God's new work through Jesus Christ, the unique son of Abraham. Only secondarily, and only on this basis, is Abraham an example of the faith to which Christians are called.

This divergence between NT and Jewish readings foreshadows the divergence between Christian and Muslim uses of Abraham that we will explore in the following chapters. The New Testament's *Christ-centered* narrative hermeneutic of Abraham arises from the conviction that the Christ is in fact the crucified and risen Jesus, who is the fulfiller of the promises given to Abraham. By contrast,

Islam's *prophet-centered* reading of Abraham, to which we now turn, arises from Muhammad's arrival as a prophet preaching monotheism. In this worldview Abraham is seen as a great model of monotheistic faith and prophethood.

CHAPTER 5 – ABRAHAM IN THE QUR'AN

According to the Qur'an, Islam is the very "religion of Abraham" (Q 2:130).[1] Reynolds has argued that the Quran's presentation of Abraham "as the model of its own Prophet and its emphasis on the Arabic language suggests that the emergence of Islam was connected with a conviction that the Arabs are the descendants of Abraham no less than the Jews."[2] But why does the Qur'an tell and retell *particular* Abraham episodes, and how do these episodes fit into the purpose of their respective suras and of the Qur'an as a whole?

While there is no single Abraham narrative in the Qur'an, the general shape and content of a qur'anic Abraham "narrative" can be reconstructed from the twenty-five suras in which Abraham (Ibrahim) is mentioned.[3] Consideration of this material as a whole reveals *four distinct Abraham stories* along with a variety of brief *descriptions* of Abraham, which can be grouped into eleven categories. While it is not my primary purpose to examine the reconstructed Abraham narrative in chronological order, it is helpful to notice that three of the four stories fit three major geographical[4] foci in his life, as understood in Islamic tradition:

1) Events in Mesopotamia – the story of Abraham disputing with idolaters.
2) Events in Syria/Canaan – the story of angels visiting Abraham and his wife.
3) Events in Mecca – the story of Abraham building the Kaaba with Ishmael.[5]

The fourth story, Abraham's attempted offering of his son, is notoriously difficult to locate in the sequence and is reported only once in the Qur'an.[6] This is further complicated by the fact that the Qur'an does not name the son. It is generally placed in the third period with Ishmael as the son being offered, though some (early) Muslim exegetes have judged the son to be Isaac[7] and the location to be Syria.[8]

The four distinct qur'anic Abraham narratives are given in a variety of forms and with varying detail in fifteen different suras:

(Story 1) Disputation with idolaters.[9] This story, found in eight suras in different forms, is from the early period of Abraham's life, during which he rejects the idolatry of his kinsfolk and derides their foolishness and blindness in worshipping anything other than the Creator. In some of the accounts, Abraham is cast into a fire by his antagonists but is miraculously protected by God. Fundamental to this story in its various permutations is Abraham's declaration of allegiance to the one Creator God and consequent separation from his idol-worshipping clan. Though this material has no real parallels in the canonical biblical Abraham narrative, there are many in later Jewish para-biblical writings.[10] Table 5.1 sets out the elements of Abraham's disputes with idolaters.

Figure 5.1 – Qur'anic Abraham Story 1

Qur'anic accounts:	6:74-87	19:41-50	21:51-73	26:69-102	29:16-27	37:83-100	43:26-28	60:3-6
Story 1 - Early Disputes with Idolaters								
1 Introduction. consider Abraham		19:41	21:51	26:69		37:83-84		
2 Challenges his father and people regarding idols	6:74	19:42-45	21:52-56	26:70-76	29:16	37:84-87	43:26	60:4
3 Abraham discerns that star, moon, sun not God	6:75-78							60:4
4 Father argues with Abraham and threatens to stone him		19:46						
5 Abraham proposes to pray for his father		19:47						60:4
6 Declares that he 'quits' their idols, rejecting 'associates'	6:78-81	19:48-49					43:26-27	60:4
7 Affirms allegiance to the one creating, sustaining God	6:79-80		21:56	26:77-82	29:17			
8 People dispute with Abraham	6:80				29:18			
9 Abraham (and followers) prays for favor and forgivness				26:83-89		37:100		60:4-5
10 Breaks idols, mocks questioners under trial			21:57-67			37:88-96		
11 Abraham cast into fire and delivered			21:68-70		29:24	37:97-98		
12 Warns people of judgment and day of resurrection		19:45		26:90-102	29:25			
13 Leaves to go to the Promised Land (joined by Lot)		19:49	21:71		29:26	37:99		
14 God rewards Abraham with posterity (esp. Isaac & Jacob)	6:84-87	19:49-50	21:72-73		29:27		43:28	

FIGURE 5.2 – QUR'ANIC ABRAHAM STORY 2

Qur'anic Accounts::	11:69-83	15:51-77	29:31-32	37:112-113	51:24-37
Story 2 - Abraham hosts visiting angels					
1 Introduction		15:51			51:24
2 Messengers come greeting Abraham: 'peace'	11:69	15:52	29:31		51:25-27
3 Angels don't eat offered food but allay Abrahams fears	11:70	15:53			51:28
4 Sent to Lot's people	11:70				
5 Angels announce special son Isaac's (and Jacob's) birth	11:71b	15:53		37:112-113	51:28
6 Wife laughs, doubts	11:71a, 72				51:29
7 Abraham questions due to old age		15:54			51:30
8 Angels confirm God's purpose of blessing	11:73	15:55			
9 Abraham affirms faith (not despair)		15:56			
10 Abraham asks messangers their business		15:57			51:31
11 Angels announce they are sent to sinful people in judgment		15:58	29:31		51"32-34
12 Abraham intercedes for Lot's people, compassionate	11:74-75		29:32		
13 Abraham told no change is possible in command	11:76				
14 Angels announce they will deliver Lot's family except for his wife		15:59-60	29:32		51-35-37
15 Lot and the judgment of his people	11:77-83	15:61-77			

FIGURE 5.3 – QUR'ANIC ABRAHAM STORY 3

Qur'anic Accounts:	2:124-141	3:95-97	14:35-41	22:26-33
Story 3 - Abraham Builds the Kaaba				
1 Introduction				
2 God appointed the Kaaba to be a place of pilgrimage	2:125	3:96		22:26
3 Bekka/Mecca a "holy place and a guidence"		3:96		
4 "Abraham's station" is to be the place of prayer	2:125	3:97		
5 Covenant with Abraham and Ishmael to purify it for pilgrimage rites	2:125			22:26
6 Duty of all to make pilgrimage to the house		3:97		22:27-29
7 Requirements for venerating God's "sacred things" and "waymarks"				22:30-33
8 Abraham prays for the land around the Kaaba to be fruitful	2:126			
9 Abraham and Ishmael raise the foundations of the House	2:127			
10 Prayer of dedication, for seed to be kept from idolatry	2:127		14:35-38	
11 Prayer for selves and their seed, and for the 'holy rites'	2:128		14:39-40	
12 Prayer for a Messenger to be sent	2:129			
13 Prayer for forgiveness for himself, his parents, and the believers on the Day			14:41	

(Story 2) Hosting angelic visitors.[11] The second narrative is recounted in five different suras. Abraham warmly welcomes angelic messengers with a meal, which they do not eat. After allaying Abraham's concern about this odd behavior, they announce the impending birth of a special son, Isaac, causing both the prophet and his wife to question them. The angels confirm God's purpose of blessing, and then announce that their primary mission is to bring judgment to the people of Lot and to deliver his family (with the exception of his wife). In two suras, the visit is directly followed by the story of the judgment of Lot's people. This Abraham narrative parallels Genesis 18-19 to a degree and is the only story common to both the Bible and Qur'an that the Qur'an recounts more than once (the other common story is the near-offering of Abraham's son). For this reason, it is more amenable for direct comparison than either the first or the third story.[12]

(Story 3) Constructing the Kaaba.[13] We find elements of the third story in four suras. God appoints the Kaaba to be a pilgrimage site at Bekka/Mecca, declaring it to be "a blessed place; a source of guidance for all people" (3:96). "Abraham's station" is to be the place of prayer, and God makes a covenant with Abraham and Ishmael to purify it for pilgrimage rites. It is the duty of all to make the pilgrimage to the House, according to the requirements for venerating God's "sacred things" and "waymarks." The other major feature is Abraham and Ishmael's prayer of dedication as they raise the foundations of the House which is to be devoted to worship. They pray for the land around the Kaaba to be fruitful, and in dedicating the holy place, they pray for themselves and their seed to be kept from idolatry and to keep the "holy rites." Finally, Abraham prays for God to send a Messenger to the people of Mecca and seeks forgiveness for himself, his parents, and the believers on the Day of Judgment.

(Story 4) The offering of Abraham's son.[14] This famous story is found in only one sura and is not clearly located within the received Abraham narrative in terms of either chronology or setting. After Abraham leaves his father and people in Mesopotamia, he prays that God will grant him a "righteous son." God announces the birth of an unnamed "patient son" (presumably Ishmael). This son grows to the age of helping his father in work. Abraham tells his son of a dream in which he sees himself sacrificing his son. The boy states his willingness to obey God, and both are found "surrendered," ready to go through with the sacrifice. At the last moment, God intervenes, affirming that the prophet has passed the test and "ransoms" the boy with a "mighty sacrifice." God rewards Abraham with a posterity who will "bless" him. Isaac's birth is then announced (possibly indicating that the first son was Ishmael), and God pronounces a blessing on Abraham and Isaac and some of their descendants. This story occupies common ground with the Genesis narrative and has frequently been compared with it.[15]

The second and fourth of these stories have significant correlation with the biblical narrative itself as well as with later exegetical material, while the first story of early events in Ur has parallels only with later Jewish exegetical narrative. The third story of events in Mecca has no clear parallel with either.[16]

We will look at each of these stories in their sura contexts in more detail below (see Appendix 5 for my extended analysis).

Qur'anic descriptions of Abraham

In addition to the four narratives summarized above, I have identified eleven discrete descriptions of Abraham:

(1) *Chosen and guided* (2:130; 3:33-34; 6:83-87; 16:121; 19:58; 21:51; 38:45-47). Abraham is chosen in this world and will rank among the righteous in the Hereafter (2:130). He is mentioned first in an extended list of prophets who are chosen and guided (6:83-87). God gave Abraham his righteousness or proper course beforehand, because he "knew him." Abraham, Isaac, and Jacob are among "the elect, the truly good" whom God caused to be devoted to him through their "sincere remembrance of the Final Home" (38:45-47). Abraham is often said to be "guided," a concept closely related to prophethood.

(2) *Tested* (2:124). Abraham was "tested with words" and fulfilled them.[17] Although Abraham's testing is frequently referred to in Jewish writings, the content of his testing differs significantly in Islamic interpretive tradition (see Apendix 5 on 2:124 and 37:105-06). This description coincides with Islamic conviction that human life on earth is primarily a test, including the lives of prophets, who are model humans. Mir says, "The concept of trial is basic to Qur'ānic thought. The very purpose of human life is conceived in terms of trial."[18] The Qur'an puts it this way: "Exalted is He . . . who created death and life to test you and reveal which of you does best" (67:2).

(3) *An example of prayer or intercession* (2:126-129, 260; 9:114; 11:74-76; 14:35-41; 26:83-102; 29:32; 37:100; 60:4). The Qur'an records a number of Abraham's prayers. He prays for his seed, requesting a secure land and fruits. He prays that God will send a Messenger. He intercedes for his father until it is clear that he is an enemy of God, and for Lot's people, at which he is told to cease. He prays that he and his descendants will be kept from idolatry and perform the prayer. He offers praise to God for giving him Ishmael and Isaac in his old age. He seeks forgiveness for himself, his parents, and the believers on the day of resurrection and reckoning when idolaters will be cast into Hell with Iblis (Satan), desiring to be joined with the righteous and inherit the Garden of Bliss (26:84-89).[19]

(4) *One who "submitted/surrendered" to God* (2:131-32; 37:103). Abraham is perhaps the prime example of those who are surrendered or submitted to God. The word *islam* means devoted submission to God alone, and Muslims are "submitters."[20] Thus the Qur'an says, "True Religion, in God's eyes, is *islam*" (3:19). While dedicating the Kaaba with Ishmael, Abraham prays, "O our Sustainer! Make us surrender ourselves unto Thee" (2:128, Asad). Likewise, "When his Sustainer said to him, 'Surrender thyself unto Me!' – he answered, 'I have surrendered myself unto [Thee,] the Sustainer of all the worlds'" (2:131, Asad).[21] So for example, when asked to sacrifice his son, he "surrenders" along with him. All the prophets are examples of those who are surrendered to God (e.g. 2:128; 5:111; 10:72; 12:101).

Submission is the essence of the religion of Islam, as Ahmad expresses: "all notable prophets including Sayyidna Ibrahim (Abraham) . . . were followers of al din or Islam. . . . Without exception they called themselves Muslims."[22]

(5) *Head of "the people of Abraham"* (2:133; 3:67; 4:54; 6:84-86; 9:70; 12:6; 16:120; 21:71-73; 22:43; 37:108-112; 43:26-29; 57:26). The term "people of Abraham" can refer to his father's clan who rejected Abraham's efforts to turn them from idolatry (6:83; 9:70; 22:43). Here I am referring to Abraham's descendants. When Jacob charges his sons to surrender to God, they respond, "We will serve thy God and the God of thy fathers Abraham, Ishmael and Isaac, One God" (2:132-33). God gives the people of Abraham "the Book and the Wisdom, and... a mighty kingdom" (4:54; cf. 2:258), and appoints the Prophecy and the Book to be among their seed (57:26). Various passages refer to blessing being on the house of Abraham who is described as a "nation obedient unto God" (16:120), but at the same time some are doers of good, and some clearly those who "wronged themselves" (37:113). Abraham makes his decision to worship God alone, and his words of confession are bequeathed to his (Arab) posterity (43:28).

(6) *Neither Jew nor Christian* (2:135, 140; 3:67; 42:13-14). In Muhammad's disputes with Jews and Christians it becomes apparent that both groups claim Abrahamic authority for their religion. But God assures him that the creed of Abraham preceded the others and warns them not to doubt or "scatter" (divide) over this (42:13-14). As it is evident that the Torah and Injil were sent after Abraham, he was neither Jew nor Christian (3:65-67). Abraham and all the prophets are affirmed to be Muslims (e.g. 3:67).

(7) *Exemplar of the religion of Abraham* (2:130; 3:83-85, 95; 4:125; 6:161; 12:38; 16:123; 22:78; 42:13). While all the prophets are Muslims, the Qur'an identifies Islam with Abraham in a particular way. We read that no one "but a fool would forsake the religion of Abraham" (2:130).[23] Believers are to follow the one religion or "creed" of Abraham without divisions (2:135; 3:84-85, 95; 16:123; 22:78). There is no fairer religion than his who submits his will to God and who follows this straight path, the right religion, the creed of Abraham (4:125; 6:161-62). Joseph says, "I follow the faith of my forefathers, Abraham, Isaac and Jacob" (12:38). God laid down for Muhammad as "matters of faith" (*din*), that pure creed previously entrusted to Noah, Abraham, Moses, and Jesus (42:13).

(8) *A man of pure faith, a "hanif"* (2:135; 3:67, 95; 4:125; 6:79, 161; 16:120, 123; 19:41). The Arabic term *hanif*, notoriously difficult to translate,[24] is repeatedly applied to Abraham, who refused to join other gods to the one God.[25] Christians as well as pagan Arabs are suspected of committing this great sin (4:171; 5:73). Muhammad is warned: "They say, 'Become Jews or Christians, and you will be rightly guided.' Say [Prophet], 'No, [ours is] the religion of Abraham, the upright [hanif], who did not worship any god besides God'" (2:135). Abraham is the only person unequivocally identified with the term in the Qur'an. Reynolds notes that the term *hanif* is frequently followed by the clarifying phrase "who did not worship any god besides God."

When Abraham embraces the worship of God alone, he announces that he is "a *hanif*, not one of the idolaters" (Q 6.79), a phrase that becomes a refrain in the qur'anic material on Abraham (2.135; 3.67, 95; 6.79, 161; 16.120, 123). Among other things, it seems to be a way of separating Abraham from Judaism and Christianity, as when the Qur'an declares: "Abraham was not a Jew, and not a Christian, but rather *hanif*, a muslim" (Q 3.67a).[26]

Turkish commentator Yazır argues that it means something like "cleansed from *küfür* (impiety) and *şirk* (shirk)," thus explicitly distanced from Jewish and Christian errors.[27] Moving in a different direction, based on studies of the Syriac cognate word *hanpa* (meaning pagan or gentile), Reynolds and Sydney Griffith understand this difficult term to mean something like "gentile monotheist" or "faithful gentile" respectively.[28]

(9) *Friend of God – Khalilullah (4:125)*. To the identification of Abraham as a man of pure faith is added the statement that "God took Abraham for a friend." My survey question regarding why Abraham received this exalted title was often answered in terms of Abraham's submission to God, and I was told on more than one occasion that each of the prophets had a special title, and that *Khalilullah* was Abraham's title.[29] See further comments at 4:125.

(10) *Recipient of revelation as other prophets (2:136; 3:84; 4:163; 19:41; 33:7; 53:36-37; 57:26; 87:19)*. The Qur'an speaks of that which was "sent down on" various prophets, listing in addition to Abraham also Noah, Ishmael, Isaac, Jacob, the Tribes, Moses, Jesus, Job, Jonah, Aaron, Solomon, and David (2:136; 3:84; 4:163). This refers to divine revelation received.[30] The Qur'an also speaks of the scrolls of Abraham[31] and Moses (53:36-37; 87:18-19). God sent messengers with clear signs, including the Book, Balance (justice) and Iron (enforcing power). He specifically sent Noah and Abraham, and established in their line Prophethood and the Book (57:25-26). In addition to this general assertion of Abraham receiving revelation, the Qur'an records some instances where God speaks to Abraham in conversational dialogue in which God speaks, Abraham asks, God answers, etc. (2:124-131, 260).

(11) *Exemplar of faith seeking understanding (2:259-260)*. Abraham wishes to understand how God gives life to the dead. Two examples are given of people seeking for understanding in this way, the second of which is Abraham.

Qur'anic textual coherence

In contrast with the Bible, the Qur'an is not structured around a narrative framework. Its one hundred fourteen *suras* of rhymed prose are arranged largely in order of length, comprised of what seem to many readers to be relatively disconnected oracles. Scholars routinely make note of this basic distinction. For example, Ruthven says, "The most obvious difficulty for those brought up on the chronological sequences of the Bible . . . is the absence of sustained narrative. The subject matter . . . appears to be jumbled and diffused throughout the text."[32] This however does not indicate a lack of purpose, especially in an oral didactic and liturgical context. Indeed, Ruthven argues, "The seemingly chaotic organization of the material ensures that each of the parts in some way represents the whole . . .

any one of the *surahs* will contain, in a more or less condensed form, the message of the whole."[33] It does however make serious comparison with the biblical Abraham narrative a more complicated task.

In the following survey, I consider passages referring to Abraham as whole paragraphs or discourse units within their sura contexts. However, it is a matter of debate among Islamic scholars as to whether suras of the Qur'an can rightly be studied as coherent units.[34] Mir summarizes the majority position:

> With most Muslim exegetes, the basic unit of Qur'an study is one or a few verses taken in isolation from the preceding and following verses. This approach led to the widely-held belief (or the belief may have caused the approach) that the received arrangement of qur'anic verses and surahs is not very significant for exegetical purposes.[35]

Against this common approach Mir argues in agreement with Farahi and Islahi, scholars of the Indian subcontinent, that there is indeed textual coherence or "nazm"[36] in the Qur'an.[37] Barlas also affirms the internal coherence of the Qur'an, stating "the Qur'an asks us to read it as a whole (thus, intratextually)."[38] Farrin has recently mounted an argument for the overall symmetry and coherence of the Qur'an, building on the work of various scholars working in the area of modern textual criticism since the 1980s. He presents evidence that each qur'anic sura forms an organic whole, that suras tend to occur in pairs, and that the sura pairs and certain individual chapters form coherent groups, all generally arranged in concentric "rings." He concludes, "The Qur'an is a text whose form perfectly supports its meaning. . . . Correspondences are numerous and dense, to be sure, but overall they follow a single concentric plan. Parallels and symmetries throughout underscore a greater unity."[39] Whether or not such a qur'anic structure is present, overall *thematic* coherence is evident. In their sura introductions, Maududi and Yusuf Ali presume that each sura deals with an overarching theme addressed in related topics.

My working assumption is that there is general coherence within suras that makes it fruitful to consider the Abraham material in relation to its surrounding verses, particularly its immediate discourse-unit context. My approach to understanding the qur'anic worldview also presumes that to reach a clear understanding of a theme or repeated narrative it is best to consider all the related verses systematically and analyze their interconnectivity before reaching a conclusion. Duderija identifies approaches such as this, which offer a "systematic, thematic, holistic, corroborative, inductive approach to qur'anic interpretation," with methodologies used by "progressive Muslims."[40]

Muhammad and the Abraham Stories in Qur'anic Context

When examined in their sura contexts, the four distinct Abraham stories, recounted in various versions, reveal a deep conceptual connection between Abraham and Muhammad. In the qur'anic presentation, Abraham serves as a particular model and encouragement for Muhammad, and the religion God gives Muhammad is nothing other than the "religion of Abraham." The following summary is based on my sura-by-sura analysis of every Abraham reference in the Qur'an, which may be seen in Appendix 5. Each sura contributes detail and color to the qur'anic portrait of Abraham in Muhammad's likeness.

Story 1—A model for bold proclamation of tawhid

Sura 6:74-87. In a situation where Muhammad is being mocked by idolaters, God reminds him, "Messengers have been mocked before you [Muhammad], and those who mocked them were engulfed by the very punishment they had mocked" (6:10). He gives Muhammad words and arguments with which to confute unbelieving opponents. More than 30 times God commands him to "Say . . ." as he instructs him in this process (e.g. 11, 12, 14, 161, 162, 164). Abraham's dispute with the idolaters of his father's people models this effective argumentation (6:74-87). God shows Abraham the power and the laws of the heavens and the earth, "so that he might be a firm believer" or "true believer [*hanif*]" (6:75-79),[41] and so that he might use the argument of creation to refute his opponents (6:83). God instructs Muhammad to say that God has guided him into the true way, "a straight path, an upright religion, the faith of Abraham" (6:161).

Sura 19:41-50. God tells Muhammad to recount "the story of Abraham," who pleads with his father to cease the worship of inanimate idols, by which he will find himself worshipping Satan. He warns his father of punishment from the Lord if he persists as Satan's companion. This underscores the significant role given to Iblis or Satan in the Qur'an: "We have sent messengers before you [Muhammad] to other communities, but Satan made their foul deeds seem alluring to them" (16:63). The Qur'an frequently warns people, as Abraham warns his father, that they must not follow Satan (e.g. 2:168, 208; 6:142; 12:5; 17:53; 18:50; 35:6). Believers should pay attention to the qur'anic guidance, seeking God's protection: "[Satan's] power is only over those who ally themselves with him and those who, because of him, join partners with God" (16:98-100).

Sura 21:51-75. Abraham's story assured Muhammad of eventual success through divine intervention. All the previous prophets encountered opposition, but these opponents were always defeated in the end (21:41; 6:38; 12:109-110). The dispute between Abraham and his father's idolatrous people (21:51-73) exemplifies both the opposition and the subsequent divine intervention. Abraham challenges his father and people regarding idols and affirms his allegiance to the one God. He breaks their idols and mocks his questioners when brought to trial (21:52-67). Ultimately he is cast into the fire, but is miraculously delivered (21:68-70).[42]

Sura 26. As part of its argument against disbelievers who belittle the Qur'an, sura 26 recounts several stories of earlier prophets, including Abraham's dispute with his idolatrous kinsfolk (26:69-104). These stories are told to encourage Muhammad with the understanding that what is happening to him now is only what has happened in the past to others (26:3-6). Abraham stands as a model messenger, who challenges his people regarding idols (26:70-76), affirms his allegiance to the one God (26:77-82), prays for favor and forgiveness for his people (26:83-89), and warns them of judgment and the day of resurrection (26:90-93). It is difficult to determine where God moves from narrating prophet stories to exhorting Muhammad, but if 26:94-104 are part of Abraham's story, then the announcement of the punishment of those who reject is also included in his warning.

While some elements vary, in every version of this story Abraham calls his idolatrous people to worship the true God. Abraham is a model prophet, fulfilling his duty to warn his hearers, just as Muhammad is to do. Muslim exegetes agree that the central issue in this story is the bold proclamation of monotheism:

> Each commentator emphasizes *tawhid* at different parts of the story, whether it is the various debates that Abraham engages in with his people or the prayers he says before he is thrown into the fire. They all also portray Abraham as a model believer who embodies the teachings of *tawhid* and challenges the foundations of *shirk* in his society. Because of his belief in *tawhid* and his resolute faith in God, Abraham is seen to be miraculously saved by God from the fire as a sign to all believers.[43]

Sura 37:83-100. Three separate Abraham narratives follow a lengthy description of the Day of Judgment and support the general defense of Muhammad's prophethood and the hereafter. "See how those who were warned met their end! Not so the true servants of God" (37:69-74). The prophet stories thus illustrate these "true servants of God" (37:75-148). God says of Abraham, "truly he was one of Our faithful servants" (37:111). The first story concerns his father's people in Mesopotamia who reject his arguments against worshipping idols. When they throw him into the blaze, God "humiliates" them, but nothing is said of punishment. In fact, the only note of punishment for Abraham's people who reject his warnings is eschatological: "Hell will be your home and no one will help you" (29:25). In this Abraham is closer to Muhammad than to other messengers whose stories record the immediate punishment of unbelieving peoples.

In *sura 42*, complete continuity among all the scripture-receiving messengers is strongly affirmed, especially the five major prophets: "In matters of faith, He has laid down for you [people] the same commandment that He gave Noah, which We have revealed to you [Muhammad] and which We enjoined on Abraham and Moses and Jesus" (42:13-15). Religious divisions are all traced to "rivalry." Muhammad is called to reject such selfish rivalry and assert that he believes in "whatever Scripture God has sent down" and mediate between them on the basis of straightforward ethical monotheism. God will reward each one on the basis of their deeds at the Day of Judgment. In light of this affirmation, there is little meaning in discussing divergence in views about the nature or activity of God.

Sura 43:26-28. Some wealthy people in Mecca claimed loyalty to their ancestors' traditions as the reason for rejecting God's messengers (43:22-23). Muhammad is shown particularly through the story of Abraham subverting the idolatrous religion of his ancestors that previous messengers faced the same issue (43:24-28).

Sura 60:4-7 and sura 9:113-114. This sura is devoted to ordering the relationship of the believers with unbelievers, focusing primarily on the 'presenting problem' of believers desiring to marry women who have converted to Islam while their husbands have not. The solution is for these women to disown their former husbands. Abraham is offered as a homiletical illustration of those compelled to break relationship with obstinate unbelievers. He said to his people, "We disown you and what you worship besides God!" (60:4). There was however one exception to this stern position: Abraham did not simply renounce his father as he did the others, but prayed for his forgiveness (cf. 19:47).

In a related issue, God will reward those who fight with Muhammad and punish those who refuse, just as he has in the past (9:111). There is to be no mercy shown to those who resist the prophet by siding with the unbelievers, even if they are relatives. Abraham's story is a model of how believers should act toward Muhammad's opponents. "It is not fitting for the Prophet and the believers to ask forgiveness for the idolaters—even if they are related to them them—after having been shown that they are the inhabitants of the Blaze: Abraham asked forgiveness for his father because he had made a promise to him, but once he realized that his father was an enemy of God, he washed his hands of him" (9:113-14; cf. 60:4).

Story 2—Encouragement from the combined Abraham–Lot "punishment story"

Sura 21:74-75 and sura 29:16-27 While the second Abraham episode does not have such obvious parallels with Muhammad as the first, it is the relationship with Lot's story which provides the connection. Suras 21 and 29 clarify Abraham's special relationship with Lot and link the first story to the second: "We saved him and Lot [and sent them] to the land We blessed for all people. . . . We gave Lot sound judgement and knowledge and saved him from the community who practised obscenities" (21:71-75). Lot believes Abraham's parting warning to his people, affirming, "I will flee to my Lord: He is the Almighty, the All Wise" (29:26). Lot challenges his people and seeks God's help when they challenge him to bring God's punishment down on them if his message is true (29:28-30). The angels who bring this punishment first visit Abraham (29:31-32), and then Lot (29:33-34), informing them of their mission to destroy the town where Lot lived and rescue him and his family. The Abraham story of the angelic visitation serves essentially as the prelude to the main event, which is the punishment of Lot's wicked people, who are destroyed after rejecting the prophetic warning. United in this way to Lot's story, the second Abrahamic episode also relates to Muhammed's situation.

Sura 11:69-83. Muhammad is encouraged with a series of seven punishment-stories[44] about messengers sent to their communities, facing the same type of situation as he faced in Mecca. One of these is the Abrahamic angel visitation story (11:69-76), included despite the fact that it has little in common with this pattern. But Abraham's story is linked to the story of Lot and his people by the messengers' opening words: "Do not fear. We have been sent against the people of Lot" (11:70). When recounted together with Lot's story, Abraham's visitation becomes a punishment story. The stories of these prophets are recounted for a stated purpose: "We have told you the stories of the prophets to make your heart firm and in these accounts truth has come to you [Muhammed], as well as lessons and reminders for the believers" (11:120). The Abraham narrative functions along with the story of the judgment of Lot's people, as a classic prophet story of warning, rejection, punishment.

Sura 15:51-77. Muhammad is to tell God's "servants" of the sure destinies of believers and unbelievers (15:26-50). He is then told, "tell them also of Abraham," following which the second Abraham story is narrated (15:51-77). The story is told in two parts, each introduced by the arrival of the messengers at the respective households of Abraham and Lot (15:52, 61). While the messengers' primary mission is to destroy Lot's people and deliver the prophet, the announcement of a son to the aged prophet Abraham comes first (15:53). This announcement encourages Muhammad to take heart and not despair, for the word of God will be fulfilled, as it was with Abraham.

Sura 51:24-37. The "story of Abraham's honored guests," who bring word of the birth of a son and the impending punishment of the people of Lot, is narrated again in 51:24-37. Abraham initially responds in fear when the angelic messengers do not eat the food he offers them and his wife reacts with incredulity to the good news of "a son who would be gifted with knowledge." The punishment that rained down on Lot's "people lost in sin" left behind the destroyed town as "a sign for those who fear the painful punishment" (51:32-37). The importance of observing such "signs" is underscored in the ensuing punishment stories of Moses and Pharaoh, the peoples of 'Ad and Thamud, and the people of Noah, which are introduced with the words "There is another sign in . . ." (51:38, 41, 43). Muhammad's verbal message is also to be "clear warning" (51:50). The story of angels visiting Abraham serves two purposes in relation to this theme of heeding the signs of God: He is an example of one who believes the messengers of God bringing news that is humanly hard to believe (the birth), and his story is a prelude to the narrative of the punishment of Lot's people, the first of the punishment "signs" recounted here.

Story 3—Origins of Islamic Rites at the Kaaba

This story regarding Abraham has many natural links with Muhammad, since it depicts what may be described as the origin of the Islamic rites centered on the Kaaba, especially the Pilgrimage. In the Qur'an only Muhammad and Abraham (together with Ishmael) are related to Mecca and the founding events that shape and focus much of religious activity at "the spiritual and ritual center of the Islamic world."[45]

Sura 2:124-141. The story of Abraham and Ishmael constructing and dedicating the Kaaba follows a series of reminders and rebukes to those refusing to believe Muhammad, drawing on prophet stories, arranged roughly in biblical order: Creation and Adam (2:30-39), Israel (2:40-86), Moses, and Jesus and their struggles with stubborn, disobedient people (2:87-121), Abraham (2:124-

141). The first reference to Abraham in the Qur'an (2:124) recalls a time when "Abraham's Lord tested him with certain commandments." The idea of Abraham being "tested" is also developed extensively in both Jewish and Muslim exegetical writings.[46] But the Qur'an itself says nothing about the context of this "testing" and the sura continues with the Kaaba construction story, which may be understood as the primary outcome of his obedience and faith in the face of testing (2:125-29). In their prayer of dedication, Abraham and Ishmael ask God to send a Messenger to the people of Mecca (2:127–29), a patent reference to Muhammad. The context of this account is a call to the "children of Israel" (2:122), Jews who are charged with wrongly appropriating Abraham for themselves and in so doing departing from the primal religion of Abraham, which is being restored through Muhammad's prophetic office: "Who but a fool would forsake the religion of Abraham?" (2:130). The qur'anic response to Jewish and Christian claims to Abrahamic heritage is that "Abraham, Ishmael, Isaac, Jacob and the Tribes" were neither Jews nor Christians, but uncompromised submitters to God (2:135-140).

Sura 3:95-97. Like the preceding one, sura 3 deals with issues raised by Muhammad's interaction with Jews and Christians, insisting that "the people who are closest to him are those who truly follow his ways, this Prophet, and [true] believers" (3:68). The only specific event narrated from Abraham's life is the founding of the House of worship, designated as the place of worship for all mankind (3:95-97). Yet there are factions of the People of the Book (understood to be the Jews of Medina) who try to obstruct the believers. Abraham's link to the Kaaba is part of the argument against the Jews, whose role as people of the Book has now passed on to the followers of Muhammad and his book. While temporarily centered on Jerusalem, the true original *qiblah* for all is Mecca, so all believers are to unite in the "religion of Abraham" and refuse all divisions and apostasy (3:95, 200).

Sura 14:35-41. In the middle of sura 14, which warns against rejecting the prophet's message, Muhammad is told to "remember" Abraham praying that God would bless the town of Mecca (14:35).[47] In particular Abraham seeks preservation from idolatry for himself and his offspring, so that they may be thankful and "keep up" the ritual prayers at the House. Uniquely in this sura, he also seeks forgiveness on the Day of Judgment for himself, his parents, and the believers (14:41). Abraham's urgent desire to be kept from idolatry serves as a warning for the idolaters in Muhammad's audience to forsake their idols immediately. Abraham's "offspring" is particularly important in this prayer, which serves as a call for all the descendants of Abraham to recognize the Kaaba as the new or renewed place of prayer. The issue of biblical particularism will be considered more fully below, but it might be noted that the Muslim focus on the Kaaba is no less particular than the Jewish focus on Jerusalem.[48]

Sura 22:26-33. According to sura 22, Muhammad's followers were being forcibly prevented from entering the shrine at Mecca, and this sura gives permission for the Muslims to defend themselves and fight for their faith. The call to forcibly establish this pilgrimage is linked with Abraham: "As for the disbelievers, who bar others from God's path and from the Sacred Mosque ... We shall make them taste a painful punishment. We showed Abraham the site of the House, saying, 'Do not assign partners to Me. Purify My House'" (22:25-26). Just as his own people opposed Muhammad in this task, so also earlier prophets, including Abraham, were opposed by their people. Yet God destroyed the disbelievers: "If they reject you [Prophet], so did the people of Noah before them, and those of 'Ad, Thamud, Abraham, Lot, Midian. Moses too was called a liar. I gave the disbelievers time, but in the end I punished them!" (22:42-45). The final verse of the sura encourages the faithful to defend their religion and relates this religion (Islam) to "the faith of your forefather Abraham. God has called you Muslims" (22:78).

Story 4 – A Supreme Example of Muslim Surrender to God

The story of Abraham sacrificing his son is recounted in the Qur'an only in *sura 37*, which contrasts the horrific fate of unbelievers and the blessed afterlife of "God's true/faithful servants" (47:40, 74, 81, 110, 122, 128, 131, 160, 169). As one of these faithful servants, Abraham shines as an example of obedient submission to God. Although it is generally placed later in his career, in its context the account is linked to the story of Abraham disputing with his people: "They wanted to harm him, but We humiliated them. He said, 'I will go to my Lord: He is sure to guide me. Lord, grant me a righteous son'" (37:98-99). In answer to his prayer, God gives him the good news of a "patient son" (37:100-101). When the unidentified boy is old enough to "work" with his father, Abraham tells him of his dream/vision in which he sees himself sacrificing his son. The son responds, "Father, do as you are commanded and, God willing, you will find me steadfast" (37:102). As in Jewish exegetical narratives, the Qur'an specifically notes that both father and son "submitted to God," marking them as exemplary servants of God. God states that Abraham has "fulfilled the dream" and passed the "test" (37:106), adding that "We ransomed his son with a momentous sacrifice" (37:107). This great sacrifice is generally taken to refer to the animal granted by God to die instead of the boy (as in Gen 22:13). In the Qur'an this story illustrates obedient submission to the will of God. It also illustrates God's testing of mankind, referred to repeatedly in the Qur'an as the life-long process, which exposes the presence or absence of genuine submissive faith.[49]

This story is unique to Abraham and has fewer textual links with Muhammad than the others, but like the third story its traditional centrality in the Kaaba-centered "Eid al-Adha" sacrifice ritual establishes the connection.[50] The annual commemoration of this event is not a sacrifice in the biblical sense, but an act recalling the obedience of Abraham.[51]

Consideration of these four Abraham stories within their sura contexts shows that, in the Qur'an, Abraham and Muhammad are inseparably related. In fact, we may say that the trajectory from Abraham to Muhammad in the Qur'an is as clear as the trajectory from Abraham to Jesus traced by the New Testament. The links are of a different sort—model-pattern rather than promise-fulfillment—but no less definite. Abraham's bold disputation in the cause of Tawhid, his visitation by angels on their way to punish an unbelieving people, his founding of the Meccan Pilgrimage rites, and his exemplary submission all epitomize aspects of the Islamic "religion of Abraham" proclaimed by Muhammad.

QUR'ANIC ABRAHAM MOTIFS

From this picture of Abraham as an exemplary prophet like Muhammad, an ideal Muslim and the restorer of the rituals at the Kaaba we can isolate seven motifs from the qur'anic Abraham material:

(1) Prophet of pure monotheism. In the Qur'an Abraham exemplifies a true prophet of God in many ways, particularly as a prophet of pure monotheism, which may be indicated by the designation *hanif.* He gladly surrenders and devotes himself to the Lord of the universe. He stands for this truth without compromise, even in the face of stiff opposition from his people. He faithfully bears the same message as all of God's prophets, the message of God and the last Day. Various aspects of his experience as a prophet coincide with those of other messengers confronting other people, as part of an identifiable qur'anic prophet pattern.

(2) Observer of the "signs" of creation. Abraham reasons from the created universe to the Creator. He observes the rising and setting of a star, the moon and the sun in succession, eventually concluding that because these set there must be an unchanging creator (6:75-79). Abraham's example in this story becomes an argument for the importance of reason in Islam. No other Islamic prophet so exemplifies this inductive reasoning from the evidence of creation to God, although the concept of all of creation as "signs" to be read is associated with all the prophets and suggests that this is the duty of all people.

(3) Bold polemicist. Abraham bears bold, confrontational, public witness to one Creator and disputes effectively with the idolaters among whom he finds himself. He breaks to pieces his father's idols and mocks his accusers by suggesting that the largest idol has broken the others. He uses his divinely given skill and wisdom to persuade his people with irrefutable proofs so they will forsake their idols and turn to the creator God. When they resist and are not persuaded, Abraham leaves them to their fate.

(4) Vindicated messenger. God, who miraculously confounds the opposition and delivers him from those who try to kill him, vindicates Abraham. The most memorable example is when the people who condemn him for breaking their idols cast Abraham into the fire. The fire does not burn him, as God tells Muhammad: "They planned to harm him, but We made them suffer the greatest loss" (21:70). God vindicates and rewards Abraham, as he does all the prophets.

(5) Ideal Muslim. Abraham exemplifies and sets the standard of a true believer, a true "muslim." He devotes himself to the Lord of the universe alone and holds firmly to this truth of God's unity. He recognizes the primacy of the Hereafter and prays earnestly not to be ashamed on that great Day of Reckoning. His obedience when tested by God stands as an example of Muslim living, since the purpose of life for believers is faithfulness in the face of trials. Abraham

also exemplifies one whom God has "guided" (16:120), which is another way of describing a true believer.

(6) Recipient of divine revelation. In a number of stories Abraham receives messages from God, thus establishing his prophethood. For example, messengers from God (angels) visit him, bringing the surprising good news of a son to be born and a heavy message of judgment on Lot's people. In another example he builds the Kaaba in obedience to a direct word of command (2:125). God also speaks to him after the near offering of his son (37:104-105). He receives written revelation referred to as "the scriptures of Abraham." In this role Abraham serves particularly as a pattern or prototype of Muhammad.

(7) Inaugurator of Meccan rites. Abraham is intimately associated with the key rituals of Islamic worship at Mecca. He and his son Ishmael construct the house of worship, the Kaaba. He prays for the surrounding land to be fruitful, dedicating the place as a shrine for the Hajj (pilgrimage) and its accompanying rites (2:127-29; 14:35-41). Muslims from around the world commemorate and reenact Abraham's attempted offering of his son every year in the Eid al-Adha festival of sacrifice. The formal Muslim prayers or *salat* are also tied to Abraham as they are performed facing toward Mecca and contain prayers patterned after Abraham's. Perhaps this is where the phrase "religion of Abraham" belongs, though it could be linked with his model believer role, a lower-case "muslim," or submitter. While Abraham's submission to God is exemplary in a general sense, his specific role in the Mecca cult is crucial. Just as receiving Muhammad as prophet is basic Muslim identity, so accepting Abraham's role in the Kaaba and the pilgrimage rites entails becoming a "Muslim" in the upper case sense.

THE HOMILETICAL FUNCTION OF QUR'ANIC ABRAHAM STORIES

The Abraham stories and descriptions support the homiletical purposes of the qur'anic discourses, functioning like sermon illustrations. God himself tells Muhammad to recall Abraham as a model for his difficult mission and for those to whom he is sent. Abraham's exemplary relationship to his idolatrous people should guide Muhammad in his prophetic challenges. As with the stories of all the qur'anic prophets, these episodes from Abraham's life provide moral and ethical patterns for response to God's message, underscoring the danger of rejecting the messengers of God.

Yet, while Abraham is a prophet of God, perhaps even the particular model for Muhammad, at a number of points he does not fit the typical "punishment story" pattern typical of the prophets in the Qur'an. It is really only in his dispute with idolaters that qur'anic Abraham stories conform to the common prophet pattern to any significant degree. While Abraham is an ideal qur'anic prophet, the narratives present a more complex picture, a composite one which recalls scenes from Genesis (chapters 18 and 22), Jewish tradition (discovering God from the stars, being cast into the fire) and pre-Islamic Arab tradition (the pilgrimage site at Mecca). All of these descriptions and stories are directed towards a common purpose, however, as homiletical illustrations for the Qur'an's message.

We can see already that the qur'anic reading of Abraham diverges significantly from the NT reading, in which the central Abrahamic themes all relate to the coming of Jesus. Abraham does not serve in the NT as a model for Jesus or any prophet, but as the recipient and believer of divine promises that are fulfilled in Jesus the Messiah for all nations. In the NT Abraham is a model of a believer redeemed through the death and resurrection of Jesus Christ, but not a model of a prophet of monotheism. The Qur'an's *prophet-centered* reading of Abraham thus has little in common with the New Testament's *Christ-centered* reading. Yet before developing this preliminary assessment through theological comparison it will be helpful to consider the way one group of contemporary Muslims use Abraham.

CHAPTER 6 – TURKISH MUSLIM USE OF ABRAHAM

In order to understand how Turkish Muslims appropriate Abraham, I interviewed nine Muslim clerics in Istanbul.[1] We discussed at length who Abraham is to them and how they utilize Abrahamic material in teaching and preaching sermons in their mosques. In their answers, my interviewees repeatedly referred to the qur'anic Abraham stories, recounting parts of them to support and illustrate their insights and their Islamic worldview. They also appealed to para-qur'anic stories to supplement the narratives and reinforce particular points.

My Turkish interviewees represent a traditional, somewhat Turkish flavored, Sunni reading of Abraham. They are not representative of the whole Turkish population, or the full breadth of Islam in Turkey. All are professional imams, trained under the Turkish government's Directorate of Religious Affairs (*Diyanet İşleri Başkanlığı*), which is seen by minority Muslim groups, such as *Alevis*, as biased against their views.[2] Thus these clergymen represent the mainstream, albeit still evolving "state Islam" that is preached in the mosques and taught in the religious classes in Turkey's public educational system.[3] They claim to speak for the Sunni majority of the population, and as state-approved teachers they also help to shape the beliefs of this majority.[4]

Turkey is both the cultural heir of the Islamic Ottoman Empire and a secular republic, now a candidate for membership in the European Union. Despite popular (but diminishing) insistence that Turkey is a secular state, Muslims constitute an estimated 99 percent of the Turkish population, and Sunni Islam is the only religion represented in the government's Directorate of Religious Affairs. As O'Mahony points out, "to the surprise of many, Turkey does not just have a secular face, often highlighted by Western observers, but is also very religious."[5]

My interviews regarding Abraham indicate that despite Turkey's reputation of being among the leaders of "Qur'an-only" approaches (see below), the traditional exegetical narratives of Sunni Islam are being taught consistently throughout the country's mosque and religious education system. This may be seen in the interviewees' extensive use of para-qur'anic Abraham stories of Islamic interpretive tradition. When asked about commentaries used and trusted most in Turkey, the nine-volume interpretation (*meal*) and commentary (*tefsir*) of *Elmalılı Muhammed Hamdi Yazır*[6] was always mentioned first as the most widely accepted and trustworthy work. First published in 1938, this famous Turkish commentary represents a traditional Sunni interpretation, following the Hanafi school of Islamic jurisprudence.[7] My interviewees also found acceptable the newer commentary from the Ministry of Religious Affairs (*Diyanet İşleri Başkanlığı Kur'an Tefsiri*), though it generally met with less enthusiasm. Although Muhammad Asad's *The Message of the Qur'an* is widely known and used in its Turkish translation (*Muhammed Esed Tefsiri*), my interviewees told me that it is criticized as reflecting Asad's Jewish background at points. This was said to be evident in its more metaphorical interpretation of certain verses. Maududi's commentary is considered by them to be good, especially in where issues of logic are at stake. Fazlur Rahman's *Major Themes in the Qur'an*, available in Turkish as *Ana Konularıyla Kur'an*, was seen as representing a modern and Western point of view at many points. Yusuf Ali, widely known in English, seemed known and deemed trustworthy.

HISTORICAL SKETCH OF TURKISH ISLAM

The Turkic peoples of Central Asia first encountered Islam through war with the Arabian caliphates whose armies were advancing eastward beyond Persia in the late seventh and early eighth centuries.[8] In addition to conversion through subjugation to Muslim conquerors and through trade, acceptance of the Islamic faith was facilitated by the Turks' previous acquaintance with other religions and their belief in a supreme creator known as *Tengri* (Tanrı in modern Turkish). Potential common ground was also available with Muslim Sufis who represented primarily a Sunni mysticism and resembled Turkish shamans in some ways.[9] In the following centuries, the Turkish Seljuk dynasty established a Sunni empire that stretched from Persia to Constantinople at the time of the First Crusade in 1095. The Ottomans, who gradually grew in strength in the centuries leading to the capture of Constantinople in 1453, replaced the Seljuks. Although Islam was the religion of the governing Ottoman polity, religious minorities subsisted under Ottoman rule with varying degrees of autonomy. Two streams were dominant in this era. The first was Sunni orthodoxy led by the *ulema*, or scholars of Islam, which emphasized *'ilm'* or knowledge of God through study of the Qur'an and the Hadith and through study of Islamic law *(fiqh)*. The second was Sufi mysticism, which emphasized *ma'rifa* or knowledge of God through personal revelation—sometimes described as "tasting" God.[10]

Under the officially secular Turkish Republic, founded in 1923, religion was not separated from state control, but brought under the firm control of the General Directorate of Religious Affairs. This allowed the state to control the building of mosques, appointing of clergy, and content of teaching within an orthodox Sunni framework. Shankland describes this new order:

> This Republican version of the faith stressed the appropriateness of moral behavior (*ahlak*) in this world, and while it rejected Şeriat, Islamic Law, broadly accepted the legitimacy of the five pillars (acknowledge the one God; pray; perform the pilgrimage; pay alms; and keep the fast). This innovation was, in effect, a puritan secular version of faith, one that stressed the Koran and the need to rid the believer of intermediaries between the self and God.[11]

Under this new structure, non-orthodox and Sufi versions of Islam were increasingly marginalized. With the passing of laws in 1925 banning all *tariqats* and religious fraternities, the Sufi orders were forced underground.[12]

In light of this background, Yavuz asks, is there a form of Islam particular to Turkey or the Turkish people today?[13] Islam is after all a worldwide religion, transcending national characteristics in a universal faith with similar practices found in every part of the world. Yet it seems clear that as Islam spread into diverse ethnic and language groups, whether through the conquest or through unforced conversion, it took on discernible forms differing from region to region. Yavuz claims that the uniformity sometimes presumed of Islam is not a reality on the ground. "I do not think that there is a homogenous religious or civilizational entity termed 'Islam.' Instead I believe that there are at least seven diverse competing and conflicting zones of political Islam. Conversion patterns, colonial legacy, types of nationalism, and political economy all factor into these evolving separate zones."[14] He identifies the following "diverse ethno-cultural" zones: Arab, Persian (Shi'i), Turkish, South Asian (Pakistan, India, Bangladesh, and Afghanistan), Malay-Indonesian, African, and Minority (Diaspora). Regarding the Turkish zone, he agrees with Ocak: "We should accept the fact that there is a specific way of being Muslim which reflects the Turkish understanding and practices in those regions [which] stretch from Central Asia to the Balkans."[15] In addition to traditional Sunni orthodoxy three significant influences on Turkish Islam are Sufism, Secularism, and the so-called "Qur'an-only" movement.

Sufism. It has been argued that some distinctive practices found in Turkish Islam have been influenced by coexistence with Christian communities. Tapper and Tapper point to some unusual features of the Turkish *Mevlüt* (Islamic memorial service) rituals that emphasize young Muhammad's intimate relationship with his mother (parallel to Jesus and Mary) and his intercession for the Islamic community during the night journey (parallel to Jesus' death, intercession, and resurrection).[16] However, if such influences have occurred, it is likely that they have been mediated through Sufism. Studies of characteristics particular to "Turkish Islam" generally point to the great Sufi orders mentioned above, which had a wide influence throughout the Turkish-speaking Muslim world.[17] I quote at length Yavuz's helpful summary of the influence of Sufism on Turkish Islam:

> By absorbing Islam into Turkish culture the Sufi networks created Turkish Islam. . . . The first factor, therefore, that defines the Turkish understanding of Islam and makes it unique is the enduring tradition of Sufism that formed its foundation and has managed to remain a dominant force despite various efforts towards its subjugation or elimination. . . . Turkey's Sufism has adopted *a nonliteral and inclusive reading of religion.* . . . Famous Sufis such as Jallaluddin Rumi, Yunus Emre and Haci Bektaşi Veli would often declare that they were beyond Islam in the belief that traditions rather than doctrine define a religion. *Turkish understanding of Islam is very much punctuated by the tolerance of Rumi, love of Yunus and reasonability of Haci Bektaşi Veli.*[18]

In recent years the influence of these Sufi orders has been felt most strongly through the Nakşibendi-rooted *Nurcu*[19] community from which the leaders of the presently dominant AK Party have emerged, under the influence of prominent cleric Fethullah Gülen.[20] My own encounters with young theology students have led to invitations to meetings of *Nurcu* Muslims gathered to read and discuss the writings of Said Nursi. They particularly emphasize growing to recognize the active sovereignty of God in every aspect of one's life, seeing the Creator in every part of creation.

The *Bektaşi* influence is primarily seen among *Alevis* (Anatolian Sufi-Shia Muslims), who make up approximately 20 to 25 percent of the population of today's Turkey.[21] The Alevis are a sect with origins in Shia Islam, who have been deeply influenced by Sufi traditions. Alevis have different beliefs from Sunnis, such as belief in an esoteric "God-Muhammad-Ali" unity, in the Twelve Imams, and in the ideal or perfect human being (*İnsani Kamil*), who has full control of his or her hands, tongue and loins (*eline diline beline sahip*). They often teach a four-step path to such perfection, beginning with Law (*şeriat*), Path (*tarikat*), Merit or Skill (*marifet*) and Truth (*hakikat*). While emphasizing moral behavior rather than religious laws and internal experience (*tasavvuf*) rather than external forms, Alevis do have traditional worship ceremonies known as "cem" held in worship houses known as "cemevis" instead of mosques.[22] Men and women worship together in music-accompanied services, presided over by hereditary leaders known as "dede" (literally grandfather). While there is something of a revival of traditional Alevi religious identity, Alevis tend to be modernist and secularist, supporting Kemalist rather than Islamist parties.[23]

Overall, despite the unarguable Sufi influence, Turkish Islam, as taught in all mosques and schools under the direction of the powerful Ministry of Religious Affairs, is predominantly orthodox Sunni, Hanafi Islam. Other forms of Islam are marginalized.

Secularism. Despite the overwhelming majority of Muslims in the population,[24] Turkish writers and spokespersons are careful to insist, "Turkey is not an *Islamic state*, but a secular state with an *Islamic* society."[25] This insistence on secularism has been one of the hallmarks of Mustafa Kemal Ataturk's legacy since the establishment of the Turkish Republic on October 29, 1923. Yet despite official secularism, it is a curious reality that the percentage of Muslims in the Turkish population has increased significantly during the past 90 years, to its present 99.8 percent. This is due in part to nation-building approaches followed by the Turkish government and participated in by segments of the population that align themselves with nationalistic "official Islam."[26] Secularism led to an emphasis on the practice of religion as a private affair for many Turks. This is evident in the catechism (İlmihal) used in religious education in Turkish schools, at least up to the year 2000: "The religious education curriculum has consistently included those aspects of Islam that affect the individual; and has excluded almost everything dealing with the social aspects of Islam."[27] At the same time, the attempts of the secular state to control religious activities have come under increasing criticism and opposition since the 1990s. In his analysis of this increasingly failed attempt to constrain religious identity to the private, individualistic realm, Keyman argues that the growing resistance is against state governing of Islamic self-identity: "The processes of sacralisation and de-privatization of religion in Turkey have arisen from the critique of state-centric secularism and its attempt to create a laicist social ethos and national identity by means of control and governmentality directed towards the Islamic self."[28] My assessment, confirmed by a recent survey, is that while these processes are continuing with ever-increasing effect, the worldview of the majority of Turkish Muslims retains many elements of secularism resulting from the century-long privatization of religion.[29]

Qur'an-only movements. Turkish theologians have been in the forefront of a "back to the Qur'an" or "Qur'an-only" movement in recent years. Edip Yüksel is one of these who came to the belief that "the Qur'an is the only legitimate source of religious guidance in Islam."[30] Influential theologian Yaşar Nuri Öztürk, among the best known of these reformers, wrote what many consider to be his most important work on *Qur'anic Islam.*[31] Another aspect of reform being advocated by some Turkish theologians is reevaluation of the hadith collections, including proposals for assessing them not only on the basis of *isnad* (the chain of transmitters of a hadith) but also on the merits of their content. "This would allow sifting of those hadith that contradict modern notions of science, human rights, and women's rights."[32] However, as I will point out below, the narrative traditions of Islamic interpretation are deeply intertwined with the qur'anic stories, at least as used by my Turkish interviewees.

During recent years we have witnessed the rise to power of the immensely successful Justice and Development Party (Turkish: *Adalet ve Kalkınma Partisi, AKP*), which developed from groups with Islamist roots. The movement has generated an increasingly religious Islamic society that looks for inspiration to the golden years of the Ottoman Empire rather than to Atatürk and the Republic.[33] There is renewed interest and pride in Turkish Islamic heritage, including the Sufi orders that had been suppressed to a large degree for the previous 90 years. The increasing conservatism is visible in women's headscarves, which were worn in November 2013 by female parliamentarians for the first time in the history of the Turkish republic. Critics of Turkey's secular program celebrate such changes as the advent of long-denied religious freedom, meaning freedom from the authoritarian oppression of a secular state.[34] At the same time there is burgeoning discourse on the need to reform Islam in light of the present world situation. Large numbers of young Turkish Islamic scholars are studying abroad as part of the effort to develop Turkey as a reformist leader in the Muslim world, able to bridge between east and west. Şentürk notes that the republican state's ideological "elimination of a clerical class (*ulema*) has meant that today reformist discourse is carried out mainly by academics."[35] As noted above, these reformist Muslims scholars are being strongly supported by the present AKP government.

RESEARCH INTERVIEWS

I conducted two sets of qualitative research interviews with nine Turkish Muslim leaders.[36] Eight of these "District Preachers" (İlçe Vaizleri) serve major mosques in Istanbul and preach in smaller mosques on a regular basis; one is a theologian, writer, and teacher of religion in a private high school. They rank above local imams and are responsible to the "mufti" of that district in organizational structure of the Turkish General Directorate of Religious Affairs (GDRA). I visited each interviewee in his own setting, and conducted lengthy (an hour or longer) conversational interviews in Turkish, while drinking the glasses of black tea without which little business is done in Turkey. I described for them my research as a Christian theologian and doctoral candidate concerning the place of Abraham in Turkish Islam. I explained that I would be asking them a series of ten questions about A) their personal impressions regarding Abraham, B) about Abraham in Islam, and C) about interfaith ideas concerning Abraham. The interviewees were asked the following questions during the first interview:

A) Personal impressions regarding Abraham

1. Who is Abraham to you?
2. Why do you think Abraham is called "the friend of God"?
3. Which of the stories from Abraham's life have affected you the most?
4. In your sermons and teaching how have you used Abraham? If as an example, then as an example of what?

B) Abraham in Islam

5. Why is Islam called the "religion of Abraham"?
6. Is Abraham mentioned in public or private worship? If so, when and in what prayers?
7. What can you say about the relationship between Abraham and other prophets?

C) Interfaith concepts of Abraham

8. Are you familiar with efforts at interfaith dialogue under the name of "Abrahamic dialogue" (between Muslims, Jews, and Christians)? If so, how do you feel about them?
9. What do you know about what Christians and Jews believe about Abraham? How would their faith be related to Abraham?
10. Do you know anything about the Abraham narratives in the Torah (Tawrat)? Have you ever read them?

With the permission of the interviewees I recorded each interview and had the audio recording transcribed in Turkish. I then summarized the various answers in a spreadsheet and analyzed them for commonality and priority among answers to the ten questions. I also noted which of the four qur'anic Abraham stories (see chapter 5) were referred to, and how many times, by each interviewee in answering each question and considered their aims in recounting or alluding to the stories. I further broke down these results by the qur'anic and para-qur'anic[37] narrative units used by the interviewees. More than a third of the Abraham stories referred to were in fact para-qur'anic. My goal in these interviews was to learn from them (as well educated Muslims who are representative of those publically shaping the faith of the majority of Turkish people) their convictions about Abraham in Islam with minimal discussion of my Christian understanding. I took particular interest in which Abraham stories and narrative details were referred to in their answers and how they made use of these narratives.

LEARNING ABOUT ABRAHAM FROM TURKISH MUSLIMS

My interviewees regarded Abraham as an ideal prophet whose impressive example has affected them in many ways and whose stories are recounted frequently in their work as preachers and leaders. While admittedly a somewhat subjective exercise, I have tried to compile and distill the primary points of agreement in the summaries below in order to give the blended flavor of their answers. These summaries of the results reflect the frequency with which the answers were given.

Responses to the Survey Questions

Personal impressions

1. To these preachers Abraham, ancestor of Muhammad and "father" of the prophets, is one of the five great prophets (*Ulul'azm Anbiya'*). He is particularly exemplary for his use of reason in seeking God, for his obedient surrender in difficult testing, and for struggling against idolatry in the cause of pure monotheistic faith. He is remembered and imitated in public prayers and during the Mecca rituals as the model and father of the "religion of Abraham."

2. Abraham is likely called "the friend of God" because of his actions, particularly his generous hospitality, his complete surrender and trust in God, and his stalwart defense of monotheism. God gave him a particular title as he did to each of the five great prophets (Noah, Abraham, Moses, Jesus, and Muhammad).

3. From Abraham's life the stories that have affected the interviewees the most are those showing his courage and complete surrender to God, namely his willingness to offer of his son, to be cast into the fire by Nimrod, and to leave Hagar and Ishmael in the desert. Also his logical, meditative reasoning approach in seeking God and persuading others made a deep impact.

4. The interviewees use Abraham as an example of many things, particularly the following: reasoning and logical persuasion, surrender, generosity, and prayer. They also draw upon Abraham in teaching about the prophets, the pilgrimage and circumcision rituals, the foolishness of idolatry, and in explaining the divergence of Judaism and Christianity from the true faith of Abraham.

Abraham in Islam

5. Islam is called the "religion/faith of Abraham" primarily because all the prophets brought the same message and religion, which is Islam, the pure monotheistic faith of the *Hanif.* Muhammad declared himself to be of Abraham's faith and was instructed by God to challenge Jews and Christians who try to claim Abraham for themselves by reminding them that he preceded them and was a "Muslim."

6. Abraham is mentioned regularly in public worship, as his prayer for forgiveness and mercy on the Day of Judgment (26:84-89) is repeated at the end of daily *Salat* prayers, along with entreating for Muhammad and his people the blessing and mercy shown to Abraham. He is also prominent in many other rituals, such as in blessings for meals, in funerals, in Hajj and Sacrifice festival activities, and in personal requests. It was noted that Abraham is of special importance during major festivals and is frequently appealed to in explaining the reason for the rituals associated with them. Chief among these is the pilgrimage to Mecca, where these preachers often lead groups of Turkish pilgrims.

7. In regard to other prophets, Abraham is perceived as one of many equal messengers, but has a special link with those of his time, Lot, Ishmael, Isaac. He heads the line of prophets descended from Isaac who comprise most of those mentioned in the Qur'an. He is also the "father" and model for all the prophets who followed him and shared common prayers and faith with them all, despite the claims of Jews and Christians to primary ownership.

Abraham in relation to interfaith dialogue

The questions concerning Abraham in relation to interfaith dialogue received shorter answers in general. These preachers were not especially interested or experienced in the field of interfaith dialogue. But if such interfaith dialogue is to happen, Abraham was perceived to be a good starting point.

8. The primary value of interfaith "Abrahamic" dialogue is in meeting the need for greater peace and mutual understanding among Muslims, Jews, and Christians. Yet differences must be discussed, with no compromise demanded. Sincere intent is essential, with no imposing of one's faith on others. While common concepts exist and common projects are possible, true Abrahamic faith is pure monotheism (Islam).

9. Regarding what Christians and Jews believe about Abraham, it is common knowledge that Jews and Christians both (wrongly) claim Abraham, and that for them Isaac is emphasized and Ishmael de-emphasized. From the perspective of my interviewees, major difficulties with other perspectives on Abraham are that they do not accept Muhammad and that today's Tawrat and Injil are of doubtful value at best.

10. Regarding their acquaintance with Abraham's place in the Hebrew Scriptures, none of my interviewees claimed good knowledge of the Abraham narratives in the Torah. Some have read them in the past, usually during training years, but don't know them well. Nor do they trust them for use in understanding Abraham, either because of their own lack of expertise or because the books are not trustworthy. The biblical narrative plays no notable role in their thinking about the prophet Abraham.

Use of qur'anic Abraham stories

I tabulated all the references to the four qur'anic stories made by each interviewee for each question. The totals for these references are shown in Figure 6.1

FIGURE 6.1 – TOTAL REFERENCES TO ABRAHAM STORIES

Interviewee No:	1	2	3	4	5	6	7	8	9	
Total for all questions										
Story #1 - Early life (discover God, dispute idolaters)	6	7	5	2	7	2	3	1	0	33
Story #2 - Angel visit (annunciation, Lot story)	2	0	1	0	1	0	1	0	0	5
Story #3 - Mecca (Hagar-Ishmael, build Kaaba)	4	1	1	1	3	2	0	2	1	15
Story #4 - Near offering of son	2	1	1	1	1	2	1	1	0	10
	14	9	8	4	12	6	5	5	1	63

It is immediately evident that by far the most references are to story 1, followed by stories 3 and 4, with only 5 references to story 2. The primary appeal was to the early life of Abraham and to the establishing of the Kaaba in Mecca with his son Ishmael. These may be set out in greater detail by looking at shorter segments of these stories that were referred to. I will group these and attend to the points being made by the interviewees as they refer to particular narratives.

(1) Disputation with idolaters. Several narratives were cited to show Abraham as a prophet with great reasoning and disputing powers. Interviewees made eight references to Abraham discovering God through looking at the stars, moon, and sun, showing him discovering the Creator through deduction (or perhaps using it in clever disputation), and four references to his silencing an arrogant ruler by challenging him to bring the sun from the west. They referred twice to him confronting his father and his people about idolatry, being threatened and proposing to pray for his father, in order to illustrate his courage in facing opposition as well as his merciful character. They made seven references to Abraham breaking the idols of his people, generally to show his fearless opposition to idolatry. Their ten references to the story of Abraham being cast into the fire, which miraculously does not burn him, show him to be a prophet of uncompromising obedience, beyond "reason," committed at any cost. One commented on two traits shown here: "On the one hand when we say 'Abraham' we see a great leader seeking God through reason, on the other a prophet for whom God does rare miracles."[38] Finally the interviewees referred twice to God telling Abraham to divide four birds which would be gathered again as evidence of God's life-giving power, which again show his eagerness to understand his faith.

(2) Abraham hosts angelic visitors. The interviewees referred three times to Abraham hosting angels who announce good news of a child to be born in his old age, showing him again as a beneficiary of miraculous events. They made two references to Abraham's generous hospitality being evident in this story. One reference was made to his being tested by God and passing every test.[39]

(3) Building of the Kaaba. The interviewees referred twelve times to Abraham building the Kaaba with Ishmael, purifying and establishing it as the place of pilgrimage (2:127), and three times to his praying for God's blessing on the town

of Mecca and for God to send a prophet to its people. Abraham is thus shown as central to the interviewees' understanding of the Hajj rituals in Mecca.

(4) Abraham offers his son. Abraham's willingness to offer his son (37:83-113) is cited ten times, by almost all of the interviewees, as an example of his surrender to the will of God and his great faith. Frequently this is seen to contrast with or to complement his reasoning ability.

Para-qur'anic stories

As noted above, this term refers to stories within the genre of traditional Islamic stories that are recognizably related to the those recounted or referred to in the Qur'an, but which are in fact distinct stories or story details. One of the noticeable results of these interviews was the extent to which qur'anic Abraham stories were supplemented by related stories not found in the Qur'an itself. These para-qur'anic stories were generally recounted without being distinguished from the qur'anic stories. This result raises the issue of how to evaluate such stories, which have become part of Islamic tradition.

Among the twenty-three distinct Abraham story units referred to by the interviewees I identified fourteen para-qur'anic stories or story details. Of these, two were not related to specific qur'anic stories. One of these two was a brief listing by one interviewee of the regions to which Abraham's journeys took him: Born in Haran, went to Egypt and back, then to Mesopotamia, and then to Arabia. Another referred briefly to Abraham under pressure from a ruler saying his wife was his sister.[40]

The remaining twelve para-qur'anic stories or details are related to and embellish the four main qur'anic stories. These may be considered under four headings:

(1) Early life. In addition to the qur'anic narrative in which Abraham discovers God through looking at the stars, moon, and sun, my interviewees referred twice to Abraham growing up miraculously fast, in a cave, separate from the idolatrous society.[41] These details amplify the sense of Abraham as a specially chosen prophet and add to the greatness of his reasoning abilities by showing he does so at an early age. Three times they recounted that after breaking the idols Abraham put his axe on the large idol that he had left intact, preparing to mock the idolaters by proposing that this idol had broken the others with the axe.[42] This detail is cited to illustrate his clever disputing ability, confounding his pagan opposition. Three times the ruler silenced by Abraham's clever argument in the Qur'an is identified as Nimrod.[43] These details support the picture of Abraham as a prophet of "reason," who silences his opponents through clever disputation and unanswerable arguments.

(2) Angelic visitors. Three times interviewees tell how Abraham not only hosts the angels who bring good news of a son to be born in his old age, but is in fact extraordinarily hospitable to all who come his way. He is known to never eat without guests. God blesses him so he will be able to host many guests. One recounted a story where God tells Abraham he has fed an ungrateful unbeliever for eighty-five years, so Abraham should do likewise. Another told

a story where Abraham feeds three hundred fire-worshippers, who encounter God through him. These stories embellish the virtues of Abraham, the "friend of God," showing him to be an astonishingly hospitable person and prophet who has been supernaturally endowed with this capacity by God. This portrait is comparable with stories of Islamic saints or "friends of God" who exhibit great love toward God and man.[44]

(3) Abraham and the Kaaba. Two interviewees relate that the Kaaba's location was a holy place in Adam's time, lost in the Noahic flood. Abraham finds or is shown the old foundation, upon which he and Ishmael construct the Kaaba as known today. Six interviewees refer to the story in which Abraham takes Hagar and Ishmael to a desert place unfit for agriculture, where he leaves them. He responds to Hagar's urgent question by affirming that God has told him to do so, at which she is satisfied. This story is frequently joined with the near-sacrifice of his son, as the prime example of Abraham's unswerving submission to the will of God. He obeys without objection even when his "reason" cannot justify the action. One interviewee put it this way:

> Abraham was a very intelligent man of reason, but when the time came God said, 'take your wife Hagar and son Ishmael to a desert place (1000km away) and leave them there.' He takes them, not asking what they will eat and drink there, just trusting God. He does not question, he does not reason, but trusts God. 'If God says so, so be it.' God says 'sacrifice your son,' so he takes his precious one and does so.

For the interviewees, this story is a prime example of Abraham's (and Hagar's) steadfast faith and willing submission to God, on a par with Abraham being willing to offer his son. Firestone considers this story (and others) at length, judging that for a non-qur'anic story to receive acceptance it must "satisfy Islamic interests."[45] In this case the interests are at least partially to fill gaps in the story and clarify the "transfer to Mecca."[46] The story is found in the Hadith (Al-Bukhari 4:583-584). Dirks raises questions about the trustworthiness of the traditional attempt to link Abraham's qur'anic prayer in Mecca (14:37) to this dramatic scene of Abraham committing Hagar and Ishmael to God's care in the desert.[47] However my interviewees considered the story trustworthy and important.

One interviewee recounts that Abraham returned to the location sometime later to find it had become a city, which becomes the location of Islamic pilgrimage ritual. Three interviewees add details of Abraham establishing the pilgrimage rites such as Hagar's running, stoning Satan, etc. These stories, which are recounted more than those in any other group, serve to substantiate the Kaaba and pilgrimage rituals through identifying them with Abraham.

(4) Abraham's offering of his son. According to one interviewee, as Abraham tries to sacrifice his son, the knife miraculously doesn't cut. This detail supports the divine approval of Abraham's complete obedience as he is only kept from slaughtering his son by divine/angelic intervention preventing the knife from cutting.[48] One interviewee mentions that Abraham prayed that he would be praised by future generations, which seems to supplement the divine approval and reward described in Q 37:108-111.

As a further illustration of the way Turkish Muslims appropriate this story, Şentürk says "from the Sufi perspective, morality, like all other issues, revolves around love of God. Humans are obliged to love and respect the rights of creation as a whole—humans, animals, plants—because God created them."[49] Abraham stories are recounted, especially of Abraham sacrificing his son, to illustrate the way of loving God above all, which requires the putting away of all other loves. In explaining this, Yaşar Nuri Öztürk lists four practices which are understood as basic to the Sufi way of life: *zuhd* (Turkish *züht*, meaning ascetic piety), *dhikr* (Turkish *zikir*, meaning remembrance), *tahajjud* (praying at night, especially after midnight), and *seeking to suffer*. He says the Qur'an teaches that "man must suffer in order to find God," citing Q 29:2-3. He then then notes the frequent Sufi appeal to Abraham in this regard, noting para-qur'anic details about Abraham's inner life:

> Why is this suffering deemed necessary? Sufis insist that the answer lies in the fact that drawing near to God necessarily entails the painful process of divorcing oneself from all but God. The Koranic story of Abraham and his son Ishmael is often cited by Sufis as an example of how difficult this divorce can be. Abu Bakr al-Wasiti (d.322/953) makes the following comments about this story: "Allah, in subjecting Abraham to the test of sacrificing his son, intended by this to erase from Abraham's heart the love of all other things. *When Abraham looked into his soul, he saw that his son Ishmael was closest to his heart, and he desired his destruction.*"[50]

The extent to which my interviewees made use of para-qur'anic narrative details shows that these teachers stand in the mainstream of Islamic interpretive tradition, where nearly all of the narratives may be found. In practice they do not conform to the "Qur'an-only" emphasis noted above. The interviewees were generally quite comfortable combining these narratives with the qur'anic ones in their explanations. Yet they showed awareness as trained experts that some of what they were recounting belonged to what one called "qur'anic culture," rather than directly from the Qur'an.

SECOND INTERVIEWS CONFIRMING RESULTS AND DISCUSSING ABRAHAM

Having reached my own tentative conclusions about the first interviews and about worldview harmony and dissonance in the Abraham narratives (see chapter 7), I submitted my ideas to my Turkish interlocutors for review during a second face-to-face discussion.[51] My purpose was to confirm my conclusions and give my partners opportunity to suggest corrections. Clooney's remarks on having comparative theological views critiqued by insiders through dialogue clarify this goal:

> Face to face encounters among concerned religious persons of multiple traditions may then be the necessary forum for airing concerns about comparative theology, as insiders to traditions under discussion are given the opportunity to critique the views of outsiders. . . . Religious insiders can then hear back from scholars about the reasons for their admittedly different approach to the same texts; not every difference is a mistake or ill-intentioned, after all. And so inter-religious dialogue may help and test comparative theology, making it more directly accountable in the court of dialogue.[52]

In these second interviews I began by briefly reviewing the results and analysis of our previous interviews, reminding my interlocutors of the four qur'anic Abraham stories they recounted and alluded to, and explaining how frequently they referred to each one. I then drew attention to the para-qur'anic stories and details that they used while telling the stories, asking for explanation of this phenomenon. Next I outlined the basic qur'anic worldview elements I had identified (*Tawhid, Prophethood, and Afterlife*) and asked for confirmation of this outline, seeking further clarification or correction as appropriate. I then reviewed with each interviewee the seven biblical Abraham motifs synthesized from chapters 4–5 and the seven Islamic Abraham motifs distilled from chapters 6–7 (see below), particularly asking for response to the Islamic motifs. Finally, I drew attention to the way these motifs may be compared under worldview categories and considered some specific examples as time permitted.

My initial hope was to have my Turkish contacts read and respond to the Genesis Abraham narrative in a second interview. This did not prove to be possible other than with three men. The others were not eager to read and discuss the biblical story, either because they did not feel they could give any expert input or because they believed the true Torah given to the prophet Moses is not faithfully preserved in the biblical text as we have it. Consequently, I changed my approach to seeking their evaluation of the preliminary results of my research, and found this to be a more acceptable discussion topic. In what follows I have brought the results of the three interviewees who read the Genesis account into the question framework of the final approach in order to analyze them together.

Second interviews were less structured than the first, in order to allow as much free discussion as possible within a limited time. Our conversations were between one and two hours in length.

Few comments were made on the tabulated results of my first interview, in which I noted that by far the majority of references to Abraham stories were to the idolatry dispute in Story 1, followed by Story 3. Two confirmed this as natural, because according to Islam the faith of Abraham is Tawhid faith. A Hadith scholar interviewee confirmed this conclusion, suggesting that the reason why stories 1, 3 and 4 are primary is that the "Tawhid struggle" is foundational and primary in Abraham, and that surrender is a key theme.

I asked my interlocutors to look at the way in which the four qur'anic Abraham episodes may be fitted into the biblical narrative. One explained that the reason for difficulty in harmonizing the two sets of stories is that the Qur'an does not aim to explain anyone's biography; the only goal is to support the prophetic message. He noted that the main difference between Genesis 18 and the qur'anic account of Abraham's angelic visitors (story 2) was that, in Genesis, God is present in a tangible way. Several noted that it is possible to correlate the narratives regarding Abraham in Mecca with Genesis 21, as Hagar and Isaac are sent into the desert and miraculously water is found. One acknowledged that the stories related to Abraham's early life are not found in Genesis but in Jewish tradition. He took every opportunity to emphasize that Abraham never worshipped idols at any stage of his life, and that Q 6:75-80 is only part of his clever dispute with his people, rather than a record of his own discovery of God from observing creation. He also located the offering of Ishmael before the construction of the Kaaba and before the birth of Isaac. In general, difficulties of timing were not seen to be of great consequence, especially conflicts with the Genesis record. The message is more important that the order of the stories.

All interviewees recognized that non-qur'anic stories were frequently used by Muslims in their use of Abraham and other prophets as examples. They argued that in order not to fall into error, the key was that material not supported by well-attested Hadith should not be used for anything other than adding interest or to illustrate good moral behavior in preaching. Binding issues such as religious worship require a qur'anic source or a sound Hadith. For this reason, folk tales about Abraham should not be used to make judgments about such issues. One was especially insistent on the importance of determining the source, as some of the examples I showed were from non-Hadith sources and therefore deemed not trustworthy. Another made it clear he rarely uses narrative material not found in the Qur'an or Hadith. Nevertheless it remained evident that my interviewees' concepts of Abraham were significantly reinforced by the para-qur'anic material which they used to make their points about him. Hagar's willingness to accept Abraham's leaving her alone with the infant Ishmael in the Meccan desert was frequently cited as an example of exemplary surrender and faithfulness, though neither this story nor Hagar's name is found in the Qur'an.

Muslim Worldview Elements: Tawhid, Prophethood, and Afterlife

One interviewee argued that while these three are correct, the order might be better if Tawhid and Afterlife came first, followed by prophethood. This supported his view that while prophets may be different, Tawhid and "the Day" form the core of Islamic belief. Another noted that these elements represent three of the five pillars of Islam, and another emphasized the importance of understanding Tawhid as implying worship of the one God in addition to the truth of creation. Regarding prophetic guidance, they confirmed my understanding that this may be placed over against the Christian concept of redemption. Every people group is sent a guide (Turkish: hidayetçi). This guidance (Turkish: hidayet), which leads to salvation (Turkish: kurtuluş), may be summarized as "God, Prophet, Islam," and this guided life that Abraham represents is above all belief in God with no element of shirk.

Abrahamic Motifs

Several notes of clarification were made regarding the Abrahamic themes I identified. One interviewee told me I should rephrase my seventh Islamic Abraham motif so that Abraham was not the original "builder" of the Kaaba or "founder" of the worship related to it, but rather the one who "rebuilt" the house and "revived" the proper worship. It existed from long before, likely built by Adam himself. He also noted that Abraham's career could be divided into his time of "reasoning," before receiving revelation as a prophet, and his period of exhibiting "obedience beyond reason," which is consequent on God's giving him difficult or "unreasonable" commands. He stated that the Hajj is not really intended for the cleansing or forgiveness of sin. Regarding revelation given to Abraham, there are "books" not named in the Qur'an. The "religion of Abraham" is not to be taken to mean the religion that Abraham founded, but the divine religion which Abraham also followed. Abraham was never an idolater, so he is not to be understood as discovering the true God at some point in his life. The difficulty with the qur'anic word "khalifa" is to understand whom Adam follows. The sin of incest attributed to Lot in Genesis simply cannot be true; after all, Lot is a prophet. The logic of this position was underscored by one who said that prophets are above all *examples* to be emulated by believers, and the attribution of such blatant sin to a prophet of God would be incompatible with this goal.

Points of Dissonance and Harmony

My interviewees identified several points of harmony between Christian and Muslim worldviews. Some conceded that Muslims also see the line of Isaac as the line of prophets. Both worldviews understand true believers to be "children of Abraham." However, my interlocutors stated points of dissonance more strongly. One made clear several times in the course of this second interview that God does not condescend or come down into his creation, but gives signs (Turkish: *tecelli*). We concluded that this did constitute an area of deep difference in the way Christians and Muslims understand the ways of God. Another said that there is no "seed" or offspring promise in the Qur'an, which has no interest in genealogy, and that the closest thing to this might be the "light" passed on from Adam through all the prophets to Muhammad, an idea found only in the Islamic mystics. He also said one could perhaps speak of a "Tawhid line" or prophetic lineage.

The idea of God "coming" into his creation is antithetical to/incompatible with his deity (Turkish: *Allahlığına ters*). In this regard it is also inappropriate to believe that Abraham saw God or that God appeared to Abraham. God does not appear to human beings, even prophets; he always uses an intermediary (Turkish: *vasıta*), usually an angel. Qur'anic passages which seem to show Abraham discoursing directly with God must be explained otherwise. One interviewee urged me to work on clarifying that the Tawhid faith is evident from all the books, since Abraham is a common prophet in all three monotheistic religions. He stated that the Qur'an is far superior in this regard, in that it declares Tawhid unmistakably, with perfect clarity.

Other Comments

One interlocutor pointed out that my research does not address Abraham's character as much as he would have expected, because for him this is one of the most important aspects of studying Abraham. At the same time he found the less-than-exemplary actions of the patriarchs in the biblical narrative disturbing.

Several areas of common ground between the two perspectives on Abraham were noted by the Turkish clerics. First there was a general comment that the Abraham of Genesis is recognizable as the same Abraham known to Muslims. A specific example was the way in which Abraham is blessed by being given sons. One said that there might be a general parallelism in the two pictures, which he gave as 80 percent in common. He also saw common ground in the concept of Abraham's "seed."

As an example of the difference in attitudes to the prophets, one noted that whereas in the Torah Moses is clearly guilty of killing an Egyptian, in Islamic sources this is always treated as an accident. Another stated that the Torah is generally quite nationalistic in its perspective. His own explanation for the preponderance of known Hebrew prophets found in the Qur'an is that only Jewish and Arab prophets would be familiar to its audience.

Regarding Muslim attitudes toward the Afterlife, one cleric affirmed that there is a sense of fear, uncertainty, and urgency about the Day of Judgment, because one does not know whether one's deeds of religious worship have been acceptable or not. This attitude agrees with the example of Abraham, who prayed urgently for his own acceptance on the great Day. We discussed how Christians tend to look forward to the coming of the Lord with eager anticipation rather than fear and uncertainty because of confidence in the redemption they believe has been accomplished on their behalf.

Summary of Turkish Muslim uses of Abraham

My sample was limited to nine government-approved, formally trained Turkish leaders. It might have yielded somewhat different outcomes if representatives of Alevi or openly Sufi-leaning people were surveyed. Sufism continues to play an explicit role in Turkish Islam through various Sufi orders of which many Turks are members. However, the imprint of Sufism is not particularly evident in the thinking of my Turkish Muslim interlocutors, except in the repeated references to Abraham's exalted character traits, which are also like those found in Sufi hagiography of the Muslim saints or "friends of God."

While the sweeping effects of Turkish secularism discussed above are evidently diminishing in the past decade, nothing was expressed to me that would support extending of religion into the political realm. The goal of dialogue and mutual awareness and tolerance was mentioned at times in this regard. My interlocutors emphasized several times that Abraham is a figure around whom a certain degree of common ground might be found as long as care is taken to avoid imposing different views upon one another. However, it seemed that this potential is located primarily in the Turkish view of Islam as tolerant of other religions, rather than in the principles of secularism enshrined in the Turkish Republic.

Despite limitations, these results highlight the aspects of Abraham's role that are primary for many Turkish Muslims. They reveal that Abraham is very important in the teaching and practice of Turkish Muslims. The importance and identity of Abraham for my interviewees can be summed up under three headings.

(1) Prophet of Tawhid. Firstly, most interviewees see Abraham as a key example of a prophet of God, one of the five most important (ulū al-ʿazm)

prophets. It was frequently mentioned that all the prophets brought the same message, i.e. Islam. Abraham is the model prophet. Numerous references were made to Abraham being a prophet of Tawhid. In particular one interviewee repeatedly emphasized to me that the faith of Abraham was fundamentally the purest monotheism, without any complications of "father and son" being added. The true religion of Abraham is only Islam; both Judaism and Christianity have complicated this pure faith. Baydar argued that "In order to dispel from minds the bigotry of the Judaism which humanizes God and the Christianity which deifies a man, their common ancestor Abraham [is] commended in the Quran."[53] It was repeatedly emphasized to me that only dialogue which maintains the Tawhid focus could ultimately be meaningful. One interviewee put it this way:

> All the [monotheistic] religions are basically one in essence, and all the prophets gave basically the same Tawhid message in essence. Some things changed according to conditions of their times—forms of worship, responsibilities, etc.—and these may be studied. But essentially belief in God, in the afterlife, Tawhid belief . . . these do not change. So in the Qur'an, in the eyes of God, the only religion is Islam.

Abraham, like all prophets, preaches Tawhid. One interviewee summed up his understanding of prophethood for me: "Prophets from Adam onward are all given the task of making the Tawhid creed dominant on the earth. What is the common characteristic of all religions? That all have put forth belief in the one God." Abraham is the prophet of sound philosophical reasoning and of unquestioning obedience to the Creator. Hence he is known in Islamic commentaries as what Baydar calls the "prince of monotheists and the precursor of the philosopher-theologians (kelâmcılar)."[54] He stands at the head of the line of great Islamic prophets of whom Muhammad is the seal.

(2) Model Muslim. Secondly, Abraham is used as a model of a faithful, surrendered monotheist, a true "Muslim." Turkish Muslims for the past 90 years in the officially secular Republic have tended to focus on private faith. For this purpose, Abraham is above all a model Muslim. This is evident in a few areas: He reasons his way to God, and disputes with idolaters using persuasive logic. My interviewees put great emphasis on this model, saying that more thinking is needed among Turkish Muslims. One bemoaned the state of believers today:

> [Abraham's example of reflective thinking] must be explained to people. His reflective thinking (tefekkür) is of top priority today in my opinion, because we have lost it and in losing it we have lost very much. Our society greatly needs such meditation and reflection. It is needed for material and spiritual reasons, for this life and the afterlife. For this reason, I make frequent use of this Abrahamic quality.[55]

Furthermore, Abraham was wholeheartedly surrendered to God, as seen in Story 1 (willing to be cast into the fire), in Story 3 (willing to leave his wife and son in the desert), and in Story 4 (willing to offer his son). He is also referred to as an example of generosity, gentleness, and prayer.

Theology teacher Ahmet Baydar is the author of the most significant modern Turkish work on Abraham I have discovered. I interviewed him twice outside of the specific interviews analyzed in this chapter. Baydar proposes an "Abrahamic reading" for living in today's world. He identifies three keys in to maintaining one's original created disposition (*fitrat*, that inner purity which preserves creationist values) in the face of family and other threatening influences, which are exemplified in Abraham's life: (1) distancing from external coercion, (2) deliverance from internal pressure, and (3) using the mind.[56] By resisting the external pressure from his idolatrous surroundings, by overcoming his natural affection in surrender to God, and by using his intellect to recognize the Creator Abraham stands as the model believer.

(3) Builder of the Kaaba. Thirdly, Abraham is inseparable from the Islamic rituals centered in Mecca, where he rebuilt and dedicated the Kaaba with his son Ishmael. In terms of tying Abraham to Islam, no point is more important than this in the thinking of my Turkish interviewees. Elements of Story 3 are taught, repeated, and enacted in the Hajj rituals. As part of their job as officials serving under the General Directorate of Religion, they have responsibility for arranging trips to Mecca, both for the annual Hajj and for other pilgrimages to the holy site during other seasons. Many of the interviewees highlight their use of Abraham throughout all the journeys to Mecca. One summarized it this way:

> The Hajj contains the essentials of the oneness of the faith. We just returned from the Hajj. While we were there we continually explained what Abraham did, both from the Qur'an and from the Hadith. How he built the Kaaba, how he established the Pilgrimage rituals. Abraham's entire life is central not only for the Hajj but for understanding and proclaiming faith in the one God.

Not only the Hajj but also the daily routines of religious Muslims are deeply affected by Abraham, as his blessing and his prayers are included in their regular worship. Abraham's place in the daily prayers was frequently mentioned in our discussions, including the prayer for Muhammad to be blessed with Abraham's blessing and the plea for mercy modelled upon Abraham's request for forgiveness on the last Day.

CORRELATION OF ABRAHAM MOTIFS FROM THE QUR'AN AND TURKISH ISLAM

The Turkish imams I interviewed seem to be Qur'an-centered Muslims whose worldview, at least insofar as it concerns Abraham, is largely derived from the Qur'an itself. While some details of the stories they related are not from the Qur'an, but reflect Islamic interpretive traditions, there is nevertheless a strong degree of correspondence between the Abraham narratives as they are used homiletically in the qur'anic discourses and their significance in Turkish Islam. We can summarize these correlations according to the seven Abrahamic themes from the Qur'an identified in chapter 5:

(1) Exemplar and prophet of pure monotheism. The Turkish imams identify Abraham first and foremost as a *prophet of Tawhid.* The faith of Abraham is fundamentally pure monotheism, without any added complications. The religion of Abraham is only to be identified with Islam, because both Judaism and Christianity have complicated this pure faith through Judaism's humanizing of God and Christianity's deifying of a man. This corresponds with the qur'anic

narrative showing Abraham devoting himself unreservedly to the Lord of creation, praying earnestly and confessing the one God even in the face of death. Like all the prophets, Abraham faithfully proclaims the message of God and the Last Day.

(2) Exemplar and prophet of reason. Abraham is understood to be the prime exemplar of sound *philosophical reasoning,* the precursor of all true monotheistic philosopher-theologians. By reading the evident "signs" of creation, he discovers and puts his faith in the true creator God.[57] This is supported by a para-qur'anic story of Abraham growing up in a cave and seeing the stars, moon and sun for the first time. For some of my Turkish interviewees versed in reasoning with naturalistic arguments, this quality, so closely associated with Abraham, is at the heart of Islam as a religion of reason.

(3) Bold polemicist for monotheism. Abraham bears witness to the Creator and with clever arguments confounds his opponents. Resisting the external pressure from his idolatrous surroundings, Abraham disputes using persuasive logic. Para-qur'anic details such as putting the axe on the largest idol are cited in support of his cleverness in argument. This Abrahamic characteristic or ability in logical disputation is highly valued and is to be pursued by Muslims today.

(4) Unquestioning obedience vindicated by God. Abraham exemplifies unquestioning obedience to the Creator, as one who was wholeheartedly surrendered to God, as seen in the qur'anic story of his willingness to be cast into the fire and to offer his son, as well as the para-qur'anic story of his willingness to leave his wife and son in the desert. By going beyond reason in such surrender to God, Abraham stands as a model believer whom God sooner or later will vindicate.

(5) Exemplar of perfect "muslim" character. Abraham's exemplary character is cited not only in relation to his faith and obedience but also in relation to his outstanding hospitality and his compassion. Para-qur'anic stories are told regarding his hosting large numbers of guests. In the qur'anic perspective the purpose of life for believers is faithfulness in the face of trials. Abraham exemplifies and sets the standard of a true believer, a "muslim" who is obedient and submissive when confronted with the "tests" given him by God. In addition to being cast into the fire, the greatest of these tests narrated in the Qur'an is the story of the attempted offering of his son.

(6) Recipient of divine revelation. Though little mentioned in answer to my survey questions, discussion confirmed that it is taken for granted that Abraham receives revelation from God. This is seen in qur'anic stories where Abraham is portrayed as conversing with God several times. The Qur'an mentions "the scriptures of Abraham" along with the scriptures of Moses, implying that Abraham received divine revelation as Moses did, though it was unclear to interviewees what this book of Abraham was.[58] Two passages seem to recount direct dialogue between God and Abraham, which interviewees interpreted to mean that angelic mediators were used.

(7) Founder-restorer of the Kaaba. Abraham is the founder of the various Islamic rituals centered in Mecca, where he rebuilt the Kaaba. Para-qur'anic

story details are cited to show examples of his actions, which are commemorated in the Hajj. For Abraham's role in Islam, no other point is more important in the thinking of my Turkish interviewees. Abraham is commemorated not only throughout the Hajj, but also in the daily routines of religious Muslims, as his blessing and his prayers are included in their regular worship. In the Qur'an Abraham and his son Ishmael build (or rebuild) the house of worship—the Kaaba. He prays for the surrounding land to be fruitful, dedicating the place as a center for the Hajj (pilgrimage) and its accompanying rites. Abraham's attempted offering of his son is recalled and celebrated every year in the *Eid al-Adha* festival of sacrifice at the end of the Hajj. Islamic prayers are oriented to this essentially Abrahamic house of worship.

NONOVERLAPPING NARRATIVES

Analysis of these interviews with Turkish clerics shows that they tend to major on the stories concerning the early life of Abraham and the establishing of the Kaaba in Mecca with his son Ishmael. Additionally, their purpose in referring to the story of Abraham offering his son is generally the same as for recounting the para-qur'anic story of his leaving Hagar in Mecca (surrender). This usage, together with the traditional identification of the nearly-offered son as Ishmael, links stories 3 and 4 together. Few references were made to the qur'anic narrative that has the most in common with Genesis, the angelic visit to Abraham. Thus the respective primary narratives (Genesis and Qur'an) and their respective uses (by Christians and Muslims) provide only limited common ground in and of themselves. Nevertheless, as we will see in the following chapter, such nonoverlapping narratives can still be compared by means of the worldview polarities framework. Juxtaposing various parts of these nonoverlapping stories according to the worldview elements that they reflect will facilitate the detailed theological comparison we are pursuing.

CHAPTER 7 – TWO WORLDVIEWS, TWO STORIES, TWO ABRAHAMS?

I understand the significance of Abraham for my faith through my reading of the Genesis narrative and its appropriation in the NT, informed by Christian theological interpretation.[1] My Turkish Muslim interlocutors understand the significance of Abraham for their faith through their reading of the Abraham stories and their application recorded in the Qur'an, informed by their Islamic interpretive tradition. Therefore, careful theological comparison requires that I clarify not only the primary harmony and dissonance of the basic Abraham material, but also the ways in which the story material forms and indicates our different worldviews. What follows is an analysis of the ways some Christians and some Muslims (in this case myself and several Turkish imams) *appeal* to Abraham within our distinct worldviews.

FIGURE 7.1 – WORLDVIEWS COMPARED

	Abraham in Genesis			Abraham in Qur'an
+	Abraham in New Testament		+	Abraham in Islamic tradition
+	my reading		+	Turkish reading
=	Abraham in a Christian worldview		=	Abraham in a Muslim worldview

Juxtaposing the primary narratives (Figure 7.2) shows that only two major story episodes are shared in common between Genesis and the Qur'an. These are the visit by angels (Gen 18; Q story 2) and the near-offering of the son (Gen 22; Q story 4). Of the remaining two qur'anic stories, story 1 clearly belongs to the period when Abraham still lived in Mesopotamia, as its Jewish narrative counterparts make clear. Story 3 has no biblical or para-biblical counterpart and may only with some creative ingenuity be related to the period following Hagar and Ishmael being expelled from Abraham's household into the desert. From the biblical narrative perspective, almost none of the episodes that comprise the Genesis Abraham story are paralleled in the Qur'an. At the same time the Qur'an does presume the existence of, or refer in passing to, some of these episodes, such as Abraham's genealogy, his wives, his move to Palestine, and Israel as the descendants of his grandson Jacob.

FIGURE 7.2 – ABRAHAM NARRATIVES JUXTAPOSED

Genesis Abraham narrative	Qur'anic Abraham narratives
Genealogy from Shem to Terah (11:10-26)	
Genealogy of Abram's clan (11:27-32)	
[Jewish para-biblical stories of Abraham's early life]	1 Abr. confronts his idolatrous people
A. Call and obedience of Abram (12:1-9)	
B. Abram, Sarai, and the king Pharaoh (12:10–13:1)	
C. Abram, Lot, and Sodom (13:2–14:24)	
D. Covenant with Abram (15:1-21)	
E. Birth of Ishmael (16:1-16)	
D'. Covenant renewed with Abraham (17:1-27)	
C'. Abraham, Lot, and Sodom (18:1–19:38)	2 Abr. visited by angels going to Lot
B'. Abraham, Sarah, Abimelech, Isaac born (20:1–21:34)	
[No biblical or significant para-biblical parallels]	3 Abr. and Ishmael build Kaaba
A'. Test and obedience of Abraham (22:1-19)	4 Abr. nearly offers son
Genealogy of Abraham's clan (22:20-24)	
Purchase of burial ground (23:1-20)	
Betrothal of Rebekah (24:1-67)	
Abraham's second marriage and death (25:1-11)	

Because of the small degree of overlap in story episodes, much of the comparison I make below involves arguments from the absence of certain Abrahamic themes in the stories on one side that are emphasized in the stories told on the other side. These absences may represent a significant aspect of the worldview in question. Let me clarify this with four additional comments about what is being compared and what is not.

First, in the Islamic Abraham themes identified above we found Turkish Muslims making significant use of traditional para-qur'anic *embellished narratives* to explain and highlight particular aspects of the qur'anic Abraham. The traditional Islamic interpretation which informs their use of the Qur'an has followed a similar approach to traditional Jewish interpretation of the Torah, insofar as the use of para-biblical *embellished (exegetical) narratives* indicate a particular reading of the primary texts.[2]

Second, as noted above, not only are these approaches similar, but the actual *stories* of the qur'anic and the para-qur'anic Abraham narratives are far closer to those found in Jewish exegetical literature than to those in Genesis. The fact that the NT reading of Abraham marginalizes or explicitly rejects this traditional Jewish material contributes significantly to the dissonance between worldviews that I set out below. To some degree it makes this a study of how the Christian worldview differs not only from the Muslim but also from the Jewish worldview. So, for example, Lowin identifies four common exegetical themes in the *Jewish and Muslim* retelling of Abraham's life: "[1] Abraham's almost-sacrifice of his son, [2] Abraham's relationship with his wife Sarah, [3] Abraham's later visit to Ishmael, and [4] motifs relating to the birth and early life of the forefather."[3] Yet as she notes clearly, only the first of these themes is actually found in Genesis and the Qur'an. The others are only common ground in secondary Jewish and Muslim exegetical writings.[4] A NT-based Christian reading like mine, which does not utilize Jewish exegetical narratives to explain Genesis, only finds explicit common ground with the son-sacrifice story.[5] So while these Jewish and Muslim secondary stories are interesting for other types of comparisons, for the purpose of comparing Abraham in *Christian and Muslim* narrative worldviews it is also necessary to focus on themes which are absent, or nearly so, in one or the other primary texts (i.e. the Genesis and qur'anic Abraham narratives). Determining how the respective dialogue partners, Christian and Muslim in this case, *use* the narratives is what matters most for direct engagement.

Third, the Qur'an does not narrate a complete life of Abraham, but refers to apparently well-known episodes of his life in support of its message. In this it is more like the NT, which cites episodes of the Genesis Abraham narrative to support its messianic message. However, the qur'anic life of Abraham must be reconstructed from its references. In Genesis the *story* is on the surface while the message must be inferred. Unlike the Qur'an, it makes no direct appeal to the reader/listener. In the Qur'an however the *message* is on the surface while the narrative must be inferred or pieced together. The Qur'an does for Muslims what Genesis (recounting the Abraham narrative) and the NT (setting out Abrahamic theology and application in light of Christ) together do for Christians. The Qur'an gives both the authoritative Abraham narratives (in sketch form at least) and also the Abrahamic application for Muslims in light of Muhammad.

ABRAHAM NARRATIVES IN A WORLDVIEW FRAMEWORK

As we begin examining these particular Abraham narratives in relation to worldview, our task is related to, but somewhat different from, considering the biblical metanarrative or the Qur'an as a whole in relation to worldview, as we did in chapter 2. The challenge here is to utilize the worldview framework to achieve useful comparison without "overriding" the actual stories in their own complexity.[6] In this study we have moved from *metanarrative* (Bible and Qur'an) to *worldview* (Christian and Muslim), and now we move from *specific small narratives* (Abraham in Genesis and the Qur'an) to comparative *worldview reading of particular stories* (Abraham in Christian and Muslim worldviews).

Creation-Fall—Tawhid Polarity in Abraham Narratives

God in Creation. The biblical story of God creating the cosmos forms part of the backdrop to the Abraham narrative. The qur'anic Abraham stories likewise presume the reality of God the Creator and Sustainer of all things, whose presence dominates the Qur'an.[7] In Genesis this is a narrative theme: God's rich provision of food in blessing and his withholding of food through famine in cursing runs throughout the narrative (e.g. abundance in Gen 13:2; 24:35; famine in Gen 12:10; 26:1).[8] The Qur'an, too, frequently points to God's provision for his creatures as evidence of his power as Creator (e.g. Qur'an 27:60-64). Abraham surrenders to "Him who created the heavens and the earth" (6:79). He prays for produce to be given to those people of Mecca who believe in God and the Last Day (2:126). Both Abraham narratives articulate this common perspective of God as the source of creation's fruitfulness. But where Genesis emphasizes *God's covenant faithfulness* in blessing Abraham and his offspring (e.g. Gen 24:1; 26:12; 30:30), the Qur'an emphasizes *human responsibility* to recognize God as Creator and be thankful, as Abraham prays, "provide them with produce, so that they may be thankful" (14:37). Despite these differences in emphasis, we see a great deal of common ground here.

We also find areas of dissonance. Genesis narrates nothing about Abraham discovering the Creator or disputing with idolaters. God is certainly known from the preceding primordial narrative as sole Creator and Judge, and Abraham's call directly follows the scattering of the idolatrous nations and he knows God as "the Lord, God Most High, Possessor of heaven and earth" (Gen 14:22) and as "the Judge of all the earth" (18:25). But he is not apparently sent to call idolaters to repentance and faith in the one Creator, but simply selected as the vessel through which God's new people would be called into existence.

By contrast, in the qur'anic narrative Abraham deduces the reality of God through the evidence of creation during his early life. His explicit rejection of idolatry is paradigmatic for the qur'anic worldview. Muhammad is told to respond to the claims of Jews and Christians with the words, "No, [ours is] the religion of Abraham, the upright, who did not worship any god besides God" (2:136; cf. 6:161-63; 16:123). After Abraham discovers the Creator, he says, "My people, I disown all that you worship beside God" (6:78-84; cf. 9:114-116; 60:4). Abraham debates with his father about idolatry, arguing that the idols have no power to do anything, either of benefit or of harm (19:42; cf. 21:52-57, 66-67; 26:74-78; 29:17, 25). This emphasis appears in the Kaaba story (story 3) as well: Abraham prays in Mecca, "Preserve me and my offspring from *idolatry*, Lord" (14:35-38), and God says, "We showed Abraham the site of the House, saying, 'Do not assign partners to Me'" (22:26, 30).

One encyclopedia entry on Abraham in Islam mistakenly asserts that "as in the Bible, [Abraham] is portrayed as an opponent of idolatry."[9] To the contrary, in Genesis, despite frequent interaction between God and Abraham, there is nothing of the discoverer of God who openly rejects idolatry, and nothing of the apologist for monotheism.[10] The Bible of course rejects idolatry,[11] but in contrast with Abraham's portrayal in later Jewish exegesis and in the Qur'an, there is no prophetic anti-idolatry activity in the canonical patriarchal narratives.[12] Abraham neither destroys idols nor defies idolatrous tyrants. He does not even explicitly turn from idols to serve the living God (though this might be deduced from Josh 24:2-3). This is not to say that he makes no public confession of allegiance to the Creator. Building altars and calling on the name of the Lord is certainly an open statement of faith in his God. His communion with Melchizedek, "priest of God Most High" and his open refusal of the pagan king of Sodom are clear evidence of this: "I have lifted my hand to the LORD, God Most High"

(Gen 14:18-23). Nevertheless, this is not part of the canonical Abraham narrative in any significant way, and Muslims who read the Genesis Abraham narrative find this characteristic to be sadly lacking.[13]

There is a second and even more profound divergence, that raises one of the key issues separating Christian and Muslim faith, namely what Cragg called "the distancing or otherwise between the divine and the human."[14] In the biblical Abraham narrative the Lord "appears" to the patriarch in four passages (Gen 12:7; 15:1-21; 17:1-22; 18:1-33). God's immanence in these accounts is not easily reducible to the closeness experienced by the spiritual mystic; rather God comes in a tangible way, appearing, visiting, eating at Abraham's table, and walking with him to the Sodom overlook before departing. Twice in the patriarchal narrative, the identity of God is explicitly stated in terms of his appearing (12:7; 35:1). As Staton points out, these appearances of God are central to the unfolding storyline.[15]

This theme corresponds with the biblical picture of the Lord as the God who "comes to" and "dwells among" his people (Abraham's descendants) in stunningly tangible ways. As Terrien says, "The reality of the presence of God stands at the center of biblical faith."[16] It is the Holy One's presence in the land that makes it "holy ground," especially the temple on the "mount of the LORD" (Gen 22:14; cf. Exod 3:5; 29:42-46; 40:34-38; Lev 26:11-13; Deut 26:1-5; Josh 5:15; 1 Kings 8:10-11). From the NT perspective the God of Abraham has appeared climactically (John 8:56-58), to dwell among his people bodily in Jesus, the new temple.[17]

The qur'anic Abraham narratives contain no such divine appearances. His immanence is understood rather as being evident throughout creation.[18] While God does speak to Abraham, he is primarily the example of reasoned commitment to the Creator whom he "discovers" in the created order. The Qur'an says nothing about God appearing to him. Whereas in Genesis God "appears" along with two angels and visits Abraham and Sarah, in the Qur'an only angels visit them. In Genesis the Lord eats along with the angels, while in the Qur'an even the angels do not partake. While later Jewish texts tend to reshape clear biblical appearances of the Lord such as this,[19] the Qur'an has no element of divine presence in its version of the event.[20] This is very significant for comparative theology, as Lodahl notes:

> The Qur'an takes the exact opposite direction; its solution to anthropomorphism is to keep the story but change the characters (angels pay a visit, not God), and then to edit the story such that God comes out looking very Godly: transcendent, almighty, omniscient—and, in a sense, effectively outside the narrative picture.[21]

Genesis recounts, "Abraham still stood before the LORD" after the two angels departed for Sodom (18:22). At the conclusion of Abraham's intercession for the "righteous" in Sodom, "the LORD went his way, when he had finished speaking to Abraham, and Abraham returned to his place" (18:23-33). On the other hand, the Qur'an simply recounts that Abraham's request was rejected, though it is not altogether clear how this rejection is communicated (11:74-76).

Consequently, these two monotheistic perspectives on the relationship of the Creator God to the creation, though sharing common ground, are differently articulated in their Abraham narratives. In the Christian perspective recognition of the Creator and rejection of false deities are not significant issues for Abraham, whereas they are central to Abraham's place in the Muslim Tawhid perspective. In the Christian reading, God's personal, visible appearances to Abraham cohere with God's condescension to reveal himself in various ways including, ultimately, incarnation. But the Muslim reading articulates a worldview in which the Creator does not "come" in person or reveal himself to Abraham in this way, and where God does not reveal himself but only his will. In fact, the Qur'an explicitly opposes the Christian worldview on this point.[22]

Humankind in Creation. In the biblical Abraham narratives, a perspective on humankind is developed largely through the story of Abraham and his descendants, the people of Israel. Humanity's situation in relation to God is exemplified and in fact embodied in this failing people and in the nations around them. By contrast, the qur'anic perspective does not single out one people as the representative of the rest of mankind in this way. Abraham's people are one among many similar peoples to whom messengers come.

Several points of comparison may be teased out. First, in Genesis to be human is to be in a particular relationship with God, which may be best described as a *covenant* relationship initiated by God the Creator. Blocher describes the Eden covenant with "the twin foci of the *place* and the *bond*."[23] This divine-human relationship, damaged in the fall, is re-established in the Abraham narrative as God initiates just such a relationship, built upon divine promises and confirmed by oath-sworn covenants (Gen 12; 15; 17; 22). God promises a *place* and spells out covenant provisions. The relationship is like a marriage *bond* between a man and a woman, so much so that God considers the unfaithfulness of Abraham's descendants to be spiritual "adultery" (e.g. Hos 1–3).

In the qur'anic narratives, there is no eternal covenant relationship between God and Abraham. A pledge is made to Abraham after he passes the divine testing (2:124), and God extracts a pledge from all the prophets (3:81). But this pledge is taken from the prophets or the community to which they are sent; it is not God's pledge to them.[24] In the Muslim worldview Abraham does not stand in an irrevocable covenant with God as he does in the Christian worldview (Rom 11:28-29).

Second, from the beginning of the Genesis creation narrative, human beings are defined particularly in the *male-female* relationship, in which together they are created in the "image of God" (1:27). They are to be fruitful and multiply and together subdue the earth. In Genesis 2 this monogamous marriage relationship takes priority over even the birth family: "Therefore a man shall leave his father and his mother and hold fast to his wife" (Gen 2:24). Abraham's story significantly begins with a call to leave his father and to a significant degree highlights his relationship with his wife Sarah.[25] Much of the narrative revolves around her barrenness and other threats to the promise of offspring that God will give Abraham through their union.

In the Qur'an, the male-female relationship is also deeply significant. It emphasizes that God created pairs (Q4:1; 39:6; 42:1; 49:13; 30:21). But the idea of leaving kin in light of marriage seems to be rejected in this context: "Beware of severing the ties of kinship" (4:1). The Qur'an says very little about Abraham's wife. The only two references are in versions of Story 2, which describe his unnamed wife's incredulous reaction to the messengers' announcement of a son to be born in her old age (Q11:71; 51:29; cf. Gen 18:9-15). Their relationship has little importance in the Muslim worldview.

Third, Genesis 2 highlights humanity's relationship to the soil of creation from which they were taken. Adam is placed in a particular place to live and work, a fruitful garden prepared by God. Abraham is promised a fruitful *land*, which God will show him, where he builds altars for burnt offerings, and which Deuteronomy describes as cared for by God himself (Deut 11:12). The curse of the fall complicates this relationship, but does not sever the link. Thus issues such as famine in the land, cursing and blessing, barrenness and fruitfulness stand out in the patriarchal narratives.

In the Qur'an the creation of Adam from clay is given as the reason Satan refuses to bow to him (Q7:12; 15:33; 17:61; 38:76). The garden in which he and his mate were placed was not on earth but in Paradise, from which they were sent down to earth in consequence of eating the forbidden fruit (Q2:36; cf. 7:24).[26] The closest equivalent to the Abrahamic land theme in the Qur'an is to be found in Abraham's prayer for Mecca after God told him to purify his house for those who circumambulate it and worship towards it. Abraham prays, "My Lord, make this land secure and *provide with produce* those of its people who believe in God and the Last Day" (2:126). In the Qur'an Abraham is identified particularly with the land around Mecca.

Fourth, in the Abraham stories we see a distinction, noted in chapter 2, between the Christian concept of humanity created in the *image* of God and the Muslim concept of humanity as God's *vicegerent*. While both include the idea of mankind representing God in governing the created world, it seems that image emphasizes the relational aspect of humanity reflecting and beholding the divine glory (1 Cor 11:7; 2 Cor 3:18), with a strong connection between *image and son* (Gen 5:1, 3; Col 1:15).[27] The Muslim concept of vicegerency is primarily concerned with man's role as God's servant. Nasr says, "we are both khalifat Allah and 'abd Allah; we are God's *vicegerents* and also *servants*, that is, we have to submit our will to God."[28] The Abraham narratives show these distinct emphases. For example, Genesis 18 narrates Abraham's strikingly familiar relationship to God, despite his awareness of being "but dust and ashes" in his presence (18:27). The Lord shares table fellowship with him, converses about his plans for the following year (to give him a son through Sarah), and makes him privy to the divine decision regarding Sodom (Gen 18:22; 19:27). Abraham intercedes with God more like a confidant than a servant. In the qur'anic account of Abraham's angelic visitors (story 2), such relational intimacy between God and Abraham is absent. God's word is delivered to him by messengers rather than in person. His fear of these angelic messengers is repeatedly mentioned. When Abraham pleads for Lot's people, he is summarily rejected (11:76). In Genesis 22, the narrative's strong emphasis on Abraham's son reaches its climax. Abraham is to offer his only son Isaac, whom he loves. God commends him with the words, "you have not withheld your son, your only son, from me" (22:12). This may allude to the father-son image that God is restoring; Abraham's descendants are God's "firstborn son" (Exod 4:22-23). In Christian perspective, Abraham participates deeply, if unknowingly, in God's purpose of "bringing many sons to glory," by not sparing his beloved son Jesus (Heb 2:10; 12:23; cf. Rom 8:29). On the other hand, the qur'anic story highlights the submission of Abraham and his son: "When they had both submitted to God." (37:103) The narrative's conclusion highlights the servant aspect of the meaning of being human: "truly he was one of Our faithful servants (37:111).

Fifth, Abraham is presented in the Bible as an example of genuine faith seen in trusting God's promise and obedience to his commands, but not as a model human being. However, in the Qur'an Abraham's role as a model human being stands out: "You have a good example in Abraham and his companions" (60:4-6). The Muslim perspective on mankind and the meaning of human life is articulated in Abraham's story in three ways: (1) In the Muslim narratives Abraham was tested in many ways and succeeded perfectly in every test, thus fulfilling the purpose of his creation. As such he is a model human being.[29] (2) In the Muslim narrative perspective Abraham surrenders himself to God from the first episode of his life, and lives every stage of his life in obedient submission to God's will. (3) For Turkish Muslims, Abraham is the prime example of a rational person who considers the created order and through reason reaches the conviction that there is a Creator. People are responsible to discern the Creator through reason and to submit to him in gratitude. This "Abrahamic reading" of the signs of creation is essential to the human situation.[30] The first two of these three Islamic themes may be found in the biblical picture as well; Abraham is tested by God, though only once is it called a test (Gen 22:1), and he does submit to the will of God obediently. However, the third theme is not found in the biblical narrative, as I have pointed out above. Abraham is not an example of such reasoning in Genesis or the NT. Rather he exemplifies believing God's saving promises.

Evil in creation. If on the one hand, as we saw in the preceding section, the Genesis Abraham narrative reflects many of the original purposes of God for mankind, on the other hand it shows many of the symptoms of the fall, even in the patriarch's own life. The covenant with Abraham is established in the midst of opposition and paganism. Abraham is not in a garden, but in a land full of pagan kings where wells must be dug for water. He is surrounded by sin and violence, with neighbors described as "great sinners against the LORD" (Gen 13:13). Kings wage war and carry off innocent people, including Lot (Gen 14). In this matter the Qur'an's perspective is not entirely different, as Abraham lives among stubborn idolaters.

The main dissonance comes in the Bible's mixed portrayal of Abraham himself, who is considered by Muslims to be a sinless prophet. In Genesis Abraham's weaknesses (lying about his wife) and his "fall" in taking Sarah's maid Hagar (see below) are part of the larger narrative of the fall and failure of even the chosen, believing line.[31] The Hebrew prophets grieve their own sinfulness. David's great psalms of shamed confession are the classic expression of this deep penitence (Pss 32; 51; 139). Isaiah cries out in the presence of the Holy One, "Woe is me! For I am lost; for I am a man of unclean lips" (Isa 6:5). In this worldview the only hope is "the LORD, who *redeemed* Abraham" (Isa 29:22). The NT shows Abraham to be as much in need of God's gift of righteousness as adulterous David or any human—for all have sinned. The "redeemed" come like Peter, who fell down at Jesus' knees, saying, "Depart from me, for I am a sinful man, O Lord!" (Luke 5:8; cf. 1 Tim 1:15). The promise of "blessing" presumes their previously "cursed" and alienated condition, which the NT describes in Rom 1.

The Qur'an, however, presents Abraham as a model of perfect righteousness, a paragon of every virtue: "Abraham was truly an example: devoutly obedient to God and true in faith. He was not an idolater" (16:120; cf. 53:37). The qur'anic Abraham's virtue is primarily identified as his purity of faith, with not being an idolater.[32] He is "the upright, who did not worship any god besides God" (2:135). Abraham's perfection in this area is of first importance in the qur'anic worldview. The main sense of evil in the narrative is stubborn idolatry in Abraham's kinsfolk who refuse to listen to his message. The unforgivable sin is *shirk* or polytheistic association of other powers with God. Evil situations, such as the persecution Abraham encounters, are within the will of God as part of the testing given to each person.

I argued in chapter 3 that the story of Ishmael's birth in Genesis 16 is narrated as a second "fall," with serious consequences for the overall story, introducing conflict between his wives and between his sons and their offspring. Genesis takes pains to narrate the subsequent divinely sanctioned exclusion of Ishmael (as well his other sons, and Isaac's firstborn, Esau) from this covenant purpose. However, Muslims see no such problem in Abraham's taking Hagar as a second wife and view Ishmael as chosen by God as a prophet. This "fall" episode is therefore a significant issue for dialogue with Muslims. It shows an area of worldview dissonance not easily harmonized.[33] The Qur'an's treatment of Abraham does not allow anything that would tend to denigrate him. My Turkish interlocutors repeatedly identified this as a deep problem with the biblical story. How, they ask, can prophets of God be guilty of serious misbehavior that undermines their *essential task as role models*? The starkness of this disagreement about what is wrong with humanity correlates directly with the solution proposed in the next polarity: For sinful humanity, redemption by God himself is necessary; for forgetful people, guidance from exemplary prophets will be enough.

Redemption—Prophethood Polarity

The issues seen in the second polarity, Redemption—Prophethood, are related to the worldview question, "What is God doing in relation to the human situation?" and the question, "Who are the people of Abraham, Christians or Muslims?" Abraham-related feasts shed light on the two perspectives.

The Bible narrates a chain of one-of-a-kind, divine *redemptive* interventions, beginning with Abraham, which continues through the narrative of Israel's history. In the NT, God intervenes once again to redeem a people for his name and to reconcile the world to himself by the offering of his Son, a story to be announced to all nations as the gospel of God. The central OT and NT saving acts of God are recalled respectively in the *Passover* feast, where the Exodus is recounted,[34] and in the *Lord's Supper*, where Christians retell the story of Jesus' death and resurrection. The promises and trajectory of the Abraham narrative are fulfilled and consummated by Jesus the Messiah.

The Qur'an portrays prophets sent to peoples throughout history, with the *guidance* needed for mankind to live according to God's will. Abraham stands in a line of great prophets of pure monotheism. The Qur'an, which is disclosed to the final prophet, describes itself as "guidance for mankind" (2:185). Muhammad is entrusted with the final word for mankind, establishing the great *Ummah* or faithful people of Islam. At the feast of *Eid al-Adha*, the sacrifice festival celebrated at the end of the *Hajj*, Abraham-related rites commemorate Hagar's desperate search for water and the divine guidance, the near-sacrifice of his son, and Abraham's construction of the Kaaba with Ishmael. The key link is between Abraham and Muhammad, whose story is also the story of Mecca and the Kaaba.[35]

Abraham stands in a particular kind of relationship to very different culminating stories (of Jesus and Muhammad respectively). Abraham's story in the Bible is the beginning of a single narrative of *redemption* continuing through Jesus, who as the Messiah brings the story to its culmination. Abraham's story in the Qur'an is the epitome of a pattern of *prophethood* in which Muhammad's story is the final, permanent stage.

(1) Recipient of promise or Prophet? The biblical God reveals himself by personally entering the story of redemption. *God comes to redeem*, and uses prophets to explain what he is doing and how his people are to respond. His "signs" in the redemption narrative are the signs of divinely initiated covenants, and Abraham's primary role is as the recipient of God's covenant promises, the "promisee," to whom God reveals himself in remarkable ways. In the Qur'an *God sends messengers who bring guidance* and call their hearers to submit to the Creator, and to heed the signs of God's creation and of judgment on prophet-rejecting peoples (e.g. Qur'an 22:45-51). Abraham's primary role is as a model prophet of God, who discerns God from the signs of nature, submits to God, and contends for him against idolatry. We can compare two understandings of how and what God communicated to Abraham, what God does through Abraham, and what God's other prophets are in relation to Abraham.

Throughout Genesis 12–50 the patriarchs receive divine *revelation*,[36] and are therefore called "prophets" (20:7; cf. Ps. 105:15). God's visible presence marked major turning points as he blessed, renamed, or sent them (12:7; 17:1; 18:1; 26:2-5, 24; 35:1, 7, 9). God drew near to reveal not just his will, but to reveal himself to this clan in a comprehensible way, allowing them to know Him. He becomes *their* God in a particular way, not just the God of all creation and all nations.

The Islamic concept of revelation is sometimes developed on the basis of Qur'an 42:51, "It is not granted to any mortal that God should speak to him except *through revelation* or *from behind a veil*, or by *sending a messenger* to reveal by His command what He will." Three modes of revelation may be suggested in this verse. First, through unmediated inspiration of an idea in the heart or through a vision. Second, from behind a veil, which evidently refers to God speaking without being seen by the hearer, as perhaps when God speaks to Moses from the bush (Q 28:30; 7:143-44). Third, by sending an angelic messenger, which is the surest and clearest mode of revelation, through which the Qur'an was revealed to Muhammad. Saeed cites the medieval Muslim scholar al-Zamakhshari as saying that Abraham received the command to offer his son through the first mode.[37] According to Rubin, in the Qur'an "revelation does not come down directly to the prophets. The intermediate agents are the angels. God sends them down with the revelations."[38] However, the Qur'an records instances where God speaks to Abraham in conversational dialogue not unlike that found in Genesis:

> When Abraham's Lord tested him with certain commandments, which he fulfilled,
> *He said,* 'I will make you a leader of people.'
> *Abraham asked,* 'And will You make leaders from my descendants too?'
> *God answered,* 'My pledge does not hold for those who do evil'. . . .
> *His Lord said to him,* 'Devote yourself to Me.'
> *Abraham replied,* 'I devote myself to the Lord of the Universe,' (2:124-131)

> And when *Abraham said,* 'My Lord, show me how You give life to the dead,'
> *He said,* 'Do you not believe, then?'
> 'Yes,' *said Abraham,* 'but just to put my heart at rest.'
> *So God said,* 'Take four birds and train them to come back to you. . . .' (2:260)

These passages seem to recount direct dialogue between God and Abraham, which goes beyond the "inner illumination" (Asad) described first in 42:51. They do not indicate any angel mediating God's speech to Abraham, though one of my interlocutors insisted it must be through an angel.[39] Further study on God's communication with Abraham in the Qur'an would be helpful. In the Qur'an God tells Muhammad, communicating in first-person speech, "God spoke to some messengers" (2:253) and conversed with the prophets Moses (7:155-56) and Jesus (3:55).

However, it is not so much the *manner* of God's communication with Abraham that differs, but the *content* of the communication. In Genesis God's primary word to Abraham is *promise*, beginning with his first words: "I will bless you" (Gen 12:1-3). God takes extra steps to confirm the unchangeableness of his purpose to bless Abraham and through him all nations, including making covenants (Gen 15, 17) and swearing an oath (Gen 22; cf. Heb 6:13-17).[40] In the NT Abraham is explicitly described as the one "who had the promises" (Heb 7:6; cf.11:17).

Al-Faruqi rejects the biblical concept of covenantal promise, which is central to the Abraham narrative, as fundamentally incompatible with the Muslim worldview.

> The covenant is a perfectly ethical notion if only all it purports to say is the truth that if man obeys God and does the good, he would be blessed. . . . Although there is plenty of talk of "the Covenant," yet the Hebrew Scripture covenant is nothing of the sort. It is, more properly, a promise, a one-directional favor-proffering by God upon "His people." This transformation of the covenant into "the Promise" is the other side of the racialization of election.[41]

Al-Faruqi's reading of the Qur'an leads him to define the covenant as "a purely ethical contract, unequivocally binding upon man and God," citing Q 2:40: "O children of Israel . . . keep your pledge to Me, and I will mine to you." He says that Islam has "recaptured the pure Semitic vision" of covenant in which every person "gets exactly what he deserves."[42] This raise the question of the basis of Abraham's election by God, for the Qur'an says clearly, "We have *chosen* [Abraham] in this world and he will rank among the righteous in the Hereafter" (2:130; cf. 16:121). The common Muslim understanding is that Abraham's exemplary early life (story 1) is understood to be the basis for his election or at least for its continuance. It is not taken as being "uncaused" or "undeserved." His testing is the ground of his being made a leader of people (2:124).[43]

It is instructive to compare God swearing by himself in the Bible (e.g. Gen 22:16), with his swearing by elements of creation in the Qur'an (e.g. on the sky and the stars in Q 86:1; 53:1; 92:1-3), to emphasize the veracity of his statements. Scholars discuss whether such oaths of Allah in the Qur'an play a literary or a theological role.[44] But in any case, God's oaths in the Qur'an do not have the same binding effect in relation to divine promises as in the Bible, where God swears by himself to bring about a certain unchangeable purpose, beginning with Abraham (cf. Ps 110:4; Isa 45:23; Heb 6:13).

Another aspect of the content of divine revelation is *what God reveals about himself.* The identity of Abraham's God is revealed by the particulars of a particular narrative; it is what might be called a "narrative identity," as Ginzberg describes:

> God is not just a general concept, but . . . has a history . . . God is talked about in terms of appearing, meeting people, speaking to them and acting in their lives. . . . YWHW, by participating in the lives of His people, attaches His identity to them. Just like a married couple, the participants become one and share the same history.[45]

The strong particularity in the biblical Abraham narrative goes beyond the generalities of God as Creator and universal Sovereign and is largely incompatible with the Muslim worldview. At the same time, the Qur'an is full of statements about God and his attributes that are compatible with Christian understanding.

Many of these appear in the Abraham narrative passages. Abraham and Ishmael pray, "You are the All Hearing, the All Knowing.... You are the Ever Relenting, the Most Merciful" (2:127-129; cf. 19:44-45). The angels reassure Abraham, "He is the Wise, the All Knowing" (51:30). Abraham prays: "Forgive us, Lord, for You are the Almighty" (60:5-7).

Yet despite common ground in titles used of God, there remains a significant distance between Christian and Muslim understandings of God's self-disclosed identity. At the heart of this dissonance is *whether God can be known or not*. Shehadi demonstrates from Ghazali's writings that ultimately God's unknowability "follows logically from the utter difference of God's nature."[46] But that God reveals not only his will but also *himself* is a central reality of the biblical narrative. God is deeply and personally involved in the action, revealing who he is by what he does and says. Oden explains, "Although God is generally knowable throughout all nature and history, God has become specially known through a particular history, the history of a people set aside, a holy place, and a salvation history."[47]

When we ask what God does through Abraham, we encounter a difference in emphasis between *redemption* and *guidance*. In his letter to the Romans Paul shows Abraham's place in the redemption narrative. Abraham, whom God *redeemed* (Isa 29:22), stands at the head of the chosen line through which God brings the redeemer into the world (Rom 1:3; 9:5; 11:28-29), and is also a prime example of one whom God redeems. All humanity is "under sin," a condition which began with Adam's one act of disobedience (1:18–3:20; cf. 5:12-21). God provides righteousness for all who believe, through Jesus Christ's death and resurrection (3:21-31). Abraham exemplifies all whom God redeems and reckons righteous in this way. God had passed over Abraham's and David's sins, but now it has been revealed that the just basis for this non-execution of divine justice was the one propitiatory offering and righteous act of Jesus on the cross (3:25-26; 5:18-19). Abraham, standing in the OT narrative between Gentiles who are without God and Jews who fail to keep God's law, typifies both groups as one saved by faith in God's promise (Rom 4).

In the Muslim worldview what God does through Abraham is send a warning about idolatry and *guidance* about the right way of faith and submission. While this "way" is common to all the prophets, it is identified particularly as the "religion" or "creed" of Abraham (2:130; cf. 3:83-85, 95; 12:38; 16:123; 22:78; 42:13). There are no wiser people than those who submit their wills to God and follow this straight or rightly guided path, the creed of Abraham (4:125; 6:161-62).

We can compare redemption and guidance through the concepts of "signs" relating to Abraham. In Genesis the main "signs" are those given in connection with God's *covenants*: the rainbow to Noah (9:12-13, 17) and circumcision to Abraham (17:11). God tells Abraham what he will do for him, and gives him the covenant of circumcision as "*a sign of the covenant*" (Gen 17:7, 11; cf. Rom 4:11), to remind the descendants of what he has promised to do for them.[48] These signs are not so much evidence of God's existence as confirmation of his one-off, covenantal acts.

Afzaal sums up the concept of "signs" in the Qur'an: "The word [*ayah*] appears in the Qur'an as referring to miracles of prophets, to the beings and phenomena of nature, to the realities found in the human soul, to major historical events, and to the verses of the Qur'an itself."[49] Turkish Islam tends to emphasize the "ordinary" signs in nature. For example, Yazıcıoğlu says these miracle stories invite the reader of the Qur'an to rethink the ordinary course of nature.

> Abraham's miraculous survival in fire by the divine command (Q. 21:69) is meant to suggest that when the fire does burn at other times, it does so because of God's command, not because of its "blind" nature and on its own ... [this is] God acting through natural causes, or natural causes acting in God's name.[50]

The Qur'an uses signs in relation to Abraham to warn of judgment. In the middle of the account of Abraham warning his people to turn from idolatry, God's own threat is interposed: "those who disbelieve in God's *signs* and the encounter with Him . . . there awaits them a painful chastisement" (29:23, Arberry). The visiting angels tell Abraham about Lot's people, "We left the town to be a *sign* for those who fear the painful punishment" (51:36-37).[51] Listing Abraham among others, God says, "We sent Our messengers with clear signs" (57:25). These are divine judgments accompanying prophets. In the Qur'an the signs of God's existence and power are seen throughout creation and throughout history.

A related comparison is the *star motif* in the respective Abraham stories. In Genesis God takes Abraham outside, and tells him to number the stars, promising, "So shall your offspring be" (Gen 15:5). The innumerable stars signify the innumerable offspring God promises to give the childless man married to an aged, barren woman. In the Qur'an, however, Abraham observes a star and says, "This is my Lord," but when it sets, he rejects such "things that set." After repeating this with the moon and the sun he says, "I have turned my face as a true believer towards Him who created the heavens and the earth" (6:75-79). The stars signify the contrast between the created order and the infinite Creator. They signify the truth of monotheism and the need to recognize creation's "signs" of the Creator.[52]

Thus in the Christian worldview Abraham stands as a recipient and channel of the redemptive acts of God and in the Muslim worldview as a model prophet bringing the guidance of God though which people learn to observe the "religion of Abraham." This does not mean that there is no ethical imperative or divine guidance for righteous living in the biblical Abraham narrative. Abraham is expected to guide his offspring into obedient living in the "way of the Lord" as God's soliloquy shows: "I have chosen him, that he may command his children and his household after him *to keep the way of the LORD by doing righteousness and justice, so that* the LORD may bring to Abraham what he has promised him" (Gen 18:17-19). However, it is clear that in the overall biblical picture this ethical training that Abraham will carry out serves the "redemptive" purpose of God to be fulfilled for all nations. As Wright puts it, "ethics stands as the mid-term between election and mission, as the purpose of the former and the basis for the latter."[53] The overall Abraham narrative has important ethical implications from the Christian perspective. Abraham is presented in the NT as the father of the faithful, and the example of his obedient faith is normative for Christians.[54] The biblical worldview entails a deep commitment to developing godly character and ethical behavior. Nevertheless, Abraham's character as reflected in Genesis proves insufficiently exemplary from a moral-ethical standpoint to satisfy the standard of near-perfection expected of a prophet of Islam.

Differing conceptions of prophecy in relation to Abraham offer a final point of comparison. The concept of prophecy is important to both the Christian and Muslim understandings of God's approach to mankind. In both the Bible and the Qur'an God communicates to Abraham as to other prophets. Yet Abraham stands in a deeply different relationship to prophecy or prophethood in the two worldviews.

In the biblical picture one of the great privileges of Abraham's descendants was that they "were entrusted with the oracles of God" (Rom 3:2). Prophecy marked Israel. The biblical prophets were for the most part not sent to idol-worshipping peoples, but to the covenant people of Abraham, who had become idolatrous, to turn them back to God.[55] Abraham himself does not fit the mold of a biblical prophet. He precedes the Law, and the Law precedes the prophets. The prophets' message calls the people of Israel to keep the Sinai covenant that was made with them as Abraham's descendants. Isaiah says to Israel, "Look to Abraham your father and to Sarah who bore you" (Isa 51:1-2). This means little without Abraham's position at the "root" of the "olive tree" (Rom 11:28-29). Abraham has a very different role than the prophets of Israel.[56] In the Bible many prophets are sent to one people, Israel, and Abraham is not a prophet in this sense.

In the Muslim worldview however, each prophet is sent to a different people with the same message. The qur'anic Abraham was a prophet in the mold of other prophets, or rather all the prophets were in the mold of Abraham. It is arguable that Abraham is the most fundamental pattern for Muhammad, despite Muhammad's many similarities to Moses. In the Qur'an Allah specifically calls Muhammad to conform to the way of Abraham (16:123; 2:136; 4:125). Using Sura 54, *The Moon*, as an example, Stewart shows how the qur'anic references to prophets follow a predictable form:

1.   God selects a prophet (implied);
2.   The prophet addresses his people (implied;)
3.   The prophet warns his people of God's wrath;
4.   They reject the warnings;
5.   God annihilates the rejecters, saving only prophet and believers.[57]

In the qur'anic narrative of his disputation with idolaters (story 1), Abraham fits this pattern fairly closely.[58] He challenges and warns his people about their idols in every version of the story.[59] His father and his people reject his warning, and when he goes on to destroy their idols, he is condemned and cast into the fire. Yet he is miraculously delivered.[60] At this point he warns them and leaves. But there is no record of the unrepentant people being destroyed.[61]

The qur'anic account of Abraham's angelic visitors (story 2) fits the pattern only because the angel visitation is recounted together with the destruction of "the people of Lot." Neither does the other main element of the story, Abraham receiving "good news" of a son, fit this pattern. In fact Abraham is almost the only prophet in the Qur'an whose offspring is announced by angels.[62] This reference to his offspring is part of the Qur'an's occasional acknowledgement of Israel's special place, and represents some common ground with the biblical narrative. Nevertheless, the Lot narrative, which follows the birth announcement, seems to be the main reason for this story's importance as a qur'anic prophet narrative.

The narrative of Abraham's restoration of the Kaaba (story 3) does not fit the punishment story pattern either. There no particular warning of a people, nor a narrative of punishment, except as Abraham's prayer of dedication, is used in conjunction with warnings to those in Muhammad's day who oppose pilgrimage to the sacred site (Q 22:25-30). This narrative relates only to Muhammad and Abraham (and Ishmael) and does not fit with any other prophet story before or after Abraham. Despite the purpose for Mecca revealed to Abraham and Ishmael, apparently none of the prophets between Abraham and Muhammad have anything to do with that pilgrimage site. There is no pilgrimage or sacred prayer direction in the other prophet stories.[63]

Abraham's near offering of his son (story 4) also shows no evidence of this pattern. No other prophet is asked to do such a thing, and consequently this story is unique among qur'anic prophet stories. It does however fit the picture of prophets who are examples of complete surrender to God.

Thus only the first episode of Abraham's life fully fits this prophet-story pattern. It seems that Abraham is not such a stereotypical prophet after all. It might be argued that these non-stereotypical elements reflect appropriation of either well-known Jewish Abraham traditions such as the divine visitation and the son-offering stories[64] or Islamic material associating Abraham with the Kaaba rituals.[65] In general it is far easier to fit Moses into the typical qur'anic prophet mold than Abraham.[66] It is clear that the Abraham of Genesis does not fit the punishment story pattern at all.

We observe a final difference in two divine statements of Abraham's relationship to the nations. On one hand the Bible says, "In you (your offspring) all the nations of the earth will be blessed" (Gen 12:2-3), indicating a redemption trajectory. On the other hand the Qur'an says, "I will make you a leader of people" or as Yusuf Ali translates more literally, "I will make thee an *Imam to the nations*" (2:124), pointing to Abraham as an example and leader in proper living and worship. In the Bible the promisee-patriarch Abraham receives the promises of redemptive acts of God. Humans are called to respond in faith. In the Qur'an, the prophet-imam Abraham brings guidance and calls men and women to confession of Tawhid and submission to Allah in ethical living.

(2) True children of Abraham: Followers of Messiah or Muhammad? In Genesis 12:2, God promises to make of Abraham "a great nation" (cf. 18:18), referring to the nation of Israel, as the biblical narrative makes clear. Yet the initial promise in Genesis also indicates that "all nations" were to be blessed through Abraham's

offspring (12:3; 18:18; 22:18). God also promises Abraham that he and Sarah will become many "nations" (17:4-6, 16). The biblical prophets indicate that only a remnant of ethnic Israel will be included in the true people of Abraham, and point to a day when many from other nations will be included (e.g. Isa 55:3-5; 56:1-7; Ps 22:27; 72:8-11, 17).[67] Identifying the legitimate people of Abraham is crucial in the NT, as we saw in chapter 4. The issues involved are at the heart of the Christian message, that all who believe and follow the risen Christ, Jews or Gentiles, become true "sons of Abraham." Their faith is not belief in the existence or sovereignty of God, but like Abraham's faith, trusting in God's goodness and faithfulness to fulfill his specific promises.[68]

Qur'anic verses do speak of God granting privileges to Abraham's descendants (4:54; 57:26). However, the Qur'an clearly identifies Muhammad's followers as the true people of Abraham: "The people who are closest to [Abraham] are those who truly follow his ways, this Prophet, and [true] believers" (3:67-68; cf. 6:161; 2:135). The qur'anic Abraham stories, like the rest of the prophet stories, sketch the portraits of two types of people: those who listen to the prophetic message, believing the prophet and submitting to God, and those who reject the message and persecute the messenger. The vision of an ideal society, the Islamic *ummah*, is seen as Abraham and Ishmael pray for a God-oriented, revelation-based society as they build the Kaaba: "Our Lord, make our descendants into *a community devoted to You. . . .* make a messenger of their own rise up from among them" (2:128-29). This messenger is Muhammad. According to the Qur'an, Abraham founded the site in Mecca around which this ideal society will be established. God specifically names the community that follows the faith of Abraham *Muslims*: "He has chosen you and placed no hardship in your religion (*din*), the faith (*millat*) of your forefather Abraham. God has called you Muslims" (22:78). Haddad says concerning this verse, "Thus God has not only guided and purified the *din*, but has also been involved in every detail of it, including the name of the community."[69]

According to the NT, Jesus, son of Abraham and son of David, is the messianic King. He announced and expounded the kingdom of God, yet showed that it would not come like political kingdoms. Rather his reign would only be fully possessed at his return at the end of the age. Only then will people from all nations sit down with Abraham in the kingdom of God (Luke 13:28-29). Abraham longed for a divinely established society that could not be established by any human leader (Heb 11:10-16). Abraham is not presented in the Bible as setting up such a society, only as believing God's promise and living as a stranger while waiting for God's fulfillment.[70] In the Christian worldview Abraham is not identified with a theocratic nation in the same way as Moses, who gives the Law of God, or as David, who establishes a kingdom under God. Abraham stands rather as the forerunner of an alien people belonging to an otherworldly kingdom. The NT church is an international pilgrim people of God, like Abraham living as "strangers and exiles on the earth" (Heb 11:13).[71] The followers of Christ participate in the Abrahamic mission to bring *blessing* to the world and, like Abraham, live by faith in the promises of God.

In the Muslim worldview, prophetic guidance is given to enable people to establish this correct order. Abraham's life is exemplary, and to maintain the divine intent he establishes the religion and worship. The Qur'an lists Abraham among the messengers sent to establish a rightly guided, just society (57:25-26). The goal of establishing a worldwide community under the rule of Islamic law requires that the guidance of God be worked out in Muslim community. The Muslim worldview sees Abraham's "people" as comprised of all who follow his faith (Islam) and avoid idolatry (2:127; 14:35-38), and whose community life and religious practices are oriented toward the Meccan house and system of worship.

(3) *Jerusalem or Mecca?* Christian and Muslim conceptions of how the problem of sin and evil is ultimately dealt with can be framed in terms of *the place* in which these provisions are made. In Genesis the Abrahamic promise includes a particular land that God will show him. As the story unfolds God tells Abraham that he and his descendants will inherit the territory where they live as migrants (12:7; 13:14-17). The mysterious king-priest Melchizedek blesses Abraham outside the city of Salem (14:17-20), which is identified in biblical tradition with Jerusalem.[72] The Lord reinforces the land promise with solemn covenants (15; 17). He leads Abraham to a hilltop in the region of Moriah (22), which the Chronicler identifies with the Temple mount outside Jerusalem (2 Chr 3:1). Abraham names this site, where God spares Isaac, "the Lord will provide," and we learn of a future-oriented saying: "on the mount of the Lord it will be provided." The NT associates the temple with Jesus' body (John 2:19-22) and sees this event in Abraham's life as foreshadowing God's "not sparing" his own Son as he became the supreme offering to take away the sin of the world (Rom 8:32; John 1:29; 3:16; Heb 10:10-14). As Strom notes, "Zion serves as the place from which Yahweh has acted."[73] Jerusalem becomes the staging point for God's mission of blessing to the whole world, as promised in the Scriptures (Luke 24:47). Deliverance from the evil that has affected humanity since the fall is provided in and around Jerusalem, with which Abraham is explicitly identified.[74]

In the qur'anic scheme, as Josua notes, "salvation no longer comes from Zion."[75] The guidance needed by human beings in order to please God is delivered in Mecca and Medina, and from thence it goes out to the world. Thus the Qur'an explicitly links Abraham with Mecca and with the construction and dedication of the Kaaba, "a blessed place; a source of guidance for all people" (3:96). Muslims rehearse aspects of this story regularly in prayers and religious rituals. According to one hadith report, forgiveness of sins is associated with sincere fulfillment of the pilgrimage to Mecca.[76] Thus rituals recalling Abraham's actions are among the deeds performed to attain forgiveness of sins. The religious and ethical imperatives on which one's judgment is based are performed in continual reference to this sacred place, no matter where one lives in what Geertz describes as the "Mecca-centered international world of Islam."[77] One version of the narrative of the founding of the Kaaba (story 3) adds, "Turn your face in the direction of the Sacred Mosque: wherever you [believers] may be, turn your faces to it" (2:143-44). Ibn al-Qass (ca. AD 975) described Mecca's importance, "The Ka'ba is the qibla for the Sacred Mosque, the Sacred Mosque is the qibla for the sacred precincts [of Mecca], and the sacred precincts are the qibla for the inhabitants of the whole world from where the sun rises to where it sets."[78] King comments that "the direction of the Ka'ba is of prime importance in numerous aspects of the life of every Muslim."[79] The story of Abraham and the Kaaba articulates the foundations of this whole cluster of Islamic rituals.

In the Christian perspective, the real importance of the land was *God dwelling* among his people in the temple. This process began with the appearances of God to Abraham and his establishment of altars, culminating in his altar on Moriah. Islam makes no claim that God ever dwelt in the Kaaba. The concept of God dwelling in a localized place on earth is incompatible with the divine transcendence that dominates the Muslim worldview.

Further, as Burge reminds us, "the New Testament applies to the person of Christ religious language formerly devoted to the Holy Land or the Temple. He is the new spatiality, the new locale where God may be met."[80] Thus from a Christian perspective, not only is the Muslim focus on Mecca jarring in light of the biblical importance of Jerusalem, but it represents a regression. With the coming of Jesus Christ the hour arrived for true worshippers to exalt God without reference to any earthly location (John 1:14-18; 4:20-24). The inheritance promised to Abraham and his offspring now includes "the world" and a heavenly city (Rom 4:13; Heb 11:13-16).

Given the transfer of divine worship to the Hijaz under Muhammad, why is the land of Palestine still so deeply significant in Islamic thinking even today? Although the city of Jerusalem[81] is not mentioned in the Qur'an, it is held to be Islam's third most sacred site, after Mecca and Medina. The basis for this, however, is not Abrahamic, but is found in the qur'anic reference to Muhammad's night journey from "the sacred place of worship" in Mecca *(al-Masjid al-Ḥarām)* to "the furthest place of worship" in Jerusalem *(al-Masjid al-Aqsā)*, and from there to heaven from a rock, on which the Al Aqsa mosque was later constructed (Q 17:1).[82] In any case, the Abraham narratives of the Bible and the Qur'an point to two different locations. In terms of places of worship, Abraham is linked only with the promised land in biblical narrative, and primarily with Mecca in the qur'anic narrative. This is not to say that the qur'anic Abraham narratives entirely ignore Palestine; "We saved him [Abraham] and Lot [and sent them] to the land We blessed for all people" (21:71; cf. 21:81). Moses says to his people, "Go into the holy land which God has ordained for you" (5:21; cf. 17:104).

Consummation—Afterlife Polarity

The biblical consummation articulated in Abraham passages is closely tied to the narrative of redemption that it brings to conclusion. Likewise, the afterlife concept seen in the qur'anic Abraham material is inseparably tied to the concept of prophetic guidance. What makes these conclusions (consummation and afterlife) "Abrahamic" in their respective worldviews is, to a significant degree, their connection with the elements of redemption and prophethood.

In Christian perspective, as Jesus argued from the Hebrew Scriptures, the resurrection is sure because of God's faithfulness to his promises to long-deceased Abraham, Isaac and Jacob, who "live to God" (Luke 20:37-38). He repeatedly declared that he himself must first die and rise again in order for these promises to be fulfilled. The central NT announcement that God has raised Jesus from the dead is inseparable from its reading of Abraham. Likewise, the promises of Jesus' return and the final resurrection of his "redeemed" are inseparable from the hope of Abraham.

In Muslim perspective, belief in the afterlife is second only in importance to belief in God, and the Qur'an repeatedly joins the two. The certainty of resurrection is not linked particularly with Abraham, but is central to the common prophetic message. Nevertheless, we can usefully compare certain motifs regarding the afterlife in the qur'anic Abraham texts. Again my comparison centers around three areas: God, humanity and evil.

(1) Return of God or Return to God? In chapter 2, I pointed out that Islamic teaching on eschatology frequently focuses on the concept of a *return to God*, while the trajectory of the biblical metanarrative moves toward what we described as the *return of God*. The great expectation for the future is that the Lord will come and dwell among his people in the new creation. The Abraham narrative hints at this purpose through God's repeated appearances and his eating at Abraham's table. The link between the promises to Abraham and God dwelling among his descendants is repeatedly made (see Exod 6:2-8 with 15:17 and 29:46). The prophets announce the "second exodus" hope that the Lord who came to Abraham and Israel in the past will come again (Isa 40:1-10; Jer 23:5-8; 31:31-34; Mal 3:1), and dwell among his people (e.g. Zeph 3:14-17). The author of Hebrews tells us that Abraham, Isaac and Jacob, "desire a better country, that is, a heavenly one. Therefore God is not ashamed to be called their God, for he has prepared for them a city" (Heb 11:9-16). The fulfillment of this longing is pictured as the "holy city, new Jerusalem"—God dwelling among his people (Rev 21:1-4; cf. Titus 2:13).

In qur'anic worldview man's return to his maker holds center stage. Islamic discussions of the stages of this "return to God" from the grave are extensive.[83] Abraham declares in one of his prayers, "You are our final destination" (Q 60:5). This is seen in the qur'anic Abraham narratives in a number of ways. When Abraham asked for understanding of how God gives life to the dead, God gives him an object lesson: "Take four birds and train them to *come back* to you. Then place them on separate hilltops, call them back, and they will come flying to you: know that God is all-powerful and wise" (2:260).[84] Likewise God will call all human beings back to him. Abraham warns his people that they will be *returned to God* (29:17).

Various qur'anic passages related to Abraham rehearse warnings about the punishment of fire and the rewards of Paradise (4:54-57, 121-25). While disputing with his father's people Abraham declares his faith in God: "He who will make me die and then give me life again; and He who will, I hope, forgive my faults on the Day of Judgment" (26:81-82). Abraham warns them to turn from idols in light of the coming Day: "He will bring the next life into being. . . . He punishes whoever He will and shows mercy to whoever He will. *You will all be returned to Him*" (29:20-21, 25). Abraham will be among the righteous in the Hereafter (2:130; 16:122). Yet Abraham prays for himself and his offspring with this day in mind: "Do not disgrace me on the Day when all people are resurrected" (14:40-41; cf. 60:4-5).

The biblical Abraham story says nothing about the afterlife or anything comparable to the "return to God." The eschatological trajectory is not toward the future of the individual soul, but the future of Abraham's offspring. God's appearances accompany promises of his future actions within history, not the Day of Judgment.[85]

(2) Humanity at the end: Abrahamic "wedding feast" or the Abrahamic "Day"? A key feature of biblical eschatology is the expected messianic banquet which God himself will host.[86] I will consider this in relation to two striking Abrahamic *table scenes* noted in chapter 3: (1) The meal with the king-priest Melchizedek in Genesis 14, and (2) the meal with the Lord himself in Genesis 18.[87] In the first scene Melchizedek, priest of the Most High God, brings out *bread and wine* and blesses Abraham following his victory (14:17-20). Melchizedek is referred to again in Ps 110, which according to New Testament usage refers to the risen and enthroned Messiah's victory over his enemies: "The LORD has sworn and will not change his mind, 'You are a priest forever after the order of Melchizedek'" (Ps 110:1, 4; cf. Matt 22:41-45; Heb 10:12-13). Canonically this Abraham episode is tied to the coming redemption through Christ who is the priest "after the order of Melchizedek" (Heb 6:20; 7:17). Jesus explains the redemptive significance of his impending death by explaining *the bread and wine* shared in the Last Supper. Through his crucifixion Jesus' body is given and his blood is shed for the forgiveness of sins. The qur'anic worldview explicitly rejects this perspective on Jesus.[88]

This priestly element in the biblical narrative cannot be minimized. We find not only prophet and king, with revelation and legislation, but also priest with altar and sacrifice. Abraham sets up altars as he calls on the name of the Lord. God calls Abraham to offer his son as a burnt offering on an altar on a particular hill. These themes run through the narrative. Christians share *bread and wine* in remembrance of Jesus' priestly self-offering and in anticipation of the eschatological feast after the resurrection: "until he comes" (1 Cor 11:26; cf. 15:23-26).[89] Abraham's meal with Melchizedek can be read as pointing to the Supper and the final feast.

In the qur'anic picture Abraham and the Kaaba are related to the feast of Eid al-Adha at the end of the Sacrifice Holiday. But this is not a redemptive sacrifice, only a memorial of Abraham's great submission in the near-offering of his son. In the Islamic worldview redemption is neither necessary nor possible. The Qur'an rejects both "intercession" and "ransom" in the "Day when no soul will stand in place of another" (2:48; cf. 6:164; 17:15). Abraham prays with this in mind: "Our Lord, forgive me, my parents, and the believers on the Day of Reckoning" (14:40-41; cf. 60:4-5).

In the second Genesis scene the Lord himself visits Abraham and along with two angels partakes of a feast at his table. From a canonical perspective this scene dovetails with table scenes in the Gospels, especially Luke's account, where the Lord visits and eats with people. In these passages the true "children of Abraham" are those like Zacchaeus who eagerly welcome the Lord to their tables, as Abraham did (Luke 19:1-10). The Genesis picture also fits the consummation in which the Lord will dwell among the redeemed of all nations and the long-awaited feast will be shared (Luke 22:16).[90] "Many will come from east and west and *recline at table* with Abraham, Isaac, and Jacob in the kingdom of heaven" (Matt 8:11; cf. 26:29). The fate of unbelievers is described in the Bible not only as "eternal fire" but as eternal exclusion from the feast, as the rich man in the flames learns when he sees Lazarus reclining with Abraham and is told by the patriarch, "between us and you a great chasm has been fixed" (Luke 16:26).[91]

In the qur'anic perspective those who are blessed in the afterlife are "rightly guided" like Abraham: "God chose him and guided him to a straight path . . . and he is among the righteous in the Hereafter" (16:120-22). Conversely those who will inhabit the Fire are identified as those who are "misguided." Abraham prays: "Do not disgrace me on the Day when the Fire is placed in full view of the misguided" (26:88-90).

The prophet Abraham warns his people about the Judgment Day and the Fire (26:90-102; 29:105). *Feasting* is a feature of the qur'anic paradise: "rivers of wine, a delight for those who drink, rivers of honey clarified and pure" (47:15; cf. 14:16). God tells Abraham, "As for those who disbelieve, I will grant them enjoyment for a short while and then subject them to *the torment of the Fire*" (2:126). The "great Fire" is among the things referred to in the "scriptures of Abraham" (87:12-18). Such descriptions are part of the common message proclaimed by all the prophets including Abraham. But there is no real equivalent to the biblical banquet theme in the qur'anic perspective.[92]

The biblical description of God's covenant relationship with his people as a "marriage" in which the Lord is the husband/groom and his people are corporately his wife/bride,[93] has its consummation in the great "wedding feast."[94] Christian exposition has sometimes linked this with the extended story of finding a bride for Isaac in Genesis 24.[95] This picture finds no corollary in the Qur'an, though the divine love is at times compared to consuming romantic love in Sufi approaches.[96] The Christian worldview emphasizes God's particular, intimate relationship with his redeemed people, and the Muslim worldview emphasizes humanity's duty to submit to the transcendent God. In the Bible, Abraham's people have the "adoption" (Rom 9:4) by which they become children of God; in the Qur'an Abraham's people have the "guidance" by which they become servants of God (Q 6:84-86).

In the Christian worldview, the coming resurrection is a source of great encouragement. As God's redeemed, who share (with Abraham) the blessedness of "those whose lawless deeds are forgiven, and whose sins are covered," they believe that (as with Abraham) "God is not ashamed to be called their God"

(Rom 4:7-9; Heb 11:16). In the Muslim worldview there seems rather to be significant trepidation about the Day. In the Qur'an Abraham prays to be joined with the righteous and made one of the "inheritors of the Garden of Bliss" (26:83-90). This prayer is frequently imitated by Muslims, who also ask not to be "degraded on the day when they are raised up" (26:87).

(3) The end of Evil: New Jerusalem or Paradise? The biblical promises of universal "blessing" find their consummation in the elimination of the "curse" introduced into the good creation by the fall (Rev 22:3). The future is pictured in terms of a perfected, heavenly, "New Jerusalem" (Rev 21:9-27; 22:1-3), bringing to consummation all the hopes associated with the promised land and the holy city, which are closely related to Abraham. This "city" is also the "bride," indicating that the city is not so much the *place* as the redeemed *people* among whom God now dwells (Rev 21:2-3). The true destination of Abraham's pilgrimage in this great "assembly of the firstborn" (Heb 11:8-16; 12:22-24; 13:14), is the place God has made ready for them (Heb 11:16).[97] While biblical garden imagery and "paradise" draw attention to the restoration of *creation* as a central category of Christian eschatological hope, its New Jerusalem imagery draws attention to the *redemption* narrative of which Abraham is a key figure.

The primary qur'anic destination for Paradise is a glorious Garden. The image of Paradise, as in the Bible, recalls the place where mankind was created (though in the Bible this is on earth, while in the Qur'an it is an otherworldly place). The Qur'an has extensive descriptions of the terrifying Day of Resurrection and Judgment, and of the luxurious bliss of the pious, especially the "best of believers" and the torments of the unbelievers.[98] The focus is on these places as the recompense for each one's labor. This is specifically related to Abraham in one passage: "written in the Scriptures of Moses and of *Abraham, who fulfilled his duty*: that no soul shall bear the burden of another; that man will only have what he has worked towards; that his labor will be seen and that in the end he will be repaid in full for it" (53:36-41). The qur'anic end game relates to its particular middle game—prophetic guidance for fulfilling one's duty toward God.

In the Qur'an, disputes among Abraham's would-be descendants, particularly regarding their understanding of Abraham, will be resolved on the Day (16:124).[99] Abraham is particularly presented as a good example of disowning and renouncing one's own kinsfolk who refuse to cease idolatry: "a good example for those who fear God and the Last Day" (60:3-6). In this respect as well as others Abraham fits the mold of the prophet of Islam, as a believer and proclaimer of judgment to come on the Last Day. But this picture finds no reflection in the biblical narrative where Abraham proclaims no eschatological warning. In summary, Abraham fits into biblical eschatology as the main starting point of the redemptive process that led to the resurrection of Jesus, and will lead to the resurrection of his people when he returns, and into qur'anic eschatology as an exemplary prophet and believer in God and "the Day."

THE IMPORTANCE OF WHAT IS ABSENT

At the beginning of this chapter I noted that what is absent in one set of Abraham narratives may tell us as much about the worldview they articulate as what is present. I conclude this comparison by briefly developing this crucial point. A juxtaposition of the Genesis and qur'anic narratives shows that all but two of fourteen sections of the Genesis narrative are absent from the qur'anic stories. Only the divine visitation scene and the son-offering scene offer common narrative ground. The main themes developed in chapters 3 and 4, including the trajectory of the biblical Abraham's extensive story (the promise of blessing for all nations through a special offspring), which grow organically into the Bible's salvation-history narrative, are completely absent from the Qu'ran. On the other hand, of the four qur'anic Abraham stories, only two are paralleled in Genesis (as just noted). The overall prophet/punishment story pattern into which Abraham fits in the Qur'an is absent from the biblical Abraham narrative.[100]

Looking through the lens of Abraham narratives, the two worldviews have little in common in terms of either plight or solution. Despite some limited overlap, Abraham stands in a different story of God's relationship to humanity. If one is true, then the other cannot be depicting the real story about these things. From the Christian perspective, to which I subscribe, the qur'anic prophethood tradition is a radically different and selective spin on the story, in which the provision of divine redemption procured by God's mighty works has been replaced with the provision of divine guidance proclaimed by God's prophets. The main storyline from Abraham to Israel to Messiah Jesus has been replaced by a repeating pattern of prophet/punishment stories among which Abraham is one of many and Muhammed is the seal. Despite ostensible reference to the same person, Abraham, and significant common ground as monotheistic systems, these two narrative worldviews are largely nonoverlapping and irreconcilable. Study of other common characters such as Moses and Jesus will reveal similar if not greater degrees of incompatibility and dissonance.

CHAPTER 8 – CHALLENGES AND OPPORTUNITIES IN ABRAHAMIC DIALOGUE

Despite some surface harmony, our examination of the Abraham narratives reveals deep discord between the biblical and qur'anic narratives and the worldviews they reflect. Doing this kind of comparative theology challenges the common notion of a broad "Abrahamic" basis for Christian-Muslim dialogue. It also sharpens our understanding of the Abraham narratives, and reveals difficulties and potential opportunities in Christian witness to Muslims. Face-to-face dialogue with Turkish clerics helped me both to understand more fully the Muslim appropriation of Abraham and to confirm my analysis of the qur'anic Abraham material through the insightful critiques of insiders.

When the biblical and qur'anic Abraham narratives are juxtaposed and carefully compared in an appropriate framework, less common ground is found than is often presumed by those who refer to Christian-Muslim interfaith commonality as "Abrahamic." It turns out that the common ground that does exist is not, in fact, particularly Abrahamic in a sense that most Christians and Muslims would recognize. Common ground is found, rather, in the belief in one creator God and this God's interaction with mankind through prophetic figures. Another common factor is found in scriptures that overlap at points. But none of this is especially related to Abraham. Despite cordial, well-intentioned discussions, my in-depth discussion of Abraham with Turkish clerics revealed more dissonance than harmony in our perspectives on the patriarch/prophet. In fact, because areas of harmony turn out to be not particularly *Abrahamic*, the term is potentially misleading for genuine dialogue.

At the same time, the figure of Abraham, although understood quite differently, is integral to both worldviews. Because narrative both shapes and shows worldview, the Christian worldview is inseparable from the biblical Abraham narrative, as I have argued in my study of Genesis and the NT. Similarly, the Turkish Muslim worldview perspective on Abraham corresponds closely to the qur'anic Abraham narratives read within their contexts. Thus, the dissonance in our respective readings of Abraham is indeed rooted in the difference between two sets of stories; it is not simply a matter of two readings of one story, as sometimes asserted. The limited areas of common ground that we find in the overlap of the Abraham stories are further diminished when we consider the purpose for which the narratives are used by Christians and Muslims. Even when two apparently similar episodes are recounted (the special visit of angels, or the near-sacrifice of a son), their appropriation within the Bible and the Qur'an, and hence within Christian and Muslim worldviews, is strikingly different.

Abraham and his stories do comprise a useful starting point for dialogue between Christians and Muslims. The biblical and qur'anic Abraham narratives supply a body of interesting material to recount and discuss. Abraham is well-known to both Christians and Muslims, and the awareness of both commonality and competing claims on the patriarch/prophet opens the way for easy conversation. I spent many hours with Turkish imams discussing Abraham and our different Abraham narratives, considering together what we share and what we do not share. This aspect of my work required the use of principles for interscriptural dialogue articulated by Scriptural Reasoning practitioners, referred to in chapter 1. With informed planning and respectful listening, biblical and qur'anic Abraham materials can be compared and contrasted in ways that help both Christians and Muslims better understand both their own faith and the faith of the other. Consequently, thoughtful use of biblical and qur'anic Abraham stories does prepare the ground for mutual understanding between Christians and Muslims and facilitates interfaith dialogue. Not only areas of harmony but also areas of dissonance can be discussed with mutual benefit. Particularly through discussions of our disagreements, I had opportunity to articulate my own understanding of how Abraham and the Christian gospel are related, which represented a form of contextualized Christian witness to Muslims.

Beginning with Abraham is thus a helpful entry point into dialogue. But the more carefully the actual narratives are considered and compared, the more clearly areas of divergence emerge. Therefore, preliminary acquaintance with the qur'anic Abraham stories and how they are appropriated by Muslims within the qur'anic worldview will enable Christians to recognize areas that lead in different directions from a NT-informed reading of the biblical Abraham. In the qur'anic perspective Abraham's story fits the pattern of all the prophet stories, particularly that of Muhammad, who (like Abraham) is linked to the Kaaba, and whose universal message is explicitly identified as the creed of Abraham. Christians involved in "Abrahamic dialogue" should not forget that the gospel of God is nothing less than the fulfillment of the Abrahamic promises of blessing and salvation for all nations, that Jesus is both uniquely identified as the Messiah, "son of Abraham" (Matt 1:1-17), and uniquely identified with the "God of Abraham" (John 8:51-58), and that the NT narrates the Christian sequel to the biblical redemption narrative beginning with Abraham. Failure to grasp this deeply messianic NT appropriation of Abraham will lead to an exaggerated sense of common ground, perhaps by focusing on Abraham's obedient faith.[1] The biblical Abraham narrative culminates in Jesus the Messiah, while in the Muslim reading the qur'anic Abraham stories culminate in Muhammad, the final Prophet for mankind. The divergence I have identified in the Abraham stories only widens further as the biblical Abraham-Jesus trajectory is compared with the Abraham-Muhammad trajectory. The much-discussed difficulty in harmonizing Jesus of the NT with Jesus of the Qur'an is in fact integrally related to the dissonance between the biblical and qur'anic Abraham stories.

We have seen that these dissonances between biblical and qur'anic Abraham narratives are connected with profound worldview questions for Christians and Muslims. The most profound of these questions relate to the revelation of who God is and how he is involved with creation, with humanity's deepest needs and with the end of history.

God and Creation

Much common ground is shared by these two theistic worldviews in the area of God and creation. Both Christians and Muslims believe that all things exist and are sustained by the power of the one, sovereign, Creator God. Idolatry is condemned by both faiths as culpable refusal to honor this God. Yet while Abraham's rejection of idols and confrontation of idolaters is central to the qur'anic stories, the Genesis Abraham narrative says nothing about this and the biblical Abraham is not an overt challenger of idolatry. The sharpest worldview dissonance is the proximity or immanence of God within creation and within the different storylines. The biblical narrative reveals God entering time and space, appearing to Abraham in tangible ways, and as the chief protagonist within the events. He is palpably "present" in various scenes, speaking, coming and going, participating in symbolic covenant-making actions, and this divine presence becomes even more striking in the ongoing story of Abraham's offspring. The Christian reading of this recounted phenomenon finds easy continuity with the NT contention that the God of Abraham has condescended to take human form as Jesus Christ (through the incarnation). On the other hand, in the Muslim worldview, the qur'anic concept of God evident in creation is seen in Abraham's reasoning to the reality of the Creator by observing the astral bodies. While God narrates the Abraham stories in the Qur'an, and some verbal interaction with Abraham is recounted, he is never seen or otherwise present. My Muslim interlocutors found these details of the biblical Abraham story unacceptable to their understanding of the transcendence of God. For them, God interacts with humanity by means of angel-mediated speech to prophets, through "signs" of creation and judgment, and reveals not himself, but only his will.

God and Salvation

The biblical redemption narrative, which begins particularly with Abraham in a messianic trajectory, recounts a long series of divine interventions to save a particular people for God's name. God makes promises to Abraham, personally establishing covenants and giving signs of his covenant purposes. While the OT focuses primarily on the people of Israel, the NT narrates the expansion and fulfillment of God's work of bringing into existence a worldwide "people of Abraham" from among all nations, through the work of Jesus Christ, crucified and risen, testified to by his Spirit-endowed followers. In the Christian worldview this is God's central mission and the core of his saving provision for all mankind.

The people of Abraham are accordingly known as the redeemed ones. There is deep dissonance between this Abraham narrative and the qur'anic picture, where Abraham is not a unique link in one ongoing chain of events, but one of many prophets sent and "guided" by God with the message of salvific "guidance" for mankind. In the Muslim worldview, divine guidance to walk the right path is humanity's greatest need, not redemption from sin and spiritual bondage in a fallen world. Abraham is a model prophet of monotheism, surrendering to the Lord of the universe, defending faith in the one God against his idolatrous people, warning them of the terrifying Day of resurrection, praying to be among the righteous at the judgment, and together with Ishmael founding or reviving the pure worship of the Creator at the Kaaba. Abraham exemplifies and proclaims the message of Tawhid and the way of Islam perfectly, in the pattern and the role of every prophet, above all Muhammad, who for Muslims is the greatest and final prophet-exemplar. In the Qur'an, all who believe in God and the Last Day are the true people of Abraham. Like him, they are the rightly guided ones.

God and the Day

Despite significant common ground regarding the resurrection and judgment of all human beings at the end of the age, a major area of dissonance arises regarding God and the Day. In the biblical worldview Abraham's people look forward expectantly to "the return of God" and the great "wedding feast" which he will host. The central reality of this hope is that the God who condescended to visit Abraham and eat at his table will dwell among his people eternally. This expectation is intimately related to the narrative of God "coming" among his people in both testaments and is based on the resurrection power of God, who both gave life to Abraham's 'dead' body and raised Jesus from the dead. In the qur'anic worldview the certainty of the Day of Resurrection is based on the creative power of God, which is shown to Abraham. The primary fact is that every soul must surely "return to God," for judgment, to enjoy bliss in the Garden or suffer torment in the Fire. This great fact of the Day of Judgment is intimately related to believing in God and is to dominate the life of all Muslims, even as it does the Abraham story.

Implications for Contextual Missiology

Part of the difficulty in interfaith communication is that we neither know the stories told by our dialogue partners nor understand why they tell them. It is thus important to learn what the stories illustrate or teach as used in practice. Having a fuller understanding of the way narrative and worldview are related will help us to ask questions that lead to deeper issues. A specific example that surfaced frequently in my study was the regular Turkish Muslim use of the qur'anic stories of Abraham's early life, when he surrendered himself to the creator and began to dispute with idolaters. Because this story has no correlation with the Genesis Abraham story it is little known to most Christians. Its similarity to Jewish exegetical narratives (like Jubilees) helps us to understand how the defense of monotheism and the concept of Tawhid are articulated by the use of this Abraham story. This in turn helps Christians to think clearly about how different the NT use of Abraham really is from the Muslim usage. It may be important to think about the use or nonuse of para-canonical narratives in developing aspects of the respective worldviews. The approach of my interviewees in this regard seems to show how Islamic exegesis of the Qur'an has followed a similar path to Jewish exegesis of the Torah, insofar as *embellished narratives* serve to communicate and reinforce interpretation. The fact that the NT reading of Abraham to a very large extent avoids this process should inform Christian witness.

If storytelling is identified as an approach with potential for Christian witness to Muslims, the Abraham story deserves to be among the stories utilized. However, as I have shown with the Abraham narrative, these stories are inseparable from the larger biblical narrative and need to be told with this in mind. Understanding how these stories articulate aspects of the Christian worldview will help to keep them from being misused. Additionally, reading or telling these stories in conjunction or comparison with Muslim stories about the same characters should be done in such a way that both harmony and dissonance are shown. My conversations with Turkish clerics about the Abraham stories, while academic in character, might be an example of setting stories side by side and working out the theological implications of their commonality and their difference.

An area of serious controversy in Christian missiology today regards the extent to which it is appropriate to use others' scriptures in the interests of Christian mission. Among the more controversial proposals is to use the Qur'an along with the Bible as a source of edification for Muslim-background believers in Jesus. Higgins, a proponent of so-called *"Insider movements*,"[2] makes three observations about the nature of the Qur'an in relation to this issue: The Quran claims to confirm the Bible; The Quran is best understood as a form of Jewish and Christian "midrash"; The Quran assumes the reader/hearer knows the Bible. He then draws the following conclusions about the use of the Qur'an:

> The Quran is best seen as a proclamation of the Bible [which] can be studied and used by followers of Jesus in a way similar to the way in which many Christians read, for example, the Apocrypha. In fact, the Quran has a stronger claim than the Apocrypha because by its OWN teaching it is pointing to and depending upon the Books of the Bible.[3]

This is an approach justifying profitable reading of the Qur'an by followers of Jesus, not an example of interscriptural dialogue between Christians and Muslims or Christian witness to Muslims. Nevertheless, Muslims are not likely to be satisfied with either Higgins' assessment of the nature of the Qur'an or the careful qualifications he adds about the prophethood of Muhammad in order to affirm that followers of Jesus can with integrity recite the Islamic creed, "There is no god but Allah. Muhammad is the messenger of Allah."[4] Turkish theologian Mahmut Aydın has strong words for some contemporary Christian evaluations of the prophethood of Muhammad, using Kenneth Cragg as an example of a Christian who uses the Qur'an in dialogue with Muslims:

Cragg's generous suggestion that Christians should regard Muhammad as 'the Prophet of the Qur'an' is not as generous as he thinks . . . Muhammad is not just a Prophet for the Arabs but a Prophet with a universal Message for all human beings. Hence, Cragg's recognition of Muhammad as 'the Prophet of the Qur'*ān*' is for Muslims nothing less than a betrayal of their faith.[5]

Further consideration is needed on the debatable subject of using your dialogue partner's scripture to prove your own position. Over the centuries Christian apologists have developed many arguments from the Qur'an that seemed compelling to them.[6] Yet often these interpretations of qur'anic verses were unacceptable to Muslim interpreters and rather than being persuasive were not taken seriously. Similarly, Muslim efforts to persuade Christians through using both the Qur'an and the Bible are plentiful in Turkey.[7] But their appeals to biblical material often betray deep misunderstanding of the text.[8]

Cate argues at length against using the other's scriptures in "witnessing" primarily because of the inconsistency of calling as witness that which you otherwise reject as untrustworthy.[9] Nevertheless he argues for the importance of reading one's partner's Scripture for mission: "There is a need for understanding each other's scripture, not to derive arguments from them, but because dialogue, proclamation and witness require commonality of language."[10] I agree with Cate on this point, but would add that it is wise to recognize that when it comes to interpretation, Muslim readings of the Qur'an must be taken as authoritative for understanding it as a whole. My study has shown that the qur'anic Abraham stories are consistent with both their traditional (Turkish) usage of them and that they reflect the qur'anic-Muslim worldview. It is nearly impossible to utilize these Abraham stories to support a Christian worldview. Attempting to treat the Qur'an like midrash seem to me to reveal an insufficient grasp of the way in which the NT distances its perspective from the Jewish readings of the Hebrew Scriptures. My relatively brief discussion of this issue in chapter 4 argues that the monotheistic "hero" reading of Abraham in the Second Temple Jewish perspective cannot be reconciled with the NT perspective. To an even greater degree the Christian and Muslim Abraham stories are irreconcilable. Since these distinct Abraham readings are inseparable from the worldviews they articulate, I suggest that it is hazardous to try to use others' scriptures except as they do.

Those pursuing Christian witness to Muslims through dialogue should keep in mind two important priorities, each corresponding to one of the "greatest commandments" identified by Jesus (Mark 12:28-31). First, serious dialogue (Abrahamic or otherwise) requires genuine respect, openness and hospitality to the "other," as entailed by what Jesus describes as the second commandment, "you shall love your neighbor as yourself." Dialogue for whatever purpose must be built on grace and respect for the other.

Secondly, serious dialogue requires genuine respect for and deep understanding of distinctives, especially in relation to God and truth. Here the relevant command is the first one: "Hear, O Israel: The Lord our God, the Lord is one. And you shall love the Lord your God with all your heart and with all your soul and with all your mind and with all your strength" (Mark 12:29-30; citing

Deut 6:4-5). Love for the God of Israel puts dialogue in a different perspective, for there can be no compromising here regarding the particularity and identity of the God of Abraham. To love God with all one's mind requires thinking deeply about the Scriptures which speak of God, as explicitly underscored in the verse following the Deuteronomy text quoted by Jesus: "And *these words* that I command you today shall be on your heart" (Deut 6:6). We have seen in this study that God's identity is revealed primarily through his acts, as recounted in the Bible, and that this particular narrative identity is inseparable from the particular Abraham narrative of Genesis. This is the crux of the issue when engaging Muslims over the qur'anic Abraham (and other) stories.

IMPLICATIONS FOR COMPARATIVE THEOLOGY

The categories of my worldview polarities model constitute a helpful framework for doing Christian-Muslim comparative theology, particularly comparison of biblical and qur'anic narrative material. For example, comparing creation and fall with Tawhid (divine unity) exposes the two faiths' approaches to such questions as God's proximity or distance from his creation (transcendence and immanence) and the existence of evil in a world held to be under the sovereign rule of a good God (theodicy). Similarly, juxtaposing the sweeping categories of redemption and Prophethood helps us to understand Christian and Muslim answers to questions about God's approach to humanity, and how people are to approach God. Comparing the worldview elements of consummation and Afterlife clarifies our respective perspectives on the meaning and goal of human history and the future. Of course this approach is not altogether different from thematic comparisons that have been done by others. However, developing the relationship between worldview and narrative as I have done adds clarity and depth to the comparison. It also facilitates better comparison of specific narrative episodes in relation to their worldviews and metanarratives. Study of particular texts is an essential ingredient in comparative theology, and narrative comprises a significant portion of scriptural texts. I see a great deal of scope for further investigation of the integral relationship between narrative (biblical and other) and worldview (Christian and other).

In developing my model for theological comparison I argued that the Abraham stories belong to a larger set of biblical and qur'anic narratives, which in turn correlate with Christian and Muslim worldviews. I proposed that this connection between narrative and worldview can be developed in order to facilitate theological comparison of even nonoverlapping story episodes. For example, I showed that an important motif in the Genesis Abraham narrative is God's promise of the land of Canaan as an eternal inheritance for Abraham and his offspring, particularly the sacred site known later as Jerusalem. The Qur'an only refers to this land in relationship to Abraham once in passing.[11] However, in the qur'anic Abraham narrative, Abraham's building and dedicating the Kaaba in Mecca is the crucial motif in terms of sacred location, while the Bible says nothing about any journey of Abraham and Ishmael to the Hijaz, let alone their rebuilding a sacred site of worship there. Either these rival stories are mutually exclusive, or the later qur'anic story simply abrogates the priority of Jerusalem for Abraham. For a more fruitful theological comparison I considered the importance of these special places in the broader framework of Christian and Muslim worldviews. I compared the significance of the land promise for Christians and the sacred site of Mecca for Muslims particularly in terms of the divine provision for dealing with sin and evil, within the redemption-Prophethood polarity. This approach not only shifts the focus from the political tinderbox of Israel-Palestine, but also provides a structure for looking at details of these rival stories. I propose that this narrative-worldview framework will facilitate theological comparison of other largely nonoverlapping biblical and qur'anic narratives.

IMPLICATIONS FOR BIBLICAL INTERPRETATION IN ISLAMIC CONTEXTS

Exegesis of individual narratives should contribute to biblical and systematic theology and ultimately to worldview. As systematic theology needs to be refined by the exegetical work of biblical theology, so Christian worldview should be shaped by study of individual biblical narratives in their canonical narrative context. This approach may be seen as a sort of hermeneutical line or loop.

FIGURE 8.1 – HERMENEUTICAL LOOP

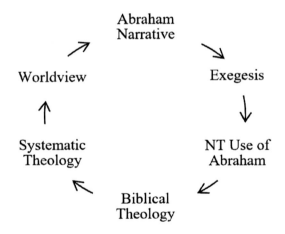

The Islamic context brings a specific set of challenges and possibilities when biblical interpretation is done with awareness of the missiological and comparative theological issues entailed by the biblical text. The Bible may arguably be approached as the product of God's mission.[12] If, as Wright contends, a "missional hermeneutic" is a key framework for interpreting the Bible as a whole, then the competing "mission" articulated in the Qur'an should be properly engaged. Reading and interpreting the Bible in the light of the qur'anic perspective on common events and characters raises many questions that need answering if the

Bible is to be explained meaningfully in Islamic contexts. Muslim background readers are particularly helped by such comparative insights. The approach I have followed in this study is one way to go about the task of biblical interpretation for those whose worldview has been shaped by Islam. As I have tried to show through the example of Abraham, the individual episodes of the biblical narrative material (to leave aside other genres) are part of a larger narrative that implicitly, and sometimes explicitly, challenges every other metanarrative, including that of Islam.[13] The biblical authors lived in pluralistic, multireligious settings and often directly or indirectly addressed these competing perspectives. The biblical text, beginning with Genesis 1, presents a storied interpretation of the cosmos and human history that diverges from all others, including the qur'anic reading. Thus the type of work I have carried out in this study is necessary to tease out the implications of the biblical text for Islamic contexts.

It is significant that the areas of deepest dissonance that I have identified are those that may properly be described as "theological." This suggests that the approach to interpretation that will delve most helpfully into the issues raised by Islamic contexts is that known as "theological interpretation" (see my Introduction). Although there are ancient and modern Muslim commentaries on biblical texts, they remain quite limited.[14] Such works may help Christians to see the Bible with new insight as they learn how it appears to Muslims. At the same time, Christian scholars pursuing theological interpretation with awareness of the Qur'an and its worldview may make a significant contribution to biblical interpretation for a variety of Muslim contexts. I hope my work in the Turkish Muslim context may contribute in a limited way to such a body of interpretive work.

SHARING ABRAHAM: OPPORTUNITIES AND CHALLENGES

To what extent do Christians and Muslims really share Abraham? My discussion of the biblical and Islamic Abraham stories with Muslim interlocutors certainly opened opportunities for interfaith encounter and dialogue. I have not found, however, that Abraham was as fruitful a starting point for Christian witness in the sense of leading to discussion of Jesus and the gospel, despite some initial expectations that it might do so. Nevertheless, I hope that this study may help encourage both beneficial Christian-Muslim dialogue and Christian witness using the Abraham narratives and other scriptural stories.

The Qur'an asserts that Abraham was a true Muslim, and directly challenges the "People of the Book" about their competing claims to Abraham:

> People of the Book, why do you argue about Abraham when the Torah and the Gospels were not revealed until after his time? Do you not understand? You argue about some things of which you have some knowledge, but why do you argue about things of which you know nothing? God knows and you do not. Abraham was neither a Jew nor a Christian. He was upright and devoted to God, never an idolater, and the people who are closest to him are those who truly follow his ways, this Prophet, and [true] believers—God is close to [true] believers. (Q 3:65-68)

I have shown that, while Abraham was of course not a Christian, the Christian Gospel is indeed inseparable from the Abraham narrative. The story of Jesus Christ, the son of Abraham, is both the continuation and the consummation of all that God initiated when he called Abraham and promised that in him all the nations of the world would be blessed. While the relationships are very different, as has been demonstrated above, it is as difficult for a Christian to separate Abraham and his story from Jesus and the NT as it is for a Muslim to separate Abraham from Muhammad and the Qur'an.

Biblical interpretation informed throughout by comparative theological insights can help Christians tell their story well, defend their faith, and engage Muslim thinking in a persuasive way. As thoughtful Christians in other eras read the Bible with a view to responding to challenges raised by other systems of thought such as Greek philosophy or Judaism, so Christians in Islamic contexts today should read the Bible with awareness of the qur'anic challenge to the biblical worldview. Muslims who read Christian interpretations of the Bible also deserve to have their perspective carefully engaged.

APPENDICES

APPENDIX 1 – BIBLICAL STORY-SUMMARY PASSAGES

Summaries: / Events:	Creation	Patriarchs	Exodus	Possess Canaan	Judges, Kingdom	Exile Return	Jesus' Ministry	Jesus' Passion	Apostolic Witness
Deut 6:20-24			x	x					
Deut 26:5-9		x	x	x					
Josh 24:2-13		x	x	x					
Neh 9:6-37	x	x	x	x	x	x			
Ps 78:12-72			x	x	x				
Ps 105		x	x	x					
Ps 135:8-12	x		x	x					
Ps 136	x		x	x					
Acts 7:2-60		x	x	x	x			x	x
Acts 10:34-43							x	x	x
Acts 13:17-39			x	x	x		x	x	x
Heb 11:3-12:2	x	x	x	x	x	x		x	

Appendix 2 – Prophets Named in the Qur'an

Prophet	2**	3**	4**	5	6	7	9**	10	11	12	14	15	17	19	21	22**	25	26	27	29	37	38	40	42	51	53	54	In list*	In all
1) Adam	1	1		2		1						1	5	11														7	9
2) Idris														10	12													2	2
3) Nuh		2	4		4	2	2	1	1		2		2	12	7	1	2	4		1	1	1	1	1	5	5	1	22	27
4) Hud ('Ad)						3	3		2		3					2	3	5		5		2	3		3	3	2	13	13
5) Salih (Thamud)						4	4		3		4	5	4			3	4	6	4	6		3	4		4	4	3	16	21
6) Ibrahim	5	3	1		1		5		4	2	5	2		4	3	4		3		2	2	9		2	1	2		19	25
7) Ismail	6	8	5		15						6			9	11							12						8	9
8) Ishaq	8	9	6		2				6	3	7			5	5						3	10						11	13
9) Lut					18	5			5			3			4			7	5	3	7	4					4	11	12
10) Ya'qub	7	10	7		3					4				6	6							11						8	9
11) Yusuf					8					1													5					3	3
12) Shu'ayb (Midian)						6	6		7			4				5		8		4		5						8	8
13) Musa	2		2	1	9	7		2	8		1		1	7	1	6	1	1	1		4		2	3	2	1		20	33
14) Harun			10		10	8		3						8	2			2			5							8	13
15) Ilyas					14																6							2	2
16) Al-Yasa					16																	13						2	2
17) Dawud	9		11	4	5								3		8				2			6						8	8
18) Sulayman	4		10		6										9				3			7						6	6
19) Ayyub			8		7										10							8						4	4
20) Dhu'l-Kifl															13							14						2	2
21) Yunus					17			4							14						8							4	6
22) Zakariyya		5			11									1	15													4	4
23) Yahya		6			12									2	16													4	4
24) Issa (Jesus)	3	7	3	3	13		1							3	17									4				9	13
Imran		4																										1	2
Number of prophets:	9	10	11	4	18	8	6	4	8	4	7	5	5	12	17	6	4	8	5	6	8	14	5	4	5	5	4		

** = Medinan suras. *This analysis does not include those found in suras where fewer than 4 names are mentioned.

The numbers represent the order in which the prophets are mentioned in the surah (though some are mentioned numerous times in one surah). The names found most frequently in surahs recounting prophet stories are Noah (in all but 7), Moses (in all but 5), and Abraham (in all but 8). Salih is found in a surprising number of surahs (21). The later prophets (after Moses) tend to be found in surahs mentioning at least 4 prophets, except Jesus. Surahs 6, 21 and 38 are the richest in prophet stories, followed by surahs 3, 4, and 19.

APPENDIX 3 – NT PASSAGES REFERRING TO ABRAHAM BY NAME

GOSPELS

1. Jesus Christ the son of Abraham and David (Matt 1:1)
2. Abraham in Jesus' genealogy (Matt 1:2; Luke 3:34)
3. Abraham – David – Exile – Messiah high points of Israel's history (Matt 1:17)
4. Jesus' birth fulfills the promise to Abraham and the fathers (Luke 1:54-55, 69-75)
5. John the Baptist: don't say, 'We have Abraham as our father' (Matt 3:7-9; Luke 3:7-8)
6. Believing Gentiles from all nations will be at table with Abraham (Matt 8:5-13; Luke 13:28-29)
7. Argument with Jews claiming Abraham as their father (John 8:31-41)
8. Jesus claims priority over Abraham who looked for his day (John 8:42-58)
9. A daughter of Abraham is freed from Satan (Luke 13:10-17)
10. Lazarus in Abraham's bosom after death, Abraham answers the rich man (Luke 16:19-31)
11. Zacchaeus a son of Abraham receives salvation (Luke 19:1-10)
12. Resurrection argument: 'I am the God of Abraham' (Matt 22:23-33; Mark 12:18-27; Luke 20:27-39)

ACTS

13. The God of Abraham has raised Jesus (Acts 3:13)
14. The covenant with Abraham is being fulfilled in Jesus (Acts 3:25)
15. Stephen narrates the story of Israel beginning with Abraham (Acts 7:2-16)
16. The Exodus from Egypt was fulfilling the promise to Abraham (Acts 7:17)
17. God identifies himself to Moses as the God of Abraham (Acts 7:32)
18. Jews addressed as "sons of Abraham's family" (Acts 13:26)

EPISTLES

19. Exegesis of Gen.15:6 showing justification by faith, not works of law (Rom 4:1-8; Gal 3:6-7)
20. Abraham was "justified" before circumcision, and before the law was given, thus uncircumcised Gentiles can be justified without circumcision or law as he was (Rom 4:9-12)
21. Abraham the father of many nations is to be interpreted as the inclusion of the Gentiles (Rom 4:13-17)
22. Abraham grows strong in faith in spite of age, fathers Isaac (Rom 4:18-22; Heb 11:11-12)

23. Justification of the Gentiles and the gift of the Spirit the fulfillment of the promise to Abraham that all nations would be blessed through him (Gal 3:8-14)
24. Promises made to Abraham find their ultimate fulfillment in Jesus Christ (using "seed" argument) (Gal 3:16)
25. Covenant made with Abraham takes precedence over the law given several centuries later at Mt. Sinai (Gal 3:17-29)
26. Not all children of Abraham are his seed; Isaac rather than Ishmael is the son of promise (Rom 9:7 Gal 4:22)
27. Paul too is of the seed of Abraham (Rom 11:1; 2 Cor 11:22)
28. Believers in Christ are offspring of Abraham (Heb 2:16)
29. God swore an oath to Abraham (Heb 6:13)
30. Abraham subordinated to Melchizedek/Christ (Heb 7:1-10)
31. Abraham, obedient "by faith" travels to and lives as stranger in the promised land, looking for eternal city (Heb 11:8-10, 13-16)
32. Abraham offers Isaac, trusting God to raise him (Heb 11:17-19)
33. Abraham's justification by faith 'fulfilled' in obedience offering Isaac (Jas 2:20-24)
34. Sarah called Abraham lord, an example of submission for wives (1 Pet 3:6)

APPENDIX 4 – THE BOOK OF JUBILEES ON ABRAHAM.[1]

Abram at age 14
Abram's turn from idolatry (11.16)
Abram defends land from ravens sent by the demon prince Mastema (11.19-21), thus ending the famine.
Abram teaches farmers to use a plough that sows seed and turns it under to be safe from birds.

Abram at age 42
Debates with father Terah over idols (12.1-5)

Abram at age 60
Burns the idol temple 12.12
Moves to Haran, lives there with Terah for 14 years 12.15

Abram at age 75
Stays up one night, observing stars for meteorological information (Will it rain this year?), realizes the foolishness of this as "a word came into his heart" that all things are in the hand of the Lord (12.16-21). Prays and confesses God Most High as his God, rejecting the evil spirits "who have dominion over the thoughts of men's hearts." He also prays for guidance about whether to return to Ur, where he is wanted, or remain in Haran. He seeks the right path from God.
Word of the Lord comes to him "through me" (the speaking angel), quoting Genesis (12:1-3 and 17:7) (12.22-25).
God commands Abram's mouth to be opened and he begins to speak Hebrew, the "original language of creation" (12.25-27).
Abram takes the "books of his fathers, and these were written in Hebrew", he transcribes them, begins to study them, the angel makes known to him what he does not understand, studies for 6 months.
He tells his father he is going to land of Canaan to scout it and return (12.28). Terah agrees, blesses him, and tells him to return to get them (12.29-31).
Journeys to Canaan (13.1-4.) Descriptions of land as fertile. Builds altar on mountain, offers on new moon date a burnt sacrifice (13.5-10). Calls on the name of the Lord: "Thou, the eternal God, are my God."
In Egypt Abram spends 5 years before Pharaoh seizes Sarai. (13.12-13).
When Abram rescues Lot he takes and gives a tenth of all to [Melchizedek understood], and this is the example for ordaining tithing to the priests. (13.25-28)

Abram around age 85-86
Gen 15 nearly quoted in full. Covenant made with Abram, he offers the pieces, and fire devours them. Covenant and festival of Noah renewed with Abram forever. (14.19-20)
Abram rejoices, tells Sarai, expects a child, but she does not bear. So Sarai suggests Hagar, Ishmael born (14.21-24). The rest is skipped over.

Abram 100 years old
Abram celebrates the feast of first-fruits, details of his offerings (15.1-2).
At this time the Lord appears to him as in Gen (17.15.3-25). Names changed to Abraham and Sarah. The covenant of circumcision is said to be "ordained and written on the heavenly tablets" (15.26). Angels of the presence and angels of sanctification said to be created circumcised (if I understand right) (15.27).

Abraham's descendants chosen, over Israel no angel appointed as with all the other nations, rather the Lord himself is their ruler. (15.31-32)

Foretells that Israel will not stay faithful to circumcise their children and this will bring wrath, and no forgiveness for "this eternal error." (15.34)

Genesis 18 recounted, but here it is "we" who appear to Abraham. Isaac announced, name taken from the heavenly tablets. Angels to visit her again. Note how the Lord is missing from the chapter. No intercession for Sodom, only judgment. (16.5-6)

Extra judgment, "commanded and engraved on the heavenly tablets, to remove them and root them out, and to execute judgment on them like the judgment of Sodom," detailed for descendants of Lot as a result of his sin with his daughters (16.9)

Abram moves from Hebron, the Lord visits Sarah as promised, she conceives and bears a son "in the third month, in the middle of the month . . . on the festival of the first fruits of the harvest." Isaac is circumcised on the 8th day (16.10-14)

Another angelic appearance detailed (16.16-19), announcing Isaac's future and that from the sons of Isaac "one should become a holy seed, and should not be reckoned among the Gentiles. For he should become the portion of the Most High, and all his seed had fallen into the possession of God, that it should be unto the Lord a people for (His) possession above all nations and that it should become a kingdom and priests and a holy nation." This is a fascinating reference!

Abraham rejoices, celebrates the very first feast of Tabernacles/Booths. (16.20-24). Further messianic-like promise "from him would arise the plant of righteousness for the eternal generations and from him a holy seed, so that it should become like him who had made all things (16.26-27)

Abraham 110 years old (?)

Weaning feast, celebration, more rejoicing, Ishmael dancing and his father rejoicing (17.1-3). Sarah becomes jealous. Follows Gen 21 closely, but there is nothing here of the mystery involved in the angel of the Lord's appearance to Hagar (17.4-14)

Abraham praised by voices in heaven. Evil angel/accuser? Like Satan in Job 1, Mastema accuses Abraham of loving Isaac more than all else and suggests God test Abraham. (17.16) This scene provides the unstated reason for the son-offering story in the next chapter (fills the perceived gap before Gen 22:1).

This is not entirely unlike the Islamic Sufi interpretation of the reason for Abraham's offering his son. Among the four practices enjoined by the Koran which are regarded as basic to the Sufi way of life is suffering.[2]

God knew Abraham was faithful, because he had already been tested repeatedly (17.17-18). Abraham the faithful exemplar stands before us here, as the "test" of Gen 22:1 is read back into every stage of his life (see Watson on this). Following the phrase "The Lord knew that Abraham was faithful in all his afflictions," a list of "tests" is recited: "for He had tried him… 1st through his country and 2nd with famine, and had tried him with 3rd the wealth of kings, and had tried him again 4th through his wife, when she was torn (from him), and 5th with circumcision; and had tried him 6th through Ishmael and Hagar, his maid-servant, when he sent them away. And in everything wherein He had tried him, he was found faithful, and his soul was not impatient, and he was not slow to act; for he was faithful and a lover of the Lord." (This "testing" or "trying" of Abraham comes in Qur'an 2:124.) A total of 10 trials given in (19:8). (10) with the death of his wife Sarah 19:3-8. Presumably 9th is the offering of his son 18:1-16, but it is not clear to me what the 7th and 8th trials are.

Jacob learned to write. (19:14) Perhaps emphasizing the superior value of Torah study.

Abraham loved Jacob, but Isaac loved Esau. (19:15-16) Abraham commands Rebecca regarding the blessing of Jacob, pronouncing a blessing upon him (19:17-30) (Gen 25:28).

Abraham calls Ishmael and Keturah's sons and charges them with keeping the law, circumcision included. (20:1-10) Arabs and Ishmaelites mingled. (20:13)

Abraham's death at 175 years old

Abraham calls Isaac, affirms that he has hated all idols (21:3-6), and that God hates all who break the law and covenant. Commands Isaac to offer sacrifices correctly (20:17-20), warns him to avoid the sins of mankind and keep the commandments to be blessed (20:21-26).

Abraham blesses and charges Jacob extensively on his deathbed (22:1–23:8). Jacob is lying in bed beside Abraham at his death.

APPENDIX 5 – SURA BY SURA ANALYSIS OF QUR'ANIC ABRAHAM MATERIAL

Considering each qur'anic Abraham passage in its own sura context helps us understand how Abraham is appropriated. My limitations are obvious, as a non-Muslim attempting to comment on even this restricted qur'anic theme.[1] The reflections below are therefore based largely on widely received Muslim exegesis (*tafsir*) as summarized in running commentary notes found in English and Turkish interpretations (*meal*) of the Qur'an. I have consulted the English notes provided by Yusuf Ali,[2] Muhammad Asad,[3] Abdel Haleem,[4] Syed Abu-Ala' Maududi[5] and Shaykh Muhammad al-Ghazali.[6] Those of Asad, Maududi, and al-Ghazali are available in Turkish and are taken seriously by Turkish theologians.[7] I have occasionally consulted the works of contemporary Turkish *mufassir* (authors of tafsir): Bayraktar Bayraklı[8] and Tahsin Emiroğlu,[9] recommended to me at the Center for Islamic Studies in Istanbul (İslam Araştırmaları Merkezi), as well as the notes of the revered Elmalılı Hamdi Yazır.[10] I have occasionally referred to the commentary notes of the Turkish Ministry of Religious Affairs (*Diyanet* İşleri *Bakanlığı*) in Ankara.[11] Nevertheless, the following reflections are primarily my own assessment and interpretation of the qur'anic Abraham material. As noted in chapter 1, my approach broadly correlates with Turkish efforts to understand Islam primarily according to the Qur'an, rather than through "through the eyes of the scholars of Islamic jurisprudence."[12]

2. Al-Baqara.

More descriptions of Abraham are found in this long sura than in any other, including 10 of my 11 identified descriptions. The sura opens with the declaration that the Qur'an is "guidance" for those who are "mindful of God" (2:2; and "for all mankind" 2:185), showing the way to salvation.[13] It refers often to the concept of divine guidance (2:5, 16, 38, 120, 159, 175, 185, and 256). This wide-ranging sura is said to sum up the whole teaching of the Quran (Ali), and to refer to all five central principles of the religion of Islam.[14]

Sura 2 refers to three events in Abraham's life, among which only the Kaaba story is narrated in detail (2:124-29). The first verses divide mankind into three groups: The God-fearing, the unbelievers, and the hypocrites, depending on how they respond to God's guidance. Then follows a series of reminders and rebukes to those refusing to believe Muhammad, drawing on prophet stories, arranged roughly in biblical order: Creation and Adam (2:30-39), Israel (2:40-86), Moses and Jesus and their struggles with stubborn, disobedient people (2:87-121), Abraham (2:124-141). Following a major section on the Kaaba and ordinances for the Islamic community, more stories are rehearsed which roughly parallel stories from the biblical narrative concerning the Judges, Samuel, Saul, David and Goliath (2:246-

253). All of the narratives are adduced as examples of the divine guidance sent by God, especially to the Jews. Abraham is presented as one of the "rightly guided" ones (2:137), whose example the Jews and Christians should follow: "They say, 'Become Jews or Christians, and you will be rightly guided.' Say [Prophet], 'No, [ours is] the religion of Abraham, the upright, who did not worship any god besides God" (2:135).

The first reference to Abraham in the Qur'an (2:124) recalls a time when "Abraham's Lord tested him with certain commandments. Here as elsewhere Abraham's story is presumed to be familiar to the audience, in this case local Jews, addressed as the "children of Israel" (2:122).[15] Through God's answer to Abraham's prayer for his descendants, the Jews are warned that neither their descent from Abraham nor any intercession on their behalf will mean anything if they themselves are not obedient: "God answered, 'My pledge does not hold for those who do evil'" (2:124). In this passage, God selects Abraham as "a *leader* for the people" because of his obedience to certain commands or tests. This phrase is literally, "I will make you an *imam* to the nations" (Ali, Ahmed), or "an imam to humankind" (Ayoub). "Imam" is usually interpreted as containing at least two meanings: guided leader and model/pattern.[16] Abraham's surrender is the prototype of Islamic submission to God.[17]

Bayraklı entitles 2:124 "no appointing without testing."[18] The idea of Abraham as being "tested" is also developed extensively in Jewish writings (beyond the one explicit statement in Gen 22:1). Jewish Pseudepigrapha identifies various points in the biblical narrative at which Abraham was tested.[19] However there is little consensus among Muslim interpreters as to the content of this testing. Some Muslim interpreters cite ritual tests such as trimming body hair, as well as tests in relation to pilgrimage rites.[20] Others point to a series of tests of his obedience when God called him to leave his people, when Nimrod cast him into the fire, when the angels visited and when he was commanded to offer his son, and finally the greatest test was when Allah called him to surrender himself (see 2:131).[21] Emiroğlu also mentions disagreement among commentators as to whether Abraham's testing preceded or succeeded his appointment as prophet.[22]

The Kaaba narrative which follows may be understood as the primary outcome of such acts of obedience and faith in the face of testing (2:125-29). Maududi argues that by reminding them of Abraham this passage reinforces the claim that true religion is now with those who receive the prophet who has arisen in Mecca, rather than with the Jews (or others) who reject him.

The Jews have been exhorted to follow Prophet Muhammad, who had come with the same Guidance and who was a descendant and follower of Prophet

Abraham whom they highly honored as their ancestor, and professed to follow as a prophet. (Maududi)

Verse 130 refers to the "religion of Abraham," thus identifying his faith or creed directly with the Meccan site of worship focused on the Kaaba, which Asad calls "Abraham's Temple." God appoints this House to be a place of pilgrimage, and "Abraham's station" to be a place of prayer (where Abraham was supposed to have prayed).[23] He makes a covenant with Abraham and Ishmael to purify it for pilgrimage rites (2:125), and Abraham prays for the land around the Kaaba to be fruitful (cf. 14:35-41). That Abraham and Ishmael "raise the foundation" of the House may mean that the house—"beyt"—existed long before Abraham's time and that he and Ishmael were "renewing" this ancient place of worship.[24] They dedicate it to God and pray for themselves and their "seed" to be made submissive to God, and that he will show them their holy rites. They also ask God to send a Messenger to the people of Mecca (2:127–29). Reynolds draws attention to the importance of this prayer in relating Muhammad to Abraham and the Arabs to Abraham's "nation":

The notion of an Abrahamic nation seems to be at the center of the Qur'an's message. The Qur'an is the Arabic scripture given to Abraham's children. To this end the Qur'an has Abraham and Ishmael pray together that God will form a holy nation from their offspring and raise up a divine messenger from that nation. . . . The Arabs are that holy nation, and their messenger is Muhammad.[25]

The context of this account of Abraham is a call to the Jews (2:122). Following the Mecca narrative, they are charged with wrongly appropriating Abraham for themselves and in so doing departing from the primal religion: "Who but a fool would forsake the religion of Abraham?" (2:130). Abraham is represented as devoting himself to the Lord of the universe and charging his sons to do the same, as Jacob his grandson subsequently charges his sons in a deathbed scene (2:132-33). Whereas Genesis records no deathbed scene for Abraham as it does for Jacob, Jubilees 22:1–23:8 has a deathbed scene in which Abraham blesses his grandson Jacob, charging him to remain separate from idolaters.[26]

These instructions for responding to other monotheistic claims to Abrahamic heritage are framed with two identical references to the previous generations of Abraham's descendants: "That community passed away. What they earned belongs to them, and what you earn belongs to you: you will not be answerable for their deeds" (2:134, 141). Each individual and generation is responsible for their own deeds. No special privilege is to be sought in genealogical relationship to Abraham.[27] Since Abraham preceded both

Judaism and Christianity, their special claims to the patriarchs are empty. The pure religion of Abraham is being restored through Muhammad's prophetic office, and if hearers were honest they would acknowledge this. The Qur'an mounts a strong challenge to Jews and Christians who claim Abraham, asserting that "Abraham, Ishmael, Isaac, Jacob and the Tribes" were neither Jews nor Christians, but uncompromised submitters to God (2:135-140).[28]

Two short stories from Abraham's life are referred to briefly in close proximity near the end of the sura (2:258, 260). In the first Abraham confounds an opponent in a dispute in which the proud ruler claimed he too, like Abraham's god, could give or take life (by freeing and executing two prisoners). Abraham challenges him to bring the sun from the west since God brings it from the east. In the second story, Abraham seeks understanding of how God gives life to the dead, and is told to cut in pieces four birds, which God then miraculously brings back together. Yazıcıoğlu sees Abraham's question as a "request to move up from one certainty level to a higher one."[29] Abraham's reason for questioning God is "just to put my heart at rest," which may not carry the same negative implications of requesting a sign from God as that of sceptics.[30]

3. Al 'Imran.

This sura evidently has a complementary relationship with the previous one.[31] Both suras deal with issues raised by Muhammad's interaction with Jews and Christians. Abraham is introduced into the sura at four points (3:33, 65-67, 81-91, 95-97). The only specific event narrated from his life is a brief reference to the founding of the House of worship at "Bekka" (3:96-97), which is likely another name for Mecca.[32] The first reference to Abraham is at the beginning of a discourse on the occasion of the visit of a deputation from the Christians of Najran. The story of the "family of 'Imran" is recounted as a warning example to those who reject faith and turn back (3:33-63). "God chose Adam, Noah, Abraham's family, and the family of 'Imran, over all other people, in one line of descent" (33-34). 'Imran is the father of Moses' brother Aaron, but the story apparently deals with his distant priestly offspring: "A *woman of 'Imran*" (the mother of Mary), *Mary* (mother of Jesus), *Zachariah* (father of Yahya/John) into whose care Mary was entrusted, and *Jesus* who was created like Adam without father and who worked many miraculous signs as an apostle to Israel." This reference to the special election of a line of descent is perhaps the clearest qur'anic statement that could be taken to confirm the NT focus on the line of descent from Adam to Abraham to Jesus (Matt 1:1-17). Yet this seems incidental in the Qur'an; the focus of the narrative is on the disastrous outcome for those who resist the truth.

The second set of references follows immediately, as the "People of the Book" are confronted regarding disputation over Abraham: "Why do you argue about Abraham when the Torah and the Gospels were not revealed until after his time?" (3:65, 67). Abraham is called a *hanif,* understood as a pure Muslim monotheist.[33] This description generally involves the two primary components of Islamic monotheism: complete surrender to Allah and not joining gods to Allah. All people, particularly the People of the Book and those listening to Muhammad, are called to follow the example of Abraham and other revelation-receiving prophets: "Say [Muhammad], 'We [Muslims] believe in God and in what has been sent down to us and to Abraham, Ishmael, Isaac, Jacob, and the Tribes'" (3:84; identical with 2:136).

They are called to follow the "religion of Abraham" (3:95). As in Al-Baqara, the guidance of Allah is promised for those who submit to his message. But those who divide and dispute after receiving "Clear Signs" will be dreadfully penalized. The House built by Abraham is the appointed place of worship for all mankind (3:95-97), yet there are factions of the People of the Book (understood to be the Jews of Medina) who try to obstruct the believers. A central call is to unity in the faith of Abraham, without allowing distinctions and factions. Abraham's link to the Kaaba is part of the argument against the Jews, whose centrality as people of the Book has now passed on to the followers of Muhammad and his book. While temporarily centered on Jerusalem, the true original 'qiblah' for all believers is Mecca.

Abraham is brought into the argument of the sura primarily as an example for the faithful followers of the prophetic message, who are declared to be the "nearest of kin to Abraham" (3:68). They are to unite in the religion of Abraham and refuse all divisions and apostasy (3:200).

4. An-Nisa'.

Al-Ghazali says that the overall subject of the fourth sura is human social relations and how they are to be conducted and regulated.[34]Abraham is referred to in 4:54, 125, and 163 to emphasize the importance of these arrangements. Following a series of directions regarding care of orphans, inheritance, sexual propriety, marriage, fair trade, and generosity, events from the lives of people from previous eras are cited as warnings against disobeying. In 4:44-57 the "People of the Book" are described as those "who were given a portion of the Book" and are blamed for twisting their Scriptures and for believing in sorcery and evil. Muslims are warned against their schemes. In 4:54 "the people of Abraham" apparently refers to the people of Israel, to whom God gave "the Book and Wisdom, and conferred upon them a great kingdom." The previous verse speaks of those who claim "a share in the kingdom," which Asad calls "an allusion to the Jewish belief that they occupy a privileged position in the sight of God." The Qur'an is careful to point out that among Abraham's descendants are some who believe and others who reject God's "signs" and are to be cast into the Fire.

In 4:125 Abraham is presented as the one who is "true in faith" (*hanif*). Believers are exhorted to follow the "way" or "creed" of Abraham, who is the great example of one who submits his whole self to Allah and does good deeds. Further incentive is given in the extraordinary phrase "For God took Abraham as a friend." Mainstream Islamic interpretation treats this distinguished title (*Khalilullah*) as simply the expression or divine affirmation of Abraham's pure faith and consistently righteous conduct.[35] But in Sufi traditions concerning the concept of Islamic sainthood this is developed much further, as revered mystics are often referred to as "the friends of God."[36]

The third reference to Abraham in 4:163 is one of numerous verses listing recipients of divine revelation.[37] As the table below shows, this verse is the most complete listing of names where Abraham is the common denominator. His importance in the qur'anic line of prophets receiving divine revelation is evident despite uncertainty about the "book" he received (87:19).[38]

2:136	3:84	4:163	19:58	33:7	42:13	53:36-37	57:26	87:19
			Adam					
		Noah	Noah	Noah	Noah		Noah	
Abraham	Abraham	Abraham	Abraham	Abraham	Abraham	Abraham	Abraham	Abraham
Ishmael	Ishmael	Ishmael						
Isaac	Isaac	Isaac						
Jacob	Jacob	Jacob	Israel					
Tribes	Tribes	Tribes					"Others"	
Moses	Moses			Moses	Moses	Moses		Moses
Jesus	Jesus	Jesus		Jesus	Jesus		Jesus	
Prophets	Prophets							
		Job						
		Jonah						
		Aaron						
		Solomon						
		David						

6. Al-An'am.

This sura is held to be the first revealed at Mecca, and exhibits the marks of Muhammad's struggle with unbelieving opponents as he is given words and arguments with which to confute them. More than 30 times God commands Muhammad to "Say . . ." as he instructs him in this process (e.g. 11, 12, 14, 161, 162, 164). During Abraham's dispute with the idolaters of his father Azar's people (6:74-87), God shows Abraham the power and the laws of the heavens and the earth, "so that he might be a firm believer"

(6:75). This apparently refers to his experience in the following verses, where he sees a star and says, "This is my Lord," but when it sets, he says, "I do not like things that set," eventually declaring that he believes only in the one Creator: "I have turned my face as a true believer towards Him who created the heavens and the earth. I am not one of the polytheists" (6:76-79).[39] Nevertheless it seems Abraham did not reach this conclusion by himself. Rather God gave it to him to use in such disputes (6:83).

There is disagreement about whether Abraham discerned the existence of the one Creator God by observing the setting moon and sun or if he only used this reasoning process to convince the idolaters in his dispute. Those supporting the latter argue that a prophet of God would have been kept from considering the moon or sun worthy of worship, even in his early years in an idolatrous context. For example, Yusuf Ali says "This shows the stages of Abraham's spiritual enlightenment; it should not be supposed that he literally worshipped stars or heavenly bodies." One of the imams I interviewed likewise argued strongly that Abraham was at no point in his life to be considered an idolater. The statement in 6:83, "We raise in rank whoever we will," may support the interpretation that his observation of the heavenly bodies was part of the training of the prophet. Others see it as self-evident in the text that Abraham reasoned his way to monotheism. For example, Rahman says, "Abraham arrives at monotheism by a gradual process of eliminating astral gods (6:76)"[40] Similarly Dirks, "Abraham's own natural reasoning abilities and contemplation . . . led him to reject polytheistic astral worship and idolatry. In so doing, his attention shifted from the created to the Creator."[41] Whichever interpretation is correct, the qur'anic Abraham stands as a prime example of one endowed by God with powers of reason and argumentation in defense of Tawhid.

In the second reference to Abraham in this sura, God instructs Muhammad to say that Allah has guided him into the true way, "a straight path, an upright religion, the faith of Abraham" (6:161). The term hanif, which appears again here in relation to Abraham, is translated as "a man of pure faith" by Abdel Haleem. As Stewart notes, "In general the term is closely associated with Abraham (2:135; 3:67, 95; 4:125; 6:79, 161; 16:120, 123; 22:31) and contrasts with shirk 'polytheism.'"[42] The emphasis in the passage is on the monotheistic faith of Abraham, and therefore hanif may refer as much to his way as to Abraham himself.[43]

A central idea in this sura regarding Abraham is that God *guides* him and others like him. Abraham ponders the stars and moon, and says, "If my Lord does not *guide* me, I shall be one of those who go astray" (6:77). He confronts his people with the words, "How can you argue with me about God when He has *guided* me?" (6:80; cf. 26:77-78; 43:26-27). He warns them, "It is those who have faith, and do not mix their faith with idolatry, who will be secure, and it is they who are rightly *guided"* (6:82). In three additional verses the divine guidance given to Abraham is affirmed (6:84, 87, 161). God's guidance is the way in which people are delivered from idolatry and enabled to reach the hoped-for place in the afterlife. Abraham stands out as one rightly guided.

9. At-Tawba.

Abraham is referred to three times in sura 9 (in verses 70 and 114), which is largely concerned with stirring up the believers to fight in the cause of Allah.[44] In the first reference a list of those peoples who rejected and insulted the messengers of God are given, with the understanding that these rejecters were overthrown and destroyed in punishment: "Have they never heard the stories about their predecessors, the peoples of Noah, 'Ad, Thamud, Abraham, Midian, and the ruined cities?" Muhammad's listeners are to take warning: "Do they not know that whoever opposes God and His Messenger will go to the Fire of Hell and stay there?" (9:63). The argument of the sura is that God will reward those who fight with Muhammad and punish those who refuse, just as he has in the past (9:111).

There is to be no mercy shown to those who resist the prophet by siding with the unbelievers, even if they are relatives. Tender-hearted Abraham at first desired to seek forgiveness for his idolatrous father, but when he saw his father's hardness of heart he washed his hands of him (9:114; cf. 60:4). Abraham's story is a model of how believers should act toward Muhammad's opponents. "It is not fitting for the Prophet and the believers to ask forgiveness for the idolaters—even if they are related to them" (9:113).

11. Hud.

This sura is heavy on warning, emphasizing that God is aware of all that mankind does: "your Lord is never unaware of what you [people] are doing" (11:123). Al-Ghazali notes a feature of this sura that distinguishes it from the rest: "It is full of intensely personal, direct and indirect instructions addressed to Prophet Muhammad, using the first personal pronoun."[45] It is thus not surprising to find Muhammad encouraged with a series of seven punishment-stories about messengers sent to their communities, facing the same type of situation as he faced in Mecca: Noah (24-48), Hud (50-60), Salih (61-68),[46] Abraham (69-76), Lot (77-83), Shu'ayb (84-95), and Moses (96-99). For the most part, these stories recall God's judgment on peoples who reject the prophet sent to them. Welch notes that these stories follow a common form, with certain repeated features adding rhetorical weight to the heavy warnings:

Their basic plot is that God sends or selects a messenger from among the people of a tribe or town, who urges his people to serve only the true God, warns them that they will be destroyed if they reject his message, which the majority do, and then God rescues the messenger and those who believe him and destroys those who do not. Punishment-stories occur in groups, usually featuring four or more peoples or towns that were destroyed after most of the people rejected a messenger sent by God from among themselves. [47]

In certain respects Abraham is not like the others whose stories are recounted. He is not described in this section as warning his people, nor is the fate of his people recorded. However, Abraham's story is tied to the following story of Lot and his people by the messengers' first word to him: "Do not fear. We have been sent against the people of Lot" (11:70). Thus united with Lot's story, the mention of Abraham fits the punishment story pattern.

The narrative's primary focus is on the reactions of Abraham and his wife to the mysterious messengers who bring announcements of judgment on Lot's people and of a son to be born to the aged couple. Abraham's hospitality is evident: "without delay he brought in a roasted calf" (11:69). But here and in 51:27-28, Abraham becomes uneasy when he sees that they do not eat, a feature found in some para-biblical Jewish stories. [48] The messengers ask if she is "astonished" at God's pronouncement. When Abraham's fear passes, he attempts unsuccessfully to intercede for Lot's people.

At this point in the narrative, his wife laughs. [49] The narrated order of events (she laughs before receiving the news of Isaac, not after) has caused considerable discussion about the reason for Sarah's laughter. [50] While most Islamic commentators seek a cause for the "laughter" that does not impute incredulity to her, it seems probable that the background for this allusion is the biblical text in which Sarah and Abraham both laugh at seeming impossibility of their having a child at their age. Within the sura as a whole and the punishment-stories in particular, however, the point of the event is unmistakable: do not doubt the messengers of God! Their message is true and must be heeded.

The stories of these prophets are recounted for a stated purpose: "We have told you the stories of the prophets to make your heart firm and in these accounts truth has come to you [Muhammed], as well as lessons and reminders for the believers" (11:120). The fate of the communities who rejected the messengers sent to them stands as an object lesson for the community to whom Muhammad is sent. Stewart explains that "The narratives are present not as mere histories, but as didactic examples to serve as a warning to a contemporary audience, that of the Prophet Muhammad.

Both the introductory and the final sections are set in the present and relate the punishment stories to the contemporary situation."[51] But in Muhammad's case, the punishment in view for those who reject his message is at the Day of Judgment, rather than immediate.

The final section of the Abraham story in this sura is his prayer for Lot's people: "He pleaded with Us for Lot's people, for Abraham was forbearing, tender-hearted, and devout." But God's answer is unyielding: "Abraham, cease your pleading: what your Lord has ordained has come about" (11:76).

12. Yusuf.

The story of Joseph is the longest and most detailed in the Qur'an. Joseph is the only character named. Understanding the point of this particular narrative is helpful for understanding the qur'anic use of narrative in general, as the conclusion makes clear:

> *"All the messengers We sent before you [Muhammad] were men to whom We made revelations, men chosen from the people of their towns… When the messengers lost all hope and realized that they had been dismissed as liars, Our help came to them: We saved whoever We pleased, but Our punishment will not be turned away from guilty people. There is a lesson in the stories of such people for those who understand." (12:109-11)*

Joseph is an example of one such messenger of God, rejected by the people to whom he was sent and helped by God at the last moment. The narration of his story serves to encourage the prophet to whom it is revealed and to warn those who are rejecting him. It is intended to provide teaching for all who desire to learn: "There are lessons in the story of Joseph and his brothers for all who seek them" (12:7).

Waldman's comments on the Joseph story are helpful for understanding the motive of qur'anic narrative as a whole, including the Abraham stories: "Within the overall purposes of the Qur'an, the Joseph story serves. . . . as a didactic vehicle, in this case to show how God sends signs and constantly guides and rewards the God-fearing."[52] After presenting a list of seven largely common characteristics of messengers in the Qur'an, she concludes that "The qur'anic story of Joseph is structured to emphasize his fit with these characteristics, which in turn are related to other key elements in the qur'anic worldview."[53]

Abraham is mentioned twice in the extended Joseph narrative. In 12:6 Jacob explains to his son the purpose of the dream he has seen: "This is about how your Lord will choose you, teach you to interpret dreams, and perfect His blessing on you and the House of Jacob, just as He perfected it earlier on your forefathers Abraham and Isaac." Joseph's ability to interpret dreams will be one of the evidences or signs that he is a valid messenger. It is unclear whether the gift of interpretation was also the means of God's perfecting blessing on the forefathers. Nevertheless the linking of "blessing" with the line of Abraham through Isaac and Jacob may be an area of common ground with the biblical narrative where this is central.

In his second mention of Abraham, Joseph uses the opportunity of interpreting the dreams of Pharaoh's servants to declare his belief in his ancestors' God: "I reject[54] the faith of those who disbelieve in God and deny the life to come, and I follow the faith of my forefathers Abraham, Isaac, and Jacob" (12:38). Rahman argues that Muhammad's situation is often "mirrored" in the earlier prophet-stories and concludes:

That this religion of pure monotheism which is pre-eminently attributed to Abraham was primarily developed against the cult of pagan deities is obvious from 12:37-40. . . . It is, then, in a solidly Meccan context with pagans as its addressees that the Qur'an develops its image of Abraham as the super-prophet and arch-monotheist.[55]

The primacy of Muhammad's biography as a basis for interpretation is contested by Reynolds, who argues for greater use of the "biblical subtext" to properly understand qur'anic "homily."[56] Whatever the historical background, it is clear that the Qur'an consistently declares that the faith proclaimed by all the prophets was the pure monotheism of Abraham (2:130; 3:83-85, 95; 4:125; 6:161; 12:38; 16:123; 22:78; 42:13). The story of Abraham's descendant Joseph serves as an extended illustration of the way in which God guides his prophets in this straight path and vindicates them in the face of idolatrous opposition.

14. Ibrahim.

In the middle of this sura, which warns against rejecting the prophet's message, Muhammad is told to "remember" Abraham praying that God would bless the town of Mecca (14:35). This prayer concludes a story of his establishment of the Kaaba with his son Ishmael, which is narrated in four different suras (see above). In particular Abraham seeks preservation from idolatry for himself and his offspring, so that they may be thankful and "keep up" the ritual prayers at the House. Uniquely in this sura, he also seeks forgiveness on the Day of Judgment for himself, his parents, and the believers (14:41). Abraham's urgent desire to be kept from idolatry serves as a warning for the idolaters in Muhammad's audience to forsake their idols immediately. The link between Abraham and Muhammad is particularly strong in this sura. Not only are the punishment-story events similar, but in this case the actual setting is the same—the town of Mecca. Abraham's longing gives expression to that of Muhammad.

Abraham's "offspring" is particularly important in this prayer. After praying for all of his offspring, Abraham mentions having settled "some of his offspring" close to the Kaaba, which would refer to the descendants of Ishmael. He then praises God for granting him *Ishmael and Isaac* in his old age and asks that all his offspring (including Isaac's) would keep up the prayer (presumably at or toward the Sacred House). This is a call for all the descendants of Abraham to recognize the Kaaba as the place of prayer, rejecting the priority given Isaac's descendants in the biblical narrative. According to al-Ghazali,

> *Human beings are all equal, and are only distinguished by their closeness to, and fear of, God. Abraham's legacy belongs to all his offspring, and it is simply below God Almighty to designate a particular piece of land as the sole property of Jacob's children in perpetuity.*[57]

Al-Ghazali's reaction appears to express frustration at the modern Palestine-Israeli conflict. The issue of biblical particularism will be considered more fully in the following chapter, but might be noted that the Muslim focus on the Kaaba is no less particular than the Jewish focus on Jerusalem.[58]

15. Al-Hijr.

The qur'anic picture of response to God's messenger in this sura shows that messengers meet with stubborn rejection from their hearers, who refuse to be convinced in spite of the evidence of creation (15:10-25). Satan's refusal to bow to Adam and his subsequent banishment is related to encourage the prophet; Satan will have no power over God's servants, and Muhammad is to tell these "servants" of the sure destinies of believers and unbelievers (15:26-50). He is then told, "tell them also of Abraham," following which the second Abraham story, the account of angelic visitors, is narrated in 15:51-77, in a form roughly parallel to its telling in suras 11 and 51. The story is told in two parts, each introduced by the arrival of the messengers at the respective households of Abraham and Lot (15:52, 61). While the messengers' primary mission is to destroy Lot's people and deliver the prophet, the announcement of a son to the aged prophet Abraham comes first (15:53). This announcement encourages Muhammad to take heart and not despair, for the word of God will be fulfilled, as it was with Abraham. When Abraham questions the possibility of fathering a child in his old age he is told that the news is true and that he should not "despair." Abraham answers that only the "misguided" despair of God's mercy. In this he functions as an ideal prophet and Muslim who maintains his trust in Allah despite difficulties and delays.

The birth of Isaac is not narrated in the Qur'an, but he is referred to as a son "granted to" Abraham in his old age (6:84; 12:39; 19:49; 21:72), and listed with other righteous men or prophets (2:136, 140; 3:84; 4:163; 12:6, 38; 38:45). The "good news" of a son (11:112; 15:53; 29:31; 37:112-113; 51:28) is brought by the angelic messengers in all five versions of the story. Why is it "good news"? Nothing more seems to be involved than the son being a special one, a gifted and blessed son.[59] It is notable that the Islamic commentaries I have consulted on this pair of stories devote much space to the Lot story, with little explanation of the annunciation of Isaac.

16. An-Nahl.

The sura warns all people to observe the evidence of creation or nature and be "thankful" to the Creator. The "signs" of nature are corroborated by the "signs" of the Qur'an (e.g. 16:79; 10:5-6). Abraham is an "example" for the Muslim community to follow, one who was devoutly obedient to God and true in faith (16:120-23). He is an example of one who is not an idolater, but rather one who is "thankful" for the blessings of God. Thankfulness is a primary mark of a believer (16:78, 114; see also 5:89; 14:5, 7; especially Abraham's request in 14:37). Abraham is specifically identified as the one whose "creed" Muhammad is to follow.

19. Maryam.

Named for the story of Mary in verses 16-35, this sura narrates snippets from a number of prophet stories, including Abraham. In verses 41-50 God narrates to Muhammad "the story of Abraham," described as a *siddiq* (faithful or loyal one, Turkish: *sadık*).[60] Abraham pleads with his father to cease the worship of inanimate idols, by which he will find himself worshipping Satan. He warns his father of punishment from the Lord if he persists as Satan's companion. This underscores the significant role given to Iblis or Satan in the Qur'an. He appears as the main source of temptation or perhaps, as Rahman argues, as "the principle of evil which the Qur'an often personifies."[61] The Qur'an frequently warns people, as Abraham warns his father here, that they are in danger and must keep from following Satan (e.g. 2:168, 208; 6:142; 12:5; 17:53; 18:50; 35:6). The way to do this is to pay attention to divine guidance. Abraham says to his father, "knowledge that has not reached you has come to me, so follow me: I will guide you to an even path" (19:43).

When his father refuses and threatens to stone him, Abraham tells his father he will leave him to his idols and will pray to the Lord to forgive him. When he leaves his people to serve the creator, he is rewarded: "We granted him Isaac and Jacob and made them both prophets: We granted Our grace to all of them, and gave them a noble reputation" (19:49-50). Ishmael is not mentioned as a son "granted to" him; but is listed among those prophets to be mentioned along with Moses, Aaron, and Idris. Ishmael is primarily found with Abraham in the narratives of the construction of the Kaaba.[62] The prophets are mentioned under three heads: "from the seed of Adam, of those We carried in the Ark with Noah, from the seed of Abraham and Israel" (19:58). While this is the only passage where Abraham is seen in such direct conjunction with "Israel," there are a number of others that refer to the biblical Abraham lineage through Isaac and Jacob (6:84; 12:38; 19:49; 21:72; 29:27; 38:45).[63]

The story of Abraham's stubborn father may relate to the Mary narrative as an example of the state of those who have drifted into idolatry. The brief list of prophets is followed by the comment that "there came after them generations who neglected prayer and were driven by their own desires" (19:59). Christians may be implicated in this accusation, as those whose "factions have differed among themselves" (19:37).

21. Al-Anbiya'.

The sura takes its name from the prophets listed in 21:48-91: Moses, Aaron, Abraham, Lot, Noah, David and Solomon, Job, Ishmael, Idris, Dhu'l-Kifl,[64] and Zachariah (the father of John the Baptist/Yahya). It gives the story of Abraham's disputing with idolaters is given in greatest detail. The phrase "those who went before me" (21:24) draws attention to the qur'anic concept of the same prophetic actions and messages in every era.[65] God's unvaryingly sends the same message with each messenger: "We never sent any messenger before you [Muhammad] without revealing to him: 'There is no god but Me, so serve Me'" (21:25). Opposition was encountered by all the previous prophets, but these opponents were always defeated in the end (21:41; see also 6:38; 12:109-110).

The dispute between Abraham and his father's idolatrous people (51-73) exemplifies this opposition and the subsequent divine intervention. Abraham challenges his father and people regarding idols and affirms his allegiance to the one creating, sustaining God. He breaks the idols and mocks his questioners when brought to trial (21:52-67). Ultimately he is cast into the fire, but is miraculously delivered (21:68-70).[66] Following this deliverance, Abraham leaves with Lot for "the land We blessed for all people" (21:71), where he is rewarded with posterity through Isaac and Jacob. As noted above, the offspring "granted to" Abraham is generally identified with this line.

22. Al-Hajj.

Muhammad's followers were being forcibly prevented from entering the shrine at Mecca, and this sura gives permission for the Muslims to defend themselves and fight for their faith. Harsh threats of divine punishment are levelled at these disbelievers (22:19-22, 55, 57, 72). The call to forcibly establish this pilgrimage is linked with Abraham:

"As for the disbelievers, who bar others from God's path and from the Sacred Mosque. . . . We shall make them taste a painful punishment. We showed Abraham the site of the House, saying, 'Do not assign partners to Me. Purify My House." (22:25-26)

Little detail is given here of Abraham's role other than "purifying the house." The following verses set forth the duty of all to make pilgrimage to the House and the requirements for venerating God's "sacred things" and "waymarks" (26-33). Just as Muhammad was opposed by his own people in this task, so also earlier prophets including Abraham were opposed by their people. Yet God destroyed the disbelievers: "If they reject you [Prophet], so did the people of Noah before them, and those of 'Ad, Thamud, Abraham, Lot, Midian. Moses too was called a liar. I gave the disbelievers time, but in the end I punished them. How I condemned them!" (22:42-45).

The final verse of the sura encourages the faithful to defend their religion and relates this religion or faith (Islam) to "the faith of your forefather Abraham. God has called you Muslims" (22:78). Interpreters note that this sura gives the rightful heirs of Abraham permission to wage war in defense and to rule those whom they defeat. Maududi's paraphrase of the instructions for Muslims is typical:

The Believers have been officially given the name of "Muslims," saying:

> *"You are the real heirs to Abraham and you have been chosen to become witnesses of the Truth before mankind. Therefore you should establish salat and pay the zakat dues in order to become the best models of righteous life and perform Jihad for propagating the Word of Allah."* *(Maududi)*

It is central to the qur'anic worldview that "God chooses messengers from among the angels and from among men" (22:75).

26. ash-Shu' ara'.

As part of its argument against disbelievers who belittle the Qur'an, this sura "recounts several stories of earlier prophets, the reactions of their people, and punishments that afflicted them, ending by confirming the divine origin of the Qur'an."[67] Abraham's dispute with his idolatrous kinsfolk occupies some thirty five verses of this sura (26:69-102). These stories are told to encourage Muhammad with the understanding that what is happening to him now is only what has happened in the past to God's other messengers (26:3-6). At times the faithful messengers are rejected as being "possessed" (26:27), or "sorcerers" (26:34-35), "liars" (26:105, 123, 141, 160, 176, 186, 189), and "bewitched" (26:153, 185).

Abraham's story does not quite fit the pattern, in that there is no account of the punishment of those who reject his warning, though this may be implied. Rather Abraham stands as a model messenger, who challenges his people regarding idols (26:70-76), affirms his allegiance to the one God (26:77-82), prays for favor and forgiveness for his people (26:83-89), warns them of judgment and the day of resurrection (26:90-93). If the verses from 94 to 104 are part of Abraham's story, rather than a parenthetical addition, the announcement of the punishment of those who reject is also included in his warning. The wicked are called the "misguided" (26:91); they say to their idols, "We were clearly *misguided* when we made you equal with the Lord of the Worlds" (26:97-98).

29. Al-ʿAnkabut.

This sura combines into one narrative two distinct Abraham stories that are generally related in different suras: Abraham's disputation with his people (29:16-27), and the visit of angels announcing the birth of Isaac and the impending punishment of Lot's people (29:28-32).[68] In both of these stories Abraham's nephew Lot plays a role, first believing and departing with his uncle (29:26), and then confronting "his people"[69] with their wicked acts (29:28-29).

The phrase "We also sent Abraham" (29:16)[70] seems to parallel the account of Noah, which begins: "We sent Noah" (29:14). While Abraham is not literally "sent," God's superintendence of Abraham's life from cradle to confrontation may be understood as a divine "sending" process. The salient point is that as with Noah, so with Abraham. The calling and experiences of the prophets resemble one another.

Abraham calls his people to turn from idols to give thanks to the true God, who alone can meet their needs and to whom all will return. He also warns them by reminding them of previous peoples who rejected God's message (29:18). Abraham stands as a model prophet, fulfilling his duty to warn his hearers. Muslim exegetes agree that the central issue in this story is that of warning his people to turn from idolatry to Tawhid:

> Each commentator emphasizes tawhid at different parts of the story, whether it is the various debates that Abraham engages in with his people or the prayers he says before he is thrown into the fire. They all also portray Abraham as a model believer who embodies the teachings of tawhid and challenges the foundations of shirk in his society. Because of his belief in tawhid and his resolute faith in God, Abraham is seen to be miraculously saved by God from the fire as a sign to all believers.[71]

Verses 19-23 seem to be a parenthetical comment to Muhammad, expressing the sad reality that people do not see the universal evidence of God's creating life in this world and the next. The Abraham story resumes with his being thrown into the fire, and his rescue from the fire is a "sign" for those who believe, as Noah's rescue from the flood was "a sign for all people." Abraham departs with a warning that those who have chosen idols will face the penalty on the Day. Lot believes and accompanies him. The twin endowments of "prophethood and Scripture" are given to the offspring of Abraham (29:27; see also 57:26).

As in Genesis 18, the angels who announce the birth of a son also announce their mission to punish the people of the city where Lot lives (29:31). Here however, the divine intervention is God's answer to Lot's appeal for help against those who refuse his warning and taunt him to bring God's judgment as threatened (29:29-30). The final reference to Abraham in this sura is his intercession on behalf of Lot, to which the angels respond that it is already determined that Lot and his household will be saved.

Following Abraham and Lot, other prophet stories come in quick succession: Shu'ayb sent to Midian, then the tribes of 'Ad and Thamud, Moses sent with signs to Qarun, Pharaoh, and Haman. God punished each of these peoples for their sins. The Abraham narrative functions along with the story of the judgment of Lot's people, as a classic prophet story of warning, rejection, punishment.

33. Al-Ahzab.

Abraham is referred to once in this sura. God says he has taken a special pledge from the prophets, among whom Abraham is mentioned along with Muhammad, Noah, Moses, and Jesus (33:7; cf. 3:81). The next verse implies that even the prophets will be held accountable for the sincere fulfillment of their pledged service.[72] These pledges stand as an example for all believers. Those who put their lives in danger fighting for the cause of truth are said to be men "who honored their pledge to God" (33:23).[73]

37. As-Saffat.

This sura records three separate Abraham narratives among stories of the earlier prophets: the dispute with his relatives (37:83-99), the sacrifice of his son (37:100-111), and the angels' visit (37:112-113). These follow a lengthy description of the Day of Judgment and support the general defense of Muhammad's prophethood and the hereafter. "See how those who were warned met their end! Not so the true servants of God" (37:69-74). The prophet stories thus illustrate these "true servants of God" (37:75-148).[74] God says of Abraham, "truly he was one of Our faithful servants" (37:111). Like the first four prophet stories, Abraham's concludes with the announcement that in reward for his faithfulness, posterity would praise him: "We let him be praised by succeeding generations: 'Peace be upon Abraham!'" (37:109-111). Each of these stories recalls God's punishment of the people who reject the messenger sent to them and his rescue of the prophet. In Abraham's case, the first story concerns his father's people in Mesopotamia, who reject his arguments against worshipping hapless idols they have carved with their own hands. When they build a pyre and throw him into the blaze, God "humiliates" them, but nothing is said of punishment. In fact the only note of punishment for Abraham's people who reject his warnings is eschatological: "Hell will be your home and no one will help you" (29:25). In this Abraham is closer to Muhammad than to others whose stories contain records of immediate punishment of unbelieving peoples.

The story of Abraham sacrificing his son is recounted in the Qur'an only here.[75] Generally placed later his career, in its context the account is linked to the story of Abraham disputing with his people: "They wanted to harm him, but We humiliated them. He said, 'I will go to my Lord: He is sure to guide me. Lord, grant me a righteous son" (37:98-99). Apparently some years intervene here. In answer to his confidence in God's guidance and his prayer, God gives him the good news of a "patient son" (37:100-101),[76] whose identity is not given. An argument can be made that this announcement refers to Ishmael, since Isaac's birth is announced later, in verse 112. On the other hand, the "good news" of a son to be born to Abraham elsewhere refers to Isaac, not Ishmael (11:71; 15:53; 51:28; as in 37:112).[77] When the boy was old enough to "work" with his father, Abraham tells him of his dream/vision in which he sees himself sacrificing his son.[78] The son responds that he is ready to do God's will: "Father, do as you are commanded and, God willing, you will find me steadfast" (37:102). As in Jewish exegetical narratives,[79] the Qur'an specifically notes that both father and son "submitted to God," marking them as exemplary Muslims. God states that Abraham has "fulfilled the dream" (rather than his command[80]) and tells his servant, "This is how We reward those who do good" (37:105). This "reward" may refer to the deliverance from having to sacrifice his son, or to the honor of being so greatly tested.[81] Finally God recounts his intervention, "We ransomed his son with a momentous sacrifice" (107). This great sacrifice is generally taken to refer to the sheep granted by God to die instead of the boy (as in Gen 22:13), but Asad suggests that it could also refer to the annual sacrifice appointed for Muslims. The commemoration of this event is not a sacrifice in the biblical sense, but an act recalling the obedience of Abraham.[82]

In the Qur'an this story illustrates obedient submission to the will of God. It also illustrates the God's testing of mankind which is referred to repeatedly in the Qur'an, which exposes the presence or absence of genuine faith which perseveres and submits wholly to God.[83] Sufis cite the story of Abraham and his son as an example of relinquishing all other loves for the sake of the love for God.

The final Abraham story is a brief summary of the angels' visit to announce the birth of Isaac: "We gave Abraham the good news of Isaac—a prophet and a righteous man—and blessed him and Isaac too" (37:112-13). As elsewhere, care is taken to make clear that despite God's blessing, not all of Abraham and Isaac's offspring will be blessed: "some of their offspring were good, but some clearly wronged themselves."

A central theme of the sura is seen in an excuse by the unbelieving pagans that they are disadvantaged by not having scriptures like previous people: "[The disbelievers] used to say, 'If only we had a scripture like previous people, we would be true servants of God,' yet now they reject [the Qur'an]" (37:167-170). Abraham functions in the sura then as the prime example of one who had no such earlier case to look to, but who nevertheless stood firm in the face of testing and surrendered himself to the Creator.

38. Saad.

According to Asad, "this *sūrah* is devoted almost entirely to the problem of divine guidance and its rejection by those who are 'lost in false pride, and [hence] deeply in the wrong' (verse 2)." A number of earlier prophets are mentioned and their rejection by the people whom they attempted to warn is recounted as encouragement to Muhammad. Generally, people to whom prophets were sent "rejected the messengers and they were deservedly struck by My punishment" (38:14).[84] Abraham's story is not part of this group of prophets and he is mentioned only briefly (38:45-48), following accounts of David (38:17-26), Solomon (38:30-40) and Job (38:41-44), who are given as examples of those who "cried to" or "turned to" God, particularly in repentance, seeking forgiveness for errors (38:17, 24, 30, 35, 41, 44; cf. 66:8). Abraham, Isaac and Jacob are described as "men of strength and vision," whom God caused to be devoted to Him through "their sincere remembrance of the Final Home" (38:45-46).[85] Much of what follows in the sura concerns the final abode, which will be either paradise, with its gardens of bliss, or hell, the place of fire and torment which God will fill with Iblis and other arrogant ones. Thus Abraham is seen as among those whose righteous ways are shaped by deep awareness of God and the Day of Reckoning.

42. Ash-Shura.

Abraham is referred to only in verse 14 of this sura. In this passage complete continuity between all the scripture-receiving messengers is strongly affirmed: "In matters of faith, He has laid down for you [people] *the same commandment* that He gave Noah, which We have revealed to you [Muhammad] and which We enjoined on Abraham and Moses and Jesus" (42:13-15).[86] God's sovereignty stands out in the description of Abraham: "God chooses whoever He pleases for Himself and *guides* towards Himself those who turn to Him" (42:13). Abraham exemplifies the rightly-guided messengers.

The one command given to all the messengers is to maintain the unity of faith (42:13); divisions are all traced to "rivalry." Muhammad is called to reject such selfish rivalry and assert that he believes in "whatever Scripture God has sent down" and mediate (bring justice) between them on the basis of straightforward ethical monotheism. God will reward each one on the basis of their deeds at the Day of Judgment. After this basic acknowledgement is made, there is no meaning in arguments about the nature or activity of God. This makes discussion of distinctions difficult.

43. Az-Zukhruf.

Yusuf Ali's summary is helpful for understanding the way in which this sura appropriates Abraham as well as Moses and Jesus. He says that Abraham is cited to appeal to the pagan Arabs (who revere Abraham as their ancestor), that Moses is cited to appeal to the Jews, and that Jesus is cited to appeal to the Christians. In each case the Qur'an argues that Islam is the same religion as that of these revered prophets. In light of this, as Ali paraphrases, "They should give up their sectarian attitude and follow the universal religion, which shows the Straight Way."

The argument addresses stubborn disbelievers who give loyalty to the way of their ancestors as the reason for rejecting God's messengers (43:23). Muhammad is to argue that the faith of the messengers God sent to people in every era was the same, and that these messengers warned against blindly following traditions. The story of Abraham disputing with his people and renouncing their idolatrous ancestral religion shows this (43:26-28). Abraham expresses confidence in God's *guidance*.

51. Ad-Dhariyat.

The "story of Abraham's honored guests," who bring word of the birth of a son and the impending punishment of the people of Lot, is narrated again in 51:24-37. Abraham initially fears when the angelic messengers do not eat the food he offers them and his wife reacts with incredulity to the good news of "a son who would be gifted with knowledge."[87]

The punishment rained down on Lot's "people lost in sin" leaves the destroyed town as "a sign for those who fear the painful punishment" (51:32-37). The importance of observing such "signs" is underscored in the ensuing punishment stories of Moses and Pharaoh, the peoples of 'Ad and Thamud, and the people of Noah, which are introduced with the words, "There is another sign in . . ." (51:38, 41, 43). This sura also gives several "signs" of nature as evidence for the Resurrection, such as the winds scattering both dust and rain (from which the sura takes its name) and the stars in their paths (51:20-22). The prophet's verbal message is also to be "clear warning" (51:50). All of these visible "signs" are intended to draw mankind to recognize the invisible, all-powerful Creator.

The story of Abraham serves two purposes in relation to this theme of heeding the signs of God: He is an example of one who believes the messengers of God bringing news that is humanly hard to believe (the birth), and his story is a prelude to the narrative of the punishment of Lot's people, the first of the punishment "signs" recounted here.

53. An-Najm.

In this sura Abraham is referred to once (53:37). Muhammad is told to consider an unbeliever who "turns away" and asked if he has not been "told what was written in the Scriptures of Moses and of Abraham" (53:33-37). In 87:19 the Books of Moses and Abraham are mentioned together again.[88] Abraham is referred to here as the one "who fulfilled his duty" or "engagements," or "who to his trust was true" (53:37). This could refer to the testing of Abraham with various commandments (2:124) or be a more general affirmation of his faithfulness. Immediately following this is the strong affirmation that "no soul shall bear the burden of another; that man will only have what he has worked towards (53:38-40). This basic principle, that no soul shall bear the burden of another, appears in the Qur'an five times (cf. 6:164, 17:15, 35:18, 39:7). Interpreters take this string of statements to indicate that there can be no vicarious atonement (Ali, Asad). Therefore, Abraham is an example of faithful obedience rewarded by God.

54. Al-Qamar.

This sura does not mention Abraham, but does record the story of the destruction of the people of Lot (54:33-39), which is generally connected with the visit of the angels to Abraham. This comes in the middle of what are referred to as "warning tales that . . . have come down to them" (54:4-5). The implication is that these stories were known to the Arab people comprising Muhammad's audience. Perhaps Abraham is not mentioned because there is no record of a punishment befalling his people.

57. Al-Hadid.

God has sent his apostles with revelation to give the knowledge of right and wrong: "We sent Our messengers with clear signs, the Scripture and the Balance, so that people could uphold justice" (57:25). Abraham is mentioned here as an example along with Noah and Jesus, primarily to stress that not all of their descendants were true believers: "We sent Noah and Abraham, and gave prophethood and scripture to their offspring; among them there were some who were rightly guided, but many were lawbreakers. . . . We sent Jesus, son of Mary: We gave him the Gospel and put compassion and mercy into the hearts of his followers. . . . We gave a reward to those of them who believed, but many of them were lawbreakers" (57:26-27). True believers are those who have been "rightly guided." So the Qur'an shows a series of prophets, similar chronologically to the biblical history, running from Noah and Abraham to Jesus. This prophetic order is strengthened by the words "We sent other messengers to follow in their footsteps," between Abraham and Jesus, who is introduced with the words "After those We sent Jesus." Nevertheless, the Qur'an rejects the claims of Jews and Christians to be recipients of God's grace: "The People of the Book should know that they have no power over any of God's grace and that grace is in the hand of God alone" (57:29). The Qur'an portrays a pattern of prophets with similar experiences, rather than a chosen line or special nation.

60. Al-Mumtahanah.

This sura is devoted to ordering the relationship of the believers with unbelievers, focusing primarily on the presenting problem of believers desiring to marry women who have converted to Islam while their husbands have not. The solution is for these women to disown their former husbands.[89] Abraham is a model for those compelled to break relationship as the result of their faith, when he said to his people, "We disown you and what you worship besides God!" (60:4). There was however one exception to this stern position; Abraham did not simply renounce his father as he did the others, but prayed for his forgiveness (cf. 19:47). He and his companions also prayed for protection from the unbelievers whom they were disowning. Again we see various parts of well-known prophet stories being used as homiletical illustrations.

87. Al-A'la.

Abraham is referred at the end of the sura, concluding an argument that the Hereafter is better than this life. This truth is said to be found in "the earlier scriptures, the scriptures of Abraham and Moses" (87:18-19; cf. 53:36, which has the reverse order).[90] Yusuf Ali says that "no book of Abraham has come down to us," though he does mention *the Testament of Abraham* known in Jewish writings. Muhammad Asad, on the other hand, argues in his notes that these two names are given here "only as examples of earlier prophetic revelations, thus stressing, once again, the twofold fact of continuity in mankind's religious experiences and of the identity of the basic truths preached by all the prophets." God's earlier revelation to Abraham is described as containing the same message about the superiority of the life to come, calling for living life in this world with religious devotion in order to attain prosperity in the Hereafter. "You [people] prefer the life of this world, even though the Hereafter is better and more lasting" (87:15-17).

APPENDIX 6 – SUMMARY OF ABRAHAM IN CHRISTIAN AND MUSLIM WORLDVIEWS

			ABRAHAM IN CHRISTIAN WORLDVIEW		ABRAHAM IN MUSLIM WORLDVIEW	
1. CREATION - FALL		GOD	The Creator God is actively immanent in creation, reveals himself visibly to Abraham, and is involved in the narrative.	↔ ↔ ↔	God is evident in creation, is discovered by Abraham's reasoning from stars, and narrates the stories of Abraham.	**1. TAWHID**
		MAN	The human story continues in the biblical Abraham story, now treated as primarily as the chosen people and the rest of the nations. Abraham exemplifies the person of faith in covenantal relationship with God.	↔ ↔	The human story is traced paradigmatically (peoples, prophets), and Abraham is an example of human beings as they should be. All humankind belongs to God; all things happen in accordance with his will. Abraham is a true 'vicegerent.'	
		EVIL	The Abraham narrative continues and reflects the creation-fall narrative in which sin and evil are pervasive. The patriarchal narratives describe morally questionable actions by the patriarchs, including Abraham, which is consistent with the Christian "fall" idea.	↔ ↔ ↔	God is the author of both good and evil, through which mankind is tested. Satan seeks to turn people from the true path. Abraham's kinsfolk and the tyrant oppose Abraham and his message. The greatest and fundamental evil is idolatry.	
2. REDEMPTION		GOD	God speaks and appears to Abraham, personally establishing covenants and giving signs of his covenant purposes. From the Christian perspective God is known by his acts of redemption, culminating in Christ's work, through which God reveals himself.	↔ ↔ ↔	In the Qur'anic framework God 'guides' his chosen prophets and sends them with 'guidance' to remind people of their Creator and warn them of idolatry. Abraham brings this same message of Tawhid. God reveals his will, but not himself.	**2. PROPHETHOOD**
		MAN	Abraham believes God's promises, which are ultimately fulfilled in Christ and the people of Abraham taken from all nations. God's promises to Abraham are fulfilled in all who are redeemed by God through Christ's death and resurrection.	↔ ↔	All who believe in God and the Last Day like Abraham are the true people of Abraham. Abraham is the imam of the nations, with guidance for true Muslim character (submission, obedience, success in testing). Abraham prays for the messenger from among the Meccans, which is answered in the coming of Muhammad.	
		EVIL	The land promised to Abraham is the place of the altar and of the son nearly offered; the long-term solution is centred on Jerusalem, the city of Melchizedek. Victory over evil is accomplished in the atoning death of Christ, whose "day" Abraham saw.	↔ ↔ ↔	Mecca and Medina, particularly the Kaaba rebuilt by Abraham and Ishmael, are the focus of the rightly guided life and religion of Abraham. The sacrifice during the *Eid al-Adha* festival at the end of the Hajj recalls Abraham's offering of his son, but is not atoning.	
3. CONSUMMATION		GOD	Certainty of resurrection is based on the power of God, who gave life to Abraham's "dead" body and raised Jesus, and culminates in Jesus' return (the "return of the") resurrection of Abraham's people.	↔ ↔ ↔	Certainty of the Day of Resurrection is based on creative power of God, which is shown to Abraham, who in turn warns of the Last Day. The focus is on every human being's "return to God," which was also proclaimed by Abraham.	**3. AFTERLIFE**
		MAN	The 'redeemed' people of Abraham await resurrection to be with Christ at his coming. They are together with Abraham at the messianic banquet, which is also the wedding of the Lamb/Bridegroom.	↔ ↔	The "rightly guided" and chosen people of Abraham will be rewarded in the Garden. These are those who believe the prophetic message regarding God and the Last Day and who succeed in the test of life.	
		EVIL	The Biblical narrative ends as the curse is removed and blessings consummated in the new creation. The promises are fulfilled in the city/country for which Abraham longed, which is a picture of the final state where God dwells among his people.	↔ ↔ ↔	The Day is when all props are removed and each person is judged for their deeds. Like all the faithful, Abraham prays to be forgiven and not disgraced on the great Day of Reckoning. At that time the rightly guided people will receive their reward among the righteous in the Hereafter.	

ENDNOTES

ACKNOWLEDGMENTS

1   George F. V. Bristow, "Abraham in Narrative Worldviews: Doing Comparative Theology through Christian-Muslim Dialogue in Turkey" (PhD Diss., Vrije Universiteit Amsterdam, 28 May 2015), http://dare.ubvu.vu.nl/handle/1871/52738.

INTRODUCTION

1   For this reason, "its waters and fish are considered to be sacred and in no way edible by the people and are protected." Aysel Bekleyen and Erdogan Ipek, "Composition and Abundance of Zooplankton in a Natural Aquarium, Lake Balikligol (Sanliurfa, Turkey) and New Records," *JAVA* 9, no. 4 (2010): 682.

2   Many of these churches are represented by the "Türkiye Protestan Kiliseler Birliği" (Turkish Protestant Churches Union), which is a member of the European Evangelical Alliance. This union was officially established as a legal association on 23.01.2009 as the "Protestan Kiliseler Derneği" (see www.protestankiliseler.org) For a history and survey of the churches in this movement see M. Numan Malkoç, *Türkiye'de Protestanlik Ve Protestan Kiliseleri (Protestantism and Protestant Churches in Turkey)* (Istanbul: Yalin Yayincilik, 2011), which was his doctoral thesis.

3   Advocating_the_mere_tolerance_of_difference_between_women. (n.d.). Columbia World of Quotations. Retrieved June 10, 2014, from Dictionary.com website: http://quotes.dictionary.com/. From comments made on September 29, 1979, at the Second Sex Conference in New York City.

4   Marianne Moyaert, "Interreligious Dialogue and the Debate between Universalism and Particularism: Searching for a Way out of the Deadlock," *SID* 15, no. 1 (2005): 15.

5   I devote more space to CM here because many issues related to CT will be addressed in considering the related Scriptural Reasoning (SR) movement in chapter 1. For a comparison of these two approaches (CT and SR) to engaging the Scriptures of other faith traditions, see Michael Barnes, "Reading Other Religious Texts: Intratextuality and the Logic of Scripture," *JES* 46, no. 3 (2011).

6   Kirsteen Kim, "Missiology as Global Conversation of (Contextual) Theologies," in *11th International Conference of the International Association for Mission Studies (IAMS)*(Port Dickson, Malaysia, 2004), 1-2.

7   Richard Treloar, *Theological Anthropology: A Collection of Papers Prepared by Faith and Unity Commissioners of the National Council of Churches in Australia* (National Council of Churches in Australia, 2005), 2.

8   Matt 28:16-20; Mark 16:15-16; Luke 24:44-49; John 20:21-23 and Acts 1:1-8. Acts 13:1-3 is the classic example of this commissioning process from the standpoint of the sending community, while Acts 9:15; 22:14-21; and 26:15-23 recount from various standpoints the risen Jesus' initial commissioning of Paul, later enacted by the church at Antioch.

9   See Matt 24:14; Rom 1:5; 16:25-26.

10   For a definition of mission reflecting this approach see Eckhard J. Schnabel, *Early Christian Mission* (2 vols.; vol. 1; Downers Grove: InterVarsity Press, 2004), 11.

11   See C. René Padilla, "The Ebb and Flow of Kingdom Theology," in *Evangelical and Frontier Mission: Perspectives on the Global Progress of the Gospel* (eds. Snodderly and Moreau; Eugene, Oreg.: Wipf & Stock, 2011), 285.

12   Christopher J. H. Wright, *The Mission of God: Unlocking the Bible's Grand Narrative* (Nottingham: Inter-Varsity Press, 2006), 23. DeYoung and Gilbert's recent evaluation of various approaches to the church's mission differs from Wright at several points. Kevin DeYoung and Greg Gilbert, *What Is the Mission of the Church?: Making Sense of Social Justice, Shalom, and the Great Commission* (Wheaton: Crossway, 2011), 62.

13   This movement of God's love in bridging contexts is most profoundly "contextual" in the incarnation, as the eternal Word became one of us "for us and our salvation" (Nicene Creed).

14   Dean E. Flemming, *Contextualization in the New Testament: Patterns for Theology and Mission* (Downers Grove: InterVarsity Press, 2005), 19.

15   A. Scott Moreau, "Evangelical Models of Contextualization," in *Local Theology for the Global Church : Principles for an Evangelical Approach to Contextualization* (ed. Cook; Pasadena: World Evangelical Alliance Theological Commission, 2010), 169. Cited at http://jacksonwu. org/2013/05/24/how-do-evangelicasl-define-contextualization/.

16   Ida J. Glaser, "Reading Genesis in the Context of Islam: Windows on the Texts," *STT* V (2010).

17   Richard Showalter, "All the Clans, All the Peoples," *IJFM* 13, no. 1 (1996): 11.

18   Ralph Winter's introductory chapter identifies Genesis 12 as the starting point of God's mission: "From Genesis 12 to the end of the Bible, and indeed until the end of time, there unfolds the single, coherent drama of 'the Kingdom strikes back.'" Ralph D. Winter, et al., *Perspectives on the World Christian Movement: A Reader* (Pasadena: William Carey Library, 2009), 7.

19   Three significant examples may be found in Richard Bauckham, *Bible and Mission: Christian Witness in a Postmodern World* (Carlisle: Paternoster, 2003), 35-36, Andreas J. Köstenberger and Peter T. O'Brien, *Salvation to the Ends of the Earth: A Biblical Theology of Mission* (11; Leicester: Apollos, 2001), especially pp. 28-31, and Wright, *The Mission of God*, 194-95.

20   David Hesselgrave, "Great Commission Contextualization," *IJFM* 12, no. 3 (1995): 143 Tom A. Steffen, "Storying the Storybook to Tribals: A Philippines Perspective of the Chronological Teaching Model," *IJFM* 12, no. 2 (1995).

21   LCWE, *Making Disciples of Oral Learners: To Proclaim His Story Where It Has Not Been Known Before* (Lima, NY: International Orality Network, 2005), 26.

22   Tom A. Steffen, *Reconnecting God's Story to Ministry: Cross-Cultural Storytelling at Home and Abroad* (Waynesboro, Ga.: Authentic Media, 2005), 134-35.

23   On the role of storytellers (*meddahs and kıssahans*) in Ottoman social gatherings, see Zeynep Tarım Ertuğ, "Entertainment and Social Gathering at the Ottoman Court in the Sixteenth Century," *UİBD* 4, no. 1 (2007).

24   Many popular books include these stories. Banu Kopuz, *Allah Dostları: Büyük Evliyalar (Friends of God: The Great Saints)* (İstanbul: İki Dünya Yayınevi, 2007), is a Turkish example.

25   I borrow the term "transforming worldview" from Paul G. Hiebert, *Transforming Worldviews: An Anthropological Understanding of How People Change* (Grand Rapids: Baker Academic, 2008), and use it to refer to the deep "renewal of the mind" referred to in the NT, which is the intended outcome of God's work in those who believe in Christ (e.g. Rom 12:1-2; 2 Cor 3:18).

26   LCWE, *Making Disciples of Oral Learners: To Proclaim His Story Where It Has Not Been Known Before*, 33.

27   See Hans M. Weerstra, "A Call for Worldview Transformation," *IJFM* 25, no. 3 (2008): 122.

28   James L. Fredericks, "A Universal Religious Experience? Comparative Theology as an Alternative to a Theology of Religions," *Horizons* 22, no. 1 (1995).

29   The movement is represented by the Journal of Comparative Theology at Harvard Divinity School, described as "an online publication in which graduate students and emerging scholars share articles that seek to understand a particular faith in theological dialogue with one or more other religious traditions." http://www.comparativetheology.org/?page_id=49.

30   Francis X. Clooney, "Comparative Theology," in *The Oxford Handbook of Systematic Theology* (eds. Webster, et al.; Oxford: Oxford University Press, 2007), 654. Clooney's own area of comparative theological study has been Hinduism.

31   Clooney, "Comparative Theology," 654.

32   Clooney, "Comparative Theology," 657.

33   Barnes, "Reading Other Religious Texts: Intratextuality and the Logic of Scripture," 394. Barnes notes that the Jesuits use Thomas Aquinas' approach to engaging other faiths, seeking to demonstrate "that truth which faith professes and reason investigates." However, contemporary CT owes more to the major changes in interfaith relations introduced by Vatican II. Barnes, "Reading Other Religious Texts: Intratextuality and the Logic of Scripture," 403.

34   Francis X. Clooney, "Comparative Theology and Inter-Religious Dialogue," in *The Wiley-Blackwell Companion to Inter-Religious Dialogue* (ed. Cornille; Malden: John Wiley & Sons, Ltd., 2013), 56. See Marianne Moyaert, "Scriptural Reasoning as Inter-Religious Dialogue," in *Wiley-Blackwell Companion to Inter-Religious Dialogue* (ed. Cornille; Malden: Wiley & Sons, 2013), 82 n2.

35   Barnes, "Reading Other Religious Texts: Intratextuality and the Logic of Scripture," 403. See my discussion in chapter 1.

36   Kevin J Vanhoozer, "Introduction," in *Dictionary for Theological Interpretation of the Bible* (ed. Vanhoozer; Grand Rapids: Baker Academic, 2005), 24.

37   For a brief introduction to narrative criticism see Robin Parry, "Narrative Criticism," in *Dictionary for Theological Interpretation of the Bible* (ed. Vanhoozer; Grand Rapids: Baker Academic, 2005), 528-31, and the bibliography at the end of the entry.

38   See Christopher Seitz, "Canonical Approach," in *Dictionary for Theological Interpretation of the Bible* (ed. Vanhoozer; Grand Rapids: Baker Academic, 2005), 100-102, and my comments in chapter 4.

39   Adis Duderija, *Constructing a Religiously Ideal "Believer" and "Woman" in Islam: Neo-Traditional Salafi and Progressive Muslims' Methods of Interpretation* (New York: Palgrave Macmillan, 2011), 3. This differs from what he terms "textual segmentalism." Nevertheless, some of the interpreters I refer to may be in what Duderija would classify as "Neo-traditional Salafi."

40   For a survey of seven areas of epistemology and methodology where the neo-traditional and the progressive Muslims differ in their approach, see Duderija's post on the International Qur'anic Studies Assc. https://iqsaweb.wordpress.com/2015/03/23/duderija_hermeneutics/.

41   On the issue of qur'anic textual coherence see the section in chapter 5.

42   Duderija, *Constructing a Religiously Ideal "Believer" and "Woman" in Islam*, 190-91.

CHAPTER 1 – ABRAHAMIC DIALOGUE

1   The *Lubar Institute for the Study of the Abrahamic Religions* at the University of Wisconsin–Madison is one example. Their mission statement is representative of this approach: "Through encouraging people belonging to and/or interested in the Abrahamic traditions to engage each other and to find out more about both of these several traditions and their intersections, the Lubar Institute is dedicated to strengthening the values of religious pluralism so vital for sustaining American civil society and peaceful international discourse." http://lisar.lss.wisc.edu/welcome/mission.html.

2   I use the term Judaism for convenience in this study with the awareness that some Jewish scholars argue that the notion of Judaism as a "faith" or religion is largely a Christian construct serving the need for Christian self-definition in the fourth century CE. Daniel Boyarin, "Rethinking Jewish Christianity: An Argument for Dismantling a Dubious Category (to Which Is Appended a Correction of My Border Lines)," *JQR* 99, no. 1 (2009): 35-36.

3   D. R. Parks, "Abraham, the 'First Christian' and the 'First Muslim': Hermeneutics of a Religious Symbol in Western Christianity and Sunni Islam" (PhD Dissertation, Southwestern Baptist Theological Seminary, 1987). See also Norman Solomon, et al., *Abraham's Children: Jews, Christians, and Muslims in Conversation* (London: T & T Clark, 2005), 37.

4   Karl-Josef Kuschel, *Abraham: a Symbol of Hope for Jews, Christians, and Muslims* (London: SCM Press Ltd., 1995), 3.

5   Moyaert, "Interreligious Dialogue and the Debate between Universalism and Particularism: Searching for a Way out of the Deadlock," 15.

6   Michael S. Kogan, "Abrahamic Faith: Calling and Response in Jewish Narrative Theology," in *Abrahamic Faiths, Ethnicity and Ethnic Conflicts* (eds. Peachey, et al.; Washington: The Council for Research in Values and Philosophy, 1997), 96.

7   Models for a Christian theology of religions are examined by Paul F. Knitter, *Introducing Theologies of Religions* (Maryknoll: Orbis Books, 2002), 19–237. He argues that these models diverge primarily on issues of whether or not God has revealed himself in and through all major religious traditions and whether interreligious dialogue can be regarded as a common search for religious truth. Harold A. Netland, *Dissonant Voices: Religious Pluralism and the Question of Truth* (Grand Rapids: Eerdmans, 1991), 290–94.

8   Hanna N. Josua, "Ibrahim, Khalil Allah: Eine Anfrage an Die Abrahamische Ökumene" (PhD Dissertation, Evangelisch-Theologischen Facultat, 2005) 585. See also Paul Joyce. "Abraham from a Christian perspective," in *Abraham's children: Jews, Christians, and Muslims in conversation* (eds. Solomon, et al.; London ; New York: T&T Clark, 2005), 26.

9   Pim Valkenberg, *Sharing Lights on the Way to God: Muslim-Christian Dialogue and Theology in the Context of Abrahamic Partnership* (Amsterdam: Rodopi, 2006), xiv-xv.

10   The Fethullah Gülen movement is widely seen as the power originally behind the controlling AKP party, led by Recep Tayyip Erdoğan. However, events in 2013–14 severed the relationship between the reclusive cleric Gülen and Erdoğan, who won Turkey's first direct presidential elections on 10 August 2014, after a decade as prime minister.

11   *Abraham Meetings* (2009 [cited 7 May 2009]); available from http://www.abrahammeetings. org/index.php?l=en.

12   The papers were published in Cemal Uşak ed, *Hazret-I İbrahim'in Izinde* (İstanbul: Gazeteciler ve Yazarlar Vakfı Yayınları, 2001), in Turkish.

13   Hassan Azzouzi, "Kur'an-ı Kerim'de 'İbrahimî Tevhid'e Çağrı (the Abrahamic Tawhid Call in the Qur'an)," in *Hazret-I İbrahim'in Izinde* (ed. Uşak; İstanbul: Gazeteciler ve Yazarlar Vakfı Yayınları, 2001), 36.

14   *All hand-in-hand in Solidarity (Dayanışmadan yana hep yan yana)*, program booklet of the Halil İbrahim Buluşmaları (Abraham Meetings) organized by the governor of the Şanlıurfa province (Şanlıurfa Valiliği), 22–25 May, 2009. www.halilibrahim.org or www. abrahammeetings.org.

15   http://taswheaton.org/event-view/abrahamic-traditions-dinner-march-19-2015/. The Niagara Foundation is related to the above-mentioned Gülen movement.

16   A. Ekrem Ülkü, *Ulusların Babası İbrahim: Avram, Abraham, İbrahim (Abraham Father of Nations)* (İstanbul: Yeni İnsan Yayınevi, 2012), 12.

17   T. J. Winter, "Introduction," in *Abraham's Children: Jews, Christians, and Muslims in Conversation* (eds. Solomon, et al.; London: T & T Clark, 2005), 6.

18   Winter, "Introduction."

19   B Breiner, "Christian-Muslim Relations: Some Current Themes," *ICMR* 2, no. 1 (1991).

20   Susan Thistlethwaite and Glen Stassen, "Abrahamic Alternatives to War: Jewish, Christian, and Muslim Perspectives on Just Peacemaking" (Washington: United States Institute of Peace, 2008), 1.

21   Sybil Sheridan, "Abraham from a Jewish Perspective," in *Abraham's Children: Jews, Christians, and Muslims in Conversation* (eds. Solomon, et al.; London: T & T Clark, 2005), 16.

22   Irene Pabst, "The Interpretation of the Sarah-Hagar-Stories in Rabbinic and Patristic Literature: Sarah and Hagar as Female Representations of Identity and Difference," in *Lectio Difficilior: European Electronic Journal for Feminist Exegesis* (vol. 1 of; Berlin: Theol. Fakultät der Universität Bern, 2003), 13.

23 Kent Davis Sensenig, "An Abrahamic Paradigm for Just Peacemaking," *TNN* 56, no. 1 (Spring 2009): 3/6.

24 The patriarchs' interaction with pagan nations forms a significant part of the Genesis drama: Abraham returns peacefully to Canaan from Egypt even after deceiving Pharaoh (12:10-20), intervenes in a war between two alliances of local kingdoms, after which he is blessed by the king of Salem (ch. 14), intercedes with God for the condemned city of Sodom (18:16–19:29), lives among the Philistines (ch. 20), makes a treaty with Abimelech (21:22-34), and purchases a burial ground for Sarah from the sons of Heth (ch. 23).

25 While this statement refers to Sodom's people, it is broadened to include Gomorrah in 18:20. A general charge of idolatry and abominable practices is repeated throughout the Pentateuch (e.g. Exod 23:23-24; Deut 20:17-18).

26 Stephen R. Goodwin, "Fractured Land, Healing Nations: A Contextual Analysis of the Role of Religious Faith Sodalities Towards Peace-Building in Bosnia-Herzegovina" (PhD Dissertation, University of Edinburgh, 2005) 271.

27 Stephen R. Prothero, *God Is Not One: The Eight Rival Religions That Run the World—and Why Their Differences Matter* (New York: HarperOne), 3.

28 Ramazan Hurç, "Dinler Arası Diyalog Bağlamında Hz. Muhammed'in Hıristiyanlarla İlişkileri (Muhammad's Relationships with Christians in the Context of Inter-Religious Dialogue)," *FÜSBD* 12, no. 2 (2002): 392.

29 Fazlur Rahman, "Islam's Attitude toward Judaism," *MW* 72, no. 1 (1980): 13.

30 Abdulaziz Sachedina, "The Qur'an and Other Religions," in *The Cambridge Companion to the Qur'an* (ed. McAuliffe; Cambridge: Cambridge University Press, 2006), 301.

31 Sachedina, "The Qur'an and Other Religions," 299.

32 Sachedina, "The Qur'an and Other Religions," 300.

33 Sohail H. Hashmi, "The Qur'an and Tolerance: An Interpretive Essay on Verse 5:48," *JHR* 2, no. 1 (2003): 96.

34 Hashmi, "The Qur'an and Tolerance: An Interpretive Essay on Verse 5:48," 81. In fact he asserts that in this verse, "the Qur'an affirms that the problem of religious and moral diversity is not a hindrance to be overcome, but an advantage to be embraced—a necessary facet of God's unknown plan for humanity" (101).

35 Hashmi, "The Qur'an and Tolerance: An Interpretive Essay on Verse 5:48," 100.36 Kuschel, *Abraham: A Symbol of Hope*, xvi-xvii. Yet the Genesis narrative underscores the reality that in God's purposes Ishmael and Isaac cannot share the inheritance. Not much peace and understanding are seen between Sarah and Hagar.

37 Kuschel, *Abraham: A Symbol of Hope*, 72.

38 See Michael R. Licona, *The Resurrection of Jesus: A New Historiographical Approach* (Downers Grove: IVP Academic, 2010), and N. T. Wright, *The Resurrection of the Son of God: Vol. 3 in Christian Origins and the Question of God* (Minneapolis: Fortress Press, 2003), for full treatments of this subject.

39 Kuschel, *Abraham: A Symbol of Hope*, 115-16.

40 The "dominant approach" to John's Gospel assumed uncritically by Kuschel, which sets John at odds with the Synoptics and with history, is seriously challenged by Richard Bauckham, *The Testimony of the Beloved Disciple: Narrative, History, and Theology in the Gospel of John* (Grand Rapids: Baker Academic, 2007), and the claim of anti-Judaic attitudes in the fourth Gospel is refuted by Ronald E. Diprose, *Israel in the Development of Christian Thought* (Rome: Instituto Biblico Evangelico Italiano, 2000), 36-38.

41 He argues that Arabs, "belonging to the Abrahamic stock . . . came first in God's program of visitation to the nations. . . . This was a primary reason why Paul visited Arabia first in his missionary activities as apostle to the Gentiles (Gal 1:15-17)." Tony Maalouf, *Arabs in the Shadow of Israel: The Unfolding of God's Prophetic Plan for Ishmael's Line* (Grand Rapids: Kregel (Academic & Professional), 2003), 217-18.

42   See the detailed study by Jonathan Culver, "The Ishmael Promises in the Light of God's Mission: Christian and Muslim Reflections" (PhD Dissertation, Fuller Theological Seminary, 2001). Also see Shmuel Bar, "The Religious Sources of Islamic Terrorism," *PR* 125, no. June/July (2004): 1-53.

43   Yusuf Talal Delorenzo, "Ibrahim: A Family Portrait," in *Abrahamic Faiths, Ethnicity and Ethnic Conflicts* (eds. Peachey, et al.; Washington: The Council for research in Values and Philosophy, 1997), 134.

44   See Richard Bauckham, *God Crucified: Monotheism and Christology in the New Testament* (Grand Rapids: Eerdmans, 1998), and Adam Dodds, "The Abrahamic Faiths? Continuity and Discontinuity in Christian and Islamic Doctrine," *EvQ* 81, no. 3 (2009).

45   For a careful attempt to argue that there are nevertheless no insuperable barriers to believing that Christians and Muslims worship the same God, see the work of Miroslav Volf, who reminds Christians that "Muslim objections to the doctrine of the Trinity and the uncompromising affirmation about oneness from which these objections stem are not, in themselves, good enough reasons for Christians to think that they have a radically different understanding of God than Muslims." Miroslav Volf, *Allah: A Christian Response* (New York: HarperOne, 2011), 143. See however the critical review by Imad Shehadeh, "Review of Miroslav Volf. Allah: A Christian Response," *Them* 36, no. 2 (2011). I question this premise from a different angle in chapter 2, specifically the inseparability of the biblical narrative and the identity of God.

46   Theodore Pulcini, "Of Flesh and Faith: Abraham as a Principle of Inclusion and Exclusion in Christian Thought," in *Abrahamic Faiths, Ethnicity and Ethnic Conflicts* (eds. Peachey, et al.; Washington: The Council for research in Values and Philosophy, 1997), 115, 117.

47   Kuschel, *Abraham: A Symbol of Hope*, 90. See also Istvan Tatai, *The Church and Israel: In Search of a New Model in Post-Holocaust Theology* (Printed by CreateSpace Independent Publishing Platform, 2014), for a recent survey of many of these issues, especially in post-Holocaust European Christian thinking.

48   Josua, "Ibrahim, Khalil Allah," 590.

49   For the results of this symposium see Brian M. Hauglid, "On the Early Life of Abraham: Biblical and Qur'anic Intertextuality and the Anticipation of Muhammad," in *Bible and Qur'an: Essays in Scriptural Intertextuality* (ed. Reeves; vol. 24 of *Society of Biblical Literature Symposium Series*; Leiden: Brill, 2004).

50   See Michael Ipgrave, *Scriptures in Dialogue: Christians and Muslims Studying the Bible and the Qur'an Together: A Record of the Seminar "Building Bridges" Held at Doha, Qatar, 7-9 April 2003* (London: Church House Pub., 2004), for an overview.

51   http://etext.lib.virginia.edu/journals/jsrforum/syllabi/richardsonsyllabus1.html. This site contains several examples of ways in which teachers are introducing SR into their classrooms.

52   Ida J. Glaser and Gregory M Anderson, "Building Respect, Seeking Truth: Towards a Model for Muslim-Christian Dialogue," *CSR* 34, no. 4 (2005). See the vision and ethos of the CMCS at http://cmcsoxford.org.uk/.

53   See Ida J. Glaser, "Toward a Mutual Understanding of Christian and Islamic Concepts of Revelation," *Them* 7, no. 3 (1982): 22.

54   Basit B. Koshul and Steven Kepnes, *Scripture, Reason, and the Contemporary Islam-West Encounter: Studying the "Other", Understanding the "Self"* (New York: Palgrave, 2007), Introduction, xi-xii.

55   "The contributors understand . . . that 'overcoming conflict' is not their main goal for that can too easily be reduced to a search for some underlying unity or overarching principle that can unite the three monotheistic traditions. Rather the goal of the contributors is to replace a situation of stagnant conflict with dialogue and respect for difference." Koshul and Kepnes, *Scripture, Reason, and the Contemporary Islam-West Encounter*, xii.

56   David F. Ford, "An Interfaith Wisdom: Scriptural Reasoning between Jews, Christians and Muslims," *MT* 22, no. 3 (2006): 345.

57 Steven Kepnes, "A Handbook for Scriptural Reasoning," *Modern Theology* 22, no. 3 (2006).
58 Ford, "An Interfaith Wisdom," 349.
59 Ford, "An Interfaith Wisdom," 361. Of course the rabbis did not differ significantly over what writings actually constitute "Scripture." A different definition is required for this exercise, one referring to writings received as sacred/inspired by any faith community.
60 Ford, "An Interfaith Wisdom," 349-50.
61 Ford, "An Interfaith Wisdom," 351-57.
62 Melanie Prideaux, "Muslim-Christian Dialogue: The Gap between Theologians and Communities," *IJPT* 3(2009): 464.
63 These can be accessed at http://etext.virginia.edu/journals/abraham/about.html and http://etext.lib.virginia.edu/journals/ssr/.
64 http://www.interfaith.cam.ac.uk/en/academic-work/activities/scriptural-reasoning. Their Abrahamic Texts Translation Programme (ATTP) is "a long-term project [the purpose of which is] to identify and translate the most important texts in Judaism, Christianity and Islam, for the traditions' mutual use. . . . The kinds of text fall into four groups: (1) Explicit commentary on Tanakh, Bible, Qur'an, (2) Explicit commentary on Talmud, Patristics, Hadith, (3) Major philosophical and theological works in the three traditions, (4) Major intellectual sources in the three traditions, including poetry and drama." http://www.interfaith.cam.ac.uk/en/cap/scholarly-outreach.
65 Ford, "An Interfaith Wisdom," 357.
66 Kepnes puts it this way: "That Christians regard the Torah as revelation is certainly the major warrant for why Christians want and need to be in dialogue with Jews. However, from a Jewish perspective, there is an obvious imbalance in the relation. For where Christians see the Jews and their scriptures as holy, Jews do not see Christians as the rightful heir to the promises of the Torah nor do they see the New Testament as holy scriptures of revelatory for them." Steven Kepnes, "Hagar and Esau: From Others to Sisters and Brothers," in *Crisis, Call, and Leadership in the Abrahamic Traditions* (eds. Ochs and Johnson; New York: Palgrave Macmillan, 2009), 34.
67 Daniel W. Hardy, "The Promise of Scriptural Reasoning," *MT* 22, no. 3 (2006): 533.
68 Hardy, "The Promise of Scriptural Reasoning," 533.
69 Also spelled Da'wah, this refers to Islamic missionary work, preaching or "summons" to faith. The related Turkish word "davet" means "invitation." For a careful comparison of the two see David A. Kerr, "Islamic Da'wa and Christian Mission: Towards a Comparative Analysis," *IRM* 89, no. 353 (2000).
70 See Angelika Neuwirth, "Structural, Linguistic and Literary Features," in *The Cambridge Companion to the Qur'an* (ed. McAuliffe; Cambridge: Cambridge University Press, 2006), 108.
71 For example, Turkish scholar Turan sees both Christianity and Islam as religions with universal claims and suggests that Christian missiology should be studied in Turkey for insights into training religious workers for service in Islamic Da'wa. Süleyman Turan, "Misyoloji: Hristiyan Misyon Bilimi," (Istanbul: Sarkaç Yayınları, 2011), 239.
72 Ford, "An Interfaith Wisdom," 363.
73 "The now standard description of forms of inter-faith dialogue in the Roman Catholic Church puts 'the dialogue of theological exchange' alongside 'dialogue of life', 'dialogue of action' and 'dialogue of religious experience'." Barnes, *Theology and the dialogue of religions* (Cambridge, U.K. ; New York: Cambridge University Press, 2002), 21.
74 Christopher J. H. Wright, "The Christian and Other Religions: The Biblical Evidence," *Them* 9, no. 2 (1984): 14-15. See also Daniel Strange, *'For Their Rock Is Not as Our Rock': An Evangelical Theology of Religions* (Leicester: Inter-Varsity), for a recent biblical examination of perspectives on the purpose of other religions in God's providence.
75 Richard Cimino, "'No God in Common:' American Evangelical Discourse on Islam after 9/11," *RRelRes* 47(2005): 162.

76   Cimino, "No God in Common," 169.

77   Valkenberg, *Sharing Lights on the Way to God: Muslim-Christian Dialogue and Theology in the Context of Abrahamic Partnership*, xii.

78   Jonathan Sacks, *The Dignity of Difference: How to Avoid the Clash of Civilizations* (London: Continuum, 2002), 47.

79   Dr Glaser is responsible for the academic and research activities of the Centre for Muslim-Christian Studies in Oxford. The motto of this centre is "building respect and seeking truth," and the approach is to provide Christians, Muslims, and others with opportunity to read and discuss the Bible and the Qur'an together.

80   Ida J. Glaser, "An Experiment in Contextualised Comparative Hermeneutics: A Reading of Genesis 1-11 in the Context of Parallel Qur'anic Material and Christian Mission Amongst Muslims in Elswick, Newcastle Upon Tyne." (PhD dissertation, University of Durham, 1994) 9.

81   Glaser, "An Experiment in Contextualised Comparative Hermeneutics," 10.

82   Evelyne Reisacher, "Evangelical-Muslim Peacemaking: Drink Lots of Cups of Tea," *ThNN* 56, no. 1 (Spring 2009): 21. She considers the 2007 "Common Word" initiative by Muslim scholars, clerics, and intellectuals and the Christian response "Loving God and Neighbor Together: a Christian Response to 'A Common Word.'"

83   Michael Barnes, *Theology and the Dialogue of Religions* (Cambridge: Cambridge University Press, 2002), 237-39.

84   Mohamed Al-Nowaihi, "The Religion of Islam," *IRM* 55, no. April (1976): 216.

85   John Azumah, "The Integrity of Interfaith Dialogue," *ICMR* 13, no. 3 (2002): 274.

86   Christopher J. H. Wright, "Interpreting the Bible among the World Religions," *Them* 25, no. 3 (2000): 47.

87   See Neuwirth, "Structural," 108.

88   http://www.scripturalreasoning.co.uk/fatwa_english.pdf.

89   Karl. Barth, *Church Dogmatics* (trans. Bromiley; vol. II.2 The Doctrine of God; Edinburgh: T. & T. Clark, 1975), 520-21. Barth's definition of apologetics here is narrower than that which I envision in interscriptural apologetics.

90   John G. Stackhouse, *Humble Apologetics: Defending the Faith Today* (Oxford: Oxford University Press, 2002), 127.

91   "Religion is the translation of God into a particular language and thus into the life of a group, a nation, a community of faith. In the course of history, God has spoken to mankind in many languages: through Judaism to Jews, Christianity to Christians, Islam to Muslims.... How could a sacred text convey such an idea? It would declare that *God is God of all humanity, but no single faith is or should be the faith of all humanity.*" Sacks, *The Dignity of Difference*, 55. Italics added. This is not unlike the common Islamic affirmation that God has sent many prophets with similar monotheistic calls to different peoples. See also Q 5:48.

CHAPTER 2—NARRATIVE AND WORLDVIEW

1   Brian J. Walsh and J. Richard Middleton, *The Transforming Vision: Shaping a Christian World View* (Downers Grove: InterVarsity Press, 1984), 64.

2   Bauckham uses the term metanarrative in this way: "the Bible as a whole tells a story, in some sense a single story." It is "a metanarrative, a narrative about the whole of reality that elucidates the meaning of the whole of reality." Bauckham, *Bible and Mission*, 12.

3   Kathryn Greene-McCreight, "Rule of Faith," in *Dictionary for Theological Interpretation of the Bible* (ed. Vanhoozer; Grand Rapids: Baker Academic, 2005), 704.

4   Cited in Greene-McCreight, "Rule of Faith," 703.

5   Paul M. Blowers, "The Regula Fidei and the Narrative Character of Early Christian Faith," *PE* 6, no. 2 (1997): 202.

6   An extensive bibliography on worldview at http://www.leaderu.com/philosophy/worldviewbibliography.html includes works considering worldview in relation to each of the following topics: Theology and Biblical Studies, Missions and Evangelism, Philosophy,

Natural Science, Anthropology and Folklore, Psychology, Sociology, and Education. See David K. Naugle, *Worldview: The History of a Concept* (Grand Rapids: Eerdmans, 2002), for a history and critical engagement of worldview.

7   Albert M. Wolters, *Creation Regained: Biblical Basics for a Reformational Worldview* (Grand Rapids: Eerdmans, 2005), 2.

8   Clement Vidal, "Wat Is Een Wereldbeeld? (What Is a Worldview?)," in *Nieuwheid Denken. De Wetenschappen En Het Creatieve Aspect Van De Werkelijkheid* (eds. Van Belle and Van der Veken; Leuven: Acco, 2008), 3. Vidal's stated interest is to develop an "integrative scientific worldview" where worldview is the highest manifestation of philosophy, addressing the deepest questions of meaning and value.

9   N. T. Wright, *The New Testament and the People of God, Vol. 1 in Christian Origins and the Question of God* (Minneapolis: Fortress Press, 1992), 132. See also Walsh and Middleton, *The Transforming Vision*, 35. Sire lists eight questions: "What is prime reality—the really real? What is the nature of external reality, that is, the world around us? What is a human being? What happens to a person at death? Why is it possible to know anything at all? How do we know what is right and wrong? What is the meaning of human history? What personal, life-orienting core commitments are consistent with this worldview?" James W. Sire, *The Universe Next Door: A Basic Worldview Catalog* (Downers Grove: InterVarsity Press, 2009), 22-23.

10   Esther L. Meek, "Working Implications of the Subsidiary Nature of Worldviews" (paper presented at Midwest Regional Evangelical Theological Society Conference. Lincoln Christian College, March 19, 2004, 3.

11   Gordon D. Fee and Douglas Stuart, *How to Read the Bible for All Its Worth* (Grand Rapids: Zondervan, 2003), 90. The authors identify three levels of biblical narrative: The top level is the "metanarrative" or overall biblical story from creation to new creation (Genesis to Revelation); the second level is the story of God's covenant people (in two stages, OT and NT) and the "first" level is made up of all the individual and compound story-units that make up the other two levels.

12   Wright, *The New Testament and the People of God*, 123, 132, 243. See the extended discussion of this issue in Wright, *The New Testament and the People of God*, 31-80.

13   Jens Brockmeier, "Remembering and Forgetting: Narrative as Cultural Memory," *CP* 8, no. 1 (2002): 27-28.

14   See my comments in chapter 3 under "Presuppositions regarding biblical narrative."

15   In this statement I am following the traditional narrative of Islamic origins reflected in the biographic material of Muhammad known as the *Sirat Rasul Allah* (or the *Sīra*) and the *Hadith*, which is held by most Muslims. See Fred M. Donner, "The Historical Context," in *The Cambridge Companion to the Qur'an* (ed. McAuliffe; Cambridge: Cambridge University Press, 2006), 23-40. The relationship between the Qur'an and the *Sīra* is contested, as Brown outlines: "The prophetic biography functioned as a commentary on the Qur'an, and [traditional Muslim scholars] used it as such. Their assumption, however, was that the history of the Prophet's life could explain scripture because it described what actually happened. As we have seen, however, many of the traditions which find their way into the Sīra can be shown to have *originated* out of efforts to understand obscure passages of the Qur'an. In other words, the nature of the Qur'an and the need to understand it comprised a potent shaping force on the development of the biography of Muhammad." Daniel W. Brown, *A New Introduction to Islam* (Chichester, UK: Wiley-Blackwell, 2009), 92.

16   Wright, *The New Testament and the People of God*, 216.

17   For example, "He has sent the Scripture down to you [Prophet] with the Truth, confirming what went before: He sent down the Torah and the Gospel earlier" (Q 3:3; cf. 2:91; 3:81; 5:48; 10:37; 12:111; 46:12, 30).

18   Reza Aslan, "Qur'anic Clues to the Identity of Muhammad's Community in Medina," (International Qur'anic Studies Association, 2014), 3/6.

19   Albert M. Wolters, "On the Idea of Worldview and Its Relation to Philosophy," in *Stained Glass: Worldviews and Social Science* (eds. Marshall, et al.; Lanham, Md.: University Press of America, 1989), 18-19.

20   Vidal, "Wat Is Een Wereldbeeld? (What Is a Worldview?)," 3. Italics in the original.

21   "Postmodernism refuses to believe the Enlightenment is without a creed."James K. A. Smith, "A Little Story About Metanarratives: Lyotard, Religion, and Postmodernism Revisited," *FP* 18, no. 3 (2001): 362.

22   Ian Logan, *Reading Anselm's Proslogion: The History of Anselm's Argument and Its Significance Today* (Farnham: Ashgate, 2009), 22-24.

23   This objection was suggested to me by my supervisor Andrew Kirk in personal correspondence.

24   D. A. Carson, "Systematic Theology and Biblical Theology," in *New Dictionary of Biblical Theology* (eds. Alexander and Rosner; Leicester: Inter-Varsity Press, 2000), 15/19. Italics mine.

25   Sayyid Qutb, *Basic Principles of the Islamic Worldview* (North Haledon, N.J.: Islamic Publications International, 2006), 45.

26   He argues that "this relevance [of a worldview approach] can be judged by the degree of Muslim and Western attitudes toward modernity since most of the contemporary scholars have been devoting their energies to respond to challenges imposed by Western modernity." Kyoichiro Sugimoto, "The Variance of Muslim Attitudes toward Western Modernity: A Worldview Discourse," in *International Seminar on Islamic Thought* (ed. Long, et al.; Universiti Kebangsaan Malaysia, Selangor Darul Ehsan, Malaysia: Department of Theology and Philosophy, Faculty of Islamic Studies, 2004), 596.

27   J. Mark Bertrand, *Rethinking Worldview: Learning to Think, Live, and Speak in This World* (Wheaton, Ill.: Crossway Books, 2007), KL 594-1874. Under his first approach, "worldview as starting point," the doctrines that hold up the Christian belief system are creation, order, rationality, and fear of God. These are broadly congruent with Islam's worldview, which holds to creation by the sole work of God, believes in an order imposed on all things by God's will, exalts rational discovery of God through creation, and defines proper relationship to God as submission. His second approach is "worldview as system," in which worldviews are perspectives on relationship to God, to others, and to the world. Here also, these elements do not immediately stand out as incongruent with Islam.

28   Personal correspondence, 13 July, 2014. Brown argues elsewhere that "without the biography of Muhammad there would be no Islam that we would recognize as such." Brown, *A New Introduction to Islam*, KL 2766.

29   For example, Wolters, *Creation Regained: Biblical Basics for a Reformational Worldview*, 12; Walsh and Middleton, *The Transforming Vision*. See also N. T. Wright, *Surprised by Hope: Rethinking Heaven, the Resurrection, and the Mission of the Church* (New York: HarperOne, 2008), 94-97. A representative summary statement is this: "The Bible's main plot is the story of how God restores a creation that had been disfigured by sin: first comes the creation followed by the fall, and then comes the restoration." Michael W. Goheen and Craig G. Bartholomew, *Living at the Crossroads: An Introduction to Christian Worldview* (Grand Rapids: Baker Academic, 2008), 32.

30   For example, Christopher J. H. Wright, *The Mission of God's People: A Biblical Theology of the Church's Mission* (Grand Rapids: Zondervan, 2010), KL 456.

31   Lesslie Newbigin, *The Gospel in a Pluralist Society* (Grand Rapids: Eerdmans, 1989), 89.

32   As noted above I am using the term "biblical" to refer to the Christian canon as a whole, and "biblical worldview" in the broad sense of elements generally held in common by all major streams of Christian tradition.

33   Orthodox theology distinguishes between image and likeness: "However sinful we may be, we never lose the image; but the likeness depends upon our moral choice, upon our 'virtue', and so it is destroyed by sin." Timothy Ware, *The Orthodox Church, New Edition* (London: Penguin Books, 1993), 218. For Protestant positions see Victor P. Hamilton, *The Book of*

Genesis: Chapters 1-17 (Grand Rapids: Eerdmans, 1990), 134-37, and Bruce K. Waltke and Cathi J. Fredricks, *Genesis: A Commentary* (Grand Rapids: Zondervan, 2001), 65-67.

34   For the link between sonship and image of God see Stephen G. Dempster, *Dominion and Dynasty: A Biblical Theology of the Hebrew Bible* (15; Leicester, England; Downers Grove, Ill.: Apollos; InterVarsity Press, 2003), 58-59.

35   Blocher argues that God's commandment regarding the tree of life and the tree of the knowledge of good and evil form the main provisions of a "covenant agreement." Henri Blocher, *In the Beginning: The Opening Chapters of Genesis* (Leicester: Inter-Varsity Press, 1984), 111-34.

36   Both Jewish and Islamic sources seek to fill this and other seeming "gaps" in the Genesis narrative. Ida J. Glaser, "Qur'anic Challenges for Genesis," *JSOT*, no. 75 (1997): 10. The NT explicitly identifies "that ancient serpent" as the great being "who is called the devil and Satan, the deceiver of the whole world" (Rev 12:9).

37   This focus on human sin does not dismiss the role of the serpent but highlights the unique role given to man created in God's image and charged to rule the rest of creation (Gen 1:26-28; Ps 8:4-8). For this reason, in Christian understanding the redemption of creation requires a second "Adam," to whom all things will finally be subjected (Rom 5:12-21; 1 Cor 15:21-28; Eph 1:19-22). Traditionally the first statement of this purpose is found in Gen 3:15, where ultimate victory is promised. See Gregory K. Beale, *A New Testament Biblical Theology: The Unfolding of the Old Testament in the New* (Grand Rapids: Baker Academic, 2011), 219-21. For a defense of the messianic reading of Gen 3:15, see Jack Collins, "A Syntactical Note (Genesis 3:15): Is the Woman's Seed Singular or Plural?," *TynBul* 48, no. 1 (1997).

38   For the Reformed thinking that the fall was in a certain sense determined by God, see Herman Bavinck, "The Development of the Doctrine of Predestination among the Reformed (Continued): The Controversy in Regard to Infra- and Supralapsarianism," *RPM* 9, no. 6 (2007): 4/7. For a strong rejection of this reading see Orthodox theologian David B. Hart, *The Doors of the Sea: Where Was God in the Tsunami?* (Grand Rapids: Eerdmans, 2005), 86-87. Hart says, "In the New Testament, our condition as fallen creatures is explicitly portrayed as a subjugation to the subsidiary and often mutinous authority of angelic and demonic 'powers,' which are not able to defeat God's transcendent and providential governance of all things, but which are certainly able to act against him within the limits of cosmic time." Hart, *The Doors of the Sea: Where Was God in the Tsunami?*, 65.

39   Kaminski argues against seeing a singular "fall" from a perfect state to a sinful one, describing Genesis 3–11 as a "series of linked narratives that describe the ongoing corruption of human beings." Joel S. Kaminski, "The Theology of Genesis," in *The Book of Genesis : Composition, Reception, and Interpretation* (eds. Evans, et al.; vol. 152 of *Supplements to Vetus Testamentum*; Leiden: Brill, 2012), 640.

40   Walter J Houston, "Sex or Violence? Thinking Again with Genesis About Fall and Original Sin," in *Genesis and Christian Theology* (eds. MacDonald, et al.; Grand Rapids: Eerdmans, 2012), KL1810-1811. Houston finds evidence that creation has fallen from the intention of God in the spread of *violence*. Levenson presents the more optimistic rabbinic view of the human situation, saying that "the major weapon in that war is the Torah itself." Jon D. Levenson, *Creation and the Persistence of Evil: The Jewish Drama of Divine Omnipotence* (Princeton: Princeton University Press, 1994), 40. Ware says that while the Orthodox picture of fallen humanity is less somber than the Augustinian or Calvinist view, "they certainly agree with the west in believing that human sin had set up between God and humanity a barrier which humanity by its own efforts could never break down." Ware, *The Orthodox Church*, 224-25.

41   Wright's comments on Deut 4:32-34 clarify what is at stake: "What God did in the events of the exodus and Sinai was unprecedented (God had never done such a thing at any other time) and unparalleled (God had never done such a thing anywhere else for any other nation)." Wright, *The Mission of God's People*, KL 3059-3064. God does remind his rebellious

people that he not only brought up "Israel from the land of Egypt," but also brought up "the Philistines from Caphtor and the Syrians from Kir" (Amos 9:7), yet his promise to raise up the fallen booth of David shows the special commitment to his purpose for this line (9:11; cf. 3:1-2).

42   For example, see Pss 50:3-4; 96:12-13; 98:8-9; Isa 40:2-6; 24:23; 25:6-10; 35:3-6, 10; 40:3-5, 9-11; 42:7-10; 52:7-10; 59:15-17, 19-21; 60:1-3; 62:1, 3, 5, 9; 66:12, 14-16, 18-19; Ezek 43:1-17; Hag 2:6-9; Zech 2:4-5, 10-12; 8:2-3; 14:1-5, 9, 16; and Mal 3:1-3. See N. T. Wright, *Jesus and the Victory of God, Vol. 2 in Christian Origins and the Question of God* (London: SPCK, 1996), 615-21.

43   Jewish theologian Sweeney sees two distinctive readings of the Hebrew Bible, determined by different canonical arrangements: "Whereas the Tanak is structured according to a cyclical pattern of the institution of ideal Jewish life, the disruption of Jewish life, and the restoration of that ideal, the Christian Old Testament is structured according to a linear principle that posits the revelation of Christ as the culmination of human history." Marvin A. Sweeney, *Tanak: A Theological and Critical Introduction to the Jewish Bible* (Minneapolis: Fortress Press, 2012), 24. Yet the OT book sequence is as much a LXX (Jewish) arrangement as a Christian one. See Karen H. Jobes and Moisés Silva, *Invitation to the Septuagint* (Grand Rapids: Baker Academic, 2000), 79-85. In both arrangements (in the Jewish Tanakh and the Christian OT) this narrative is carried by the Torah and the "former prophets," whose sequence is virtually the same in both arrangements and whose future-orientation is evident. See T. D. Alexander, "Royal Expectations in Genesis to Kings: Their Importance for Biblical Theology," *TynBul* 49, no. 2 (1998). Dempster finds the culmination of this eschatological "plan, purpose and plot" in Chronicles, the final book in the Tanakh. Dempster, *Dominion and Dynasty*, 45-50, 227.

44   See Gregory K. Beale, "The Eschatological Conception of New Testament Theology," in *'The Reader Must Understand': Eschatology in Bible and Theology* (eds. Brower and Elliott; Leicester: Apollos, 1997), 11-52.

45   Beale argues that Christ's resurrection is the inauguration of the promised new creation, which will be consummated at the end of this present age in the glorious garden-temple-city of God, Beale, *A New Testament Biblical Theology*, 227-356.

46   I heard this illustration from Üçal many years ago and confirmed it during a discussion via Skype 11.7.2014.

47   Sachiko Murata and William C. Chittick, *The Vision of Islam* (New York: Paragon House, 1994), xxvii. The Turkish curriculum or catechism for religious education is structured around these three dimensions, given as "faith, worship, and ethics." Recep Kaymakcan, "Religious Education Culture in Modern Turkey," in *International Handbook of the Religious, Moral and Spiritual Dimensions in Education* (ed. De Souza; vol. 1 of; Dordrecht; London: Springer, 2006), 451-52.

48   Murata and Chittick, *The Vision of Islam*, xv-xvi.

49   Murata and Chittick, *The Vision of Islam*, 43.

50   For such guidance Muslims look not only the Qur'an but also to the prophetic Sunna, as embodied in the Hadith. "Indeed the rulings of sharia are based more often on the hadith than the Quran (a book with few practical instructions)." Gabriel Said Reynolds, *The Emergence of Islam: Classical Traditions in Contemporary Perspective* (Minneapolis: Fortress Press, 2012), KL 4383-4384.

51   Abdelaziz Berghout, "Toward an Islamic Framework for Worldview Studies: Preliminary Theorization," *AJISS* 24, no. 2 (2007): 23. In this paper Berghout provides a comprehensive list of Muslim contributors to worldview studies.

52   Abdullah and Junaid Nadvi, "Understanding the Principles of Islamic World-View," *Dialogue* VI, no. 3 (2011): 282. Elsewhere in his paper Navdi uses the combined term "value-principles."

53   Fazlur Rahman, *Major Themes of the Qur'an* (Chicago: The University of Chicago Press, 2009), xv.

54 See for example Asad Zaman, "Developing an Islamic World View: An Essential Component of an Islamic Education," *LJPS* 1, no. 1 (Jan–July, 2007): 105-06.
55 Yvonne Y. Haddad, "Ghurba as Paradigm for Muslim Life: A Risale-I Nur Worldview," *MW* 89, no. 3-4 (1999): 297-98. "All three sought to realize their vision through the creation of an educated society at once conversant with the technology, science and learning of the West and with a reinterpreted, rational, revitalized Islam capable of managing the modern world." Haddad, "Ghurba as Paradigm for Muslim Life: A Risale-I Nur Worldview," 300. See Syed Naquib al-Attas, "The Worldview of Islam: An Outline," in *Islam and the Challenge of Modernity* (ed. Al-Attas; Kuala Lumpur: International Institute of Islamic Thought and Civilization, 2005), and Ismail R. Al Faruqi, *Al Tawhid: Its Implications for Thought and Life* (4; Herndon, VA: International Institute of Islamic Thought, 1992), for more recent examples.
56 J. Mark Halstead, "An Islamic Concept of Education," *CE* 40, no. 4 (2004). This article is available in Turkish: J. Mark Halstead, "Islam Eğitim Anlayışı (an Islamic Concept of Education)," *OMÜİFD* 32 (2012). An analysis of the work of this influential movement's two leading scholars is found in Rosnani Hashim and Imron Rossidy, "Islamization of Knowledge. A Comparative Analysis of the Conceptions of Al-Attas and Al-Faruqi," *ID* 8, no. 1 (2000). Also Syed Naquib al-Attas, "Islamic Philosophy: An Introduction," *JIP* 1, no. 1 (2005): 14.
57 See Nasr Abu Zayd, "Towards Understanding the Qur'an's Worldview: An Autobiographical Reflection," in *New Perspectives on the Qur'an: The Qur'an in Its Historical Context 2* (ed. Reynolds; vol. 12 of *Routledge Studies in the Quran*; New York: Routledge, 2011), where he highlights the units of qur'anic "discourse," which are larger than verses and shorter than suras. He proposes that these somewhat independent discourse-units, identified through consideration of speaker-addressees and mode of discourse, should be structured in a "chronological arrangement of discourse, a project that needs to be accomplished in the future." Abu Zayd, "Towards Understanding the Qur'an's Worldview," 85.
58 Malise Ruthven, *Islam in the World* (Oxford: Oxford University Press, 2006), KL1212-15.
59 Ramadan says that "there is no "Islamic theology." Tariq Ramadan, *Western Muslims and the Future of Islam* (Oxford: Oxford University Press, 2004), 11.
60 See the discussion in Katharina Völker, "Quran and Reform: Rahman, Arkoun, Abu Zayd" (PhD Dissertation, University of Otago, 2011) 168-72. Navdi argues, "The Islamic worldview is . . . based on three fundamental principles which are: tawhîd (theism), khilâfah (Vicegerency), and 'adâlah (Justice). These principles not only frame the Islamic worldview, but they also constitute the fountainhead of the maqasid (objectives) and the strategy of Man's life in this world." Nadvi, "Understanding the Principles of Islamic World-View," 271.
61 M. A. S. Abdel Haleem, *The Qur'an* (Oxford: Oxford University Press, 2004), KL 327. Farrin sees these main themes in the Qur'an's opening sura, "monotheism (v. 4), guidance by means of revelation (vv 5-6), and the Hereafter (vv 1-3)." Raymond Farrin, *Structure and Qur'anic Interpretation: A Study of Symmetry and Coherence in Islam's Holy Text* (Ashland, Oreg.: White Cloud Press, 2014), KL 301-302.
62 William C. Chittick, "Muslim Eschatology," in *The Oxford Handbook of Eschatology* (ed. Walls; Oxford: Oxford University Press, 2007), 135. So also Marcia Hermansen, "Eschatology," in *The Cambridge Companion to Classical Islamic Theology* (ed. Winter; Cambridge: Cambridge University Press, 2008), 309.
63 In most summaries these elements remain constant. When a fourth is added it may include "Divine Decree and Determining (al-qada and al-qadar)" or "Instruction in Law." Umeyye Isra Yazicioglu, "Learning to Ask Questions: The Cases of Abraham and Noah (P) in the Quran," *JSR* 5, no. 1 (2005): 9 n3. Justice is often listed in Turkish Islam. See Ian S. Markham and Suendam Birinci Pirim, *An Introduction to Said Nursi: Life, Thought and Writings* (Farnham: Ashgate, 2011), 24.
64 Ramadan, *Western Muslims and the Future of Islam*, 203.
65 Nadvi, "Understanding the Principles of Islamic World-View," 271.

66   Al Faruqi, *Al Tawhid*, 17. Similarly Qutb said, "The Oneness of God is the primary constituent of the Islamic concept, for it is also the fundamental truth in the Islamic creed. . . . It extends to the way in which the Muslim sees the universe and his own active role within it, to the ordering of every aspect of human life, the hidden and the visible, the small and the great, the petty and the portentous, ritual and law, belief and action, the individual and society, this world and the hereafter." Qutb, *Basic Principles of the Islamic Worldview*, 203-04.

67   This twofold definition of the oneness of God is attributed to Ali, cousin and son-in-law of Muhammad. Vincent J. Cornell, "God: God in Islam," *Encyclopedia of Religion* 5:3561.

68   Ahmed Afzaal, "Tawhid (Oneness of God)," in *The Encyclopedia of Religion and Nature* (eds. Taylor and Kaplan; London: Thoemmes Continuum, 2005), 1623. Ahmad concurs: "*Tawhīd* is not simply a statement of belief. It is an assertion of the ultimate universal truth and reality about the Creator and Sustainer of the universe. It furnishes man with a new vision of the cosmos, humanity, knowledge, morality, and eschatology." Anis Ahmad, "Reorientation of Islamic History: Some Methodological Issues," in *Islam: Source and Purpose of Knowledge: Proceedings and Selected Papers of 2nd Conference on Islamization of Knowledge*, (Herndon, Va.: International Institute of Islamic Thought, 1982), 303.

69   Unpublished personal communication from W. C. Smith, cited in Jane I. Smith, "Reflections on Aspects of Immortality in Islam," *HTR* 70, no. 1-2 (1977): 86.

70   These thoughts come from discussion with Turkish doctoral candidate Cengiz Kanik on 10/9/2012 at the İslam Araştırmaları Merkezi (İSAM, Islamic Studies Center) in İstanbul.

71   Ammar Fadzil, "Significance of the Knowledge of Muham Al-Ikhtilaf in Understanding the Qur'an," *BJQH* 4, May (2006): 28.

72   Compare Afzaal, "Tawhid (Oneness of God)," 1623.

73   See Col 1:16 for the same categorization of created realms in the Bible.

74   "According to the vision of *Tawhid*, everything other than God is a portent or pointer that signifies God . . . the Qur'an puts particular emphasis on directing the reader's attention to the innumerable and easily accessible beings and phenomena of nature as so many signs through which God may be known." Afzaal, "Tawhid (Oneness of God)," 1623.

75   Yamina B. Mermer, "Sacred Text and Revelation" (paper presented at Religious Identity and Renewal: Jewish, Christian and Muslim Explorations. Seattle University School of Theology & Ministry, August 10–14, 2014), 7.

76   Emphasis added. Asad paraphrases the qur'anic question with the words, "Will you not recognize the miracle of planned and purposeful creation?" (note on 28:72).

77   Asad (on 16:36) says this could mean "'at every period,' since *ummah* has this significance as well. In its wider sense, it may also be taken here to denote "civilization," thus comprising a human group as well as a period of time."

78   Thus believers are exhorted to say, "We believe in God and in what was sent down to us and what was sent down to Abraham, Ishmael, Isaac, Jacob, and the Tribes, and what was given to Moses, Jesus, and all the prophets by their Lord. We make no distinction between any of them, and we devote ourselves to Him" (2:136).

79   William J. Hamblin, "Pre-Islamic Arabian Prophets," in *Mormons and Muslims: Spiritual Foundations and Modern Manifestations* (ed. Palmer; Provo, Utah: Religious Studies Center, Brigham Young University, 2002), 135.

80   Abu Zayd, "Towards Understanding the Qur'an's Worldview," 66. Ruthven shows that this understanding is also found in the prophets and saints among the lineages of Sufi sect leaders. Ruthven, *Islam in the World*, KL 3510-3512.

81   "Narratives develop into retribution legends or punishment stories, serving to prove that divine justice is at work in history, the unjustly harassed being rewarded with salvation, the transgressors and the unbelievers punished by annihilation." Neuwirth, "Structural," 106. On these prophetic moral examples, see John Renard, *Friends of God: Islamic Images of Piety, Commitment, and Servanthood* (Berkeley: University of California Press, 2008), 14.

82   Rahman, *Major Themes*, 60.

83 Asad says, "The designation 'apostle' (rasūl) is applied to bearers of divine revelations which comprise a new doctrinal system or dispensation; a 'prophet' (nabī), on the other hand, is said to be one whom God has entrusted with the enunciation of ethical principles on the basis of an already-existing dispensation. . . . Hence, every apostle is a prophet as well, but not every prophet is an apostle" (on 22:52). See Uri Rubin, "Prophets and Prophethood," in *The Blackwell Companion to the Qur'an* (ed. Rippin; Malden: Blackwell, 2006), 240-41.

84 al-Attas, "Islamic Philosophy: An Introduction," 11. *Dünya* in Turkish means world, and *Ahiret* means afterlife. See also the explanation of these categories by M. A. Abdel Haleem, "Qur'an and Hadith," in *The Cambridge Companion to Classical Islamic Theology* (ed. Winter; Cambridge: Cambridge University Press, 2008), 129.

85 Rahman, *Major Themes*, 114. Of course, as Rahman notes, the prophets all bring essentially the same message.

86 4:136; 4:150; 57:19; 65:8. The singular, "God and his messenger" is found dozens of times, referring to Muhammad. The phrase "believe in God and his messenger" is found in 4:171; 7:158; 24:62-63; 48:9, 13.

87 2:8, 62, 126, 177, 228, 232, 264; 3:114; 4:39; 5:69; 9:18-19, 29, 44-45, 89; 33:21; 58:22; 60:6; 65:2.

88 Jane Dammen McAuliffe, *The Cambridge Companion to the Qur'an* (Cambridge: Cambridge University Press, 2006), 3.

89 The Qur'an over and over declares that God alone is the omnipotent Creator of everything. He is the Creator of the heavens and (the) earth (6:14, 101-102; 12:101; 14:10; 15:85-86; 35:1; 39:46; 42:11), he is the Creator of all things (6:102; 13:16), the best and most gracious Creator (23:12-16; 37:124-125; 39:62, 52:34-35), to give just a few examples.

90 Michael E. Lodahl, *Claiming Abraham: Reading the Bible and the Qur'an Side by Side* (Grand Rapids: Brazos Press, 2010), KL 871-872, 904-906.

91 So John Kaltner, *Ishmael Instructs Isaac: An Introduction to the Qur'an for Bible Readers* (Collegeville, Minn.: Liturgical press, 1999), 31-32. Also Glaser, "Qur'anic Challenges for Genesis," 11.

92 On this issue see Glaser, "Qur'anic Challenges for Genesis," 11. See also Lodahl, *Claiming Abraham*, KL 1555-1656.

93 So Kaltner, *Ishmael Instructs Isaac*, 34-35. See also Glaser, "Qur'anic Challenges for Genesis," 12. However, a Christian canonical perspective minimizes this difference; elsewhere the Bible is clear that the serpent is Satan. (Rev 12:9; 20:2; cf. Rom 16:20; Isa 27:1). See James M. Hamilton, "The Skull Crushing Seed of the Woman: Inner-Biblical Interpretation of Genesis 3:15," *SBJT* 10, no. 2 (2006).

94 This exile-from-God's-presence theme continues in Cain's story (4:14) and Israel's story.

95 On the philosophical and theological issues related to this position see K. Scott Oliphint, *God with Us: Divine Condescension and the Attributes of God* (Wheaton: Crossway, 2012), who highlights the "condescension" inherent in God's theophanic presence.

96 This term comes from Terrien's whole-Bible study of God's presence, where he asserts, "the reality of the presence of God stands at the center of biblical faith." Samuel L. Terrien, *The Elusive Presence: Toward a New Biblical Theology* (26; San Francisco: Harper & Row, 1978), xxvii.

97 See my notes on Jubilees in chapter 4. Juncker's study of the "Angel of the Lord" in intertestamental literature shows how the LXX uniformly translates theophany texts to minimize any identity between the Lord and the appearing messenger. Gunther H. Juncker, "Jesus and the Angel of the Lord: An Old Testament Paradigm for New Testament Christology" (PhD Dissertation, Trinity Evangelical Divinity School, 2001) 279-80.

98 Zulfiqar Ali Shah, *Anthropomorphic Depictions of God: The Concept of God in Judaic, Christian and Islamic Traditions: Representing the Unrepresentable* (Herndon, Va.: International Institute of Islamic Thought, 2010), 661.

99 Shah, *Anthropomorphic Depictions*, 515.

100 Islamic theological (*kalām*) and philosophical (*falsafa*) traditions examine the question of how the actions of the timeless Creator are related to the actions of time-bound creatures. See David B. Burrell, "Creation," in *The Cambridge Companion to Classical Islamic Theology* (ed. Winter; Cambridge ; New York: Cambridge University Press, 2008), 141-58.

101 On this polarity of divine transcendence and immanence see William P Brown, "Manifest Diversity: The Presence of God in Genesis," in *Genesis and Christian Theology* (eds. MacDonald, et al.; Grand Rapids: Eerdmans, 2012), KL 461-462.

102 Other sections of the Hebrew Scriptures do teach the oneness, transcendence, and utter uniqueness of God, classically Deut 6:4 and Isa 40-48. While a distinct anti-idolatry polemic, defending God's majesty as creator, is present in the Genesis creation narrative, it is not on the surface. Still, those acquainted with the astral deities of the ANE will feel the anti-mythical force of God creating the heavenly bodies by his word in Gen 1. See Hamilton, *Genesis 1-17*, 123-140.

103 Other explanations are possible, such as the "divine council," but this seems more difficult to reconcile with the clear statement that God made man in his own image (Gen 1:27; 5:1). Hamilton says, "What we often so blithely dismiss as 'foreign to the thought of the OT' may be nothing of the kind. . . . If the narrator had meant the [council], then we would expect, 'So God created man in *their* image.'" Hamilton, *Genesis 1-17*, 134-36. But see the discussion in Michael S Heiser, *The Unseen Realm: Recovering the Supernatural Worldview of the Bible* (Bellingham: Lexham Press, 2015), 672-75.

104 On this see Andreas J. Köstenberger and Scott R. Swain, *Father, Son, and Spirit: The Trinity and John's Gospel* (24; Nottingham, England; Downers Grove, Ill.: Apollos; InterVarsity Press, 2008), and Richard Bauckham, *Jesus and the God of Israel: God Crucified and Other Studies on the New Testament's Christology of Divine Identity* (Grand Rapids: Eerdmans, 2008), with their bibliographies.

105 On the relationship of the creation account in Gen 1:1–2:3 to the following narrative, see Ian Hart, "Genesis 1:1-2:3 as a Prologue to the Book of Genesis," *TynBul* 46, no. 2 (1995).

106 See Jason S DeRouchie, "The Blessing-Commission, the Promised Offspring, and the *Toledot* Structure of Genesis," *JETS* 56, no. 2 (2013): 222-25.

107 Carol M. Kaminski, *From Noah to Israel: Realization of the Primaeval Blessing after the Flood* (413; London: T & T Clark International, 2004), 94, 110. She points to Gen 35:22b-26 as the point where the line seems to reach its fulfillment in all 12 sons of Israel, but this seems to me to miss the emphasis on Judah and subsequent genealogies.

108 See 1 Cor 15:21-22, 45-47; Rom 5:14-19; Heb 2:5-15. Luke carefully traces this genealogy backwards from Jesus, following the baptismal declaration of Jesus as God's "beloved Son," to Adam, "the son of God" (3:22-38). The Qur'an makes little of this messianic-Adamic storyline other than asserting that Jesus' miraculous birth was like that of Adam, a unique creative act of God: "In God's eyes Jesus is just like Adam: He created him from dust, said to him, 'Be', and he was" (3:59).

109 Hermansen, "Eschatology," 310.

110 Ramadan, *Western Muslims and the Future of Islam*, 12.

111 Kaltner, *Ishmael Instructs Isaac*, 32. Italics added. However, Nasr argues that Islam "does stress the theomorphic nature of man." Seyyed Hossein Nasr, "Who Is Man? The Perennial Answer of Islam," *SCR* 2, no. 1 (1967): 3.

112 Roth notes that Ibn Haz began his attacks on the Bible's anthropomorphisms with Gen 1:26. Norman Roth, "Forgery and Abrogation of the Torah: A Theme in Muslim and Christian Polemic in Spain," *PAAJR* 54(1987): 219.

113 On man as *Khilāfah (Vicegerency or Caliphate)* in the Islamic worldview, see Nadvi, "Understanding the Principles of Islamic World-View," 273-74.

114 Glaser, "Qur'anic Challenges for Genesis," 11, 14.

115 See Peter J Gentry, "Kingdom through Covenant: Humanity as the Divine Image," *SBJT* 12, no. 1 (2008): 194-97. Jesus, the last Adam, is presented as both the Son of God, one with the

Father, and as the Image of the invisible God (e.g. John 1:18; 10:30; Col 1:15-16; Heb 1:3). Through him human beings are "born of God," to grow into the same likeness (John 1:12-13; Rom 8:29).

116 "The macrostructure of Genesis 1-11 shows that the author intended the judgments of Gen. 3:14-19 as something more than what happens to any disobedient individual. Adam's sin had a real effect on his descendants." Stephen Kempf, "Genesis 3:14-19: Climax of the Discourse?," *JTT* 6, no. 4 (1993): 374-75.

117 Joseph, however, resists the temptation. Timothy J. Stone, "Joseph in the Likeness of Adam: Narrative Echoes of the Fall," in *Genesis and Christian Theology* (eds. MacDonald, et al.; Grand Rapids: Eerdmans, 2012), 62-73.

118 For example, Stump devotes a large section of her extensive work on theodicy to the consideration of four narratives—Job, Samson, Abraham and Mary of Bethany. Eleonore Stump, *Wandering in Darkness: Narrative and the Problem of Suffering* (Oxford: Oxford University Press, 2010), 175-367.

119 Stump, *Wandering in Darkness*, 4.

120 Duane A. Miller, "Narrative and Metanarraative in Christianity and Islam," *SFM* 6, no. 3 (2010): 503. Miller develops a number of significant distinctions based on his reading of Q 20:115-124 in comparison with the Genesis Adam narrative.

121 Ruthven, *Islam in the World*, KL 1484-1486.

122 Hart, *The Doors of the Sea: Where Was God in the Tsunami?*, 61-62.

123 7 May 2014 interview.

124 Willem A. Bijlefeld, "Eschatology: Some Muslim and Christian Data," *ICMR* 15, no. 1 (2004): 46.

125 Muhsin Akbaş, "The Problem of Evil and Theodicy in Jewish, Christian, and Islamic Thought" (PhD dissertation, University of Wales, 1999), 191.

126 Akbaş, "The Problem of Evil and Theodicy in Jewish, Christian, and Islamic Thought," 281.

127 Osman Demir, "'Things Are Known through Their Opposites': A Survey on the Reasons and Sources of Evil in Muslim Axiology," (Inter-Disciplinary.Net, 2013), 2/8. He argues: "In many verses of Qur'an, Allah mentions opposite concepts such as day and night, light and darkness, faith and disbelief, gratitude and ingratitude, difficulty and ease together. Thus He indicates their presence of each other in harmony and order." Demir, "'Things Are Known through Their Opposites': A Survey on the Reasons and Sources of Evil in Muslim Axiology," 6/8.

128 Similarly, Turkish theologian Aydın presented Said Nursi's views on this subject in a 1995 conference paper on the problem of evil. "Bediuzzaman states that things are known by their opposites. . . . [He] tries to find a solution based on the mystery of unity." Mehmet Aydin, "The Problem of Evil in the Risale-I Nur" (paper presented at Third International Bediüzzaman Symposium: The Reconstruction of Islamic Thought in the Twentieth Century and Bediuzzaman Said Nursi. Istanbul, 24–26 September, 1995), 4/11. Nursi's perspective reflects the Sufi classics.

129 See Walter C. Kaiser, Jr., *Grief and Pain in the Plan of God: Christian Assurance and the Message of Lamentations* (Ross-shire: Christian Focus, 1980), for a Christian worldview approach.

130 Wright, *The New Testament and the People of God*, 132 Also Sire, *The Universe Next Door*, 23.

131 Miller notes, "The concept of *guidance* is a metatheme in Islam, just as *redemption* is for Christianity." Miller, "Narrative and Metanarrative in Christianity and Islam," 504.

132 Bauckham gives the following list of summary passages along with their varying scope: Deut 6:20-24; 26:5-9; Josh 24:2-13; Neh 9:6-37; Ps 78; 105; 135:8-12; 136; Acts 7:2-50. Richard Bauckham, "Reading Scripture as a Coherent Story," in *The Art of Reading Scripture* (eds. Davis and Hays; Grand Rapids: Eerdmans, 2003), 41, to which I add Acts 10:34-43; 13:17-39; and Heb 11:3-32.

133 The closest thing in the Bible to the qur'anic lists and series of prophets is Hebrews 11, where exemplars of faith are set down in biblical order. But these differ from qur'anic prophet stories

in that the common element in the stories is not their being sent to a particular people with a common message, but their common faith in God's promises.

134 Most notably 2:133, 136, 140; 3:84; 4:163-164; 6:83-86; and 42:13.

135 **Sura 3**: Zachariah (37-41); John (38-39); Mary and Jesus (42-57); **Sura 7**: Adam (10-27), Noah (59-64), Hūd (65-72), Salih (73-79), Lot (80-84), Shu'ayb (85-91), Moses and Aaron (103-162); **Sura 10**: Noah (71-73), Moses and Aaron (75-93), Jonah (98); **Sura 11**: Noah (25-49), Hūd (50-60), Salih (61-68), Abraham, (69-76), Lot (77-83), Shu'ayb (84-95), Moses (96-99); **Sura 14**: Noah, Hūd, Salih (9-18); **Sura 15**: Adam and Iblis (26-49), Abraham (51-60), Lot (61-77), Shu'ayb (78-79), Salih (80-84); **Sura 19**: Zachariah, John, Jesus (2-35), Abraham (41-50), Moses (and Aaron, 51-53), Ishmael (54-55), and Idris (56-57); **Sura 21**: Moses and Aaron (48), then separately Abraham, Isaac, Jacob and Lot (72-75), Noah (76-77), David and Solomon (78-82), Job (83-84), Ishmael, Idris, and Dhu'l-Kifl (85-86), Jonah (87-88), Zachariah, John and Jesus (89-91); **Sura 25**: Moses' audience (35-36), Noah's people (37), 'Ad (Hūd 's people), Thamud (Salih's people), and al-Rass (37-39); **Sura 26**: Moses and Aaron (10-67), Abraham (69-89); then separately Noah (105-121), Hūd (123-140), Salih (141-159), Lot (160-175), Shu'ayb (176-190); **Sura 27**: Moses (8-14), David and Solomon (15-44); then separately Salih (45-53) and Lot (54-59); **Sura 29**: Noah (14-15). Abraham and Lot (16-35 the peoples of Shu'ayb (36-37), Hūd (38), Salih (38) and Moses (39); **Sura 37**: Noah (75-83), Abraham and Isaac (83-113), Moses and Aaron (114-122), Elijah (123-132), Lot (133-138), Jonah (139-148); **Sura 38**: David (17-26), Solomon (30-40), and Job (41-44), followed by a call to remember Abraham, Isaac, and Jacob, (45-46), and Ishmael, Elisha, and Dhu'l-Kifl (47); **Sura 51**: Abraham and Sodom (24-36), Moses and Pharaoh (38-40), 'Ad (41-42), Thamud (43-45) and Noah's people (46); **Sura 53**: Moses (36), Abraham (37), 'Ad (50) and Thamūd (51), Noah's people (52).

136 Often the list of prophets is continuous between the OT and NT, as in suras 3, 4, 6, 19 and 21. The Qur'an makes no distinction between them, seeing them all as prophets sent to particular peoples in the eras before Muhammad.

137 "The Qur'an maintains that all of the prophets are sent with the same message: their stories, and indeed their own characters, are part of a grand meta-narrative." Gabriel Said Reynolds and Emran El-Badawi, "The Qur'an and the Syriac Bible," *OISO* (2013): 2/6.

138 Brannon M. Wheeler, *Prophets in the Quran: An Introduction to the Quran and Muslim Exegesis* (London: Continuum, 2002), considers in their traditional order all the prophets referred to in the Qur'an and classical Muslim sources. According to the traditions compiled by Wheeler, Hud and Salih were said to be messengers sent to the Arab peoples of Ad and Thamud. Idris is sometimes identified with the biblical Enoch, Hūd with Eber, Shu'ayb with Jethro who was sent to the people of Midian, and Dhu'l-Kifl with Elijah or Ezekiel.

139 For the way this sura holds together as a ring composition with the pivotal centre point on the replacing of Jerusalem with Mecca as the *qibla*, or prayer direction (2:104-141), see Raymond Farrin, "Surat Al-Baqara: A Structural Analysis," *MW* 100, no. 1 (2010).

140 Wright, *The Mission of God*, 65.

141 Shabbir Akhtar, *The Quran and the Secular Mind: A Philosophy of Islam* (New York: Routledge, 2007), 244.

142 Muhammad Abu-Hamdiyyah, *The Qur'an* (London: Routledge, 2002), 46. See the discussion in Abu Zayd, "Towards Understanding the Qur'an's Worldview," 84-85. See also Kate Zebiri, "Towards a Rhetorical Criticism of the Qur'an," *JQS* 5, no. 2 (2003).

143 Neuwirth, "Structural," 97-98.

144 Kaltner, *Ishmael Instructs Isaac*, 123. Likewise Wansbrough: "Analysis of the qur'anic application of these [materials] shows that they have been adapted to the essentially paraenetic character of that document, and that, for example, originally narrative material was reduced almost invariably to a series of discrete and parabolic utterances." John E. Wansbrough and Andrew Rippin, *Quranic Studies: Sources and Methods of Scriptural Interpretation* (Amherst, N.Y.: Prometheus Books, 2004), 1.

145 See Angelika Neuwirth, "Qur'an and History—a Disputed Relationship. Some Reflections on Qur'anic History and History in the Qur'an," *JQS* 5, no. 1 (2003): 15. She says, "the divine trials of the past are to be considered 'types' of the Last Judgement that will supersede everything preceding it, the dispatchment of earlier prophets in a way 'prefigure' Muhammad's activities."

146 Marilyn R. Waldman, "New Approaches to 'Biblical' Materials in the Qur'an," *MW* 75, no. 1 (1985): 12.

147 This is demonstrably true for all in the Bible, with the exception of Jesus, who is explicitly identified as the uniquely sinless (John 8:46; 2 Cor 5:21; 1 Pet 2:22; 1 John 3:5).

148 See Alford T. Welch, "Formulaic Features of the Punishment Stories," in *Literary Structures of Religious Meaning in the Qur'an* (ed. Boullata; Richmond: Curzon, 2000), 106-07.

149 "Typically, the Qur'an tells the story of a major prophet not in one but in several places. . . . The portion of a story related in a given place will be closely connected with the theme or subject being treated in that place." Mustansir Mir, "Some Aspects of Narration in the Qur'an," in *Sacred Tropes: Tanakh, New Testament, and Qur'an as Literature and Culture* (ed. Sabbath; vol. 98 of *Biblical Interpretation*; Leiden: Brill, 2009), 97.

150 Reynolds and El-Badawi, "The Qur'an and the Syriac Bible." If this assessment is correct, it becomes important to distinguish between the typological usage found in this later Christian literature and that found in the NT. I argue in chapter 4 that the NT does not primarily present a typological reading of the Abraham narrative, but emphasizes a promise-fulfillment reading. In this, it depends on the chronological narrative integrity of the whole story. The NT reading differs from later Christian readings even as it does from the Jewish exegetical narrative embellishments which find their way into those readings.

151 Ismail R. Al Faruqi, "A Comparison of the Islamic and Christian Approaches to Hebrew Scripture," *JBR* 31, no. 4 (1963): 286, 290. Ahmad similarly disallows any involvement of God in human history. Ahmad, "Reorientation of Islamic History," 287.

152 Al-Faruqi misrepresents or misunderstands the Christian position at points, using the word "favoritism" and setting up a straw man: "Islam therefore is safe against ever having to rely upon a *deterministic theory of history* in order to justify itself." Al Faruqi, "A Comparison," 286. Italics added. Biblical history is not simply "deterministic," but is the account of the sovereign will of God and the free will of human beings in conflict and cooperation. God has entered into relationship with human events in history-making ways that do not remove this autonomy in the process. While God's purposes generate the overarching narrative, the inclusion of individuals into these purposes involves their own will (e.g. Gen 50:20).

153 Nasr Abu Zayd, "The Qur'anic Concept of Justice," in *Forum for Intercultural Philosophy* (Tübingen, 2001), para 13.

154 In Genesis, repeated cycles of divine blessing in creation/re-creation, followed by human failure and rebellion, seems to testify on the macro-scale to human bondage to sin subsequent to the original "fall." See Beale, *A New Testament Biblical Theology*, 58-62. The NT sums up this teaching in Rom 5:12; 8:20.

155 Nasr says, "Islam rejects the idea of original sin. It appeals, not to the will of man which has been warped since that event or act which Christianity so profoundly describes as original sin, but to his intelligence which lies within the primordial nature of man (*al-fitrah*), the inner nature which man possessed before his fall on earth and which man still carries deep within himself. . . . religion in its universal sense (al-din) is then inherent to the human state." Nasr, "Who Is Man? The Perennial Answer of Islam," 3-4.

156 Fazlur Rahman, "Islamization of Knowledge: A Response," *AJISS* 5, no. 1 (1988): 4.

157 Abu Zayd says, "The experience of Adam's forgetting his Lord's 'convention' establishes the need for a Divine reminder. All prophets, including Prophet Muhammad himself, are, accordingly, representatives of 'reminders'; the Qur'an is simply called *dhikr*, reminder . . . and Muhammad is only *mudhakkir* (88:21)." Abu Zayd, "The Qur'anic Concept of Justice,"

paragraph 13. See Q 2:37-38. For this reason, various practices of *dhikr* [Turkish: *zikir*] or "remembrance" are central to Islamic religious life.

158 "The citations of Isaiah 53 in the NT show the Church, following the lead of Jesus, using the passage to work out the meaning of Jesus' death and resurrection." K. D. Litwak, "The Use of Quotations from Isaiah 52:13-53:12 in the New Testament," *JETS* 26, no. 4 (1983): 388. The "blood of the Lamb" becomes a significant NT theme, related to redemption and the forgiveness of sins (e.g. Matt 26:28 and par; Rom 3:25; Eph 1:7; Heb 9-10; 1 Pet 1:19; Rev 7:14). See John R.W. Stott, *The Cross of Christ* (Downers Grove: InterVarsity, 1986), for aspects of the the cross in Christian understanding.

159 Hermansen, "Eschatology," 317. However, the biblical meaning of the cross is not simply related to "original sin" as rejected by Islam in this quote, but to human "sins" *in toto*. For example, "Christ died for our *sins* according to the Scriptures" (1 Cor 15:3; cf. 1 Pet 3:18). Likewise, human guilt before God is not simply attributed to original sin, but to our own "trespasses and sins" which have made a separation between us and God (e.g. Isa 59:1-2; Eph 2:1-3).

160 The Qur'an may give the possibility of divinely permitted intercession: "Who is there that can intercede with Him except by His leave?" (2:255; cf. 19:87; 20:109; 43:86; and 53:26). Hermansen, "Eschatology," 317.

161 Angelika Neuwirth, "Two Views of History and Human Future: Qur'anic and Biblical Renderings of Divine Promises," *JQS* 10, no. 1 (2008): 14. These two passages are particularly apt for comparison due to their similar use of a repeated refrain throughout. The Q55 refrain, "Which, then, of your Lord's blessings do you both [mankind and jinn] deny?" correlates to the refrain of Psalm 136, "for his steadfast love endures forever."

162 Hermansen, "Eschatology," 308. Italics added.

163 Study of the NT use of the "coming of God" passages in the OT show that these are frequently identified with Jesus' "first" coming (e.g. Isa 40:1-10 and Mal 3:1 in Mark 1:1-3). The last days associated with the coming of the Lord have thus begun, but the Lord's climactic coming in power and judgment is still located in the future (e.g. Zech 12:10-12 in Rev 1:7). On the NT monotheistic inclusion of Jesus in the identity of the God of Israel, see Bauckham, *God Crucified*.

164 "Most Sufis and many philosophers ... justify their approach by stressing the need to actualize the return to God here and now, before one is compelled to meet God simply by the unfolding of the cosmos." Chittick, "Muslim Eschatology," 138. Muhammad's "ascent to heaven (*al-mi'raj*) became to the Sufi the example of how cosmological elements are stripped away until only the real divine image is apparent." Abu Zayd, "Towards Understanding the Qur'an's Worldview," 66.

165 In chapter 4, I will show how the Abrahamic promises are also correlated in the NT with the certainty of resurrection.

166 This is the understanding of my Turkish interviewees. But historically there has been a range of Islamic interpretations of Q 4:157, as to Jesus not dying but being "raised up" to God. "Mahmoud M. Ayoub, "Towards an Islamic Christology, Pt 2 : The Death of Jesus, Reality or Delusion (a Study of the Death of Jesus in Tafsīr Literature)," *MW* 70, no. 2 (1980).

167 Gabriel Said Reynolds, *The Qur'an and Its Biblical Subtext* (10; London ; New York: Routledge, 2010), KL 5752-5758.

168 Abdel Haleem says, "the Qur'an invariably presents arguments based on premises that it takes to be universally accessible." Abdel Haleem, "Qur'an and Hadith," 31.

169 Neuwirth, "Two Views of History," 14.

170 William J. Dumbrell, *The End of the Beginning: Revelation 21-22 and the Old Testament* (Eugene, Oreg.: Wipf and Stock Publishers, 2001), develops each theme in its OT context, its fulfillment in Christ and its consummation in Rev 21-22.

171 Hermansen identifies four aspects of the relationship between creation and eschatology in the Islamic worldview: 1) *The creation motif: "Am I not your Lord?"* referring to the return to God as a process in this life and in the end. 2) *Cosmic creation and the end of convention*, referring to the undoing and remaking of nature itself. 3) *The creation of Adam and the Garden*,

referring to the restoring of the ideal stature and God-consciousness each is created with. 4) *The creation motif: humans accepting the Trust*, pointing to the judgment of individuals at the resurrection and of nations within history to whom prophets were sent. Hermansen, "Eschatology," 309-14.

172 See Gregory K. Beale, *The Temple and the Church's Mission* (Leicester: IVP, 2004), for a full development of this theme.

173 Aziz Al-Azmeh, "Rhetoric for the Senses: A Consideration of Muslim Paradise Narratives," *JALit* 26, no. 3 (1995): 228-31.

174 Hermansen, "Eschatology," 320.

175 The "Lamb" refers to the crucified, risen, and exalted Jesus Christ (Rev 5:6-14; 21:27).

176 Rahman, *Major Themes*, 109.

CHAPTER 3 – ABRAHAM IN GENESIS

1 These formulaic phrases are best understood as superscriptions to what follows, meaning something like "this is the account of the line of . . ." and introducing material concerning what becomes of the named ancestor's descendants. For arguments for this conclusion see Matthew A. Thomas, *These Are the Generations: Identity, Covenant, and the Toledot Formula* (551; New York: T & T Clark International, 2010), 37-47. DeRouchie differs from Thomas on the implications of the formulas for structure but concurs that it is a heading. DeRouchie, "The Blessing-Commission," 22-29.

2 Abram/Abraham's name appears 181 times in Gen 11:26–25:10 out of a total of 237 in the Hebrew Bible.

3 As my focus is on the Abraham narrative in Gen 11–25, this survey is minimal. Two works which consider this material in detail are Thomas Römer, "Abraham Traditions in the Hebrew Bible Outside the Book of Genesis," in *The Book of Genesis: Composition, Reception, and Interpretation* (eds. Evans, et al.; vol. 152 of *Supplements to Vetus Testamentum*; Leiden: Brill, 2012) and Wright, *The Mission of God*, 222-64.

4 Exod 4:5; Josh 24:2; 1 Kgs 18:36; 1 Chr 29:18; 2 Chr 30:6; Ps 47:9.

5 See the discussion of this verse in Römer, "Abraham Traditions," 161-64.

6 Bauckham, *Bible and Mission*, 31.

7 Mark J. Boda, "'Declare His Glory among the Nations': The Psalter as Missional Collection," in *Christian Mission: Old Testament Foundations and New Testament Developments* (eds. Porter and Westfall; Eugene: Pickwick Publications, 2010), KL 526-527. Cf. Pss 72:17; 87:4-6.

8 Klinghoffer says, "The sages hold that the Torah is cryptic, containing innumerable instances of what appear to be errors, inconsistencies, and editorial blunders. Each is like a pointing finger, urging us to consult the tradition. Called Oral Torah, this explanatory tradition was originally passed down by word of mouth and includes elaborations on the biblical text." David Klinghoffer, *The Discovery of God: Abraham and the Birth of Monotheism* (New York: Doubleday, 2003), KL 921-925.

9 See T. D. Alexander, *From Paradise to the Promised Land: An Introduction to the Pentateuch, Third Edition* (Grand Rapids: Baker Academic, 2012), 82-83. For example, the "doublets" which have been seen as evidence of multiple sources, have been shown to have clear purpose within a careful structure by Devora Steinmetz, *From Father to Son: Kinship, Conflict, and Continuity in Genesis* (Louisville, Ky.: Westminster/John Knox Press, 1991), 63ff.

10 See my notes on "theological interpretation" in the introduction. Hans Frei argued that "the text means what it says." Hans W. Frei, "Response to 'Narrative Theology: An Evangelical Appraisal'," *TrinJ* 8, no. 1 (1987): 22. I take this to be true in relation to what it says about God and humanity.

11 As Wright argues, "It is possible for real history to be told as a good story, and for a good story to be grounded in real history. The 'having happenedness' of the biblical story is very important and should not be lost sight of when we look at the art by which that story was written." Wright, "Interpreting the Bible," 45.

12   D. Gooding, *According to Luke: A New Exposition of the Third Gospel* (Leicester: Inter-Varsity Press, 1987), 13-15, 358-59. For a detailed application of Gooding's approach in OT studies see Dominique Barthélemy, et al., *The Story of David and Goliath: Textual and Literary Criticism: Papers of a Joint Research Venture* (73; Fribourg, Suisse: Éditions universitaires; Vandenhoeck & Ruprecht, 1986), 55-86, 99-106, 114-120, 145-154.

13   J. Gerald Janzen, *Abraham and All the Families of the Earth: A Commentary on the Book of Genesis 12-50* (Grand Rapids: Eerdmans, 1993), 1. Plunket interacts helpfully with these issues, discussing Child's "canonical" approach as well as Van Seters and Whybray. Rodney L. Plunket, "'Between Elim and Sinai': A Theological Interpretation of Exodus Sixteen Shaped by Its Canonical Context." (PhD Dissertation, Durham University, 1996) 10-16.

14   For a statement of this position see Iain W. Provan, et al., *A Biblical History of Israel* (Louisville: Westminster John Knox Press, 2003), 102.

15   For structures of Genesis using these headers as the basis see John H. Walton, *The NIV Application Commentary: Genesis* (Grand Rapids: Zondervan, 2001), 39-41, Hamilton, *Genesis 1-17*, 2-11, and Waltke and Fredricks, *Genesis: A Commentary*, 17-21.

16   "The animating principle and fundamental moving energy in this story is the generative power of which conception and birth are the prime embodiment." Janzen, *Abraham and All the Families*, 3.

17   Gordon J. Wenham, *Genesis 1-15* (vol. 1; Waco: Word Books, 1987), 259. Arguments supporting the unity of the narrative as we have it may be found in Anthony Abela, *The Themes of the Abraham Narrative: Thematic Coherence within the Abraham Literary Unit of Genesis 11,27 - 25,18* (Malta: Studia Editions, 1989), and T. D. Alexander, *Abraham in the Negev: A Source-Critical Investigation of Genesis 20:1-22:19* (Carlisle, Cumbria: Paternoster, 1997), 102-110.

18   In support of this division see Alexander, *Abraham in the Negev*, 102-103. See also Steinmetz, *From Father to Son*, 166.

19   "The two outermost episodes represent the first and last times that God speaks to Abraham; those speech acts define the limits of Abraham's mission." Steinmetz, *From Father to Son*, 166.

20   See the similar analysis in Rachel Yudkowsky, "Chaos or Chiasm? The Structure of Abraham's Life," *JBQ* 35, no. 2 (2007): 110–11. Others argue that chapters 15–16 balance 17:1–18:15, each section comprised of a covenant and a birth announcement, e.g. K.S. Hong, "An Exegetical Reading of the Abraham Narrative in Genesis: Semantic, Textuality and Theology" (University of Pretoria, 2007) 247. I see chapter 16 as a single central section, and keep 18:1-15 with the section formed by chapters 18–19, in agreement with Wenham, *Genesis 1–15*, 263 and Alexander, *Abraham in the Negev*, 105.

21   Mary Douglas, *Thinking in Circles: An Essay on Ring Composition* (New Haven: Yale University Press, 2007), 16.

22   Klinghoffer, *Discovery of God*, KL 2685-2686.

23   See notes below on chapter 16 showing that there are numerous links with Gen 3 which intimate that this event is intended to be the account of another game-changing failure or "fall."

24   Keith N. Grüneberg, *Abraham, Blessing and the Nations: A Philological and Exegetical Study of Genesis 12:3 in Its Narrative Context* (vol. 332; Berlin: Walter de Gruyter, 2003), 9-10. "It is the promise of a son that is central to the Abraham story, and most of the episodes are related in some way or another to that promise." Wenham, *Genesis 1-15*, 262. See also Alexander, *Abraham in the Negev*, 103-05.

25   Larry R. Helyer, "The Separation of Abram and Lot: Its Significance in the Patriarchal Narratives," *JSOT* 26 (1983): 80.

26   This connection is supported by repetition of the "blessing" theme. Edward Noort, "Abraham and the Nations," in *Abraham, the Nations, and the Hagarites: Jewish, Christian, and Islamic Perspectives on Kinship with Abraham* (eds. Goodman, et al.; vol. 13 of *Themes in Biblical Narrative*; Leiden: Brill Academic Publishers, 2010), 19.

27   Ronald Hendel, *Remembering Abraham: Culture, Memory, and History in the Hebrew Bible* (New York: Oxford University Press, 2005), 36.

28   Penley argues for a known historical background for these events. Paul T Penley, "A Historical Reading of Genesis 11:1–9: The Sumerian Demise and Dispersion under the Ur III Dynasty," *JETS* 50, no. 4 (2007): 714.

29   Waltke and Fredricks, *Genesis: A Commentary*, 199.

30   Stump, *Wandering in Darkness*, 263.

31   The divine rejuvenation of barren Sarah and aged Abraham prefigures the restored Edenic abundance of Zion in later Hebrew Scripture (Isa 51:2-3). The spiritual "barrenness" of Sarah's physical offspring will be an important issue in the future, requiring another act of God to bring offspring to bereaved "lady Zion" (Isa 49:19-21; 54:1). See John L. Ronning, "The Naming of Isaac: The Role of the Wife/Sister Episodes in the Redaction of Genesis," *WTJ* 53(1991): 16-17.

32   No clear winner has emerged in the debate between scholars over which Ur was Abram's homeland (southern Iraqi Ur or northern Ur close to Haran). See Walton, *The NIV Application Commentary: Genesis*, 390-91. Turks are certain that ancient Urfa is the birthplace of Abraham, and many thousands visit the site annually.

33   "Islamic tradition likewise identifies Urfa as the birthplace of the patriarch Abraham, hence it is a major pilgrimage site for Muslims. Inside the courtyard of the Mevlid-i Halil Camii [mosque] is the cave where, according to tradition, Abraham was born." Mark Wilson, *Biblical Turkey: A Guide to the Jewish and Christian Sites of Asia Minor* (Istanbul: Efe Yayınları, 2010), 49. Hamilton summarizes the arguments for both locations and concludes that the balance of evidence favors a northern Ur. Hamilton, *Genesis 1-17*, 363-65.

34   For support for the now traditional Sumerian site in Iraq, see Wenham, *Genesis 1-15*, 272. Dirks also assumes the Sumerian Ur location and argues that Abraham was of Akkadian origin. Jerald Dirks, *Abraham: The Friend of God* (Beltsville, Md.: Amana Publications, 2002), 23-28, 208-17.

35   These have much in common with Jewish exegetical narrative of the period. See Shari L. Lowin, "The Making of a Forefather: Abraham in Islamic and Jewish Exegetical Narratives" (PhD Dissertation, The University of Chicago, 2002).

36   It is interesting that while this passage figures prominently in Christian interpretation, it is "largely disregarded in ancient Judaism." George H. von Kooten and Jacques T. A. G. M. van Ruiten, "Introduction," in *Abraham, the Nations, and the Hagarites: Jewish, Christian, and Islamic Perspectives on Kinship with Abraham* (eds. Goodman, et al.; vol. 13 of *Themes in Biblical Narrative*; Leiden: Brill Academic Publishers, 2010), xviii. Jewish tradition emphasizes Abraham's early role as the father of monotheism, to which this call is seen an additional stage.

37   This is the meaning when the final phrase is understood as a passive. Recent studies reach different conclusions as to whether this final phrase is reflexive ("by you all the families of the earth shall bless themselves") or passive as understood in the LXX and the NT ("by you all the families of the earth will be blessed"). Williamson concludes that a "middle" sense of the verb is best, which yields a meaning like "Through you all the families of the earth may/ will experience blessing." Paul R. Williamson, *Abraham, Israel, and the Nations: The Patriarchal Promise and Its Covenantal Development in Genesis* (Sheffield: Sheffield Academic Press, 2000), 220-28. In support of the reflexive, see Noort, "Abraham and the Nations," 24-30. Moberly also favors the reflexive, citing parallels with Jer 24:8-9 and 29:21-23. R. W. L. Moberly, *The Theology of the Book of Genesis* (Cambridge ; New York: Cambridge University Press, 2009), KL 1526-1531. For a monograph length study which supports the passive meaning of Gen 12:3, see Grüneberg, *Abraham, Blessing and the Nations*, 70-90. Also in support of the passive see Benjamin J. Noonan, "Abraham, Blessing, and the Nations: A Reexamination of the Niphal and Hitpael of Brk [Hebrew Characters] in the Patriarchal Narratives," *HS* 51(2010).

38 So Noort says, "The fact that Gen 12:3 concerns the entire world and all peoples, bears witness to a universalism which, even in comparison with the latter prophets, is unequalled." Noort, "Abraham and the Nations," 19.

39 On the importance of the Table of Nations in the Hebrew perspective on the nations in relationship to God's purpose, see James M. Scott, "Luke's Geographical Horizon," in *The Book of Acts in Its Graeco-Roman Setting* (eds. Gill and Gempf; Grand Rapids: Eerdmans, 1994), 499-522.

40 Noort, "Abraham and the Nations," 20.

41 In the creation narrative God blessed the creatures (Gen 1:22), mankind (1:28; cf. 5:3) and the seventh day (2:3).

42 See 3:17; 4:11; 5:29; 8:21 and 9:25. "It seems quite likely, based on the heavy use of the root for 'bless,' employed five times in vv. 2-3, that Abraham and his descendants are the ones who will undo the earlier divine curses connected to human evil doing." Kaminski, "The Theology of Genesis," 644.

43 Janzen, *Abraham and All the Families*, 5.

44 In Jewish tradition Abraham is pictured as leaving Haran with many converts to monotheism won through his missionary efforts. This extrabiblical picture is extrapolated from the reference to "the souls that they had obtained in Haran" (Gen 12:5), which may be rendered "souls they had made," by conversion. So Klinghoffer, *Discovery of God*, KL 786-838. However, this same primitive root *asah* is used to mean "acquired" in a number of other passages (Isa 15:7; Ezek 22:13; 28:4; 38:12), and need not mean "made" or "begotten" here.

45 Stump, *Wandering in Darkness*, 266-67.

46 On the appearances of God in Genesis see Brown, "Manifest Diversity: The Presence of God in Genesis," 3-25. It seems that one strand of tradition in Second Temple times understood that the initial appearance and call recorded in 12:1-3 occurred while the patriarch was still in Mesopotamia (Acts 7:2).

47 See Cecil P. Staton, Jr., "'And Yahweh Appeared . . .': A Study of the Motifs of 'Seeing God' and of 'God's Appearing' in Old Testament Narratives" (PhD Dissertation, University of Oxford, 1988).

48 For the identity of "the Angel of the Lord/God," see Juncker, who concludes, "A cumulative and fairly convincing case can be made that the Angel of the Lord in a number of at texts is YHWH himself." Juncker, "Jesus and the Angel of the Lord," 186. In the OT text the temporary appearances of the Lord merge rather naturally with the appearances of his messenger, to the extent that it is sometimes difficult to determine who is appearing.

49 Dempster, *Dominion and Dynasty*, 78. Other scholars see evidence here that these altar locations (12:6-8; 28:21) were "perfectly orthodox and innocuous normal shrines in the Yahwistic cult," which were later condemned under Deuteronomistic spirituality. Hendel, *Remembering Abraham*, 25-26.

50 "This pilgrim-like activity was like planting a flag and claiming the land . . . for God and Israel's future temple, where God would take up his permanent residence in the capital of that land." Beale, *The Temple and the Church's Mission*, 99.

51 12:7 follows his journey; 13:14-17 follows his granting Lot first choice; 15:1 follows his refusal of the king of Sodom's reward; 22:15-18 follows his willingness to offer up Isaac.

52 Stephen B. Chapman, "Food, Famine and the Nations: A Canonical Approach to Genesis," in *Genesis and Christian Theology* (eds. MacDonald, et al.; Grand Rapids: Eerdmans, 2012) develops the significance of food and famine in Genesis as a unifying theme of the book.

53 This seems clear despite Jewish, ancient Christian, and Muslim efforts to clear Abraham of guilt in the situation. See Tammi J. Schneider, *Sarah: Mother of Nations* (New York: Continuum, 2004), 33, Mark Sheridan, *Genesis 12-50* (ed. Oden; vol. 2; Downers Grove: InterVarsity Press, 2002), 6-9, and Klinghoffer, *Discovery of God*, KL 1479-1481. Notice however, that the accusatory question "What have you done?" is used in biblical narrative where real guilt

is evident (Gen 3:13; 4:10; 26:10; Josh 7:19). Mark E. Biddle, "The 'Endangered Ancestress' and Blessing for the Nations," *JBL* 109, no. 4 (1990): 604.

54   Lesslie Newbigin, *The Open Secret: An Introduction to the Theology of Mission* (Grand Rapids: Eerdmans, 1995), 72.

55   Frequently the sins of pagan Egypt's ancient ancestor Ham are highlighted in this regard. See Steinmetz, *From Father to Son*, 170. However accurate, the picture of pagan sinfulness is not emphasized in this narrative or in chapter 20. Rather the patriarch is rebuked by the pagan ruler in both scenes.

56   "His war was not one based on religion or land, as those of Moses and Muhammad were. Indeed Abraham refuses to take even the normal spoils of war (v. 23-24)." Lowin, "The Making of a Forefather," 296. Wenham observes, "Taken as a whole the book of Genesis offers a very powerful condemnation of violence." Gordon J. Wenham, "Review of R. W. L. Moberly *the Theology of the Book of Genesis*," *JTS* 62, no. 1 (2011): 263. He cites Genesis 4 along with 6:11, 13; 9:5-6, and 49:5-7.

57   "The view that Melchizedek's Salem in Gen. xiv 18 was Jerusalem remains the most probable interpretation of the available evidence." John A. Emerton, "The Site of Salem, the City of Melchizedek (Genesis Xiv 18)," in *Studies in the Pentateuch* (ed. Emerton; vol. 41 of *Supplements to Vetus Testamentum*; Leiden: E. J. Brill, 1990), 70. Jewish tradition agrees with this identification. See Klinghoffer, *Discovery of God*, KL 1920-2017.

58   For a recent defense of this ancient tradition, see Scott W. Hahn, "Kinship by Covenant: A Biblical Theological Study of Covenant Types and Texts in the Old and New Testaments" (PhD Dissertation, Marquette University, 1995) 171-81.

59   As argued by David Elgavish, "The Encounter of Abram and Melchizedek King of Salem: A Covenant Establishing Ceremony," in *Studies in the Book of Genesis: Literature, Redaction and History* (ed. Wénin; vol. 155 of *Bibliotheca Ephemeridum Theologicarum Lovaniensium*; Leuven: University Press; Uitgeverij Peeters, 2001), 495-508.

60   Helyer, "The Separation of Abram and Lot," 83. Several lines of evidence are presented to support the "probability that Lot was viewed by Abram as his heir."

61   Terence E. Fretheim, *Abraham: Trials of Family and Faith* (Columbia: University of South Carolina Press, 2007), 35.

62   Throughout Genesis the patriarchs receive divine revelation (though without the "word of the Lord" formula, which does not recur in the Biblical narrative until 1 Sam 15:10). They are probably called "prophets" for this reason (20:7; cf. Ps 105:15).

63   Wenham, *Genesis 1-15*, 328-29.

64   Heiser argues that "the word of the Lord" appears visibly here, and that this is part of the background of the divine Word appearing in flesh in John's gospel. Heiser, *The Unseen Realm*, KL 2377-2425. See also Daniel Boyarin, "The Gospel of the Memra: Jewish Binitarianism and the Prologue to John," *HTR* 94, no. 3 (2001): 276.

65   Hamilton suggests that the word *hasab* "is used to demonstrate Yahweh's reckoning of Abram's act of faith as the deciding factor in his relationship with Abram," Hamilton, *Genesis 1-17*, 427. See R. W. L. Moberly, "Abraham's Righteousness," in *Studies in the Pentateuch* (ed. Emerton; vol. 41 of *Supplements to Vetus Testamentum*; Leiden: E. J. Brill, 1990), and the discussion in Francis Watson, *Paul and the Hermeneutics of Faith* (London: T & T Clark International, 2004), 179: "YHWH intends that his relationship to Abraham should in future be exclusively determined by that promise." Moberly and Watson examine Gen 15:6 in relation to Ps 106:31.

66   This alternate approach is found in rabbinic Judaism, cited by Klinghoffer, *Discovery of God*, KL 2192-2197. See also the discussion in K. Seybold, "*Hāšab*," in *Theological Dictionary of the Old Testament* (eds. Botterweck and Ringgren; Grand Rapids: Eerdmans, 1974), 243-44.

67   Bo Johnson, "Who Reckoned Righteousness to Whom," *SEA* 51-52.

68   Tom Holland, *Romans: The Divine Marriage: A Biblical Theological Commentary* (Eugene, Oreg.: Pickwick Publications, 2011), 114.

69   See also Exod 6:6; 13:3; 15:13; Lev 19:36; Deut 5:15; 7:8; 13:10; 15:15; 26:6-8, for this emphasis on God redeeming Israel by bringing them out of bondage.

70   Nahum M. Sarna, *Understanding Genesis* (New York: Jewish Theological Seminary of America, 1966), 127. However, this covenant is different from the Sinai covenant, which was binding on both God and Israel: "This covenant . . . is a promissory oath made by God alone . . . The nearest parallel to this form is the royal land grant made by kings to loyal servants." Wenham, *Genesis 1-15*, 333.

71   See Hamilton, *Genesis 1-17*, 437.

72   Walton argues that "Genesis represent[s] the history of the establishment of the covenant" and that this multi-phased covenant is best seen as "representing the revelatory plan of God. Its purpose is to provide a means whereby God will reveal himself to the world." Walton, *The NIV Application Commentary: Genesis*, 37.

73   On the matrix of covenant-making passages coming together in the theophany in Judges 2:1-5 and Mal 3:1 among others, see Juncker, "Jesus and the Angel of the Lord," 121-25, 180-85.

74   Walter C. Kaiser, Jr. and Moisés Silva, *An Introduction to Biblical Hermeneutics : The Search for Meaning* (Grand Rapids: Zondervan, 1994), 71.

75   "From God's perspective, however, Ishmael is not the apex—he is the pivot on which the story turns." Yudkowsky, "Chaos or Chiasm?," 112.

76   See Hamilton, *Genesis 1-17*, 444.

77   Years later Abraham's grandson Jacob responds angrily to Rachel's impatience in the same situation: "Am I in the place of *God, who has withheld from you* the fruit of the womb?" (30:2). His question alludes to Gen 3:1-6, where the woman is tempted to be in the place of God. Ronning notes, "Besides the verbal allusion, there is a thematic similarity to Gen 3 in this sin, in that it is motivated by dissatisfaction with God's providence—the attitude that God is withholding something good from people, so they must take action on their own." John L. Ronning, *The Jewish Targums and John's Logos Theology* (Peabody, Mass.: Hendrickson Publishers, 2010), 101.

78   Culver, "The Ishmael Promises in the Light of God's Mission: Christian and Muslim Reflections," 39. Flint argues agains this position: "the way Sarai announces her plan, however, suggests a defiant attempt to circumvent the LORD's purposes." Bar, "The Religious Sources of Islamic Terrorism," 10.

79   Gordon J. Wenham, *Genesis 16-50* (vol. 2; Dallas: Word Books, 1994), 12. For correlations between the two events see John Sailhamer, *The Pentateuch as Narrative: A Biblical-Theological Commentary* (Grand Rapids: Zondervan, 1992), 153. The clause "listened to the voice" is used in only these two texts. George V. P. Campbell, "Rushing Ahead of God: An Exposition of Genesis 16:1-16," *BSac* 163, no. July–Sep (2006): 282. Ronning presents a series of parallels with Genesis 3 showing that Gen 16:1-6 is indeed about a "fall." John L. Ronning, "The Curse on the Serpent (Genesis 3:15) in Biblical Theology and Hermeneutics" (PhD Dissertation, Westminster Theological Seminary, 1997) 193-97. Also Stone, "Joseph in the Likeness of Adam: Narrative Echoes of the Fall," KL 965-68.

80   Klinghoffer locates the importance of this turning point within Abraham's internal life: "With Ishmael's birth, perhaps even earlier in the sexual relationship with Hagar, something changed in Abram... after Ishmael's birth, he seems focused on his Egyptian family— Hagar and Ishmael." Klinghoffer, *Discovery of God*, KL 2687-2689. But this reading neglects the importance of Sarah and her son in the ongoing narrative.

81   "The earlier chapters are the foundation and the continuing frame of reference for [the patriarchal narratives]. If they are not often explicitly referred to in Gen. 12-50, that is because they are everywhere presupposed and echoed." Janzen, *Abraham and All the Families*, 6.

82   Wenham, *Genesis 16-50*, 9.

83   Abraham too draws attention to God's "seeing" in naming the mount where Isaac is spared (22:24).

84   Darrell D. Hannah, *Michael and Christ: Michael Traditions and Angel Christology in Early Christianity* (109; Tübingen: Mohr Siebeck, 1999), 19. Similarly, Kaiser says,

"Frequently He receives the respect, worship and honor reserved only for God, yet He was consistently distinguished from God. He carried an identity with God; yet He was also sent from Him!" Walter C. Kaiser, Jr., *Toward an Old Testament Theology* (Grand Rapids: Zondervan, 1981), 85.

85 On the other hand, this phrase may be seen as announcing Ishmael's freedom from servitude: "He will not be under anyone's power (hand), but will enjoy parity with those who act against him; and he will dwell alongside his own kin." Janzen, *Abraham and All the Families*, 45.

86 Wenham, *Genesis 16-50*, 10. Also Fretheim, *Abraham: Trials*, 97.

87 See Hamilton, *Genesis 1-17*, 454-55.

88 "In biblical narrative the link between name and plot is pervasive; suffice it to mention the bearing of Ishmael's, Isaac's, and Jacob's names on the plot of Genesis." Jean-Pierre Sonnet, "'Ehyeh Asher Ehyeh' (Exodus 3:14): God's 'Narrative Identity' among Suspense, Curiosity, and Surprise," *PoeT* 31, no. 2 (2010): 332.

89 Kepnes, "Hagar and Esau," 35. Kepnes mines this rich narrative to argue that scripture "neither thoroughly demonizes the other nor does it leave her narratives out. On the contrary, it preserves the memories and stories of the others and says, in fundamental ways, that these others are related to us. The others, indeed, are us!" Kepnes, "Hagar and Esau," 38-39.

90 Kepnes, "Hagar and Esau," 36.

91 Ishmael's descendants are Arabs, but not necessarily Muslims. Esau's descendants are Edom.

92 Kepnes, "Hagar and Esau," 39.

93 This text stands as a warning to the people of God against becoming like Sarai and oppressing the outsider, as Israel will learn when they are oppressed in Hagar's homeland (Exod 1-2). To do so will be to oppose the God who sees, hears, and cares for the afflicted.

94 That Abram has placed his hopes in Ishmael seems indicated by his exclamation, "Oh that Ishmael might live before you!" (17:18).

95 "As the text stands, this must be understood as a fuller unfolding of the covenant of Gen. xv." Moberly, "Abraham's Righteousness," 120.

96 This incidentally shows that the nation which comes from Ishmael is not considered one of this multitude of nations. Culver argues that, "Essentially 17:20 is a genealogical corollary to 17:6 as witnessed by the similarity between fecundity, nations and kings in the Abrahamic promise (17:6); and fecundity, princes and nation in the Ishmaelite promise (17:20)." Culver, "The Ishmael Promises in the Light of God's Mission: Christian and Muslim Reflections," 76. However, there is a closer parallel with God's promise regarding Sarah (17:15-16). Not only the *name change*, but the promises of a plurality of *nations* and of *kings*, ties them together and distinguishes them from the Ishmael promise: princes are not kings, and a great nation is not many nations.

97 The "royal promises" (17:6, 16; 35:1) share two common features: 1) characters receive new names; 2) the promise of kings is linked with themes of fruitfulness, seed, and land. Daniel S. Diffey, "The Royal Promise in Genesis: The Often Underestimated Importance of Genesis 17:6, 17 and 35:11," *TynBul* 62, no. 2 (2011).

98 Notice for example Exod 29:45-46; Lev 26:11-12; Num 35:34; Deut 2:12; 1 Kgs 6:13.

99 For the phrase "royal lineage" see Alexander, *From Paradise to the Promised Land*, 134-45. Isaac's son Esau, the father of the Edomites, is likewise excluded from the covenant blessings in spite of physical descent from Abraham, though in his case specific disinterest in his birthright is underlined (Gen 25:29-34; 27:30-40). Somewhat like his uncle Ishmael, restless Esau is promised eventual independence (16:12; 27:40).

100 Williamson, *Abraham, Israel, and the Nations*, 61-62.

101 This is seen in the parallel announcements: "...whom Sarah shall bear to you *at this time next year*" (17:21), and "I will surely return to you *about this time next year*, and Sarah your wife shall have a son.... At the appointed time I will return to you, *about this time next year*" (18:10, 14). When the fulfillment of the promise is described in chapter 21, his "returning to" Sarah is described as a "visitation": "Yahweh *visited* Sarah as he had said, and Yahweh did to Sarah as he had promised" (21:1).

102 There are inadequate grounds in the text for finding in the "three men" standing in front of Abraham (18:2) "a symbol or prefiguration of the Trinity" (three men = Father, Son and Holy Spirit) as sometimes done in church history. Sheridan, *Genesis 12-50*, 61.

103 Rabbinic readings often separate the visit of Yahweh from that of the angels. For example, Genesis Rabbah "describes God along with his retinue coming to visit Abraham following his circumcision . . . stating that Abraham saw the Shekinah and *then* saw the angels." Emmanouela Grypeou and Helen Spurling, "Abraham's Angels: Jewish and Christian Exegesis of Genesis 18–19," in *The Exegetical Encounter between Jews and Christians in Late Antiquity* (eds. Grypeou and Spurling; Leiden: Brill, 2009), 186. The earliest Christian commentators generally saw the Lord as one of the three visitors: "The interpretation of the episode of Mamre as a revelation apparition of the pre-incarnate Christ accompanied by two angels was widely accepted in the patristic literature. The Trinitarian interpretation . . . became more prominent in the later exegetical tradition." Grypeou and Spurling, "Abraham's Angels," 196.

104 Ronning argues that God not only makes it possible for Sarah to conceive but in the process miraculously "rejuvenates" her physically to the extent that at 89 years of age she is as desirable to the pagan king Abimelech as she was decades earlier to Pharaoh. Ronning, "The Naming of Isaac," 13-14. He points to Paul's linking the miraculous rejuvenation of Abraham and Sarah's physical bodies with the resurrection of Jesus from the dead. Thus the rejuvenation becomes a sign of the resurrection. Ronning, "The Naming of Isaac," 16-17.

105 Jewish exegesis suggests that the third angel who appeared to Abraham, sometimes identified as Michael, returned to heaven after completing his mission of announcing the birth of Isaac. Grypeou and Spurling, "Abraham's Angels," 187. The preceding verse, however, records rather that "the LORD went his way, when he had finished speaking to Abraham" (18:33).

106 On Lot's righteousness see T. D. Alexander, "Lot's Hospitality: A Clue to His Righteousness," *JBL* 104, no. 2 (1985).

107 This also points to his role as a prophet of God (Amos 3:7). Yet Abraham is never portrayed as warning the people of Sodom or any other pagan center of their need to repent. Rather his role is intercession (cf. 20:7, 17).

108 This and other details parallel with the flood narrative, where God "remembered Noah" (8:1). The effects of the "Fall" continue to effect the human race, and even Abraham's nephew is rescued with difficulty due to his hesitant lingering in spite of the angels' urgings (19:16).

109 For arguments demonstrating that these are accounts of two separate events see T. D. Alexander, "Are the Wife/Sister Incidents of Genesis Literary Compositional Variants," *VT* 42, no. 2 (1992). Also see Steinmetz, *From Father to Son*, 63-64.

110 Biddle, "The 'Endangered Ancestress' and Blessing for the Nations," 602. Ronning argues that Abraham's actions in this incident and the previous one are part of a pattern seen in Genesis where the new Adam figures are disqualified by virtue of their sins and sons. "The rebuke of the king in each of these incidents (12:18: 'What is this you have done to me?'; 20:9: 'What have you done to us?') is reminiscent of the LORD's words to Eve, 'What is this you have done?' (3:13)." Ronning, *The Curse on the Serpent*, 101. Lodahl draws attention to the tendency of later readings to minimize or eliminate failures and sins of the patriarchs: "The hagiographic overhaul of the biblical characters is typical of the Qur'an—and before the Qur'an, of Jewish and Christian interpretive traditions as well" Lodahl, *Claiming Abraham*, KL 2195-2196. Whatever later Christian tradition may do, the NT does not "whitewash" even the most prominent believers in the Hebrew Scriptures, but rather presents them as examples of those "blessed" ones whose sins have been not counted against them, and have become heirs of "the righteousness that comes by faith." Abraham, David, and Noah are all considered this way (Rom 4:1-8; Heb 11:7).

111 It has been suggested from ancient times that Ishmael may have been inferring that Isaac was an illegitimate child, the result of Sarah's stay in Abimelech's harem. Ronning, *The Curse on the Serpent*, 101 n27. For details see Klinghoffer, *Discovery of God*, KL 3737-3814.

112 Campbell, "Rushing Ahead of God," 277.
113 This brief notice contrasts with the elaborate story of the finding of a wife for Isaac, wife who is carefully brought from among Abraham's people (ch 24) with divine guidance.
114 S. Nikaido, "Hagar and Ishmael as Literary Figures: An Intertextual Study," *VT* 51(2001): 221-22.
115 Nikaido, "Hagar and Ishmael as Literary Figures: An Intertextual Study," 240.
116 Note that Isaac returns there when famine strikes again (26:1).
117 This has however been questioned by Reuven Firestone, "Comparative Studies in Bible and Qur'an: A Fresh Look at Genesis 22 in Light of Sura 37," in *Judaism and Islam: Boundaries, Communication and Interaction: Essays in Honor of William M. Brinner* (ed. Brinner: Brill, 2000), 169-84.
118 Abela, *The Themes of the Abraham Narrative*, 72-73. He notes the number of times "son" (*bēn*) is used in the narrative as evidence of the focus on the father and son relationship: 22:2, 3, 6, 7, 8, 9, 10, 12, 13, 16.
119 "Is not this the obvious key to the language of Genesis 1:26f.? God created man as a sort of earthly son, who represents him and responds to him." Blocher, *In the Beginning*, 89.
120 Holland argues that Isaac may function as the "firstborn," the heir and family redeemer figure. See his discussion of "the Firstborn and the Jewish Cult" in Tom Holland, *Contours of Pauline Theology: A Radical New Survey of the Influences on Paul's Biblical Writings* (Ross-shire: Mentor, Christian Focus Publications, 2004), 237-73.
121 "Here the same root, 'see, provide,' is used in the niphal, which is regularly used of the LORD appearing to men (cf. 12:7; 17:1; 18:1), thus making a link backward with Abraham's past experience and forward to Israel's future experiences on the mountain of God (Exod 3:1-2,16; Lev 9:4,6, etc.)." Wenham, *Genesis 16-50*, 111.
122 The importance of the place is likely seen in the name Moriah. "The name anticipates Abraham's experience that 'the LORD will provide' (v 14; cf. v 8) *ra'ah* 'provide, see' is a key word of the narrative, and here in the name of the place to which Abraham must take his son, there is the first hint of salvation." Wenham, *Genesis 16-50*, 104-05. Kalimi argues that "the Temple Mount was identified with the site of the Aqeda during the period of the First Temple (Gen 22:14b)." Isaac Kalimi, "The Land of Moriah, Mount Moriah, and the Site of Solomon's Temple in Biblical Historiography," *HTR* 83, no. 04 (1990): 350.
123 To "possess the gate" of one's enemies is to conquer their cities. Wenham, *Genesis 16-50*, 112.
124 Note that the final reference in verse 17 is singular: "*his* enemies." See James M. Hamilton, "The Seed of the Woman and the Blessing of Abraham," *TynBul* 58, no. 2 (2007): 262. Also Collins, "A Syntactical Note," 139-148. Alexander concludes that "if the immediately preceding reference to 'seed' in 22:17 denotes an individual, this must also be the case in 22:18a, for there is nothing here to indicate a change in number. The blessing of 'all the nations of the earth' is thus associated with a particular descendant of Abraham.... The book of Genesis not only intimates that this lineage will eventually give rise to a royal dynasty, but also anticipates that a future member of this line will conquer his enemies and mediate God's blessing to the nations of the earth." T. D. Alexander, "Further Observations on the Term 'Seed' in Genesis," *TynBul* 48, no. 2 (1997): 366, 368.
125 Rashi cites earlier traditional sources concerning the atoning value of the near sacrifice of Isaac: "Its contextual (*peshuto*) meaning is according to the Targum: God will choose and see for himself this place to cause his presence to dwell there and to cause sacrifices to be offered there. And there is an aggadic Midrash: God will see this binding to forgive Israel in every year and to rescue them from disaster, so that in this day and in all future generations it will be said: 'On the mountain God will see the ashes of Isaac piled up as an atonement.'" Cited in Devorah Schoenfeld, *Isaac on Jewish and Christian Altars: Polemic and Exegesis in Rashi and the Glossa Ordinaria* (New York: Fordham University Press, 2012), 108. On the NT allusions to this passage see chapter 4.
126 Dempster, *Dominion and Dynasty*, 85, n.47.

127 Judith Frishman, "'And Abraham Had Faith': But in What? Ephrem and the Rabbis on Abraham and God's Blessings," in *The Exegetical Encounter between Jews and Christians in Late Antiquity* (eds. Grypeou and Spurling; Leiden; Boston: Brill, 2009), 177. Italics added.

128 R. W. L. Moberly, "Christ as the Key to Scripture: Genesis 22 Reconsidered," in *He Swore an Oath: Biblical Themes from Genesis 12-50* (eds. Hess, et al.; Eugene, Oreg.: Wipf and Stock Publishers, 2007), 161. This divine incorporation of the human faith-obedience in the accomplishing of God's mission is a profound concept that for Christian readers reaches its deepest meaning in the son of Abraham's one act of righteousness (Rom 5:19). See chapter 4.

129 Janzen concludes, "The various specific steps in Abraham's life implicitly embody the same sort of day-by-day, situation-by-situation response to God that the various specific laws later call for." Janzen, *Abraham and All the Families*, 100. Jewish traditions take these verses in a different direction, finding in them evidence that Abraham kept the Mosaic Law in full, even before it was revealed on Sinai.

130 This is in line with Clines' proposal that the "theme of the Pentateuch is the partial fulfillment —which implies also the partial non-fulfillment—of the promise to or blessing of the patriarchs." David J. A. Clines, *The Theme of the Pentateuch* (10; Sheffield: Dept. of Biblical Studies, University of Sheffield, 1978), 29.

131 Sean M. McDonough, "'And David Was Old, Advanced in Years': 2 Samuel 24:18-25, 1 Kings 1:1, and Genesis 23-24," *VT* 49, no. 1 (1999): 129.

132 Walton, *The NIV Application Commentary: Genesis*, 534

133 Esther Fuchs, "Structure and Patriarchal Functions in the Biblical Betrothal Type-Scene: Some Preliminary Notes," in *Women in the Hebrew Bible: A Reader* (ed. Bach; New York: Routledge, 1999), 46.

134 Janzen, *Abraham and All the Families*, 90.

135 Wenham argues that this phrase, a direct quote from 16:12, "probably hints at the later antagonism between the bedouin-like Ishmaelites and the more settled Israelites." Wenham, *Genesis 16-50*, 165. But an argument also can be made that the primary meaning of this phrase (literally "before the face of") implies not hostility, but only geographic proximity "in the presence of" or "in front of." Maalouf, *Arabs in the Shadow of Israel: The Unfolding of God's Prophetic Plan for Ishmael's Line*, 73-77.

136 "The depiction [in Gen 26:5] of Abraham as a Torah-observant Jew is one that will reverberate in Jewish biblical interpretation through the centuries." Jon D. Levenson, *Inheriting Abraham: The Legacy of the Patriarch in Judaism, Christianity, and Islam* (Princeton: Princeton University Press, 2012), 143. Cf. R. W. L. Moberly, "The Earliest Commentary on the Akedah," *VT* 38, no. 3 (1988): 305.

137 "The reference to Abraham's obedience in Gen 26,5 lacks reference to Torah (note the plural). As the orthodox Jewish commentator, Benno Jacob [B. Jacob, *Das Erstr Buch der Tora*, 1934, 548], pointed out, this reverence must refer to the Noachian prohibitions, circumcision (Gen 17) and the general laws of humanity. What is omitted in Gen 26,5 is the reference to *hukkah* and *Torah*, the very terms needed to support [the idea that Abraham exemplifies living by torah]." Brevard S. Childs, "Critique of Recent Intertextual Canonical Interpretation," *ZAW* 115, no. 2 (2003): 180. Jewish tradition found "two Torahs" in the plural *tôrôtāy*, the oral and the written. Victor P. Hamilton, *The Book of Genesis: Chapters 18-50* (Grand Rapids: Eerdmans, 1995), 194 n.26.

138 Regarding the unflattering story of Judah in Gen 38 Goldin says, "The election of the younger is God's inscrutable device of choosing whom He will, the last-born in place of the first." Judah Goldin, "The Youngest Son or Where Does Genesis 38 Belong," *JBL* 96, no. 1 (1977): 43-44.

139 See Alexander, *From Paradise to the Promised Land*, 134-60.

140 Sonnet, "'Ehyeh Asher Ehyeh,'" 339.

141 Watson summarizes, "The question of who God is can best be answered by reference to what God does—just as, in a narrative, a character may be individualized by reference to

significant actions within a specific history rather than through immanent attributes or dispositions. Divine being and divine action are inseparable." Francis Watson, "The Triune Divine Identity: Reflections on Pauline God-Language, in Disagreement with J. D. G. Dunn," *JSNT*, no. 80 (2000): 105.

142 Adam's firstborn Cain is set aside while Abel (and then Seth in his place) is chosen; Isaac's firstborn Esau is set aside in as Jacob is chosen; Jacob's firstborn Reuben (along with Simeon and Levi) are passed over in favor of Judah; Joseph's firstborn Manasseh is passed over in favor of his brother Ephraim.

143 "The doctrine of the land emerges unmistakably in the foundation document of Judaism—the Tanakh." W. D. Davis, "Reflections on Territory in Judaism," in *Sha'arei Talmon: Studies in the Bible, Qumran, and the Ancient near East Presented to Shemaryahu Talmon* (eds. Fishbane and Tov; Winona Lake: Eisenbrauns, 1992), 339.

144 Some OT examples of texts with echoes of the promise of "blessing for all nations" are: Pss 22:27-28; 47:9; 67; 72:17; 86:9; 87; 96; 102:15, 21-22; 117; Isa 19:19-25; 45:22-23; 56:3-8; 60; Jer 4:1-2; Amos 9:11-12; Zech 2:10-11. On these passages see Wright, *The Mission of God*, 222-64.

CHAPTER 4 – ABRAHAM IN THE NEW TESTAMENT

1 Examples of the wide variety of appeals to Abraham in patristic writers, generally praising his virtues or using his story as a typological picture of the believer's journey or character, may be seen in Frances M. Young, *Biblical Exegesis and the Formation of Christian Culture* (Peabody, Mass.: Hendrickson, 2002), 106-110, 260.

2 Carson argues that "with time this historically grounded typology gave way to a more thematically controlled typology." D. A. Carson, "Theological Interpretation of Scripture: Yes, But . . ." in *Theological Commentary: Evangelical Perspectives* (ed. Allen; London; New York: T & T Clark International, 2011), 201.

3 For a helpful definition of the Great Tradition, see Roger E. Olson, *The Mosaic of Christian Belief: Twenty Centuries of Unity and Diversity* (Downers Grove: InterVarsity Press, 2002), 33-39.

4 See my discussion of theological interpretation of the Bible in the Introduction.

5 Comprehensive book-by-book engagement with much of this literature can be found in Gregory K. Beale and D. A. Carson eds, *Commentary on the New Testament Use of the Old Testament* (Grand Rapids: Baker Academic, 2007). Other significant studies include Richard B. Hays, *Echoes of Scripture in the Letters of Paul* (New Haven: Yale University Press, 1989); Kenneth Berding and Jonathan Lunde, *Three Views on the New Testament Use of the Old Testament* (Grand Rapids: Zondervan, 2008); Richard N. Longenecker, *Biblical Exegesis in the Apostolic Period* (Grand Rapids: Eerdmans, 1999); Douglas J. Moo, *The Old Testament in the Gospel Passion Narratives* (Sheffield: The Almond Press, 1983) and Douglas J. Moo, "Paul's Universalizing Hermeneutic in Romans," *SBJT* 11, no. 3 (2007). Various approaches are compared in Gregory K. Beale ed., *The Right Doctrine from the Wrong Texts? Essays on the Use of the Old Testament in the New* (Grand Rapids: Baker Books, 1994); A helpful introduction is also found in Grant R. Osborne, *The Hermeneutical Spiral: A Comprehensive Introduction to Biblical Interpretation* (Downers Grove: InterVarsity Press, 2006), 323-44.

6 Although several additional Jewish books composed in Greek during the Hellenistic era were often included with collections of Greek translations of the Hebrew Scriptures, my consideration is limited to the books of the Hebrew canon (comprising 24 books in the Tanakh, 39 in the Protestant OT). While for the (Eastern) Orthodox Church the authoritative OT text is the Septuagint (LXX), and the canon includes additional Jewish books composed in Greek, commonly termed "Deutero-Canonical" by Orthodox and Catholics and "Apocryphal" by Protestants), "most Orthodox scholars of the present day . . . consider that the Deutero-Canonical books, although part of the Bible, stand on a lower footing than the rest of the Old Testament." Ware, *The Orthodox Church*, 200. See also Jobes and Silva, *Invitation*, 85.

7   Regarding the existence of a canonical Hebrew Scripture in the time period of the NT writings I am adopting the position defended by Dempster, which draws attention not only to the contested conclusion of the OT canonization process (likely by the end of the first century), but also to the internal evidence of "canonical consciousness" within the biblical texts themselves. Stephen G. Dempster, "Canons on the Right and Canons on the Left: Finding a Resolution in the Canon Debate," *JETS* 52, no. 1 (2009): 69-76. See also Zipora Talshir, "Several Canon-Related Concepts Originating in Chronicles," *ZAW* 113, no. 3 (2001).

8   See for example, David Klinghoffer, *Why the Jews Rejected Jesus: The Turning Point in Western History* (New York: Doubleday, 2005), 3.

9   See Lee M. McDonald and James A. Sanders, *The Canon Debate* (Peabody: Hendrickson Publishers, 2002), and Michael J. Kruger, *Canon Revisited: Establishing the Origins and Authority of the New Testament Books* (Wheaton: Crossway, 2012), for overviews of the issues involved.

10   His first works were Brevard S. Childs, *Biblical Theology in Crisis* (Philadelphia,: Westminster Press, 1970) and Brevard S. Childs, "Old Testament as Scripture of the Church," *CTM* 43, no. 11 (1972) His work provoked strong reaction by Oxford scholar James Barr, who, defending a historical critical approach and convinced that canon was an artificial concept, contended that Childs' work would play into the hands of fundamentalists. James Barr, "Childs' Introduction to the Old Testament as Scripture," 16 (1980): 23. For a helpful review of the Childs-Barr debate see Richard R. Topping, "The Canon and the Truth: Brevard Childs and James Barr on the Canon and the Historical-Critical Method," *TJT* 8, no. 2 (1992). See also Iain W. Provan, "Canons to the Left of Him : Brevard Childs, His Critics, and the Future of Old Testament Theology," *SJT* 50, no. 1 (1997).

11   Christopher Seitz, "The Canonical Approach and Theological Interpretation," in *Canon and Biblical Interpretation* (eds. Bartholomew and Thiselton; Grand Rapids: Zondervan, 2006), KL 2664-2665.

12   See the essays in "Part Three: The New/Second Testament Canon" in McDonald and Sanders, *The Canon Debate*, 267-579.

13   Michael J. Kruger, "The Definition of the Term 'Canon': Exclusive or Multidimensional?," *TynBul* 63, no. 1 (2012): 14. He develops this argument in greater detail in his most recent work, Michael J. Kruger, *The Question of Canon: Challenging the Status Quo in the New Testament Debate* (Downers Grove: IVP Academic), 27-46. He argues for an "ontological" definition, in addition to the "exclusive" definition (a fixed, final, and closed lists of books) and the "functional" definition (a collection of books functions as a religious norm).

14   See Luke 1:2; John 19:35; 21:24; Acts 10:38-39, 43; 13:31; 1 Cor 15:1-11; Eph 2:20; 3:5; Heb 2:3-4; 5:1; 2 Pet 3:2; 1 John 1:1-2.

15   Eugene E. Lemcio, *The Past of Jesus in the Gospels* (Cambridge: Cambridge University Press, 1991), 127-28.

16   As Bird argues, "the claim that Jesus was 'the Messiah' became one of the central and defining characteristics of the new movement from its earliest phase." Michael F. Bird, *Jesus Is the Christ: The Messianic Testimony of the Gospels* (Downers Grove: InterVarsity Press, 2012), KL 502-503.

17   See Matt 16:16; Mark 1:1; Luke 1:35; John 20:31; Acts 2:36; 9:20; 10:36; Rom 1:4; 10:9; 1 Cor 12:3; Heb 1:2; 4:14; Jas 2:1; 1 Pet 3:15; 1 John 4:15; 2 John 9; Rev 1:5; 2:18; 19:16. The case for this understanding and the way Jesus is included within the "divine identity" is argued by Bauckham, *Jesus and the God of Israel*, 1-59.

18   Kevin J Vanhoozer, "Interpreting Scripture between the Rock of Biblical Studies and the Hard Place of Systematic Theology: The State of the Evangelical (Dis)Union," in *Renewing the Evangelical Mission* (ed. Lints; Grand Rapids: Eerdmans, 2013), 212-13.

19   Vanhoozer also argues that "beyond the historical unity of the single drama of redemption and the literary unity of the continuous biblical narrative is the properly theological unity implicit in the idea that God is the ultimate communicative agent speaking in Scripture." Kevin J Vanhoozer, *The Drama of Doctrine: A Canonical-Linguistic Approach to Christian Theology* (Louisville: Westminster John Knox Press, 2005), 177.

20   Denis Farkasfalvy, "The Apostolic Gospels in the Early Church: The Concept of Canon and the Formation of the Four-Gospel Canon," in *Canon and Biblical Interpretation* (eds. Bartholomew and Thiselton; Grand Rapids: Zondervan, 2006), KL 3201-10.

21   For the hermeneutical and theological presuppositions of the NT see Gregory K. Beale, "Did Jesus and His Followers Preach the Right Doctrine from the Wrong Texts? An Examination of the Presuppositions of Jesus' and the Apostles' Exegetical Method," in *The Right Doctrine from the Wrong Texts?: Essays on the Use of the Old Testament in the New* (ed. Beale; Grand Rapids: Baker Books, 1994), 391-92.

22   Hundreds of direct citations, allusions, and verbal parallels of OT passages in the NT are listed in the indexes at the back of Kurt Aland, et al., *The Greek New Testament* (Stuttgart: Deutsche Bibelgesellschaft, 1998), 887-901.

23   Peter Enns, *Inspiration and Incarnation: Evangelicals and the Problem of the Old Testament* (Grand Rapids: Baker Academic, 2005), 115. See the review of Enns by D. A. Carson, "Three More Books on the Bible: A Critical Review," *TJ* 27, no. 1 (2006): 18-45.

24   For opposing and affirmative arguments engaging the question "Did the NT authors respect the context of the OT text?" see the nine essays collected in Beale, *The Right Doctrine from the Wrong Texts?: Essays on the Use of the Old Testament in the New*, 137-276.

25   For approaches seeking to demonstrate this trajectory see Dempster, *Dominion and Dynasty*, and Beale, *A New Testament Biblical Theology* Part 1, especially chapter 5: "The eschatological storyline of the OT in relation to the NT."

26   These are in 69 verses (two references in Matt 3:9; two in Luke 3:8; three in John 8:39), making a total of 73 references. Oddly enough, Abraham is found 69 times in the Qur'an. See Appendix 3 for a list of passages.

27   William Baird, "Abraham in the New Testament: Tradition and the New Identity," *Int* 42, no. 4 (1988): 368.

28   Because Mark's single reference to Abraham is paralleled in Matthew and Luke, I will not treat it separately.

29   John Nolland, "Genealogical Annotation in Genesis as Background for the Matthean Genealogy of Jesus," *TynBul* 47, no. 1 (1996). Luke also gives the genealogy, but goes past Abraham to Adam, "the son of God" (Luke 3:23-38).

30   On the fulfillment theme see Craig L. Blomberg, *Matthew* (22; Nashville: Broadman Press, 1992), 30-32.

31   For the reading of "offspring" as singular see Alexander, "Further Observations."

32   For example, the child Jesus' exile-like journey to and from Egypt fulfills the words of Hos 11:1, where God refers to the Exodus of Israel: "Out of Egypt I called my son." For a recent discussion of this hermeneutical approach see Gregory K. Beale, "The Use of Hosea 11:1 in Matthew 2:15: One More Time," *JETS* 55, no. 4 (2012). This may be why the exile is underscored as the second major turning point in the threefold 14-generation genealogy structure (Matt 1:1-2, 17).

33   Craig S. Keener, *A Commentary on the Gospel of Matthew* (Grand Rapids: Eerdmans, 1999), 120-21.

34   Evidence of this concept is seen in Second Temple times. "Josephus has Nehemiah declare that 'G-d cherishes the memory of our fathers Abraham, Isaac, and Jacob, and because of their righteousness does not give up His providential care for us' (*Ant.* 11.169)." Louis H. Feldman, *Josephus's Interpretation of the Bible* (27; Berkeley: University of California Press, 1998), 224. See the excursus on "Personal and Ancestral Merits in Jewish Texts" in Keener, *Matthew*, 125-27.

35   Wright, *The Mission of God's People*, 243-44.

36   Robert C. Tannehill, *The Narrative Unity of Luke-Acts: A Literary Interpretation. The Gospel According to Luke. (Foundations and Facets)* (2 vols.; vol. 1; Philadelphia: Fortress Press, 1986), xiii, 2.

37   Studies of Abraham motifs in Luke–Acts may be found in Robert L. Brawley, "Abrahamic Covenant Traditions and the Characterization of God in Luke–Acts," in *The Unity of Luke-*

Acts (ed. Verheyden; Leuven: Leuven University Press: Peeters, 1999), and Robert L. Brawley, "For Blessing All Families of the Earth : Covenant Traditions in Luke-Acts," *CurTM* 22, no. 1 (1995): 18-26. Also the recent PhD dissertation by Hyochan M. Kim, "From Israel to the Nations': A Critical Study of the Abraham Motif in Luke-Acts" (PhD Dissertation, Trinity Evangelical Divinity School, 2007).

38 Matthew points to this *remnant* theme with his selection of OT "fulfillment" quotations in chapters 1–2, and with Jesus' descriptions of the "meek" and "little ones" who will form his people. See Stein's discussion of how "the early Christian proclamation was that the promises made to Abraham, Isaac, Jacob and the Prophets have been fulfilled." Robert H. Stein, *Luke* (24; Nashville: Broadman Press, 1992), 40-42. On Isaiah's remnant theme in these and other verses see John Oswalt, *The Book of Isaiah. Chapters 1-39* (Grand Rapids: Eerdmans, 1986), 190-91, and John Oswalt, *The Book of Isaiah. Chapters 40-66* (Grand Rapids: Eerdmans, 1998), 640.

39 It would be possible to identify Abraham as one of "the prophets" from this verse, but it is more likely that the patriarchs and are seen as two separate and honoured groups venerated by those who will not be with them.

40 David P. Moessner, *Lord of the Banquet: The Literary and Theological Significance of the Lukan Travel Narrative* (Harrisburg: Trinity Press International, 1998), 162.

41 The same Greek phrase ἡ πιστις σου σεσωκε σε is translated variously "your faith has *saved you*" or "your faith has *made you well*" depending on whether forgiveness of sins or physical healing is concerned. See also Luke 8:50.

42 Cohn-Sherbok maintains that "Jesus' answer . . . is not based on any of these [rabbinic] rules, and is thus defective from a rabbinic point of view. Though some scholars have mistakenly regarded Jesus' response as typically rabbinic, it is not remarkable that Jesus could use such a defence since the Gospel tradition suggests that he was not skilled in the argumentative style of the Pharisees and Sadducees." Dan Cohn-Sherbok, "Jesus' Defence of the Resurrection of the Dead," *JSNT*, no. 11 (1981): 71-72. On the contrary, Jesus was neither unskilled nor unfamiliar with Tannaitic exegetical ways, but he openly challenged these approaches as "defective," as I am arguing here. Downing argues against Cohn-Sherbok from Philo's *de abrahamo (X-XI) 50-55.* F. Gerald Downing, "The Resurrection of the Dead: Jesus and Philo," *JSNT*, no. 15 (1982): 47.

43 So Richard B. Hays, "Reading Scripture in Light of the Resurrection," in *The Art of Reading Scripture* (eds. Davis and Hays; Grand Rapids, Mich.: Eerdmans, 2003), 227. However, if this were the argument, it would not strictly speaking be for "resurrection" in the biblical sense of resurrection of the body, but for some sort of ongoing life after death. See the discussion by I. Howard Marshall, *The Gospel of Luke* (Grand Rapids: Eerdmans, 1978), 742-43.

44 Edwards says, "Jesus' argument for the reality of resurrection is based on the assumption that the call of God establishes a relationship with God, and once a relationship with God is established, it bears the promise of God and cannot be ended, even by death." James R. Edwards, *The Gospel According to Mark* (Grand Rapids: Eerdmans, 2002), 369.

45 J. Gerald Janzen, "Resurrection and Hermeneutics: On Exodus 3.6 in Mark 12.26," *JSNT* 23 (1985): 55. Janzen also notes the relationship between resurrection and the Abraham narrative in the Epistles: "In both Romans 4 and Hebrews 11, resurrection is associated with the ancestors, not in terms of their own physical demise and subsequent resurrection, but in terms of their sterility and subsequent death, and in terms of the power of God in bringing life from their death through the offspring given to them. Nevertheless, their story is read as scriptural backing for the NT witness to resurrection of the individual following death." Janzen, "Resurrection and Hermeneutics," 53.

46 Beginning from this verse Brawley develops his thesis that, in Luke–Acts, "God's promise to bless all the families of the earth is fundamental for the characterization of God." Brawley, "Abrahamic Covenant Traditions," 110.

47 Scott, "Luke's Geographical Horizon," 530. In a fascinating article, Scott suggests that the structure of Acts may follow the three groups of nations descended from the sons of Noah: Shem (Acts 2:1–8:25), Ham (8:26-40), and Japheth (9:1–28:31). If this is so, the spread of the gospel in Acts can be seen clearly fulfilling the promise of God to Abraham which is the divine answer to the scattering of the nations of the earth.

48 For a consideration of supposed "difficulties as to chronological sequence, historical numbers and the use of biblical quotations in Stephen's address," which attributes them to the "conflations and inexactitude of popular Judaism," see Richard N. Longenecker, *Acts* (ed. Gaebelein; 12 vols.; vol. 9; Grand Rapids: Zondervan, 1981), 340. For a harmonizing approach and more detail see "the use of scripture in Stephen's speech," in David Peterson, *The Acts of the Apostles* (Grand Rapids: Eerdmans, 2009), 270-75.

49 Peterson notes that special attention is given to the elements of *land* (vv. 2-4), *offspring* (vv. 5-7a), *worship* (v. 7b), and the *covenant of circumcision* (v. 8). "All of these are 'basic elements in Jewish self-understanding.' The rest of the speech concerns the fulfillment of the promises and Israel's failure to respond appropriately." Peterson, *The Acts of the Apostles*, 246.

50 On this reading see Craig L. Blomberg, "The Globalization of Biblical Interpretation: A Test Case—John 3-4," *BBR* 5 (1995): 9.

51 Levenson, *Inheriting Abraham*, 151.

52 Bruner lists nine different incidents in Abraham's life which have been seen as the referent of Jesus' words. F. Dale Bruner, *The Gospel of John: A Commentary* (Grand Rapids: Eerdmans, 2012), 555-58. See the extensive literature referred to in Andrew C. Brunson, *Psalm 118 in the Gospel of John: An Intertextual Study on the New Exodus Pattern in the Theology of John* (Tübingen: Mohr Siebeck, 2003), 290-95.

53 Brunson also finds allusions to Ps 118:24, where *rejoice, be glad* and *the day* are all found in a psalm used in the Feast of Booths celebration, which is the setting of John 7–8. Brunson, *Psalm 118 in the Gospel of John: An Intertextual Study on the New Exodus Pattern in the Theology of John*, 298, 300.

54 Ronning, *The Curse on the Serpent*, 210.

55 Craig S. Keener, *The Gospel of John: A Commentary* (Peabody: Hendrickson, 2003), 768.

56 "What, after all, could be more explicit than Gen 15:1, 'And it was after these things that the Word of God appeared to Abraham'? And in v. 6, where it says that 'Abraham believed in God and he reckoned it for him as righteousness,' the Targum has, 'Abraham believed the Memra of God.'" Boyarin, "The Gospel of the Memra," 276.

57 See D. A. Carson, *The Gospel According to John* (Grand Rapids: Eerdmans, 1991), 357. In support of this position is the link between Isaac in the Aqedah and the firstborn in the Passover, both of which pointed in different ways to the death of Jesus. See Holland, *Contours of Pauline Theology*, 254-62. John 6:53 and 19:36 also highlight Jesus' identity as the Passover Lamb.

58 Keener argues that Jesus' claim "clearly refers to a Jewish name for God" (see Keener, *The Gospel of John*, 770.) In these words Jesus, the son of Abraham, claims to be the God of Abraham much as he presents himself in the later temple confrontation as both David's son (Messiah) and David's Lord through the use of Ps 110:1 (Matt 22:41-46).

59 Bruner, *The Gospel of John: A Commentary*, 553.

60 In fact the Melchizedek discussion also supports the argument that in God's purposes the new covenant has superseded the old and that salvation is not by the law but by Christ.

61 Regarding the transitional phrase introducing Abraham in 4:1, see Richard B. Hays, "'Have We Found Abraham to Be Our Forefather According to the Flesh?': A Reconsideration of Rom 4:1," *NovT* 27(1985). Hay's argues that Paul's point is that physical descent from Abraham is a matter of no consequence for either Jew or Gentile. Moo disagrees with Hays: "Paul asks his readers to contemplate with him what Abraham has found to be the case regarding the matters he is discussing." Douglas J. Moo, *The Epistle to the Romans* (Grand Rapids: Eerdmans, 1996), 259, n. 13.

62   I take "justification" in the forensic sense of having right standing before God, holding that such standing is inseparable from the "obedience of faith" (Rom 1:5; 15:18; 16:26). While this entails inclusion in the people of God, it first refers to deliverance, for Jews and Gentiles alike, from sin's reign and God's wrath, into a state of "peace with God" (Rom 5). As Moo says, "faith is the means not only of entering into relationship with God, but also of maintaining that relationship and of confirming that relationship on the day of judgment." Douglas J. Moo, "Justification in Galatians," in *Understanding the Times: New Testament Studies in the 21st Century: Essays in Honor of D. A. Carson on the Occasion of His 65th Birthday* (eds. Köstenberger and Yarbrough; Wheaton: Crossway, 2011), 192. Moo presents a thorough study of the language of justification and detailed interaction with contemporary controversies, including the so-called New Perspective, represented by N. T. Wright, *Justification: God's Plan and Paul's Vision* (Downers Grove: IVP Academic, 2009), who is answering John Piper, *The Future of Justification: A Response to N. T. Wright* (Wheaton: Crossway, 2007), and other defenders of a more traditional Reformed perspective. Moo's footnotes make a substantial bibliography.

63   People's belief or "faith" in Jesus seems intended rather than the "faithfulness of Jesus," as sometimes argued by modern commentators. Moo argues, "the consistent use of *pistis* throughout 3:21–4:25 to designate the faith exercised by people in God, or Christ, as the sole means of justification. Only very strong reasons would justify giving to *pistis* any other meaning in this, the theological summary on which the rest of the section depends." Moo, *Romans*, 225.

64   See the parallels between Rom 3:27-31 and Abraham in Rom 4, regarding *boasting* (3:27a; 4:1-2); justification by *faith, not works* (3:27b-28; 4:3-8); *circumcised and uncircumcised united* under one God and as children of Abraham (3:29-30; 4:9-17). Moo, *Romans*, 244-45.

65   Paul links Abraham with David, against whom God did not "count his sin" (adultery, murder) and whose grateful words in Ps 32 reveal the flip side of justification: forgiveness of lawless deeds and covering of sins (4:6-8).

66   See the discussion of possible meanings in Moo, *Romans*, 274.

67   See P. Church ed., *The Gospel and the Land of Promise: Christian Approaches to the Land of the Bible* (Eugene, Or.: Pickwick Publications, 2011), for recent Christian engagement with this issue from the perspective of a universalizing of the land promises. On a literal land promise yet to be fulfilled see H. Wayne House ed., *Israel, the Land and the People: An Evangelical Affirmation of God's Promises* (Grand Rapids, MI: Kregel, 1998), especially pages 231-300.

68   Watson argues that Paul's conclusion about the Law's inability to give life is based on his reading of the Pentateuch. Watson considers Exodus, Leviticus, and Numbers in turn, showing that Paul develops their narratives of salvation, law, and judgment to show that the Law's offer of life is doomed to failure because of the sinfulness of even the chosen people and that only in the God of salvation is there hope. Watson, *Paul and the Hermeneutics of Faith*, 273-411.

69   Among Paul's reasons for asserting that the Law "dispensed death" are these two: 1) the law prescribes death as the penalty for sin (Rom 5:12-21); and 2) The law exposes the sinful character of wrongdoing by revealing it to be conscious, active rebellion against God. Its effect is to increase transgression, which leads to death (Rom 5:20). David E. Garland, *2 Corinthians* (29; Nashville: Broadman & Holman, 1999), 171-72.

70   This phrase refers to his age by the time of Gen 17, as well as perhaps to Sarah's barrenness which has been a factor from the beginning of the story.

71   Wagner summarizes: "Enjoyment of the blessings graciously bestowed on Abraham has always come through promise and election rather than solely through physical descent." J. Ross Wagner, *Heralds of the Good News: Isaiah and Paul "in Concert" in the Letter to the Romans* (Leiden: Brill Academic Publishers, 2003), 47.

72   So Moo: "As Paul develops this metaphor, he compares the root of the tree to the patriarchs and the promise of God to them, the 'natural branches' to Jews, and 'wild olive tree shoots' to the Gentiles." Moo, *Romans*, 698.

73 Wagner, *Heralds*, 51.

74 Van der Lans suggests that Paul's argument may be part of a larger "debate about the promises made to Abraham in Genesis and the identity of Abraham's seed." Birgit Van der Lans, "Belonging to Abrahams Kin: Genealogical Appeals to Abraham as a Possible Background for Paul's Abrahamic Argument," in *Abraham, the Nations, and the Hagarites: Jewish, Christian, and Islamic Perspectives on Kinship with Abraham* (eds. Goodman, et al.; vol. 13 of *Themes in Biblical Narrative*; Leiden: Brill Academic Publishers, 2010), 308. Longenecker compares and assesses several different perspectives on Galatians in Bruce W. Longenecker, *The Triumph of Abraham's God: The Transformation of Identity in Galatians* (Nashville: Abingdon Press, 1998), 175-82.

75 Moises Silva, "Galatians," in *Commentary on the New Testament Use of the Old Testament* (eds. Beale and Carson; Nottingham: Apollos, 2007), 793.

76 Chee-Chiew Lee, "The Blessing of Abraham and the Promise of the Spirit: The Influence of the Prophets on Paul in Galatians 3:1-14" (PhD Dissertation, Wheaton College, 2010) 302-05.

77 For arguments supporting the singular meaning in Gen 22:17-18 see Jo Ann Davidson, "Abraham, Akedah and Atonement," in *Creation, Life, and Hope: Essays in Honor of Jacques B. Doukhan* (eds. Doukhan and Moskala; Berrien Springs, Mich: Old Testament Department, Seventh-day Adventist Theological Seminary, Andrews University, 2000), 70, and Alexander, "Further Observations," 363-67.

78 See Lee's extensive argument that "God's promise to Jacob of 'a nation and a company of nations' coming from him finds its fulfillment eschatologically when the salvation of the nations is included at the restoration of Israel." Chee-Chiew Lee, "[Hebrew Characters] in Genesis 35:11 and the Abrahamic Promise of Blessings for the Nations," *JETS* 52, no. 3 (2009): 479-80.

79 "The point of the quotation . . . is to stress the link that believers enjoy not so much with Sarah precisely, but with the new, redeemed Jerusalem." Silva, "Galatians," 809. That this verse directly follows the victory of the Suffering Servant in Isa 53, who "shall see his offspring," makes Paul's usage more plausible.

80 Karen H. Jobes, "Jerusalem, Our Mother: Metalepsis and Intertextuality in Galatians 4:21-31," *WTJ* 55 (1993): 300.

81 Longenecker argues that Paul is picking up on his opponents' use of this familiar narrative against him and turning it against them. "Paul's allegorical treatment of the Hagar-Sarah story is for polemical purposes, countering, it seems, the Judaizers' own contemporization of that story not his but their message is the Ishmaelian form of truth." Richard N. Longenecker, *Galatians* (ed. Metzger; vol. 41; Dallas: Word Incorporated, 1990), 199-200. See also Troy A. Miller, "Surrogate, Slave and Deviant? The Figure of Hagar in Jewish Tradition and Paul (Galatians 4.21-31)," in *Early Christian Literature and Intertextuality, Volume 2: Exegetical Studies* (eds. Evans and Zacharias; London: T & T Clark, 2009), 154.

82 Hebrews 4 argues from the biblical storyline running from God's creation "rest" to his new creation "rest." Joining Psalm 95:11 to Genesis 2:2, the writer refers to God's original creation "rest," to the incomplete "rest" achieved in Joshua's day, to the "rest" evidently still future in the psalmist David's day, and to the great final "Sabbath rest" still to come, into which his readers are urged to strive to enter by faith (Heb 4:3-11).

83 See below on Second Temple Jewish use of Abraham.

84 This key theme is developed carefully throughout the book (Heb 5:6, 10, 20; 7:1-10, 11, 15, 17).

85 Nicholas Perrin finds hints of this theme in the Last Supper, comparing Jesus' and Melchizedek's use of bread and wine in a covenant-making ceremony." Nicholas Perrin, "Covenantal Consciousness in Jesus' Last Week," (Wheaton College, 2009). Sent to me in personal correspondence 12/18/2009.

86 Gareth Lee Cockerill, "The Better Resurrection (Heb. 11:35): A Key to the Structure and Rhetorical Purpose of Hebrews 11," *TynBul* 51, no. 2 (2000): 229.

87 "Abraham's faith, in its relationship to righteousness, found its ultimate significance and meaning in Abraham's life of obedience." Douglas J. Moo, *The Letter of James* (PNTC; Grand Rapids: Eerdmans, 2000), KL 2146.

88 Later Jewish sources link the two as examples of proselytes as well as those who offered hospitality. Moo, *James*, KL 2219-22. See Roy B. Ward, "Works of Abraham: James 2:14-26," *HTR* 61, no. 2 (1968).

89 Abraham's act of offering his son as a burnt offering would in fact by any Mosaic standard be flagrant disobedience to the law, which states clearly in relation to human beings: "you shall not kill."

90 Craig A. Evans, "Genesis in the New Testament," in *The Book of Genesis: Composition, Reception, and Interpretation* (eds. Evans, et al.; vol. 152 of *Supplements to Vetus Testamentum*; Leiden: Brill, 2012), 492-93. Additionally it may be plausibly argued that "Paul refers to the initial declaration of a sinner's innocence before God; James to the ultimate verdict of innocence pronounced over a person at the last judgment." Moo, *James*, KL 2195.

91 For further examples, see the section on "New Testament Echoes of Abraham" in Wright, *The Mission of God*, 243-52. Richard Hays lists seven criteria for such "echoes": "Availability, volume, recurrence, thematic coherence, historical plausibility, history of interpretation, and satisfaction." Hays, *Echoes of Scripture*, 29-32. See also Beale's "definitions of quotations and allusions and criteria for discerning them," among which he includes those given by Hays. Gregory K. Beale, *Handbook on the New Testament Use of the Old Testament: Exegesis and Interpretation* (Grand Rapids, MI: Baker Academic, 2012), 29-40.

92 "The climactic text . . . 15:7-13, makes God's confirmation of his promises to the patriarchs basic to the inclusion of the Gentiles (vv.8-9)." Moo, "Paul's Universalizing Hermeneutic," 77.

93 Andreas J. Köstenberger, "John," in *Commentary on the New Testament Use of the Old Testament* (eds. Beale and Carson; Grand Rapids: Baker Academic, 2007), 430. In Genesis Jacob's dream of the ladder or stairway likely alluded to the ziggurat tower of Babel, "with its top in the heavens." DeWitt has argued that "the *raison d'être* for Sumerian temple-towers was the reunion of heaven and earth." Dale S. DeWitt, "The Historical Background of Genesis 11:1-9: Babel or Ur?," *JETS* 21, no. 1 (1979): 21.

94 Mark A. Seifrid, "Romans," in *Commentary on the New Testament Use of the Old Testament* (eds. Beale and Carson; Grand Rapids: Baker Academic, 2007), 634. Holland contends that "while there may be an echo of the *Aqedah* in this verse, the reference is better seen as a reference to the death of Jesus as the Passover victim. . . . In the Christian Passover, the firstborn Son is not spared but is given up by the father." Holland, *Romans: The Divine Marriage*, 286.

95 The LXX often uses *agapetos* in place of *monogenes*. "The seminal event in OT history is Abraham's offering of Isaac, who in Genesis 22:2, 12, 16 is called Abraham's 'one-of-a-kind' (*yahid*) son." Köstenberger, "John," 422.

96 Köstenberger and Swain, *Father, Son, and Spirit*, 128. Alternatively, the image of the sin-bearing "lamb" here could allude to the Passover lamb (John 6), to the Suffering Servant (Isa 53:7) or to the apocalyptic Lamb (Rev 5:6). For proposed backgrounds see Keener, *The Gospel of John*, 452-54. See also George Carey, "The Lamb of God and Atonement Theories," *TynBul* 32, no. 4 (1981): 101-07, and Davidson, "Abraham, Akedah and Atonement," 68-69.

97 John 12:38 quotes Isa 53:1 and the same word is used for "lamb" in Isaiah 53:7 LXX and in John 1:29, 36.

98 Levenson takes issue with Christian attempts to see in the Aqedah a *type* of God the Father willingly giving his son. Jon D. Levenson, "Abusing Abraham: Traditions, Religious Histories, and Modern Misinterpretations," *Judaism* 47, no. 3 (1998). While not primary, as I argue above, nevertheless the typological use is common, as Wenham notes: "In his miraculous birth and his description as the one beloved by his father, Isaac is easily linked typologically with Jesus whose virgin birth is narrated and who is called beloved by God. It is not far-fetched to draw the connections between Isaac and Jesus in the scenes in which they willingly go to death at the will of their respective 'fathers.' Certainly this typology is very widespread in the

NT and therefore must be extremely early and probably reflects Jesus' own self-interpretation of his mission." Wenham, *Genesis 16-50*, 117.

99   Robert L. Brawley, "Evocative Allusions in Matthew: Matthew 5:5 as a Test Case," 59, no. 3 (2003): 608-16. Brawley contends that "the understanding of the Abrahamic promise as the whole earth appears in Sir 44:19-21; *Jub* 17:3; 19:21; 22:14; 32:18-19; Rm 4:13; 1 Cor 6:2; Heb 2:5." Brawley, "Evocative Allusions," 610.

100 Jesus is presented as the "heir" in the parable of the vineyard (Matt 21:38 par.). See Baird, "Abraham in the New Testament," 369-76.

101 Charles H. H. Scobie, "Israel and the Nations: An Essay in Biblical Theology," *TynBul* 43, no. 2 (1992): 297-98. For the missiological implications of this link see Showalter, "All the Clans, All the Peoples."

102 Wright, *The Mission of God*, 213.

103 Gregory K. Beale and Sean McDonough, "Revelation," in *Commentary on the New Testament Use of the Old Testament* (eds. Beale and Carson; Nottingham: Apollos, 2007), 1108.

104 See the chapter "Monotheism and Christology in the Gospel of John" in Bauckham, *The Testimony of the Beloved Disciple*, 239-52, and his collection of essays on the application of the divine name to Jesus in the NT, in Bauckham, *Jesus and the God of Israel*.

105 Jobes notes that "because barrenness was associated with death throughout the OT, its antonym, miraculous birth from a barren woman, could aptly be associated with resurrection from death." Jobes, "Jerusalem, Our Mother," 314. She finds the association of birth with Christ's resurrection in Rom 1:4 and Col 1:18.

106 Wright provides a full discussion of alternative explanations for this pervasive hope of the early Christians and argues that "the proposal that Jesus was bodily raised from the dead possesses unrivaled power to explain the historical data at the heart of early Christianity." Wright 2003, 718.

107 Hays, "Reading Scripture," 216-38.

108 As Bauckham puts it, "this biblical God's own identity is itself a narrative identity. It is a particular identity God gives himself in the particular story of Israel and Jesus, and it is an identity which itself drives the narrative towards the universal realization of God's kingdom in all creation. God identifies himself as the God of Abraham, Israel and Jesus in order to be the God of all people and the Lord of all things." Bauckham, *Bible and Mission*, 13.

109 For a defense of the claim that "the idea of salvation supplies the key to the theology of Luke," see I. Howard Marshall, *Luke: Historian and Theologian (New Testament Profiles)* (Downers Grove: InterVarsity Press, 1998), 92.

110 As Andrew Kirk pointed out to me in personal correspondence, it may also be argued that in the prophets some non-Jews are counted as God's people. Likewise Kaiser says, "There were numerous illustrations of this historical inclusion of the Gentiles." Walter C. Kaiser, Jr., "Davidic Promise and the Inclusion of the Gentiles (Amos 9:9-15 and Acts 15:13-18) : A Test Passage for Theological Systems," *JETS* 20, no. 2 (1977): 99. Nevertheless, the idea of Gentiles being full-fledged fellow-heirs with Jewish believers is seen in the NT as a "mystery" which was "not made known to the sons of men in other generations as it has now been revealed to his holy apostles and prophets by the Spirit" (Eph 3:4-6).

111 Mark Strom, "From Promised Land to Reconciled Cosmos: Paul's Translation of 'Worldview,' 'Worldstory' and 'Worldperson'," in *The Gospel and the Land of Promise: Christian Approaches to the Land of the Bible* (ed. Church; Eugene, Oreg.: Pickwick Publications, 2011), 26.

112 Ray Pritz, *Nazarene Jewish Christianity: From the End of the New Testament Period until Its Disappearance in the Fourth Century* (37; Jerusalem: Magnes Press, 1988), argues that the Nazarenes were the heirs of the earliest Jerusalem church. Boyarin rejects the category "Jewish Christianity," arguing that the terms "Judaism" and "Christianity" were used to refer to religions only beginning in the fourth-century heresiological discourse. Boyarin, "Rethinking Jewish Christianity," 7-36.

113 Jewish scholar Peter Ochs, in the introduction and running commentary, refers to "Paul's version of Nazarene or Christian Judaism" in John Howard Yoder, et al., *The Jewish-Christian Schism Revisited* (Grand Rapids: Eerdmans, 2003), KL 158-159, though questioning the "hermeneutical and theological consistency" of this reading. See also Richard Bauckham, "The Parting of the Ways: What Happened and Why," *ST* 47, no. 1 (1993).

114 Carson, "Theological Interpretation of Scripture: Yes, But . . ." 190.

115 See George W. E. Nickelsburg, "The Bible Rewritten and Expanded," in *Jewish Writings of the Second Temple Period: Apocrypha, Pseudepigrapha, Qumran, Sectarian Writings, Philo, Josephus* (ed. Stone; *Compendia Rerum Iudaicarum Ad Novum Testamentum. Section 2, Literature of the Jewish People in the Period of the Second Temple and the Talmud 2*; Assen, Netherlands: Van Gorcum, 1984), for studies of this literature.

116 G. Walter Hansen, *Abraham in Galatians: Epistolary and Rhetorical Contexts* (29; Sheffield: JSOT Press, 1989), 187-88.

117 A partial exception is found in the *Testament of Abraham*, which along with reciting Abraham's virtues, also subverts his exemplary status by portraying the patriarch resisting the angel of death at the end of his life, showing "fear in the face of death and irrational resistance to its inevitability." Annette Yoshiko Reed, "The Construction and Subversion of Patriarchal Perfection: Abraham and Exemplarity in Philo, Josephus, and the Testament of Abraham," *JSJ* 40 (2009): 212.

118 A possible exception may be found the retrospective divine assessment of Abraham's life in Gen 26:5. See my notes on this verse in chapter 3.

119 The term "rewritten Bible" is from Daniel J. Harrington, "Abraham Traditions in the Testament of Abraham and in the 'Rewritten Bible' of the Intertestamental Period," in *Studies on the Testament of Abraham* (eds. Nickelsburg and Kraft; Missoula: Scholars Press for the Society of Biblical Literature, 1976), 196-210.

120 James C. VanderKam, *The Book of Jubilees* (Sheffield: Sheffield Academic Press, 2001), 21. My quotations of *Jubilees* are taken from R. H. Charles, *The Apocrypha and Pseudepigrapha of the Old Testament in English, with Introductions and Critical and Explanatory Notes to the Several Books* (2 vols.; Oxford: Clarendon Press, 1913), online version: http://www.pseudepigrapha.com/jubilees/index.htm. For a recent study of Jubilees see Ian Werrett, "Salvation through Emulation: Facets of Jubilean Soteriology at Qumran," in *This World and the World to Come: Soteriology in Early Judaism* (ed. Gurtner; vol. 74 of *Library of Second Temple Studies*; London: T & T Clark, 2011), 211-28.

121 VanderKam, *The Book of Jubilees*, 7.

122 William Adler, "Abraham and the Burning of the Temple of Idols: Jubilees' Traditions in Christian Chronography," *JQR* 77, no. 2-3 (1987): 95. This Syriac use of Jubilees shows the likelihood that Jubilees-based Abraham stories were well-known among the Qur'an's Arabian audience which "was to some extent bilingual, like many people of late antiquity. Many would have possessed, in addition to Arabic, some command of an Aramaic dialect—Syriac especially—which was widely spoken in the Near East at the time." Reynolds and El-Badawi, "The Qur'an and the Syriac Bible," 2/6.

123 C. T. R. Hayward, "Genesis and Its Reception in Jubilees," in *The Book of Genesis : Composition, Reception, and Interpretation* (eds. Evans, et al.; vol. 152 of *Supplements to Vetus Testamentum*; Leiden: Brill, 2012), 401.

124 In Jubilees this testing consists of a total of *ten* trials concluding with the death of Sarah (19.8). Cf. Qur'an 2:124: "Abraham's Lord tested him with certain commandments." Islamic tradition gives various lists of *ten* trials successfully endured by the prophet Abraham. Mahmoud M. Ayoub, *The Qur'an and Its Interpreters* (Albany: State University of New York Press, 1984), 152-53.

125 Leroy A. Huizenga, "The Battle for Isaac: Exploring the Composition and Function of the Aqedah in the Book of Jubilees," 13, no. 1 (2002): 43-46.

126 Many aspects of this exegetical narrative find parallels in the Qur'anic Abraham story: turning from idols to the creator, challenging his father about idols, destroying the idols, praying for his seed to be kept (see chapter 6).

127 Jon D. Levenson, "The Universal Horizon of Biblical Particularism," in *Ethnicity and the Bible* (ed. Brett Mark; Leiden: E. J. Brill, 1996), 151–52.

128 Shari L. Lowin, "Abraham in Islamic and Jewish Exegesis," *RelC* 5, no. 6 (2011): 232. Generally speaking in midrash aggadah the explanations provided by rabbis for 'problems' encountered in reading the Bible took the form of narrative expansions of the biblical account.

129 Huizenga offers a somewhat different slant on the difficulty being resolved: "For his composition of the Aqedah, the author of Jubilees found in Job a perfect solution to a great difficulty in Gen. 22—namely, the fact that it is God who is actively threatening the covenant line without cause." Huizenga, "The Battle for Isaac: Exploring the Composition and Function of the Aqedah in the Book of Jubilees," 54-55.

130 Lowin, "Abraham," 225. She is focusing primarily on a later stage of development, but as noted above, Jubilees is an early example of this approach, later developed in the rabbinic midrashim.

131 Michael Segal, *The Book of Jubilees: Rewritten Bible, Redaction, Ideology and Theology* (117; Leiden: Brill, 2007), 323. Segal finds the worldview of Jubilees in three areas: law, evil, and chronology.

132 Huizenga, "The Battle for Isaac: Exploring the Composition and Function of the Aqedah in the Book of Jubilees," 36.

133 Juncker surveys the significant writings of intertestamental Judaism and concludes that God is "much too transcendent to be wandering about the countryside as a human, or an angel, speaking to patriarchs and saints (let alone to tax collectors and sinners!)." Juncker, "Jesus and the Angel of the Lord," 278-79. He comments on this feature as seen in in Jubilees on pp. 268-71.

134 The divine voice accompanying the descent of the Spirit as a dove at Jesus' baptism (and similarly at the Transfiguration and in John 12:27) could possibly be interpreted this way, but it is not so treated. Rather it is presented as the Father's affirmation of his unique Son and the Spirit's anointing for his mission. Angels ministered to him during the temptation in the wilderness and the garden (Matt 4:11; Luke 22:43), but are not revelatory or divine appearances. In the NT angels belong to, bear witness to, and worship Jesus the Son of God.

135 Hansen, *Abraham in Galatians*, 181.

136 From a Jewish perspective Levenson compares Jewish, Christian, and Muslim interpretive traditions on Abraham in Levenson, *Inheriting Abraham*. Another Jewish study is Klinghoffer, *Discovery of God*. A Christian perspective is provided by Lodahl, *Claiming Abraham*.

137 Wright describes the sequels found in *Josephus, Sirach,* and *Maccabees*. Wright, *The New Testament and the People of God*, 217-18. He outlines the story in five acts: 1. Creation, 2. Fall, 3. Israel, 4. Jesus, and 5. NT and beyond.

138 Wright, *The New Testament and the People of God*, 218.

139 For evidence in these writings of a "judgment-of-Israel" theme, and of a "limited, exclusive soteriology" and a "conditional view of covenant," see Mark Adam Elliott, *The Survivors of Israel: A Reconsideration of the Theology of Pre-Christian Judaism* (Grand Rapids: Eerdmans, 2000), 639.

140 Lloyd G. Davies, "Christian Figural Reading and the Fashioning of Identity," (review of John David Dawson, *Christian Figural Reading and the Fashioning of Identity*) 52(2002): 87. Italics mine. He adds, "The divergence between Judaic and Christian readings of Hebrew Scriptures revolves around the importance of narrative for Christianity, so that historically 'Christianity ended up privileging *haggadah* over *halakhah*.'"

141 Van der Lans, "Belonging to Abrahams Kin," 309-12.

142 Of course the narrative itself is "torah" (instruction), intended to inform moral living in the fear of God, as shown by Gordon J. Wenham, *Story as Torah : Reading the Old Testament*

Ethically (Edinburgh: T & T Clark, 2000), yet the narrative creates a trajectory which (the NT insists) takes precedence over the law as instruction.

143 Carson, "Three More Books on the Bible: A Critical Review," 41-42.

144 Klinghoffer, *Discovery of God*, KL 168-170.

145 The NT sees this cleansing applied retroactively to people of faith from earlier eras (Rom 3:25; Heb 9:15).

146 See Longenecker, *Biblical Exegesis*.

147 See Craig A. Evans, "The Scriptures of Jesus and His Earliest Followers," in *The Canon Debate* (eds. McDonald and Sanders; Peabody: Hendrickson Publishers, 2002), as well as Harrington's conclusion that while OT apocryphal writings were appealed to by some patristic writers, attempts to show NT appropriation of them is inconclusive at best. Daniel J. Harrington, "The Old Testament Apocrypha in the Early Church and Today," in *The Canon Debate* (eds. McDonald and Sanders; Peabody: Hendrickson Publishers, 2002), 200-203.

148 NT Wright devotes two full parts of a major volume to the question of how and why Judaism and Christianity diverged. Wright, *The New Testament and the People of God*.

149 A representative sample topic of the voluminous writing on the subject can be found in the secondary literature bibliography in Wright, *Jesus and the Victory of God, Vol. 2 in Christian Origins and the Question of God*, 675-704.

150 D. A. Carson, *The Expositor's Bible Commentary: Matthew* (ed. Gaebelein; 12 vols.; vol. 8; Grand Rapids: Zondervan, 1984), 144.

151 On this move in the Synoptics see Wright, *Jesus and the Victory of God, Vol. 2 in Christian Origins and the Question of God*, 432-38. Carson argues similarly for John: "Jesus is assumed to replace Old Testament figures and institutions. He is the new temple, the one of whom Moses wrote, the true bread from heaven, the true Son, the genuine vine, the tabernacle . . . the passover. Rarely articulated, there is nevertheless an underlying *hermeneutic* at work, a way of reading the Old Testament that goes back to Jesus himself." Carson, *The Gospel According to John*, 98.

152 "It is the religious leaders of his time who represent innovation and whose misunderstandings and malpractices lead the people away from their original vocation. R. S. Good, "Jesus, Protagonist of the Old, in Lk 5:33-39," *Novum Testamentum* 25, no. 1 (1983): 20, 32.

153 Edwards, *The Gospel According to Mark*, 204.

154 Some see Paul's reading as "perverse" and "a complete rewriting of crucial passages in scripture that self-consciously give them the exactly opposite sense of what everybody would recognize as their own meaning." Troels Engberg-Pedersen, "Once More a Lutheran Paul? Francis Watson, Paul and the Hermeneutics of Faith," 59, no. 4 (2006): 460.

155 For example, Watson, *Paul and the Hermeneutics of Faith*. See the discussion of his approach below.

156 Preston M. Sprinkle, *Paul and Judaism Revisited: A Study of Divine and Human Agency in Salvation* (Downers Grove: IVP Academic Press), 238. He compares Paul and five Qumran texts to determine their emphases on either a *Deuteronomic* (repentance and return to the law precedes divine restoration) or *Prophetic* (God's unilateral act of intervention brings restoration) programs of restoration. In comparing these texts he looks in detail at their approach to five areas: restoration from the curse of the law, the eschatological Spirit, anthropological pessimism, justification, and judgment according to works. He concludes that Paul's theology, "reconstituted through his encounter with the risen Messiah, shifted from the *Deuteronomic* conventions of Moses to the *Prophetic* framework of Isaiah, Jeremiah, Ezekiel, and others, and therefore embraced a heightened awareness of divine agency and anthropological pessimism." Sprinkle, *Paul and Judaism Revisited*, 249.

157 Watson, *Paul and the Hermeneutics of Faith*, 277. Some think Watson privileges Paul's exegesis of Scripture over his Christology. D. A. Campbell, "An Evangelical Paul: A Response to Francis Watson's Paul and the Hermeneutics of Faith," *JSNT* 28, no. 3 (2006): 344-47. See

also Barry S. Crawford, "Review of Francis Watson, Paul and the Hermeneutics of Faith," *CBQ* 68 (2006): 559-60.

158 Watson, *Paul and the Hermeneutics of Faith*, 179.

159 See also Evans, for consideration of both Paul and James' nuanced awareness of various strains of Jewish appropriation of both Abraham and Phinehas. Evans, "Genesis in the New Testament," 481-93.

160 Marc Hirshman, "Origen's View of 'Jewish Fables' in Genesis," in *The Exegetical Encounter between Jews and Christians in Late Antiquity* (eds. Grypeou and Spurling; Leiden: Brill, 2009), 245. Likewise George W. Knight, *The Pastoral Epistles: A Commentary on the Greek Text* (Grand Rapids: Eerdmans, 1992), 73-74.

161 By contrast, Origen castigated straightforward readings of the failures of the patriarchs as belonging to the category of Jewish myths. Hirshman says, "Origen is steadfast in his refusal to see the saints and the patriarchs alike as anything but paragons of virtue who achieved extraordinary levels of spirituality . . . most telling is his refusal to accept the literal reading of the story of Abraham, Sarah and Abimelech and its parallels." Hirshman, "Origen's View of 'Jewish Fables' in Genesis," 246.

162 See the studies by Richard B. Hays, "'Here We Have No Lasting City': New Covenantalism in Hebrews," in *The Epistle to the Hebrews and Christian Theology* (ed. Bauckham; Grand Rapids: Eerdmans, 2009), 151-73, and by Morna D. Hooker, "Christ, the 'End' of the Cult," in *The Epistle to the Hebrews and Christian Theology* (ed. Bauckham; Grand Rapids: Eerdmans, 2009), 189-212, along with the responses to Hays in the same volume.

163 The reference to "foods" may be "a metaphor for the strange teachings" rather than a reference to Jewish food laws. Hays, "Here We Have No Lasting City," 154. Other commentators take this as a clear reference to such incursions of Jewish dietary laws that have no place in Christian spirituality. For example, Allen says, "In language reminiscent of Paul (Rom 14:17; 1 Cor 8:8; Col 2:16, 21-23), one's spiritual life is unaffected by rules about food." David L Allen, *Hebrews* (Nashville: Broadman Press, 2010), 615.

164 "These teachings may not have been unconventional or bizarre, but they were 'strange' to the gospel of Christ. The coming of Christ makes continued allegiance to what was anticipatory perverse." Gareth Lee Cockerill, *The Epistle to the Hebrews* (Grand Rapids: Eerdmans, 2012), 694.

165 Gareth Lee Cockerill, "To the Hebrews/to the Muslims: Islamic Pilgrimage as a Key to Interpretation," *MissIR* 22, no. 3 (1994). This is an issue somewhat common to both Muslim and Jewish readings. In this article the author sets out a number of parallels between the Hajj and the Christian pilgrimage, especially as seen in Hebrews 11 as a starting point.

166 S. Sandmel, "Philo's Place in Judaism. A Study of Conceptions of Abraham in Jewish Literature (Part 1)," *HUCA* 25(1954): 237. My attention was drawn to this and the following quote by Fred D. Layman, "Paul's Use of Abraham: An Approach to Paul's Understanding of History" (PhD Dissertation, University of Iowa, 1973), 1.

167 S. Sandmel, "Philo's Place in Judaism. A Study of Conceptions of Abraham in Jewish Literature (Part 2)," *HUCA* 26 (1955): 312.

CHAPTER 5 – ABRAHAM IN THE QUR'AN

1 Unless otherwise noted all quotations of the Qur'an are taken from Abdel Haleem, *The Qur'an* Kindle Edition. Although a large body of material concerning Abraham is found in the Hadith and Muslim exegetical tradition, for the purposes of this study I limit myself to qur'anic material. Substantial surveys of para-qur'anic material can be found in Shari L. Lowin, *The Making of a Forefather: Abraham in Islamic and Jewish Exegetical Narratives* (65; Leiden: Brill, 2006), Reuven Firestone, *Journeys in Holy Lands: The Evolution of the Abraham-Ishmael Legends in Islamic Exegesis* (Albany: State University of New York Press, 1990), and Kaltner, *Ishmael Instructs Isaac*, 87-131.

2 Reynolds, *The Emergence of Islam*, KL 4372-4374.

3   Qur'an suras: 2, 3, 4, 6, 9, 11, 12, 14, 15, 16, 19, 21, 22, 26, 29, 33, 37, 38, 42, 43, 51, 53, 57, 60, 87. Dirks reconstructs the life of Abraham based primarily upon Islamic sources supplemented by reference to the Bible and extrabiblical Jewish sources. Dirks, *Abraham: The Friend of God*, 218-44. While using some biblical sources to fill in gaps, he discards material which conflicts with his Islamic life of Abraham by appealing to the theory that Genesis "came into being as a literary product about 400 BCE; and was compiled from earlier literary strands in a 'cut-and-paste manner," [strands known as *J, E, and P*], Dirks, *Abraham: The Friend of God*, 8.

4   See Shosh Ben-Ari, "The Stories About Abraham in Islam. A Geographical Approach," *Arabica* 54, no. 4 (2007).

5   Islamic exegesis and history contains various reconstructions of Abraham's visits to Mecca and the events including Hagar and Ishmael which occur there, corresponding in varying degrees to Genesis 21. "According to the generally accepted chronology of the Abraham story in the medieval sources, Abraham first journeyed to Mecca at the time that he established Hagar and their suckling baby Ishmael there. After visiting Ishmael twice more when his son was to choose a wife, Abraham came a fourth time to build the Ka'ba when Ishmael was a grown man." Reuven Firestone, "Abraham's Journey to Mecca in Islamic Exegesis: A Form-Critical Study of a Tradition," *StudIsl* 76(1992): 21-22.

6   Detailed analysis of this story in Islamic exegesis, including questions of chronology and setting of the famous event, can be found in Firestone, *Journeys in Holy Lands*, 144. He has more recently argued that the story may even be out of order in the Genesis narrative; see Firestone, "Comparative Studies in Bible and Qur'an," 169-84.

7   See notes on Sura 37 below.

8   The term Syria is "Al-Sha'm, the most common medieval Arabic reference for the area roughly corresponding to today's Syria, Lebanon, Israel, and Jordan ... generally referred to in Western circles as the Holy Land." Firestone, *Journeys in Holy Lands*, 186-87.

9   Qur'an 6:74-87; 19:41-50; 21:51-73; 26:69-102; 29:16-27; 37:83-100; 43:26-28; 60:4-7.

10   Jewish interpreters developed motifs regarding this stage of Abraham's life from brief references to his calling by God from among idolaters in Josh 24:2 and Isa 29:22; 51:2. Hauglid, "Bible and Qur'an," 88. The term "para-biblical" comes from the preface, where John Reeves describes borrowing the term from some oral remarks by Robert A. Kraft "regarding the difficulty of isolating a common 'scripture' across the varieties of early Judaism and Christianity." x.

11   Qur'an 11:69-83; 15:51-77; 29:31-32; 37:99-113; 51:24-37.

12   For a recent example of such a comparison, see Michael E. Lodahl, "Disputing over Abraham Disputing with God: An Exercise in Intertextual Reasoning," *CSR* 34, no. 4 (2005).

13   Qur'an 2:124-141; 3:95-97; 14:35-41; 22:26-33.

14   37:83-113.

15   For example Norman Calder, "From Midrash to Scripture: The Sacrifice of Abraham in Early Islamic Tradition," *Mus* 101, no. 3-4 (1988). Also see Firestone, "Comparative Studies in Bible and Qur'an." And Lowin, "Abraham," 227-28.

16   Firestone sees parallels between Gen 21:9-21 and the Ibn 'Abbas version of the legend of Abraham's move to Mecca. Firestone, *Journeys in Holy Lands*, 64-65. However, he concludes, "The narrative as a complete entity exhibits all the qualities of an Islamic legend." Other versions do not exhibit such concern for consistency with the biblical story. Firestone, *Journeys in Holy Lands*, 71.

17   "This verse may be taken to be the sum of the verses following. In everything Abraham fulfilled God's wish: he purified God's house; he built the sacred refuge of the Ka'ba; he submitted his will to God's, and thus became the type of Islam" (Ali).

18   Mustansir Mir, "The Qur'ānic Story of Joseph: Plot, Themes, and Characters," *MW* LXXVI, no. 1 (1986): 6.

19 A version of Abraham's prayer for forgiveness on the great day of reckoning, cited above, is repeated at the end of each *Salat*: "O Allah! I seek refuge in You from the torment of the Hellfire, from the torment of the grave, from the trials and afflictions of life and death, and from the deception of the False-Christ. O my Lord! Grant me and my parents forgiveness, and bestow Your mercy upon them." This follows a prayer for God to bless Muhammad and the family of Muhammad as He blessed Ibrahim and the family of Ibrahim. http://islam1. org/how_to_pray/salah.htm.

20 See, for example, Abdel Haleem, "Qur'an and Hadith," 28-29.

21 Abdel Haleem translates this, "His Lord said to him, 'Devote yourself to Me.' Abraham replied, 'I devote myself to the Lord of the Universe'" and notes that "*Aslama* here means to devote oneself to the one God alone, so that Abraham will come to his Lord with his heart totally devoted to Him: 3: 64; 26: 89; 37: 84." But the commonly accepted translation is submission or surrender.

22 Ahmad, "Reorientation of Islamic History," 300.

23 "Particular attention is drawn to Abraham [in sura 2], the prophet-patriarch whose intense preoccupation with the idea of God's oneness lies at the root of the three great monotheistic religions; and the establishment of Abraham's Temple, the Ka`bah, as the direction of prayer for 'those who surrender themselves to God' (which is the meaning of the word muslimūn, sing. muslim), sets a seal, as it were, on the conscious self-identification of all true believers with the faith of Abraham." (Asad).

24 Yusuf Ali defines *hanif* as meaning "inclined to right opinion, orthodox (in the literal meaning of the Greek words.), firm in faith, sound and well-balanced, true." Ali. To this understanding Asad adds, "Already in pre-Islamic times, this term had a definitely monotheistic connotation, and was used to describe a man who turned away from sin and worldliness and from all dubious beliefs, especially idol-worship; and *tahannuf* denoted the ardent devotions, mainly consisting of long vigils and prayers, of the unitarian God-seekers of pre-Islamic times."

25 "Altogether, [the term hanif] appears twelve times in the text, ten times in the singular (2:135; 3:67, 95; 4:125; 6:79, 161; 10:105; 16:120, 123; 30:30) and twice in the plural, hunafa' (22:31; 98:5)." Devin J. Stewart, "Notes on Medieval and Modern Emendations of the Qur'an," in *The Qur'an in Its Historical Context* (ed. Reynolds; vol. 8 of *Routledge Studies in the Quran*; New York: Routledge, 2007), 238.

26 Reynolds, *The Qur'an and Its Biblical Subtext*, 72.

27 Elmalılı Hamdi Yazır, *Hak Dîni Kur'an Dili* (Ankara: Akçağ Basım Yayım Pazarlama A.Ş., 1995), on 2:135.

28 Reynolds, *The Qur'an and Its Biblical Subtext*, 75-86. Also see Sidney H. Griffith, *The Church in the Shadow of the Mosque: Christians and Muslims in the World of Islam* (Princeton: Princeton University Press, 2008), KL 5677.

29 Specifically, that Abraham is called *Khalilullah* (the Friend of God), Moses is called *Kalimatullah* (the Word of God), David is called *Khalifatullah* (the Representative of God), Jesus is called *Ruhullah* (the Spirit of God), and Muhammad is called *Rasulullah* (the Messenger of God and *Habibullah* (the Beloved of God).

30 See the discussion of revelation-receiving prophet lists below on 4:163. Ali clarifies, "These are mentioned in three groups: (1) Abraham, Isma'il, Isaac, Jacob and the Tribes: of these Abraham had apparently a Book (87:19) and the others followed his tradition: (2) Moses and Jesus, who each left a scripture; these scriptures are still extant though not in their pristine form; and (3) other scriptures, Prophets, or Messengers of God, not specifically mentioned in the Qur'ān (11:78). We make no difference between any of these. Their Message (in essentials) was one, and that is the basis of Islam." Ali.

31 On the "Book of Abraham," see notes on 87:19 below.

32 Ruthven, *Islam in the World*, 83.

33 Ruthven, *Islam in the World*, 84.

34   See the summary in Necmettin Gökkır, "Western Impact on Contemporary Qur'anic Studies: The Application of Literary Criticism," *Usûl* 3, no. 1 (2005): 73-74. In his consideration of Fazlur Rahman's attempts to develop a hermeneutical theory through which to understand the Qur'an as a unified whole comprising both its theological and its ethical sections, Gökkır refers specifically to M. A. Abdel Haleem, "Context and Internal Relationships: Keys to Quranic Exegesis," in *Approaches to the Qur'an* (ed. Hawting; Abingdon: Routledge, 1993), 71-98.

35   Mustansir Mir, *Coherence in the Qur'an: A Study of Islahi's Concept of Nazm in Tadabbur-I Qur'an* (Indianapolis: American Trust Publications, 1986), 1-2. Mir's work follows Islahi, who was in turn a student of Hamiduddin Farahi (1863–1930), a famous Islamic scholar of the Indian subcontinent. According to the website devoted to Farahi, "his greatest contribution in its study is his discovery of coherence in the Qur'an ... Farahi demonstrated ... that with a sound understanding of the Arabic language one can appreciate the coherence in the Qur'an which is certainly not a haphazard collection of injunctions. By taking into consideration, the three constituents of *nazm* (coherence): order, proportion and unity he proved that a single interpretation of the Qur'an was possible." http://www.hamid-uddin-farahi.org/index. php?option=com_content&view=article&id=62&Itemid=57.

36   The Turkish derivation of this word is *nizam*, meaning order, regularity or system, and is usually used in reference to the order to be found in the natural world (*kainattaki nizam*), which is evidence of its Creator.

37   Mustansir Mir, "The Sura as a Unity: A Twentieth Century Development in Qur'an Exegesis," in *Approaches to the Qur'an* (ed. Hawting: Routledge, 1993), 211-24.

38   Asma Barlas, *On Interpreting the Qur'an (1)* (2005 [cited 14/4/2014]); available from http://www.asmabarlas.com/EDITORIALS/Interpreting_Quran.pdf. She cites Qur'an 3:7; 15:89-93; and 6:91, arguing that "such ayat suggest that the Qur'an is a textual and hermeneutic unity and that we should not read it in a piecemeal, selective, and decontextualized way since doing so distorts its meanings."

39   Farrin, *Structure and Qur'anic Interpretation: A Study of Symmetry and Coherence in Islam's Holy Text*, KL 1364-1367. See also Michel Cuypers, *The Composition of the Qur'an: Rhetorical Analysis* (London: Bloomsbury Academic, 2015), who argues that "Semitic rhetorical analysis" reveals a careful structure using parallel, mirror and concentric elements of composition. Reynolds expresses doubts about whether this intricate structure is actually present or is created and imposed on the text by the reader. Gabriel Said Reynolds, "Review of Michel Cuypers, La Composition Du Coran: Rhétorique Sémitique," *RQR* 1, no. 2 (2015).

40   Duderija, *Constructing a Religiously Ideal "Believer" and "Woman" in Islam*, 148-50.

41   Reynolds' interpretation, that *hanif* (6:79, 161) essentially means gentile, highlights Abraham's place in the Qur'an as a symbol and a prototype of Muhammad, who was also a gentile: "'I have turned my face to the one who created the heavens and the earth, a gentile (*ḥanif*) but not a polytheist' (Q 6.79). In this way the Qur'an asserts that Abraham was in no way obliged to the People of the Book for his faith, and it thereby implies the same for its own Prophet." Reynolds, *The Qur'an and Its Biblical Subtext*, 87.

42   Some interpret this as referring to not to a literal rescue from flame but to deliverance from the metaphorical "fire" of persecution from his society (Asad on this verse; Ahmet Baydar, İbrahimî Okuyuş (Abrahamic Reading) (İstanbul: Beyan Yayınları, 2008), 38-39. But Turkish Muslims generally hold that this event literally took place in what is today the city of Şanlıurfa. The Hebrew word *Ur* (Gen 11:28, 31; 15:7) literally means fire, and in Jewish sources has been understood as Abraham's rescue from fire rather than his departure from the city of Ur: "Abram descended into the fiery furnace and was saved" (*Gen R 38:13* on Gen 11:28); "Michael descended and rescued Abraham from the fiery furnace" (*Gen R 44:13* on Gen 15:7; cf. *Gen R 44:1*). Günter Stemberger, "Genesis 15 in Rabbinic and Patristic Interpretation," in *The Exegetical Encounter between Jews and Christians in Late Antiquity* (eds. Grypeou and Spurling; vol. 18 of; Leiden; Boston: Brill, 2009), 157, says this means that God "tried" Abraham and found him faithful.

43   Younus Mirza, "Abraham as an Iconoclast: Understanding the Destruction of 'Images' through Qur'anic Exegesis," *ICMR* 16, no. 4 (2005): 428.

44   Welch, "Formulaic Features of the Punishment Stories," 78.

45   Firestone, *Journeys in Holy Lands*, 80. On the importance of this place see chapter 7.

46   Para-biblical Jewish writings identify various points in the biblical narrative where Abraham was tested beyond the one explicit statement in Gen 22:1 that "God tested Abraham" by commanding him to sacrifice Isaac. There is little consensus among Muslim interpreters as to the content of this testing. For details of both Jewish and Muslim speculation regarding Abraham's testing see the notes in Appendix 5.

47   This Abraham story is found primarily in later suras in the context of the apparent rejection of Muhammad by the Jews of Medina. The redirection of the focus of prayer from Jerusalem to Mecca may correspond with the story of Abraham as the founder of the Kaaba cult. However, Fazlur Rahman argued that the Mecca pilgrimage ordinance had nothing to do with Jews or any break with them. Rather since the Muslim community was no longer in Mecca, but Medina, they would now need to make a pilgrimage to the site. He contended there was a continuity on this matter between the Meccan and Medinan periods. Fazlur Rahman, "Pre-Foundations of the Muslim Community in Mecca," *StudIsl* 43 (1976): 20-24.

48   Against both of these we have seen the NT insistence that there is *no* central place of pilgrimage and divine worship on earth since the coming of Jesus.

49   See for example 2:124, 143, 155, 214, 249; 3:142, 154, 179, 186.

50   For an investigation of various links between Abraham's act and the Mecca rituals see Suliman Bashear, "Abraham's Sacrifice of His Son and Related Issues," *DI* 67, no. 2 (1990). Also see Firestone, *Journeys in Holy Lands*, 107-34.

51   "The Eid al-Adha, or Festival of Sacrifice . . . commemorates an event, to be sure, the supreme act of obedience by Abraham, but it differs from a simple commemoration in that the celebrant imitates the example of Abraham . . . The killing of the animal serves as the means of identifying oneself actively with the obedience of Abraham and his spirit of sacrifice." R. Marston Speight, "The Nature of Christian and Muslim Festivals," *MW* 70, no. 3-4 (1980): 262.

CHAPTER 6 – TURKISH MUSLIM USE OF ABRAHAM

1   I am grateful for the willingness of these imams to answer my questions and discuss with me who Abraham is to them and how they use the Abrahamic stories in their preaching and teaching.

2   Talip Kucukcan, "State, Islam, and Religious Liberty in Modern Turkey: Reconfiguration of Religion in the Public Sphere," *BYULR*, no. 2 (2003): 502. There are differences between Arabic-speaking *Alawites* in Syria, and Turkish, Arabic and Kurdish-speaking *Alevis* in Turkey, in terms of political and sectarian allegiance as well as religious practices. Marianne Aringberg-Laanatza, "Alevis in Turkey - Alawites in Syria: Similarities and Differences," in *Alevi Identity: Cultural, Religious, and Social Perspectives: Papers Read at a Conference Held at the Swedish Research Institute in Istanbul, November 25-27, 1996* (eds. Özdalga, et al.; Istanbul: Swedish Research Institute in Istanbul, 1998), 151-66.

3   Béatrice Hendrich uses the term "state Islam" to describe state-approved orthodox Islam in Turkey. Béatrice Hendrich, "Beyond State Islam: Religiosity and Spirituality in Contemporary Turkey," *EJTS* 13 (2011).

4   A more comprehensive study of Turkish Muslims would include *Alevis* and representatives of specific *Sufi* traditions. Nevertheless, I have attempted to include some insights related to these particular sub-streams of Turkish Islam. See under Turkish Islam and Concluding Reflections below.

5   Anthony O'Mahony, "Christianity in Modern Turkey: Some Reflections on History and Religion," in *Islam and Christianity on the Edge: Talking Points in Christian-Muslim Relations into the 21st Century* (eds. Azumah and Riddell; Victoria: Acorn Press, 2013), KL 3709.

6   Yazır, *Hak Dini Kur'an Dili*. My quotations are taken from the online version at http://www.kuranikerim.com/telmalili/.

7   According to Albayrak, Yazır "follows the *ahl al-sunna* in *aqā'id* (belief) and the Hanafi school in *amal* (actions)." Ismail Albayrak, "The Notions of Muḥkam and Mutashābih in the Commentary of Elmalı'lı Muḥammad Ḥamdi Yazır," *JQS* 5, no. 1 (2003): 20. On the early development of the four major schools—Shafii, Hanbali, Maliki, and Hanafi—see Noel J. Coulson, *A History of Islamic Law* (New Brunswick: Aldine Transaction, 2011), 36-73. For the development of Hanafism in particular, see Christopher Melchert, "How Hanafism Came to Originate in Kufa and Traditionalism in Medina," *ILS* 6, no. 3 (1999). As I have frequently been told over the years, Turkish Muslims generally adhere to the Hanafi school.

8   Peter B. Golden, *Central Asia in World History* (New York: Oxford University Press, 2011), 63-66.

9   Golden, *Central Asia in World History,* 69.

10   Colin Imber, "Islam in the Ottoman Empire," in *Europe, 1450 to 1789: Encyclopedia of the Early Modern World* (ed. Dewald; New York: Charles Scribner's Sons, 2004), 294.

11   David Shankland, *The Alevis in Turkey* (London: Routledge, 2003), 14.

12   "The law of 1925 put an end not only to the hitherto well established forms of Sufi activities but also to expressions of folk Islam like the veneration of saints at their tombs. The Societies Law of 1938 put a further constraint on any association founded with religious ambitions." Hendrich, "Beyond State Islam: Religiosity and Spirituality in Contemporary Turkey," 3.

13   M. Hakan Yavuz, "Is There a Turkish Islam? The Emergence of Convergence and Consensus," *JMMA* 24, no. 2 (2004).

14   Yavuz, "Is There a Turkish Islam?," 214.

15   Ahmet Y. Ocak, *Türk Sufiliğine Bakışlar (Approaches to Turkish Sufi Orders)* (İstanbul: İletişim, 1996), 79. Quoted in Yavuz, "Is There a Turkish Islam?," 218.

16   Nancy Tapper and Richard Tapper, "The Birth of the Prophet: Ritual and Gender in Turkish Islam," *MAN* New Series 22, no. 1: 84-85.

17   Yavuz, "Is There a Turkish Islam?." See Yaşar Nuri Öztürk, *The Eye of the Heart: An Introduction to Sufism and the Tariqats of Anatolia and the Balkans* (Istanbul: Redhouse Press, 1988), for a good survey of both Sufism and the Sufi orders.

18   Yavuz, "Is There a Turkish Islam?," 218-19. Italics added.

19   Nurcu means "followers of the light," but refers particularly to the followers of Said Nursi's teachings.

20   Political events in 2013–14 have driven a wedge between the AKP led by Recep Tayyip Erdoğan and the Gülen movement, often referred to as the *Cemaat*, or Community. An overview of the growth of this community is found in Elisabeth Özdalga, "Transformation of Sufi-Based Communities in Modern Turkey: The Nașibendis, the Nurcus, and the Gülen Community," in *Turkey's Engagement with Modernity: Conflict and Change in the Twentieth Century* (eds. Kerslake, et al.; Oxford: Palgrave MacMillan, 2010), 69-91.

21   Bedriye Poyraz, "Eu Minority Perspective and the Case of Alevilik in Turkey," in *EUI Working Papers RSCAS No. 2006/24*(Florence: European University Institute: Robert Schuman Center for Advanced Studies, 2006), 1.

22   Jamal Shah, "Evaluating Alevism in Turkey," *IJHSS* 3, no. 2 (2013): 265-66.

23   Ali Soner Bayram and Şule Toktaş, "Alevis and Alevism in the Changing Context of Turkish Politics: The Justice and Development Party's Alevi Opening," *TurSt* 12, no. 3 (2011): 423-26.

24   Only a tiny minority remains of those from other monotheistic faith traditions. In 2005 the Non-Muslims (Greeks, Armenians, Jews, others) made up 0.2% of the overall population, as opposed to 19.1% in 1914 and 2.5% in 1927. Ahmet Icduygu, et al., "The Politics of Population in a Nation-Building Process: Emigration of Non-Muslims from Turkey," *ERS* 31, no. 2 (2008): 363.

25   Cemal Karakaş, *Turkey: Islam and Laicism between the Interests of State, Politics, and Society* (vol. 78: Peace Research Institute Frankfurt, 2007), 4.

26   Icduygu, et al., "The Politics of Population," 359-60.

27   Kaymakcan, "Religious Education Culture," 454.
28   E. Fuat Keyman, "Modernity, Secularism and Islam: The Case of Turkey," *TCulS* 24, no. 2 (2007).
29   That Turkey is still largely secular in outlook is confirmed by a recent survey: http://www. pewglobal.org/2016/04/27/the-divide-over-islam-and-national-laws-in-the-muslim-world/. Nevertheless, the popular opposition which repelled the coup attempt on 15 July 2016 evidenced stong religious devotion. In an unprecedented move, announcements from Turkey's 85,000 mosques called the populace to the streets throughout the night.
30   Aisha Y. Musa, *Hadith as Scripture: Discussions on the Authority of Prophetic Traditions in Islam* (New York: Palgrave Macmillan, 2008), 100.
31   Yaşar Nuri Öztürk, *Kur'an'daki İslam (Qur'anic Islam)* (Istanbul: Yeni Boyut Yayınları, 2000), presents his reading of the qur'anic essentials of Islam.
32   Recep Şentürk, "Islamic Reformist Discourses and Intellectuals in Turkey: Permanent Religion with Dynamic Law," in *Reformist Voices of Islam: Mediating Islam and Modernity* (ed. Hunter; Armonk, N.Y.: M.E. Sharpe, 2009), 239. One interviewee led me to understand that this attempt might be more popular in Ankara, but is resisted by scholars from the influential Istanbul theology faculties. He insisted that any revision of the Hadith was confined to making them understandable for today's generation.
33   For insightful overviews of the background of these developments, see Erik-Jan Zürcher, "The Importance of Being Secular: Islam in the Service of the National and Pre-National State," in *Turkey's Engagement with Modernity: Conflict and Change in the Twentieth Century* (eds. Kerslake, et al.; Oxford: Palgrave MacMillan, 2010), and Özdalga, "Transformation of Sufi-Based Communities," 69-91. This volume contains many thoughtful studies on modern Turkey.
34   Şentürk, "Islamic Reformist Discourses," 235.
35   Şentürk, "Islamic Reformist Discourses," 243.
36   The first set of interviews was conducted between April 2011 and May 2012 and the second set between May and July 2014. For readers who are interested, my dissertation contains detailed references to interview texts and appendixes with detailed tabulation of results.
37   By "para-qur'anic" I mean that the specific narrative is not found in the Qur'an, but belongs instead to the body of Islamic narrative tradition which has grown up around the qur'anic stories. It does not mean that these para-qur'anic stories conflict with the Qur'an or the qur'anic worldview. In fact, these para-qur'anic stories are used to support and illustrate that worldview.
38   He made this comparison a number of times during the interview.
39   It is not clear that this single-verse narrative is linked with this particular story, but it can plausibly be related to this period of his life.
40   Firestone documents this non-qur'anic Islamic legend and its sources in a chapter entitled "the Tyrant." Firestone, *Journeys in Holy Lands*, 31-38.
41   Renard notes that Abraham's story is among the most extensive in the "nativity narrative" genre of Islamic hagiography. Renard, *Friends of God*, 15.
42   This detail is related in Jewish exegetical literature. See Levenson, *Inheriting Abraham*, 119.
43   This ruler's identity as Nimrod is also found in Jewish legend.
44   Examples of the lives of such saints are numerous in Turkey. For one which tells some of best known saints in the Turkish world see Kopuz, *Allah Dostları*. For an in-depth study of Islamic hagiography see Renard, *Friends of God*.
45   Firestone, *Journeys in Holy Lands*, 38.
46   "While the Qur'an refers to Abraham and Ishmael in Mecca, it provides no explanation as to how they arrived there. The traditions found in this chapter fill out the qur'anic references by establishing a context for the transition of our two main protagonists from Syria to the Hijaz. . . . Abraham personally brings Hagar and Ishmael to Mecca." Firestone, *Journeys in Holy Lands*, 63.
47   "This Hadith then goes on to quote Qur'an 14:37 as the text of Abraham's prayer delivered at this time. There are several reasons to question exactly when Abraham said this prayer. . . . Much

of this same reasoning is presented in Ibn Kathir (1998, 238-239). Dirks, *Abraham: The Friend of God*, 268.

48   Various versions of this story detail are mentioned in Firestone, *Journeys in Holy Lands*, 116-28.

49   Şentürk, "Islamic Reformist Discourses," 242.

50   Öztürk, *The Eye of the Heart*, 3. Italics added.

51   This proved to be possible only with six of my original nine interviewees.

52   Clooney, "Comparative Theology and Inter-Religious Dialogue," 58.

53   Baydar, İbrahimî Okuyuş (Abrahamic Reading), 9. Baydar charges Jews with reading "dualistically" and Christians with reading through the lens of an "undeveloped pantheism." "Keeping all of this in mind, it will not be wrong to say that Judaism and Christianity are superstitious or degenerate (*batıl*) to the degree they depart from an Abrahamic and creationist reading." Baydar 146.

54   Baydar, İbrahimî Okuyuş (Abrahamic Reading), 134.

55   He returned to this point in a number of his answers.

56   Baydar, İbrahimî Okuyuş (Abrahamic Reading),126.

57   Or he supports his argumentation with this reasoning approach as he disputes with his audience, as some interpret these verses.

58   See the discussion in Appendix 5 for perspectives on this verse in light of the fact that no book of Abraham has come down to us.

CHAPTER 7 – TWO WORLDVIEWS, TWO STORIES, TWO ABRAHAMS?

1   My understanding is also informed by the OT use of Abraham outside of Genesis, but I have not developed that material here.

2   See my overview of Jewish readings of Abraham in chapter 4.

3   Lowin, "Abraham," 227.

4   Lowin, "Abraham," 228-29.

5   Post-apostolic Christian writing does use Jewish midrashic material. Much work is being done to uncover these parallels, showing for example how the Qur'an's perspective shares Syriac Christianity's anti-Jewish polemic, notably Reynolds, *The Qur'an and Its Biblical Subtext*. See also Gabriel Said Reynolds, "On the Qur'ānic Accusation of Scriptural Falsification (Taḥrīf) and Christian Anti-Jewish Polemic," *JAOS* 130 (2010). But I contend that the NT explicitly diverges from the whole system connected with this "embellished Bible" of Jewish tradition and that the appropriation of these stories as part of canonical Christian thinking is in error.

6   See the warning regarding this difficulty in Bauckham, *Bible and Mission*, 92.

7   God is omnipresent as narrator of the Abraham narratives in the Qur'an.

8   See Chapman, "Food, Famine and the Nations," 323-33.

9   Juan Eduardo Campo, *Encyclopedia of Islam* (New York: Facts On File, 2009), 9.

10   These stories belong rather to the para-biblical legends of Abraham's early life in Ur of the Chaldees, of which nothing is recounted in Genesis 11:27-32. See George W. E. Nickelsburg, *Jewish Literature between the Bible and the Mishnah: A Historical and Literary Introduction* (Minneapolis: Fortress Press, 2005), 70. See my discussion of Jubilees in chapter 4.

11   To cite only a few OT examples, this is evident in the Genesis 1 creation account, in the first two of the Ten Commandments, in Deuteronomy's warning passages, from Israel's repeated fall into idolatry in the narratives of Judges and Kings, and from the prophetic denouncements of idolatry in the latter prophets. The NT continues the condemnation of idolatry, including Israel's idol-like blindness in the Gospels, the Gentiles turning from idols to the living God in Acts and the epistles (e.g. Acts 17; 1 Thes 1:10), and the final judgment of worldwide idolatry in Revelation. See Gregory K. Beale, *We Become What We Worship: A Biblical Theology of Idolatry* (Downers Grove: IVP Academic, 2008), for a full treatment of this theme.

12 Household idols are even found with members of Jacob's household, and it seems he did little to eliminate their presence (Gen 31:19, 34-35), although he later put them away (35:2-4). For a discussion of the evolutionary view of Israel's religion which sees pure monotheism developing only in the late exilic period and therefore not found in the patriarchal narratives, see Richard Bauckham, "Biblical Theology and the Problems of Monotheism," in *Out of Egypt: Biblical Theology and Biblical Interpretation* (eds. Bartholomew and Botha; vol. 5 of *Scripture and Hermeneutics Series*; Bletchley, Milton Keynes: Paternoster Press, 2004), 210-17.

13 This was expressed clearly by one of my interviewees who read through the Genesis Abraham narrative.

14 Kenneth Cragg, preface to Badru D. Kateregga and David W. Shenk, *A Muslim and a Christian in Dialogue* (Scottdale, Pa.: Herald Press, 2011), 15.

15 "Most prominent [in the contexts where this motif is employed] is the relationship between appearing and promise in the patriarchal traditions. Yahweh appears to each patriarch in order to affirm the promises made to Abraham (12:1-3), often at moments of tension within the larger narrative with regard to fulfillment, or when the patriarchal family is threatened (Gen 12:7; 17:1; 18:1; 26:2, 24; 35:9; 48:3)." Staton, "And Yahweh Appeared," 292.

16 Terrien, *The Elusive Presence*, xxvii.

17 The tabernacle/temple language of John 1:14-18 and 2:16-22 alludes to God's "tabernacling" among Israel, implying that Jesus is not only the temple but also the God who meets his people there. Richard B. Hays, *Reading Backwards : Figural Christology and the Fourfold Gospel Witness*, 82-86.

18 Islam has a significant if debated tradition of Muhammad's incomparable visual encounter with God, which turns primarily on the interpretation of Sura An Najm 53:1-18. Typically understood to refer to Muhammad's encounter with the angel Gabriel, this reference has been interpreted by some as a theophany, perceived either with the heart or with the eyes. See W. Wesley Williams, "Tajalli Wa-Ru'ya: A Study of Anthropomorphic Theophany and Visio Dei in the Hebrew Bible, the Qur'an and Early Sunni Islam" (PhD Dissertation, University of Michigan, 2008) 276. From my reading of Q7:143 it seems rather that Moses was shown that he could not see God.

19 "The anthropomorphism of the detail which depicts Yahweh as waiting for man appeared too gross for Judaism in the Hellenistic age." Terrien, *The Elusive Presence*, 102. For example, Exod 19:24 is a text which in the MT emphasizes the immediacy of the divine presence in the words, "I will come to you." However, "the Aramaic targumim reject the physical theophany of the deity. They consistently reject the verb of motion—the verb that defines the deity's entry into space and time—and instead render it metaphorically, so as to preserve divine transcendence." John Day, *In Search of Pre-Exilic Israel: Proceedings of the Oxford Old Testament Seminar* (406; London: T & T Clark International, 2004), 309. On this tendency, see also Juncker, "Jesus and the Angel of the Lord," 280.

20 "The Qur'an's version of the story exemplifies the theme of God's utter transcendence, certainly a dominant theme in Islam." Lodahl, *Claiming Abraham*, KL 457–459.

21 Lodahl, *Claiming Abraham*, KL 463-468.

22 In his discussion of the emergence of Islam, Reynolds argues, "The Quran's great concern with a transcendent God, and in particular its refutation of the Christian teaching of the incarnation, suggests that Islam was first preached in a context where Christian debates over theology and Christology were a topic of general interest." Reynolds, *The Emergence of Islam*, 4370-4372.

23 The *place* is the delightful garden with four rivers given by God to Adam and the *bond* is the covenant agreement with two trees which form the main provisions of the covenant agreement. Blocher, *In the Beginning*, 111-34.

24 Asad's footnote on 3:81 explains: "Lit., 'the solemn pledge of the prophets.' Zamakhsharī holds that what is meant here is a pledge taken from the community as a whole: a pledge

consisting in their acceptance of the messages conveyed through the prophets." Mention is also made in the Qur'an of covenants made by God with Israel in 4:154 and 2:83.

25   For example, in Gen 17 God changes Sarai's name to Sarah and promises a son through her; in Gen 18 the Lord announces the birth again; in Gen 20 Isaac is born, and Hagar and Ishmael are cast out; in Gen 23 she dies and Abraham purchases a special burial place for her; in Gen 25:10 Abraham is buried "with Sarah his wife."

26   For a point-by-point comparison of the creation and 'fall' stories of Adam and Eve see Torsten Löfstedt, "The Creation and Fall of Adam: A Comparison of the Qur'anic and Biblical Accounts," *SweMT* 93, no. 4 (2005).

27   Blocher draws attention to the resemblance by nature which is seen in the *relationship* of a son to his father. Blocher, *In the Beginning*, 85-89.

28   Seyyed Hossein Nasr, "Islamic Pedagogy: An Interview," *IS* 10, no. 1 (2012). Italics added.

29   Berghout says, "Thus, the creation of the universe, life, and death are all meant for humanity, who was *created for trial and test*." Berghout, "Toward an Islamic Framework for Worldview Studies: Preliminary Theorization," 32.

30   This is developed this as the central Abrahamic concept of Islam by Baydar, İbrahimî Okuyuş (Abrahamic Reading).

31   e.g. Noah's drunkenness, Lot's incest with his daughters after reluctantly leaving Sodom; Isaac's lying about his wife; Jacob deceiving his father to steal his brother's birthright; Jacob's sons selling Joseph into slavery and lying to their father to cover up, Levi and Simeon's violence, Reuben's incest with his father's concubine and Judah's with his daughter-in-law whom he thought to be a prostitute.

32   The Bible says nothing directly about Abraham not being an idolater, though statements such as "Abram called upon the name of the LORD" and "Abram believed the Lord" (Gen 12:8; 15:6) indicate his allegiance to Yahweh the Creator God.

33   Simon demonstrates that the biblical narrative's steadfast refusal to exalt the main Israelite characters is strikingly different from the writings of later Judaism (as from those of Islam). Uriel Simon, "Minor Characters in Biblical Narrative," *JSOT*, no. 46 (1990).

34   The Exodus events are explicitly linked to God's promises to Abraham (Exod 2:24; 3:6-16; 4:5; 6:3-8; 32:13).

35   The other prophet stories are told as part of a common prophet pattern, but without the connection to Mecca.

36   I use the term "revelation" in reference to the biblical and qur'anic claims that there is a God who has communicated with humanity. For Christian understanding of "revelation" see the discussion in Stephen N. Williams, "Revelation," in *Dictionary for Theological Interpretation of the Bible* (ed. Vanhoozer; Grand Rapids: Baker Academic, 2005), 678-80. For Muslim understanding of "revelation" see Abu-Hamdiyyah, *The Qur'an*, 35-39. For a concise comparison of several aspects of revelation see Glaser, "Toward a Mutual Understanding of Christian and Islamic Concepts of Revelation."

37   Abdullah Saeed, "Rethinking 'Revelation' as a Precondition for Reinterpreting the Qur'an: A Qur'anic Perspective," *JQS* 1, no. 1 (1999): 101. Regarding the third mode, he says "Revelation comes to the Prophet through a 'messenger.' This is the most indirect form of God's speech. The messenger conveys the word of God as it is, without any change and in the case of revelation to Prophets, 'sending a messenger' is the most common method of revelation." Saeed, "Rethinking 'Revelation'," 101.

38   Rubin, "Prophets and Prophethood," 237.

39   This cleric argued that this conversation must be mediated through angels even though represented as direct speech, because only Moses and Muhammad spoke directly with Allah.

40   For a fuller development of God's promise of blessing for the nations, see M. Daniel Carroll R, "Blessing the Nations: Toward a Biblical Theology of Mission from Genesis," *BBR* 10, no. 1 (2000).

41   Al Faruqi, "A Comparison," 287-88.

42   Al Faruqi, "A Comparison," 288. Qutb argues that God is not constrained even by His own promise. Commenting on Qur'an 87:7, he writes, "Every time the Qur'an states a definite promise or a constant law, it follows it with a statement implying that the Divine will is free of all limitations and restrictions, even those based on a promise from Allah or a law of His." Sayyid Qutb, et al., *In the Shade of the Qur'an* (vol. 30; London: MWH, 1979), 140, cited in Ida J. Glaser, "The Concept of Relationship as a Key to the Comparative Understanding of Christianity and Islam," *Them* 11, no. 2 (1986): 60.

43   See Reuven Firestone, "Is There a Notion of 'Divine Election' in the Quran," in *New Perspectives on the Qur'an: The Qur'an in Its Historical Context 2* (ed. Reynolds; vol. 12 of *Routledge Studies in the Quran*; New York: Routledge, 2011), 409-410.

44   M. Zakyi Ibrahim, "Oaths in the Qur'ān: Bint Al-Shāṭi's Literary Contribution," *Islamic Studies* 48, no. 4 (2009): 486.

45   Louis Ginzberg, et al., *The Legends of the Jews* (Philadelphia: The Jewish publication society of America, 1909), 111-12, 137-38. God identifies himself to Abraham with the words, "I am the LORD who brought you out from Ur of the Chaldeans" (Gen 15:7).

46   Fadlou Shehadi, *Ghazali's Unique Unknowable God: A Philosophical Critical Analysis of Some of the Problems Raised by Ghazali's View of God as Utterly Unique and Unknowable* (Leiden: Brill, 1964), 45. Al-Faruqi insists that, "In Islam, God does not reveal Himself. . . . But he can and does reveal His will; and this is wholly the ethically-imperative, the commandment, the law." Al Faruqi, "A Comparison," 286.

47   Thomas C. Oden, *The Living God* (1; San Francisco: Harper & Row, 1987), 20.

48   The rainbow will remind him of the covenant: "I will see it and remember the everlasting covenant between God and every living creature of all flesh that is on the earth" (Gen 9:16).

49   Afzaal, "Tawhid (Oneness of God)," 1623.

50   Umeyye Isra Yazicioglu, "Redefining the Miraculous: Al-Ghazālī, Ibn Rushd and Said Nursi on Qur'anic Miracle Stories," *JQS* 13, no. 2 (2011): 98-99. Yazicioglu, a member of the Society for Scriptural Reasoning, brings a Turkish perspective derived from Said Nursi. In another article, referring to Q9:70, she speaks of "the Quran's insistence on casting aside the shell of familiarity to see 'ordinary' things anew, as signs of God." Yazicioglu, "Learning to Ask Questions," 4. Italics hers.

51   Neuwirth says, "The qur'anic image of the ruined abodes . . . has a meaningful message to offer . . . it has occurred to punish evildoers who distracted their respective societies from heeding the call of their messengers." Neuwirth, "Two Views of History," 1.

52   The motif is important in both Islamic and Jewish traditions regarding Abraham's early life. Hauglid, "Bible and Qur'an," 98-100. In both Jewish para-biblical literature and Islamic tradition Abraham is led to knowledge of the one God by observing the heavenly bodies (*Jub.* 12:17-18; Philo, *Abr* 69-71; Josephus, *Ant* 1.167-168; Q 6:76-78).

53   Wright, *The Mission of God*, 368.

54   Vos argues that Abraham's virtues constitute obligations for Christians and summarizes the key ethical virtues which Abraham modeled: "While the (biblical) record does not cover up or condone (Abraham's) defects, it places, over against these, great virtues. . . . The main virtues emphasized are: hospitality, magnanimity, self-sacrifice, loyalty." Geerhardus Vos, *Biblical Theology* (Edinburgh: Banner of Truth Trust, 2012), 88.

55   Worldwide universal "prophecy" comes only with Jesus' resurrection and the Holy Spirit, who equips messengers to go in Jesus' name to all nations. Previously it was limited primarily to Israel (Matt 10:5-6).

56   Only in the phrase "Abraham called on the name of the Lord" might such a prophetic role be found (Gen 12:8; 13:4; 21:33), if translated "Abraham proclaimed the name of Yahweh." The phrase can have this meaning, as in Exod 33:19 and 34:5, but it is God proclaiming the name. A better understanding is Abraham invoking the name of the Lord in dedication of an altar (cf. Gen 4:26; 26:25). Waltke says, "This is an image of prayer." Waltke and Fredricks, *Genesis: A Commentary*, 101.

57   Devin J. Stewart, "Understanding the Quran in English: Notes on Translation, Form, and Prophetic Typology," in *Diversity in Language: Contrastive Studies in Arabic and English Theoretical and Applied Linguistics* (ed. Ibrahim; Cairo: American University in Cairo Press, 2000), 47-48.

58   While only implied in the Qur'an, Abraham's birth is accompanied by omens in the tradition, which along with his special protection as a child signifies his divine selection as a prophet. Lowin, "Abraham," 231-32. Abraham's reading in the "signs" of creation the evidence of the Creator is unique to Abraham.   .

59   6:74; 19:42-45; 21:52-56; 26:70-76; 29:16; 37:84-87; 43:26; 60:4.

60   21:56-70; 29:17-98; 37:88-96. Mirza, "Abraham as an Iconoclast: Understanding the Destruction of 'Images' through Qur'anic Exegesis," 413.

61   David Marshall, *God, Muhammad and the Unbelievers: A Quranic Study* (Richmond: Curzon, 1999), 70.

62   The others are Zachariah, father of John/Yahya (3:38-41) and Mary, mother of Jesus (3:45-47). Islamic commentators, with only a few exceptions, have not considered Mary to be a prophetess. See Jane I. Smith and Yvonne Y. Haddad, "The Virgin Mary in Islamic Tradition and Commentary," *MW* 79, no. 3-4 (1989): 177-79.

63   Q34:13 may refer to Solomon's building the first temple and 17:7 to its destruction.

64   Reynolds refers to such elements as the Qur'an's "biblical subtext," arguing that many qur'anic allusions are best understood in light of Christian and Jewish scripture. Reynolds, *The Qur'an and Its Biblical Subtext*.

65   After examining these Islamic exegetical traditions concerning Abraham building the Kaaba and calling mankind to pilgrimage, Firestone comments that "the great variety among the traditions reflects both the lack of a standardized pre-Islamic Pilgrimage ritual   and the absence of pre-Islamic traditions connecting Abraham to the Hajj." Firestone, *Journeys in Holy Lands*, 103.

66   Lowin notes this as a possible reason for embellishments of the Abraham story in the Islamic tradition. Lowin, *The Making of a Forefather*, 255.

67   Psalm 47:9 pictures a day when "the princes of the peoples gather as the people of the God of Abraham."

68   So Stump, "Abraham's faith is not a faith in the existence of God, or in the power of the being who commands the sacrifice of Isaac, or in a duty to obey God's commands, no matter what . . . The faith that makes Abraham the father of faith has its root in Abraham's acceptance of the goodness of God, Abraham's belief that God will keep his promises." Stump, *Wandering in Darkness*, 302.

69   Yvonne Y. Haddad, "Conception of the Term Dīn in the Qur'ān," *MW* 64, no. 2 (1974): 120.

70   Contra Jewish tradition that sees Abraham founding a community of proselytes. Frishman, "And Abraham Had Faith," 166.

71   Christians are to submit to the government under which they find themselves (Rom 13:1-7) and to refrain from use of force in the defense and propagation of their faith (Matt 26:52). Both the responsibility and the failure of followers of Jesus to keep to this path is considered at length by John Howard Yoder. See John Howard Yoder, *The Politics of Jesus, 2nd Ed.* (Grand Rapids: Eerdmans, 1994), and Yoder, et al., *The Jewish-Christian Schism Revisited*.

72   See Ps 76:2. According to Wenham, "The Genesis Apocryphon (22:13) and Josephus (*Ant.* 1.10.2 [1:180]) also affirm the identity of Salem with Jerusalem."Wenham, *Genesis 1-15*, 1: 316.

73   Strom, "From Promised Land to Reconciled Cosmos," 15.

74   The author of the letter to the Hebrews notes an additional theological significance in Jesus' being actually crucified outside the city (Heb 13:10-14). However, the sad fact that Jesus suffers and dies in Jerusalem is primary (e.g. Luke 13:33). It is the "great city that symbolically is called Sodom and Egypt, where their Lord was crucified" (Rev 11:8).

75   Josua, "Ibrahim, Khalil Allah," 589.

76 Sahih Bukhari, Book 27, Number 1. Several hadith are cited in studies of ways in which forgiveness of sins may be obtained. Among these is several related to the Pilgrimage. Harun Özçelik, "Hadislere Göre Günahların Bağışlanma Yolları (Ways of Forgiveness of Sins According to the Hadith)," *AÜİFD* 34 (2010). However, my interlocutors noted that all of the Islamic rites of worship are salvific in the same way as the Hajj, which is in fact not feasible for many Muslims.

77 Clifford Geertz, "The Javanese Kijaji: The Changing Role of a Cultural Broker," *CSSH* 2, no. 2 (1960): 230.

78 Cited in David A. King, *World-Maps for Finding the Direction and Distance to Mecca: Innovation and Tradition in Islamic Science* (36; Leiden: Brill, 1999), 20.

79 King, *World-Maps for Finding the Direction and Distance to Mecca: Innovation and Tradition in Islamic Science*, 47-48.

80 Gary M. Burge, *Jesus and the Land: The New Testament Challenge to "Holy Land" Theology* (Grand Rapids: Baker Academic, 2010), KL 2453-2454.

81 Jerusalem referred to as *Bayt al-Maqdis (Arabic for Jerusalem)* or *Al-Quds* in Arabic and *Kudüs* in Turkish, both meaning "holy."

82 Ghada Talhami, "Jerusalem in the Muslim Consciousness," *MW* 86, no. 3-4 (1996) The journey to Jerusalem is called the *isra'* and the journey to heaven the *mi'raj*. It is argued by some that the connection between Jerusalem and the Night Journey was only made for the first time during the Umayyad reign, when the Al-Aqsa Mosque was built. Daniel Pipes, "The Muslim Claim to Jerusalem," *MEQ*, no. Fall (2001). Pipes argues that "the stature of the city, and the emotions surrounding it, inevitably rises for Muslims when Jerusalem has political significance."

83 Smith, "Reflections on Aspects of Immortality in Islam," 91-95.

84 Abdel Haleem records that "Abu Muslim thought the important part of the image was that it is as easy for souls to come back to the body as for the birds to come back to Abraham (Razi). Cf. 'To Him you shall return', in many places, e.g. 2: 245 and 285."

85 Only the story of the destruction of Sodom raises the issue of God as "the Judge of all the earth" (Gen 18:25), and is later used as a picture of eschatological judgment (Matt 10:15; 11:23-24; 2 Pet 2:6; Jude 1:7).

86 God promises to provide a rich feast for *all peoples*, alluding to the "all nations" promise to Abraham (Isa 25:6-8). The location of this victory banquet is identified as "this mountain" (Isa 25:6-7), a likely link to the hill where Isaac was spared: "On the mount of the LORD it shall be provided" (Gen 22:14).

87 In addition, Lot gave a feast for the two angels in Sodom (19:3) and Abraham gave a feast on the day when Isaac was weaned (Gen 21:8).

88 On the possibility that Qur'an 5:114-115 refers in some way to the Lord's Supper, see Emmanouela Grypeou, "The Table from Heaven: A Note on Qur'ān, Sūrah 5,111 ff.," *CCO* 2 (2005). See also Reynolds, "On the Qur'ān's Mā'ida Passage and the Wanderings of the Israelites," in *The Coming of the Comforter: When, Where, and to Whom? Studies on the Rise of Islam in Memory of John Wansbrough* (ed. B. Lourié; Piscataway, NJ: Gorgias, 2011), 91-108. Reynolds argues that it more likely refers to unbelieving Israelites asking if God can make a banquet/table in the desert.

89 Perrin develops this complex of themes as including the eschatological judgment: "Looking at the cup, Jesus invited his followers to see a symbol of triumph ... in which Jesus himself, as the Melchizedekian priest and Zechariahan covenant-mediator [enacting Zech 9:9-10 in his triumphal entry], would somehow participate." Perrin, "Covenantal Consciousness," 8/10..

90 This is the time when God will "swallow up death forever" (1 Cor 15:54, alluding to Isa 25:8). This feast is announced again in Isa 55:1-5 in conjunction with the Davidic covenant, which advances the Abrahamic covenant. See Robin Routledge, *Old Testament Theology: A Thematic Approach* (Nottingham: Apollos - IVP, 2008), 235-36.

91   Kenneth Bailey asserts that "this [angels transporting a righteous deceased person like Lazarus to Abraham's side] is the first time this idea appears in the Jewish tradition." Kenneth E. Bailey, *Jesus through Middle Eastern Eyes: Cultural Studies in the Gospels* (Downers Grove: IVP Academic, 2008), 387 n13. The *Testament of Abraham* (dated at the earliest to second century CE) relates Abraham's soul being conveyed to heaven by angels (in version 1) or by the archangel Michael (in version 2). 4 Maccabees refers to Abraham receiving the martyrs. Cited by Marshall, *Gospel of Luke*, 636.

92   The qur'anic feast story related to Jesus (5:112-120) is not an eschatological feast but is apparently to be identified roughly with the gospel account of Jesus feeding the 5000. The name of the 5th sura, Al-Ma'ida, means "the Feast" and the sura takes its name from this feast which Jesus' disciples ask him to seek from God. For possible parallels see Lodahl, *Claiming Abraham*, KL 2867-2922. But see note 88 above.

93   For example, Ps 45; Isa 54:1-8; Ezek 16:1-14; Hos 1:2; 2:1-3; Mark 2:19; Eph 5:22-33; Rev 21:9ff.

94   See Matt 22:1-10; 25:1-13; Rev 19:9.

95   See patristic examples in Sheridan, *Genesis 12-50*, 120-37. For a Puritan example see John Cennick, *The Marriage of Isaac. A Discourse Delivered at Exeter in the Year 1744*, 4-5.

96   Examples are available in John Ryan Haule, *Divine Madness : Archetypes of Romantic Love* (Boston: Shambhala, 1990), 12-13.

97   Gareth Lee Cockerill, *Guidebook for Pilgrims to the Heavenly City* (Pasadena: William Carey Library, 2002), discusses the implications of this Abrahamic pilgrimage imagery in Hebrews.

98   E.g. Qur'an 36:51-65; 37:19-68; 55:35-78; 56:1-56; 78:31-34.

99   As noted in chapter 5, this verse seems to refer primarily to the Jews. "The implication is that the majority of the Jews had deviated from the true creed of Abraham (which is the meaning of the phrase 'those who came to hold divergent views about him') inasmuch as most of them became convinced that they were 'God's chosen people' simply because of their physical descent from that great Prophet." Asad, The Message of the Qur'an, on 16:124.

100   A one-page summary of the worldview polarities reflected in Abraham narratives which I have developed in this chapter may be found in Appendix 6.

CHAPTER 8 – CHALLENGES AND OPPORTUNITIES IN ABRAHAMIC DIALOGUE

1   Abraham's obedient faith is an important NT theme, as I pointed out in chapter 4, emphasized particularly in Hebrews and James. But this is understood within the framework of the new covenant of Christ, which makes such obedience of faith possible by the gift of the Holy Spirit to those who confess and follow Jesus as Lord. So the fulfillment of Abrahamic promises as the gospel should be kept in the forefront as primary.

2   For a brief introduction, see Timothy C. Tennent, "Followers of Jesus (Isa) in Islamic Mosques: A Closer Examination of C-5 'High Spectrum' Contextualization," *IJFM* 23, no. 3 (2006).

3   Kevin Higgins, "Muhammad, Islam, and the Quran," (Unpublished paper, 2007), 8-10, 13. This argument is open to serious challenge. The Apocrypha neither openly subverts central themes in the Hebrew canon as the Qur'an does those of the NT (e.g. denying the Father, Son, and Spirit or the centrality of the crucifixion and resurrection of Jesus), nor purports to bring a fresh and final revelation of God. As a perusal of Muslim books on the NT will show, the Qur'an's claim to confirm earlier revelation is problematic from a Muslim point of view unless it is affirmed that these books have been corrupted. There are contemporary Muslim scholars who argue that the Qur'an does not support the claim of corruption of earlier scripture; e.g. Abdullah Saeed, "The Charge of Distortion of Jewish and Christian Scriptures," *MW* 92, no. 3/4 (2002). But this does not solve the deep theological conflict between them, especially concerning Jesus. This should be a warning that the Qur'an cannot or ought not to be used as Higgins proposes.

4   Higgins, "Muhammad, Islam, and the Quran," 13-15. See the extensive evaluation and interaction with Higgins' writings in Doug Coleman, "A Theological Analysis of the Insider

Movement Paradigm from Four Perspectives: Theology of Religions, Revelation, Soteriology, and Ecclesiology" (PhD Dissertation, Southeastern Baptist Theological Seminary, 2011).

5   Mahmut Aydin, "Contemporary Christian evaluations of the prophethood of Muhammad," *Encounters: Journal of Inter-cultural Perspectives*, 6:1 (March 2000), 42. See also Azumah, "The Integrity of Interfaith Dialogue," 272.

6   See for example Sidney H. Griffith, "The Qur'an in Arab Christian Texts: The Development of an Apologetical Argument: Abu Qurrah in the Maǧlis of Al-Ma'mon," *ParOr* 24 (1999) Also Griffith, *The Church in the Shadow of the Mosque:*, KL 5152-5148.

7   For example, I. Tatlican, *Hristiyanligin Gizli Tarihi (Christianity's Secret History)* (Istanbul: Düsünce, 2005), enters into debates over the Gospels, using Christian writings to argue that the true followers of Jesus were the Ebionites and Nazarenes. He tries to show inconsistencies in the Gospels and uses the Qur'an as the court of appeal, ending his book with an invitation to Christians to accept Islam.

8   There also is a whole world of active internet-based dialogue and polemic, with sites such as *Answering Islam* and *Answering Christianity*. http://www.answering-islam.org/ and http://www.answering-christianity.com.

9   P. O'Hair Cate, "Each Others' Scriptures: The Muslim's View of the Bible and the Christian's View of the Qur'an" (PhD dissertation, Hartford Seminary, 1974) 284-85.

10   Cate, "Each Others' Scriptures," 289.

11   Q 21:71 "We saved him and Lot [and sent them] to the land We blessed for all people" [or "blessed for all times to come" in Asad's translation].

12   Wright, *The Mission of God*, 48-69.

13   Christopher Wright considers this matter helpfully in Wright, "Interpreting the Bible."

14   An ancient example is Lejla Demiri, *Muslim Exegesis of the Bible in Medieval Cairo: Najm Al-Din Al-Tufi's (D. 716/1316) Commentary on the Christian Scriptures* (vol. 19; Leiden: Brill, 2013), and a recent example is Syed Ahmad's self-published, 797-page commentary on the Gospels, "A Muslim's Commentary of the Bible," the text of which may be found at http://muslimcommentaryofbible.wordpress.com/contents-of-a-muslims-commentary-of-the-bible/254-the-death-of-jesus/. Shabbir Akhtar is currently working on an Islamic commentary on Galatians.

APPENDIX 4 – THE BOOK OF JUBILEES ON ABRAHAM

1   "Jubilees represents the triumph of the [legalistic] movement, which had been at work for the past three centuries or more . . . The Book of Jubilees was written in Hebrew by a Pharisee between the year of the accession of Hyrcanus to the high priesthood in 135 and his breach with the Pharisees some years before his death in 105 B.C." Charles, *The Apocrypha and Pseudepigrapha*, 1. More recent scholarship dates the book somewhat earlier: "It seems best to say, in view of all the evidence, that the author composed Jubilees in the period between 160-150 BCE." VanderKam, *The Book of Jubilees*, 21. In any case, it is earlier than the NT and many centuries before the Qur'an.

2   Öztürk, *The Eye of the Heart*, 2.

APPENDIX 5 – SURA BY SURA ANALYSIS OF QUR'ANIC ABRAHAM MATERIAL

1   Brown's warning is apropos: "Authoritative interpretation of the Qur'an ideally requires access to a substantial library, which would include material from all of the major branches of Muslim traditional knowledge. This should provide sufficient reason for newcomers to the text, particularly non-Muslims, to be circumspect about venturing casual opinions about what a particular passage means." Brown, *A New Introduction to Islam*, 82.

2   Abdullah Yusuf Ali, *Quran English Translation and Commentary* ([cited 17 Jan. 2012]); available from http://www.quran4u.com/Tafsiraya/Index.htm.

3   Muhammad Asad, *The Message of the Qur'an* (The Book Foundation, 2008), Kindle Edition. The notes of this Jewish convert to Islam are widely used, though banned in Saudi Arabia. The Turkish translation of Asad's interpretation (Muhammed Esed, *Kur'an Mesaji*) are widely referred to in Turkey, though with some reservations.

4   Abdel Haleem, *The Qur'an* Kindle Edition.

5   Syed Abu-Ala' Maududi, *Surah Introductions to the Qur'an* (1st) (Center for Muslim-Jewish Engagement, University of Southern California, [cited January 17 2012]); available from http://www.cmje.org/religious-texts/maududi/index.php.

6   Shaykh Muhammad Al-Ghazali, *A Thematic Commentary on the Qur'an* (trans. Shamis; Herndon, Va.: International Institute of Islamic Thought, 1997), Kindle Edition. Available in Turkish as "Kur'an'ın Konulu Tefsiri."

7   On Asad, see Meryem Demiray, "Muhammed Esed'in Kur'an Mesajı Isimli Tefsirindeki Metodu." (Yüksek lisans tezi (Postgraduate thesis), Marmara University, 2006).   On Maududi see Abdülhamit Birişik, "Ebü'l-A'lâ Mevdûdî'nin Kur'ân Yorumunu Şekillendiren Temel Dinamikler," *UÜİFD* 20, no. 2 (2011). On al-Ghazali see Mustafa Karataş, "Çağdaş Yazar Muhammed Gazâlî'nin Hadis Ve Sünnete İlişkin Görüşleri (Contemporary Writer Muhammed Gazali and His Opinions on the Hadith and Sunna)," *İUİFD* 10(2004). In his analysis, University of Istanbul theology professor Karataş generally praises Gazali's critical and Qur'an-based evaluation of the Hadith and Sunna.

8   Bayraktar Bayraklı, *Yeni Bir Anlayışın Işığında Kur'an Tefsiri (Qur'an Tafsir in the Light of a New Understanding)* (21 vols.; Istanbul: Bayraklı Yayınları, 2003), especially for Sura 2/al-Baqara.

9   H. Tahsin Emiroğlu, *Esbab-I Nüzul: Kur'an Âyetlerinin İniş Sebepleri Ve Tefsirleri (Qur'anic Verse Revelation Context and Interpretation)* (15 vols.; Istanbul: Yasin Yanınevi, 2013), especially for Sura 2/al-Baqara.

10   Yazır, *Hak Dini Kur'an Dili.* Yazır was the one commentator recommended by all of my Turkish interlocutors. My references are to the online version at http://www.kuranikerim.com/telmalili/.

11   Also known as the "Kuran Yolu" (Way of the Qur'an), this tafsir may be accessed online at the following address: http://kuran.diyanet.gov.tr/ . Some in Turkey criticise it as being too modernist in perspective, as for example its interpretation of Q2:62, which seems to decrease the essential elements of Islamic faith to three. One critic says, "This tafsir is very intent on placing non-Muslims on the way to heaven" (Bu tefsir Müslüman olmayanları cennete koymak yolunda çok gayretkeş). http://www.ihvanlar.net/2013/04/05/diyanetin-kuran-yolu-tefsirli-mealinde-skandallar-bitmiyor/. On criteria for determining the identity of "Religiously Ideal Believers" in different interpretive approaches, see Duderija, *Constructing a Religiously Ideal "Believer" and "Woman" in Islam.*

12   Kaymakcan, "Religious Education Culture," 454.

13   Bayraklı sums up the meaning of the opening as "the Qur'an is a Guide" (Kur'an bir rehberdir): "The concept of *kitap* [book] here means that it is place where sure divine knowledge is gathered. This knowledge is a guide leading those who are protected to salvation." Bayraktar Bayraklı, *Yeni Bir Anlayışın Işığında Kur'an Tefsiri (Qur'an Tafsir in the Light of a New Understanding)* (21 vols.; vol. 1; Istanbul: Bayraklı Yayınları, 2003), 169.

14   Al-Ghazali, *A Thematic Commentary on the Qur'an* page 8.

15   Kuran Yolu commentary on this verse gives an extended introduction to Abraham in Genesis, a feature rarely found in Turkish Qur'an commentaries. http://kuran.diyanet.gov.tr/Kuran.aspx#2:124.

16   Turkish Sunni commentator Bayraklı says the word *imam* here can mean prophet or exemplary leader. Bayraktar Bayraklı, *Yeni Bir Anlayışın Işığında Kur'an Tefsiri (Qur'an Tafsir in the Light of a New Understanding)* (21 vols.; vol. 2; Istanbul: Bayraklı Yayınları, 2003), 214. "In Sunni Islam, imam means 'prayer leader,' the one religiously 'in front.' . . . Among Shi'is, however, the word imam acquired the meaning of supreme spiritual guide." Khalid Duran and Abdelwahab Hechiche, *Children of Abraham: An Introduction to Islam for Jews* (Hoboken, N.J.: American Jewish Committee, KTAV Publishing House, 2001), 25.

17   Yusuf Ali on 2:124.

18 Bayraklı, *Yeni Bir Anlayışın Işığında Kur'an Tefsiri*, 213.

19 For example, Jubilees says, "He had tried him through his country and with famine, and had tried him with the wealth of kings, and had tried him again through his wife, when she was torn (from him), and with circumcision; and had tried him through Ishmael and Hagar, his maid-servant, when he sent them away. And in everything wherein He had tried him, he was found faithful" (17.17-18). See note in chapter 4.

20 See the discussion in Ayoub, *The Qur'an and Its Interpreters*, 152.

21 This is found among the meanings given in the Tafsir Ibn Kathir on 2:124, in this case Muhammad bin Ishaq reported what Ibn 'Abbas said about these words of testing. Cited by Ahmed Kalkan, *Kavram Tefsiri* (11 vols.; vol. 4), 2089.

22 H. Tahsin Emiroğlu, *Esbab-I Nüzul: Kur'an Âyetlerinin İniş Sebepleri Ve Tefsirleri (Qur'anic Verse Revelation Context and Interpretation)* (15 vols.; vol. 1; Istanbul: Yasin Yanınevi, 2013), 242.

23 According to Emiroğlu, this verse was revealed to Muhammad shortly after a suggestion from Umar that the Kaaba be designated as a place for ritual prayer (*namazgâh*). Emiroğlu, *Esbab-I Nüzul: Kur'an Âyetlerinin İniş Sebepleri Ve Tefsirleri (Qur'anic Verse Revelation Context and Interpretation)*, 244.

24 One of my interviewees articulated this understanding.

25 Reynolds, *The Emergence of Islam*, KL 3508-3517. "In this light we might understand the Qur'an's insistence elsewhere that Muhammad has a special relationship with Abraham: 'The people standing closest to Abraham are those who followed him, and this Prophet' (Q 3:68)." Reynolds and El-Badawi, "The Qur'an and the Syriac Bible."

26 According to van Ruiten, "the author of Jubilees combines Gen 25:8-10 with elements taken from Gen 49:33-50:14." Jaques T. A. G. M. van Ruiten, "Abraham's Last Day According to the Book of Jubilees (Jub. 22:1-23:8)," in *Rewritten Biblical Figures* (eds. Koskenniemi and Lindqvist; vol. 3 of *Studies in Rewritten Bible*; Winona Lake: Eisenbrauns, 2010), 87.

27 This is not entirely unlike John the Baptist's rebuke of the religious leaders of Israel in his day: "Bear fruit in keeping with repentance. And do not presume to say to yourselves, 'We have Abraham as our father,' for I tell you, God is able from these stones to raise up children for Abraham" (Matt 3:8-9).

28 Yazır notes on 2:138 that Christians were compromised by their worship of the prophet Jesus. Yazır, *Hak Dini Kur'an Dili*.

29 "He asks as someone who had asked the basic questions about the world in the light of Revelation and realized that God is all powerful. Yet, this awareness, the fact that he is a believer, does not make him suppress his question, the need of his 'heart' to actually see another example of resurrection." Yazicioglu, "Learning to Ask Questions," 6.

30 The same desire for assurance is seen in the apostles of Jesus in 5:113, though Abraham does not doubt God as they doubt Jesus and God. See Sugimoto, "The Variance of Muslim Attitudes toward Western Modernity: A Worldview Discourse," 11. Abraham's exemplary status is maintained.

31 It has been proposed that many if not most suras are arranged in *pairs* which complement each other in various ways. Mir cites Islâhî as arguing that "S. 2 deals with the theme of faith, discusses the Jews, and presents arguments from nature, while S. 3 deals with the practical implications of faith, discusses the Christians, and presents arguments based on earlier scriptures." Mustansir Mir, "Islahi's Concept of Sura-Pairs," *MW* 73, no. 1 Jan: 27. Farrin lists the chapter pairs occurring in the Qur'an in Appendix B of his study. Farrin, *Structure and Qur'anic Interpretation: A Study of Symmetry and Coherence in Islam's Holy Text*, KL 1852-2087.

32 Yazır says that it could also refer to the specific location of the Kaaba. Yazır, *Hak Dini Kur'an Dili*. Bakka may be an older name for Mecca: "The foundation of the Ka'ba goes back to Abraham, but there are place associations in the sacred territory with the names of Adam and Eve." Ali.

33   But see note above on the possible meaning "faithful gentile."

34   Al-Ghazali, *A Thematic Commentary on the Qur'an*, 55.

35   Yusuf Ali says, "Abraham is distinguished in Muslim theology with the title of 'Friend of God.' This does not of course mean that he was anything more than a mortal. But his faith was pure and true, and his conduct was firm and righteous in all circumstances." Abraham is known by this title by most Muslims. Asad paraphrases, "God exalted Abraham with His love."

36   Kopuz entitles his collection on Muslim saints "Friends of God." Kopuz, *Allah Dostları*. His is one among many Turkish collections of Islamic hagiography. Although the prophet Abraham is referred to as the friend of God, a distinction is maintained in Islamic traditions between saints or "friends" of God and prophets of God. Renard, *Friends of God*, 264-66.

37   Abraham is included in the following lists: 2:136; 3:84; 4:163; 19:58; 33:7; 42:13; 53:36-37; 57:26; 87:19. Muslim sources generally cite twenty-five prophets who are named in the Qur'an. Some distinguish between those who are prophets and those who are both prophet and messenger. I provided more on qur'anic prophet lists in chapter 2.

38   See notes on 87:19 below.

39   Reynolds' interpretation noted above, that *hanif* essentially means gentile, highlights Abraham's place in the Qur'an as a symbol and a prototype of Muhammad: "I have turned my face to the one who created the heavens and the earth, a gentile (*hanif*) but not a polytheist" (Q 6.79). In this way the Qur'an asserts that Abraham was in no way obliged to the People of the Book for his faith, and it thereby implies the same for its own Prophet." Reynolds, *The Qur'an and Its Biblical Subtext*, 87.

40   Rahman, *Major Themes*, 89. See also Turkish Baydar, İbrahimî Okuyuş (Abrahamic Reading), 96. Al-Ghazali also sees these verses recounting "Abraham's experience of his search for the one true God." Al-Ghazali, *A Thematic Commentary on the Qur'an*, KL 1696.

41   Dirks offers this additional evaluation: "The two interpretations, i.e., naturalistic observation vs. rhetorical argument, are neither mutually contradictory nor mutually exclusive." Dirks, *Abraham: The Friend of God*, 31-32.

42   Stewart, "Notes on Medieval and Modern Emendations," 238.

43   Yazır comments on 6:161 that God has guided Muhammad into "a perfectly straight religion, its 'hanif' state" ("dosdoğru bir dine yani hanif hali"). Yazır, *Hak Dîni Kur'an Dili*.

44   "The bulk of the surah deals with preparations and recruitment for the expedition to Tabuk, which took place in the heat of the summer of AH 9 (631 CE)" (Abdel Haleem).

45   Al-Ghazali, *A Thematic Commentary on the Qur'an*, 217.

46   Hud and Salih are identified as monotheistic prophets in pre-Islamic Arabia. Hamblin finds notable parallels between Hud and the prophet Lehi from the Book of Mormon. Hamblin, "Pre-Islamic Arabian Prophets."

47   Welch, "Formulaic Features of the Punishment Stories," 78.

48   Ginzberg recounts, "Abraham himself served his guests, and it appeared to him that the three men ate. *But this was an illusion. In reality the angels did not eat*, only Abraham, his three friends, Aner, Eshcol, and Mamre, and his son Ishmael partook of the banquet, and the portions set before the angels were devoured by a heavenly fire" Ginzberg, et al., *The Legends of the Jews*, 243. Italics added. Ginzberg refers to Q 11:73 in his footnote: "Koran 11.73 gives a clumsy representation of the view prevalent in Jewish sources concerning these three angels."

49   The text simply says that "Abraham's wife was standing [nearby]." This is clearly his wife Sarah. Hagar does not figure prominently in early Islam, and remarkably, she is not even mentioned in the Qur'an. Von Kooten and Van Ruiten, "Introduction," xxxiv.

50   See the discussion of "the laughter of Abraham's wife" by Reynolds, *The Qur'an and Its Biblical Subtext*, 87-97. He points to similarities between the reactions of Sarah and Mary (Q 11:71 and 3:47 respectively) and the angelic assurance that nothing is impossible for God (Gen 18:14 and Luke 1:37), especially in Christian reading of the Greek OT text, to argue that it

is "in light of the Sarah/Mary typology that the Qur'an's reference to Sarah's laughter should also be understood."

51 Stewart, "Understanding the Quran," 44.

52 Waldman, "New Approaches," 5.

53 Waldman, "New Approaches," 9. The seven characteristics Waldman identifies are these: 1) part of a set of similar individuals, 2) guided by God, 3) chosen from among their people, 4) polarize their audiences, opposed by some, believed by others, 5) two main functions are to bring good news and to warn, 6) have exemplary personal characteristics: patience, unswerving devotion, compassion, trust in God, pure faith absolutely opposed to associating (shirk) anything with God, 7) they are to be followed in conjunction with foundational beliefs and practices.

54 "I have abandoned . . ." (Yusuf Ali and Arberry).

55 Rahman, *Major Themes*, 142-43. See also M. S. Stern, "Muhammad and Joseph: A Study of Koranic Narrative," *JNES* 44, no. 3 (1985): 204.

56 Reynolds, *The Qur'an and Its Biblical Subtext*, 2.

57 Al-Ghazali, *A Thematic Commentary on the Qur'an*, 264.

58 Against both of these we have seen the NT insistence that there is *no* central place of pilgrimage and divine worship on earth since the coming of Jesus.

59 Nothing of the Genesis promise is found here, though that is why it is good news there.

60 Izutsu sees this as explaining why Abraham came to be called a *siddīq*: "Here we see Abraham described as a determined champion for monotheism against the surrounding forces of idolatrous polytheism; a zealous and fearless believer in God, who remains loyal to the last to his religion even if he is forced thereby to part with his own father and be condemned to exile. Such is a man who is fully entitled to the name of *siddīq*." Toshihiko Izutsu, *Ethico-Religious Concepts in the Qur'an* (Montreal: McGill University, Institute of Islamic Studies, McGill University Press, 1966), 93-94.

61 Rahman, *Major Themes*, 121.

62 Ishmael is mentioned as "granted to" Abraham along with Isaac in 14:38. Four times we find the listing "Abraham, Ishmael, Isaac, Jacob, and the tribes" (2:136, 140; 3:84; 4:163).

63 As in verse 49, this offspring is referred to as "granted" or "given" to Abraham in three other passages (6:84; 21:72; 29:27).

64 Some commentators suggest this refers to the prophet Ezekiel (Abdel Haleem).

65 Muhammad is told in regard to God's stern dealings with hypocrites, "This has been God's practice with those who went before. You will find no change in God's practices" (33:62).

66 Some interpret this as referring not to a literal rescue from flame but to deliverance from the metaphorical "fire" of persecution from his society (Asad on this verse; Baydar, İbrahimî Okuyuş [Abrahamic Reading], 38-39). But Turkish Muslims generally hold that this event literally took place in what is today the city of Şanlıurfa. The Hebrew word *Ur* (Gen 11:28, 31; 15:7) literally means fire, and in Jewish sources has been understood as Abraham's rescue from fire rather than his departure from the city of Ur: "Abram descended into the fiery furnace and was saved" (*Gen R 38:13* on Gen 11:28); "Michael descended and rescued Abraham from the fiery furnace" (*Gen R 44:13* on Gen 15:7; cf. *Gen R 44:1*). According to Stemberger, this means that God "tries" Abraham and finds him faithful. Stemberger, "Genesis 15 in Rabbinic and Patristic Interpretation," 157.

67 Abdel Haleem. The prophet stories recounted in this sura are those of Moses and the people of Pharaoh (26:10-68), Abraham and his people (69-102), Noah and his people (105-122), Hud and the people of 'Ad (123-140), Salih and the people of Thamud (141-159), Lot and his people/Sodom (160-175), Shu'ayb and the forest dwellers (176-190).

68 Other than here, these two narratives are related only in sura 37 (37:83-100, 112-113), though there they are separated by the story of Abraham sacrificing his son (37:99-111).

69 It is unclear who "his people" are, since Lot has presumably left Mesopotamia with his uncle when Abraham left his resistant people behind. Thus the reference must be to the people among whom he is living (Sodom).

70 This is more literally "And Abraham, when he said ..." But different interpolations are made by translators: "And Abraham, [too, was inspired by Us] when he said ..." (Asad). "And (We also saved) Abraham: behold, he said ..." (Yusuf Ali), links with the preceding sentence regarding Noah "We saved him and those with him on the Ark."

71 Mirza, "Abraham as an Iconoclast: Understanding the Destruction of 'Images' through Qur'anic Exegesis," 428.

72 "The men to whom God's Truth has been committed for promulgation will be asked in the Hereafter how the Truth fared in the world—how it was received, who opposed it, and who assisted it. Like all trustees, they will have to give a full account of their trust." (Ali)

73 "This verse is said to apply to certain of the Companions who vowed, at the time of the early campaigns, that they would fight until death at the Prophet's side (Zamakhshari); in its wider sense, however, it relates to all efforts involving a supreme sacrifice in God's cause." (Asad)

74 References to God's "true servants" are found primarily in this sura (37:40, 74, 128, 160, 169). The similar phrase "our faithful servants" is found only in this sura: used of Noah (81), Abraham (111), Moses and Aaron (122) and of Elijah (132). However, more general references to God's "servants" are found throughout the Qur'an.

75 The remembrance of this event is perpetuated through the annual Islamic feast Eid al-Adha, referred to in Turkish as "Kurban Bayramı" (holiday or festival of sacrifice).

76 This same adjective, "halim" (patient, forbearing) is used of Abraham in 9:114 and 11:75, where it refers to his intercession for Lot's people.

77 According to Bar, there was disagreement among the earliest interpreters as to whether the son was Isaac or Ishmael. See Bar, "The Religious Sources of Islamic Terrorism," 36-38. Firestone demonstrates that "Isaac was originally understood to have been the intended victim, but that this view was eclipsed by a new perspective which held Ishmael to have been intended." Reuven Firestone, "Abraham's Son as the Intended Sacrifice (Al-DhabīH, Qur'āN 37:99-113): Issues in Qur'āNic Exegesis," 34, no. 1 (1989): 115. See also F. Leemhuis, "Ibrahim's Sacrifice of His Son in the Early Post-Koranic Tradition," in *The Sacrifice of Isaac: The Aqedah (Genesis 22) and Its Interpretations* (eds. Noort and Tigchelaar; vol. 4 of *Themes in Biblical Narrative*; Leiden: Brill, 2002), 128-29.

78 In his reconstruction Dirks explains this "work" as "the serious work of spreading the message of Allah." Dirks, *Abraham: The Friend of God*, 120-22.

79 "Rabbinic-Jewish tradition takes up the essential characteristics of the short dialogues and fills in some of the textual gaps." W. J. van Bekkum, "The Aqedah and Its Interpretations in Midrash and Piyyut," in *The Sacrifice of Isaac: The Aqedah (Genesis 22) and Its Interpretations* (eds. Noort and Tigchelaar; vol. 4 of *Themes in Biblical Narrative*; Leiden: Brill, 2002), 89. The story is expanded in several texts. In 4 Maccabees, "The author mentions Isaac's willingness to die, thereby giving him an active role in the story." Robert L. Wilken, "Melito, the Jewish Community at Sardis, and the Sacrifice of Isaac," *TS* 37, no. 1 (1976): 61. In Josephus' *Antiquities*: "Isaac ... exclaimed that if he were to reject the decision of God and of his father, he would deserve never to have been born at all." Paul Maier, *Josephus - the Essential Writings*, (Grand Rapids: Kregel, 1988), 29.

80 Asad comments that "since, however, the sequence clearly shows that it was not God's will that Ishmael should be sacrificed, his and his father's 'self-surrender to God's will' can have in this context only a purely subjective meaning—namely 'to what they thought to be the will of God." Baydar understands God's statement to mean that his dream was allowed as a test, and was not in itself a divine command, even though so understood by the prophet. Baydar, İbrahimî Okuyuş (Abrahamic Reading), 62-65.

81 "A trial of this severity clearly implied that Abraham would be capable to bear it, and thus constituted a high moral distinction—in itself a reward from God." Asad.

82   "The Eid al-Adha, or Festival of Sacrifice . . . commemorates an event, to be sure, the supreme act of obedience by Abraham, but it differs from a simple commemoration in that the celebrant imitates the example of Abraham . . . The killing of the animal serves as the means of identifying oneself actively with the obedience of Abraham and his spirit of sacrifice." Speight, "The Nature of Christian and Muslim Festivals," 262.

83   See for example 2:124, 143, 155, 214, 249; 3:142, 154, 179, 186.

84   The people listed as being punished like this are these: "The people of Noah, 'Ad, and Pharaoh, Thamud, the people of Lot, and the Forest-Dwellers" (38:12-13).

85   Or "We purified them by means of a thought most pure: the remembrance of the life to come," literally "the [final] abode" (Asad).

86   This conforms with Asad's view of the sura's central theme, "the reality of divine revelation, and the fact that all prophets, at all times, preached one and the same essential truth."

87   Interpreters understand this gift of deep wisdom as divine knowledge (Ali) and/or "prophethood" (Asad).

88   Asad asserts that "the names of Abraham and Moses are cited here only by way of example, drawing attention to the fact that all through human history God has entrusted His elect, the prophets, with the task of conveying certain unchangeable ethical truths to man." One could argue that there was a written revelation given to Abraham which is not extant today (so Yusuf Ali on 87:19). There has been speculation about the existence of written revelation to Abraham also based on 2:124—"Abraham's Lord tested him with certain commandments." But generally these are understood as verbal commands. See Ayoub, *The Qur'an and Its Interpreters*, 152-53.

99   "Thus, if a wife embraces Islam while her husband remains outside its pale, the marriage is considered, from the Islamic point of view, to have been automatically annulled" (Asad on 60:10.)

90   Or, "in the ancient scrolls, the scrolls of Abraham and Moses" (Ali). "The noun ṣuḥuf (sing. ṣaïfah), which literally denotes 'leaves [of a book]' or 'scrolls,' is synonymous with kitāb in all the senses of this term (Jawharī): hence, in the above context, 'revelations'" (Asad).

INDEX OF ANCIENT SOURCES

Index of Modern Authors

INDEX OF SELECTED TOPICS

CPSIA information can be obtained
at www.ICGtesting.com
Printed in the USA
LVOW10s0039040517

533070LV00030B/590/P